Advance Praise for *Unbroken and*

"By chronicling the history of Black-led protest in America, Rev. Hawkins both reveals a tradition of struggle for a more perfect union and unmasks the lie that Black protest is 'un-American.' To receive this history is to know and know again that America would not be half the country she is if Black people had not believed her promises and worked with others to make them a reality. God bless Rev. Hawkins for telling the story and living it in his own leadership and witness today."

—Rev. Dr. William J. Barber, II, President, Repairers of the Breach, and author, *We Are Called to Be a Movement*

"Jimmie Hawkins's *Unbroken and Unbowed* uses the words by which Black Americans have named themselves—Africans, Colored, Negro, Black, African American—to trace five centuries of struggle by the sons and daughters of Africa, a struggle grounded in the radical assertion that a person cannot become a thing. Beyond the etymology of Black self-definition, this book's astonishing ambition, which Hawkins richly fulfills, is to let us see American history with heartbreaking and often inspiring clarity. Its research is as deep as the abyss of our nation's founding. From shipboard slave revolts and Reconstruction dreams, from the civil rights and Black Power movements to Rev. Dr. William Barber's Moral Mondays to Black Lives Matter, Hawkins calls every one of us to summon the courage—and love and political will—to confront this hard history and to alter its arc. 'Not everything that is faced can be changed,' James Baldwin instructs, 'but nothing can be changed until it is faced.'"

—Timothy B. Tyson, author, *Blood Done Sign My Name*

"This book is a must-read! Jimmie Hawkins's *Unbroken and Unbowed: A History of Black Protest in America* explores the history of Black protest over five hundred years in these yet-to-be United States. Articulately, definitively, and comprehensively, Hawkins shows that rather than solely victims of systemic racism and economic injustice, Black leaders are moral, political, and epistemological agents of change throughout every period of American history. This book documents that protest and resistance led by Black people has played a unique and key role in transforming the country into a more perfect union and inspires us to take action for justice and equality today."

—Liz Theoharis, cochair, Poor People's Campaign, and Director, the Kairos Center for Religions, Rights, and Social Justice, Union Theological Seminary, New York

"We finally have a careful, comprehensive, and complete history of Black protest in the United States. Hawkins follows the trajectory of Black social activism over many generations, reminding us that it is a rich and unbroken tradition. In this age of racial tribalism and reckoning, all Americans stand to benefit intellectually from reading *Unbroken and Unbowed*. It reminds us of not only how far we have come but also how far we must go to become the nation we have long claimed to be. This is a timely and immensely significant work!"

—Lewis V. Baldwin, author, *There Is a Balm in Gilead:*
The Cultural Roots of Martin Luther King, Jr.

"*Unbroken and Unbowed* is a wonderful exposition, summation, and interpretation of African American protest. Here, in a single volume, from enslaved past to engaged present, one traces the lineage and devastation of American racial animus toward Black people and the enduring African American protest against it. If, as Rev. Jimmie Hawkins rightly argues, Black protest is truth telling, this book is a scintillating record of a people proclaiming the truth of equality, in word and deed, to a country that has perpetually refused to acknowledge it. A historical survey steeped in contemporary reckoning, this book is an excellent resource for helping us understand and navigate our tumultuous time."

—Brian Blount, President, Union Presbyterian Seminary,
Richmond, Virginia, and author, *Can I Get a Witness:*
Reading Revelation through African American Culture

Unbroken and Unbowed

Unbroken and Unbowed

A History of Black Protest in America

Jimmie R. Hawkins

WJK WESTMINSTER
JOHN KNOX PRESS
LOUISVILLE • KENTUCKY

First edition
Published by Westminster John Knox Press
Louisville, Kentucky

22 23 24 25 26 27 28 29 30 31—10 9 8 7 6 5 4 3 2 1

Book design by Sharon Adams
Cover design by designpointinc.com
Cover art by Jerry Lynn. Used by permission.

Library of Congress Cataloging-in-Publication Data

Names: Hawkins, Jimmie R., author.
Title: Unbroken and unbowed : a history of black protest in America / Jimmie R. Hawkins.
Other titles: History of black protest in America
Description: First edition. | Louisville, Kentucky : Westminster John Knox Press, [2022] | Includes bibliographical references and index. | Summary: "In this compelling and informative volume, Jimmie R. Hawkins walks the reader through the many forms of Black protest in American history, from precolonial times though the George Floyd protests of 2020"—Provided by publisher.
Identifiers: LCCN 2021057729 (print) | LCCN 2021057730 (ebook) | ISBN 9780664267377 (paperback) | ISBN 9781646982332 (ebook)
Subjects: LCSH: African Americans—Politics and government—History. | African Americans—Social conditions—History. | Protest movements—United States—History. | Civil rights movements—United States—History. | African Americans—History. | United States—Race relations—History. | Anti-racism—United States—History.
Classification: LCC E184.A1 .H377 2022 (print) | LCC E184.A1 (ebook) | DDC 973/.0496073—dc23/eng/20211208
LC record available at https://lccn.loc.gov/2021057729
LC ebook record available at https://lccn.loc.gov/2021057730

Most Westminster John Knox Press books are available at special quantity discounts when purchased in bulk by corporations, organizations, and special-interest groups. For more information, please e-mail SpecialSales@wjkbooks .com.

Contents

List of Illustrations

Introduction

Colin Kaepernick (right) and Eric Reid of the San Francisco 49ers kneel in protest during the national anthem prior to playing the Los Angeles Rams in their NFL game at Levi's Stadium on September 12, 2016, in Santa Clara, California. (Photo by Thearon W. Henderson/Getty Images. Used with permission.)

Section 1

Slavers bringing captives on board a slave ship on Africa's west coast. (This file is made available under the Creative Commons CC0 1.0 Universal Public Domain Dedication.)

Section 2

"The Underground Railroad," Charles T. Webber (1825–1911), United States, 1893, oil on canvas. (Bettman Archives. Used with permission.)

Section 3

A flag hanging outside the headquarters of the NAACP (National Association for the Advancement of Colored People) in New York City in 1936 bearing the words "A Man was Lynched Yesterday." (Photo by MPI/Getty Images. Used with permission.)

Section 4

Stokely Carmichael, right, organizing local people for the Lowndes County Freedom Organization (LCFO) in Alabama in 1966. His flyer features the original LCFO black panther logo. (Photographer unknown. This file is made available under the Creative Commons CC0 1.0 Universal Public Domain Dedication.)

Section 5

Protesters kneel in prayer in the U.S. Capitol during nationwide protests sparked by the murder of George Floyd by a Minneapolis police officer in 2020. (Photo by Jimmie R. Hawkins. Used with permission.)

Acknowledgments

The author wishes to thank his family: his mother, Elsie, and his siblings; and his wife, Sheinita, his daughter, Kaela, and his son, James, for their patience on all those days I was downstairs during family time writing, sweating, stumbling, and praying. You are the inspirations in my life, and I give God thanks for each one of you. My mother, Elsie Lee, has been the rock in my life and enabled me to believe in myself.

There must be an acknowledgment of the known and unknown forebears who struggled, fought, worked, and served to make the African American experience better for those who followed. And a special mention of two mentors, the late Dr. Earlie E. Thorpe (North Carolina Central University) and the Rev. Dr. Gayraud Wilmore, PC(USA).

I give thanks to God for guiding me to write this book, and I dedicate it to God's glory in the name of God's son, Christ Jesus.

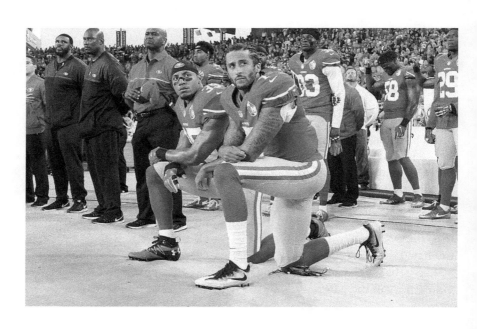

Introduction

Despite the pervasiveness of the concept of nothingness, worthlessness, inferiority, the Negro has continued to assert his worth and attempt to validate his claim to human rights. . . . The history of the black man's protest against enslavement, subordination, cruelty, inhumanity began with a seizure in African ports and has not yet ended. . . . Never having been stripped of his humanness despite all that he has endured, the Negro has continued to follow the advice of Frederick Douglass: ". . . there shall be no peace to the wicked . . . this guilty nation shall have no peace. . . . We will do all that we can to agitate! AGITATE! AGITATE!!!"[1]
—*Historian Joanne Grant*

On August 12, 2016, NFL quarterback Colin Kaepernick began a silent and at-first-unnoticed protest against police brutality. On that day he sat on the bench while other players and coaches stood during the playing of the national anthem. He did that for two more games before a reporter asked him about it. "I am not going to stand up to show pride in a flag for a country that oppresses Black people and people of color," he replied.

The next game, he kneeled in line with his standing teammates during the anthem. That got people's attention. Soon players from his and other teams were also kneeling. Criticism was swift from inside and outside the sports world. Critics blamed diminishing viewership of NFL games on fan ire against the athletes. Dallas Cowboys team owner Jerry Jones, after initially standing and locking arms in solidarity with the players, later threatened that any player kneeling during the anthem would not play and would possibly be cut from the roster. Jones declined to comment about his inattentiveness

1

when he was caught on video chatting with his son while the anthem played. The most vocal critic was President Donald Trump, who railed, "Wouldn't you love to see one of these NFL owners, when somebody disrespects our flag, they say 'get that son of a bitch off the field right now, he's fired!' Fired! That's a total disrespect of our heritage. That's a total disrespect of everything that we stand for, OK?"[2]

This was not the first time that race and the anthem resulted in controversy. Kaepernick was not the first African American player to protest racism and was not the first to resist standing during the display of the American flag. The examples are endless:

- Jackie Robinson, the first Black player to play Major League Baseball, gave public notice of his alienation from his nation's symbol. "I cannot stand and sing the anthem. I cannot salute the flag; I know that I am a black man in a white world."[3]
- On March 8, 1973, Brown University cheerleaders refused to stand for the national anthem before a game on the grounds that the flag did not represent them as citizens of color living under legalized discrimination.[4]
- That same year, at Nassau Coliseum on Long Island, New York, an Eastern Michigan University, African American runner stretched on the ground as "The Star-Spangled Banner" played. He stated that it was not arranged; he was simply stretching. Said his coach, "At our place, when they play 'The Star-Spangled Banner' at basketball games, a lot of the Black students don't stand. I guess things are different here."[5]
- In 2003, Toni Smith, a white basketball player for Manhattanville College, objected to the war in Iraq by turning her back to the flag during the playing of the anthem. ESPN writer Ralph Wiley described the impact of her actions: "But what Toni Smith doesn't know, and I hope to God she never does, is that very often these protests end with the ostracizing of the protestors rather than the evils they protest."[6]
- In 2004, professional baseball player Carlos Delgado walked into the dugout during the anthem the entire season, citing disapproval with the war. He reflected in 2016 about Kaepernick, "At this moment, he decided to take a knee during the anthem, and he will have supporters and detractors. I think the important thing is for him to be consistent with his principles and his message. It is not normal that here we are in 2016 and we still have segregation, marginalization, and the abuse that we have against minorities, religious communities, and African-American communities."[7]
- Former Denver Nuggets' player Mahmoud Abdul-Rauf viewed the American flag as a symbol of oppression and racism and refused to come out of the dressing room as the anthem played for much of his career. In a 2017 interview he reflected, "The anthem, the flag is supposed to represent the character of a people . . . in terms of freedom and justice and fairness and all this stuff. But we don't necessarily see that, especially people of color. We've never been really shielded by the rule of law."[8]

As this short list shows, African American athletes have faced severe criticism and charges of being unpatriotic for these protests. This was no less true during the Kaepernick controversy. NFL player Eric Reid, the first player to join Kaepernick in kneeling, commented in 2017,

> It baffles me that our protest is still being misconstrued as disrespectful to the country, flag and military personnel. We chose it because it's exactly the opposite . . . we chose to kneel because it's a respectful gesture. I remember thinking our posture was like a flag flown at half-mast to mark a tragedy. . . . It should go without saying that I love my country and I'm proud to be an American. But, to quote James Baldwin, "exactly for this reason, I insist on the right to criticize her perpetually."[9]

As in every other area of life, when Black athletes offered social critique, the backlash was brutal. Sociologist Steven R. Cureton said, "The challenge for the African-American male in America has been a constant struggle to reconcile the seemingly dominant social dynamic that black masculinity is significantly less human than white masculinity."[10] As long as athletes performed superbly on the playing field and were acquiescent off it, they received the temporary approval of white America. As long as they exhibited patriotic fervor and stood during the national anthem with a hand over their heart and were silent concerning racism off the field, they received measured acceptance. African Americans, the unspoken social agreement went, should be happy just to be able to live in America and be grateful for all of the opportunities afforded. They should just "shut up and play ball." Sports journalist Zach Johnk wrote, "Such acts of protest, often by black athletes and carried out recently by quarterback Colin Kaepernick and others who have knelt for the anthem at N.F.L. games, have a long history in the United States and an equally lengthy tradition of angering mostly white fans, sports officials and politicians."[11] In 1968, legendary white sportscaster Brent Musburger described John Carlos and Tommie Smith's raised fists at that year's Mexico City Olympics as done by "black-skinned storm troopers . . . destined to go down as the most unsubtle demonstration in the history of protest . . . insuring maximum embarrassment for the country that is picking up the tab for their room and board here in Mexico City. One gets a little tired of having the United States run down by athletes who are enjoying themselves at the expense of their country." He followed up five decades later by attacking the entire 49ers team and Kaepernick for taking a knee.[12]

Colin Kaepernick not only put his career on the line but backed up his on-field stand with off-the-field donations. His Colin Kaepernick Foundation provided $1 million to local charities, matched by the San Francisco 49ers. At the end of the 2016 season his teammates honored him with the Len Eshmont Award as the player who demonstrated "inspirational and courageous play." *Time Magazine* placed him on the October 2016 cover for "fueling a debate about privilege, pride and patriotism." He received the *Sports Illustrated* 2017 Muhammad Ali Legacy Award. Nike made him the face of their "Just Do It" campaign. Overlapped on his picture were printed the words, "Believe in Something. Even if it means sacrificing everything. *#JustDoIt*."[13] Amnesty International awarded him its highest honor, the 2018 Ambassador of Conscience Award.[14]

And at the end of the 2016 season, the San Francisco 49ers told Kaepernick that they would not be re-signing him because he did not fit their future plans, and he became a free agent. Despite being an elite athlete in the prime of his career, one who had led his team to a Super Bowl, Kaepernick has remained out of football since.

————————

BLACK PATRIOTIC PROTEST

Over the centuries, the right to protest in America has always been racialized. For many white Americans, there is disbelief, even denial, that the player's actions have anything to do with love of country. Whites exercise their First Amendment rights while Blacks are deemed unpatriotic, ungrateful, and contextually inappropriate.[15] In a 2017 *Washington Post* article titled "From Jimi Hendrix to Colin Kaepernick: Why Black Americans' Patriotism Often Looks Like Protest," Robyn C. Spencer wrote that "Black people have asserted their inextricable contributions to the history of this country while simultaneously protesting the racism embedded in the American nation-state since its inception. And yet, the patriotism of the Black activist has again come into question as dozens of American athletes have taken a knee during the national anthem."[16] Michael Tesler wrote in the *Washington Post*, "For many, to be American is implicitly synonymous with being white, and that whiteness and American patriotism are deeply linked." He listed studies where whites associated "being white" with patriotism while being Black equated as the opposite.[17]

Given the history of continuous oppression that Black Americans experience, the question is not "Why are Blacks unpatriotic?" Rather, one could reasonably ask, "Why are Blacks patriotic at all?" In the face of centuries of crippling structural racism and white supremacy, African Americans have proven their patriotism time and time again. There has been no other racial demographic to suffer generations of government-enforced subjugation yet retain an elevated level of patriotism. African Americans have fought in

America's wars, often at disproportionately high rates. Blacks vote in presidential elections at rates similar to whites, and in 2008 and 2012 exceeded those of whites. African Americans, even when faced with legalized oppression, retained unwavering love for their nation even as they demanded the rights of American citizenship. Blacks remained loyal to a country whose primary intent was to keep them in their place as second-class citizens, even as they did all that was asked of them out of a desire to participate in the dream called America. The jazz singer Nina Simone once said to an interviewer,

> When I was young I knew to stay alive. As a Black family, we had to work at it. We had to keep secrets. We never complained about being poor, or being taken advantage of, or not getting our share. We had to keep our mouths shut. . . . So I knew to break the silence meant a confrontation with the white people of that town. And though I didn't know I knew it, if the Black man rises up and says, "I'm just not gonna do that anymore," he stands to get murdered. But no one mentioned that, which is, indeed, quite strange.[18]

It is ironic that white men like Eric Rudolph, Timothy McVeigh, and Ted Kaczynski perpetrate extreme violence while disparaging the U.S. government as oppressive to their liberty,[19] while it has been the Black race which has faced persecution while being accused of lacking patriotism.

THE ORIGINS OF BLACK PROTEST

The Black protest movement did not begin with Colin Kaepernick. Far from it. During every period of oppression, active, deliberate, and ongoing movements have evolved to match the levels of oppression experienced. Black protest is defined as the variety of ways African Americans have resisted oppression, racial discrimination, and exploitation. It has taken place through overt resistance by public demonstrations, nonviolent and violent revolt, marches, petitions, publications, sit-ins, migration, community organizing, and boycotts. Throughout American history, the penalty for Black protest has been severe and life-threatening, so covert action was a necessary approach, especially during slavery and Jim Crow. Protest was found in the ways Blacks sought to undermine oppressive systems through teaching children how to survive, for example, and in establishing institutions of self-help and empowerment. Even philanthropy, "paying it forward," has an element of protest. A wide range of strategies and programs was used to make life better for Black Americans and oppressed people. The Anti-Defamation League states,

> There are a variety of potential goals for protest: influence public
> opinion, draw attention to and share information about a perceived
> injustice, gain a wide audience for the cause, push public policy or legis-
> lation forward, learn more about an issue, connect with others who feel
> passionate about the issue, speak one's truth and bear witness. Protests
> can also provide inspiration and a sense of being part of a larger move-
> ment. The overarching purpose of protests is to demand change.[20]

Protest movements were begun by the first African Americans and continued by their descendants each generation. According to Lerone Bennett Jr.,
"The Negro rebellion of 1960–65 is a continuation on a higher level of desperation of the evaded confrontations of the past."[21] While each generation
felt that it was the first to demonstrably rebel, all were part of a continual line
of insurgents. Alicia Garza, a cofounder of the Black Lives Matter movement,
stated,

> It is important to us that we understand that movements are not
> begun by any one person—that this movement was begun in 1619
> when Black people were brought here in chains and at the bottoms
> of boats. . . . Because there was resistance before Black Lives Matter,
> and there will be resistance after Black Lives Matter . . . a continua-
> tion of a uniquely American struggle led by Black people.[22]

Africans who were brought to the land of slavery rejected attempts to subjugate them, resisting with both reserved defiance and outright force. This
involved such things as enslaved men and women running away and indentures
working off debt to gain freedom and land rights. After permanent slavery
was instituted in the latter half of the seventeenth century, rebellions occurred
aboard slave ships and in every region slavery existed. The earliest uprisings
were in the colonial North, in cities such as New York City, and then traveled
downward throughout southern states from Virginia to Louisiana. During the
country's two internal wars, Blacks fought for the side that promised freedom.
Between 1866 and 1877, they used their freedom to pursue political office,
rewrite state constitutions, and create schools. They confronted presidents
who lacked political and moral courage. Veterans of the two world wars took
up arms to defend their homes, families, and neighborhoods against white
mobs, the police, and National Guard. In response to nationwide racial violence, they founded institutions as a form of protest to support families and
educate children. Civil rights organizations created during the 1920s and 1930s
defended a people under constant attack. The NAACP (National Association
for the Advancement of Colored People) mounted protest after protest, and,
eventually, won the judicial battle against racial segregation. During the Great
Migration, millions left the South and resettled in the North, and their voting

strength became a factor in determining presidential elections. The 1950s ushered in a period of organized protest that within a decade caused an awakening in the American consciousness about the harm inflicted by white supremacy. The final evolution was Black participation in areas previously denied to them: business, education, and politics.

The methods, strategies, and declarations have been remarkably similar in the prophetic messages and actions proclaimed over the centuries. Transportation protests, from the days of segregated stagecoaches to Montgomery buses, shared the strategies of boycott, confrontation, and disruption. The Rev. Lott Carey, of the controversial American Colonization Society, an eighteenth-century group that attempted to secure passage for Black Americans back to African countries, said, "I wish to go to a country where I shall be estimated by my merits, not by my complexion."[23] The Rev. Dr. Martin Luther King Jr. echoed those sentiments in 1963 when he spoke the famous words "I have a dream that my four little children will one day live in a nation where they will not be judged by the color of their skin, but by the content of their character."[24] Also in the 1960s, Malcolm X urged Black Americans to liberate themselves "by any means necessary." As far back as 1843 the Rev. Henry Highland Garnet urged enslaved Blacks to "use every means, both moral, intellectual, and physical."[25]

Black confrontation influenced the transformation of America from a slave-justifying nation to one that now recognizes the evils of slavery even as it grapples with the legacies of that same institution. The white population's growing awareness that human rights are due to all people owes much of this awareness to Black resistance. Blacks keenly and accurately scrutinized America's debased legal system in contrast to her stated creeds. The enslaved scoffed, both privately and publicly, at hollow, pious declarations of "Liberty or Death." Vincent Harding noted that enslaved Africans challenged the

> justice, authority, and legitimacy of their captors. Their words . . . were among the earliest forms of what we shall call the Great Tradition of Black Protest . . . if those European ships indeed represented the rising white racist nation-state and its developing systems of economic and cultural exploitation, then the black voices of the Gold Coast were also part of a beginning tradition of radical challenge to such a state. . . . They declared that for them this system had absolutely no legitimacy. . . . This was black radicalism at the outset.[26]

America marketed herself as a land of liberty and justice in the purity of daylight, yet the darkness of night revealed a more sinister, racist demeanor executed by monstrous violence. The illiterate, enslaved woman intellectually critiqued the hypocrisy of the country's revolutionary zeal. She was acutely aware of America's failure to live by her own moral and ethical standards immortalized in the Declaration of Independence that "all" are "created equal and endowed by their creator with certain inalienable rights." "All" really meant "all white men," and not even all of them, just the ones who owned property. The founding fathers mouthed pious slogans demanding political freedom from Britain yet theologically justified their enslavement of human beings as the will of God. Whites applied the demands of liberty in word only and designated it the domain "of the (white) people, for the (white) people and by the (white) people."

Through their shared experience of racial and economic exploitation, enslaved Blacks reinterpreted patriotism and inscribed upon whites the inscription of patriotic hypocrisy. Frederick Douglass wrote in a scathing essay,

> What, to the American slave, is your 4th of July? I answer: a day that reveals to him, more than all other days in the year, the gross injustice and cruelty to which he is the constant victim. To him, your celebration is a sham. . . . There is not a nation on the earth guilty of practices, more shocking and bloody, than are the people of these United States, at this very hour.[27]

Several prominent whites also subscribed to this thinking. President Abraham Lincoln privately disclosed a similar scrutiny in an 1855 letter to friend Joshua Speed: "As a nation, we began by declaring that '*all men are created equal.*' We now practically read it 'all men are created equal, *except Negroes.*'. . . . When it comes to this I should prefer emigrating to some country where they make no pretense of loving liberty—to Russia, for instance, where despotism can be taken pure, and without the base alloy of hypocrisy."[28]

Key throughout American history is the pivotal role in protest played by the masses of Black Americans. Much attention has been given in history books to national leaders such as Booker T. Washington, Ida B. Wells, W. E. B. Du Bois, and Martin Luther King Jr., but scant attention has been given to the ways in which Black people resisted in the absence of singular, national leadership. Slave insurrections, Black towns and settlements, plantation survival techniques, abolitionist activities, the Underground Railroad, mass migrations, and voting blocs demonstrate collective unity and resolve to resist oppression. Individual resistance in one area almost supernaturally mirrored actions in different locales throughout the nation. There materialized an assemblage of methods used by men and women whose identities shall forever be unknown. A spirit motivated resisters to plan rebellions and to migrate from southern killing fields. And when competent leadership appeared, thousands marched, withstood beatings, spent nights in jail, and braved threats to act in unison to resist, resist, resist. Masses of people of African descent altered the course of this nation in ways still unacknowledged. One Duke University researcher on the *Behind the Veil* project, which gathered Jim Crow–era recollections, wrote, "When you really listen to people, they were resistant to the laws and to the insults given to them by white supremacy and they resisted it in all kinds of ways, both hidden and public."[29]

The masses relied on one another, shared hardships, and developed coping techniques effective across different contexts. They relied on one another because there was no one else. While leaders sought the ears of powerful and influential whites, Black parents raised their children, started businesses, built homes, fought in wars, and even fought among themselves, but they were forever moving forward toward a better day. To quote historian Edward E. Baptist, "What mattered was to matter."[30] And that meant doing what was best for family to survive with a hope for a better future for their children and grandchildren. Life was a struggle, but it was a struggle filled with sacrifice so that their children would receive the right to live fully as American citizens.

Henry Louis Gates Jr., in *Colored People: A Memoir*, wrote, "My grandfather was Colored, my father was Negro, and I am Black."[31] A vital component of protest and resistance has been the quest for identity. One could argue that protest birthed the drive for identity. Eugene D. Genovese wrote, "The question of nationality—of 'identity'—has stalked Afro-American history from its colonial beginnings, when the expression 'a nation within a nation' was already being heard."[32] Every race, tribe, and ethnic group pursued identity formation. Other races project culture, tradition, language, and familial memory as a bond to distant lands never visited. Ethnic loyalty and education changed "Oriental" to "Asian" and "Spanish-speaking" to "Hispanic," "Latino/a," and "Latinx." Gates wrote, "In your lifetimes, I suspect, you will go from being African Americans, to 'people of color,' to being, once again, 'colored people.'. . . I have tried to evoke a Colored world of the fifties, a Negro world of the early sixties, and the advent of a Black world of the later sixties."[33] The uniqueness of the African American experience is that no other demographic has had to re-create itself time and time again. Blacks have had to forge a new sense of self-awareness for each subsequent generation, each of which had to contend with a change in status often pressured by outside forces. Attempts to overcome suppression called for the creation of a new identity, as slaves became freedmen, and as the disenfranchised became voters.

African Americans are the only people to have had their ethnic heritage permanently erased. They were left with few surviving cultural traditions as their linguistic, cultural, and familial heritages were successfully expunged on the crossing from Africa to America. Cultural underpinning was dismantled as each succeeding generation had to reimagine itself in the face of a new manifestation of white supremacy. The vast majority of Blacks not only cannot identify what part of the continent their ancestors originated from, but most don't feel a sense of connection with Africa.[34] Their only linkage is race, which has not served as a source of emotional correlation. Civil rights leader Jesse Jackson said, "Every ethnic group in this country has a reference to some land base, some historical cultural base. There are Armenian-Americans and Jewish Americans and Arab-Americans and Italian-Americans; and with a degree of accepted and reasonable pride, they connect their heritage to their mother country and where they are now."[35] Irish Americans sing "Danny Boy" at wakes. Scottish American men dress in kilts even though some Americans view them derogatively as a woman's skirt. White Americans venture to Ellis Island to locate the names of European ancestors with whom they relate. Cultural traditions generate connection, something generations of African Americans never experienced. The blockbuster 2017 movie *Black Panther* caused more barbershop conversations over the fictional African country of Wakanda than any discussions of actual African countries. To many Americans, any mention of Africa yields negative images, such as Ebola, famine, and AIDS. Nina Simone commented,

> To me, we are the most beautiful creatures in the whole world, Black people. So, my job is to make them more curious about where they came from and their own identity and pride in that identity. That's why my songs, I try to make them as powerful as possible. Mostly, just to make them curious about themselves. We don't know anything about ourselves. We don't even have the pride and the dignity of African people, but we can't even talk about where we came from. We don't know. It's like a lost race.[36]

OUTLINE

This book will briefly trace the major Black protest movements of the last five-hundred-plus years in America, dividing them into five periods: 1440–1775, 1776–1877, 1878–1954, 1955–1987, and 1988–2020. Later in the introduction the description of these time periods will be provided.

This work examines the narrative of American history from an African American perspective. It analyzes American history through an African American protest lens. American history as it is typically told is incomplete and one-sided, as people of color have been excluded from the narrative of pivotal events in which they played fundamental roles. America's narrative is told from the perspective of whites who identified an event's historical significance and noteworthy contributors. Much of American history must be recast with a mind-set to publish the complete story. As early as 1912 historian Lucy M. Salmon wrote,

> History again needs to be rewritten, in order to prune away the excrescences of tradition. . . . Another reason for rewriting history is the necessity of correcting the false assumptions of writers of history. History has often been written along the line of least resistance. . . . If a history is tainted with inaccuracy, if its conclusions rest on insecure premises, if its foundations are on shifting sands, then it must be rewritten.[37]

African Americans seek not so much to revise history as to fill in the missing pieces. They seek to have their story told from a wider vantage point—beyond victimization and with wider inclusivity and greater acknowledgment beyond slavery and Jim Crow. Blacks were present in major historical events in every decade, not just being acted upon but as actors in the unfolding of the American drama. The country has been impacted by the creative genius displayed through the inventions by Black Americans of the traffic signal, gas mask, ice cream, potato chips, plasma separation, crop rotation, and so much more. Federal and state laws, constitutional amendments, and cultural regulations were written with Black people in mind. Only in the last half-century have Blacks managed to effectively challenge the narrative and receive some recognition for their role in the American story.

In order to examine the periodic protest movements, it is important to document the oppression that was being resisted. To appreciate and understand the importance of Black protest, one must be knowledgeable about the circumstances governing the lives of the protesters. Protest was not just a matter of defiance but of survival. Each generation's protest was molded by the setting to which it was reacting. As exploitation evolved from slavery, domestic terrorism, political disenfranchisement, segregation and racial discrimination, so morphed the Black response. Each decade of life in the United States was one of constant threat to one's mental and physical well-being. Each generation faced a renewed effort to dehumanize people of African descent to justify their oppression. But there was also a stream of resistance in order to neutralize the obstacles in their path. Therefore, this work contains sections that describe with great detail the life experiences of everyday African Americans and the oppression arrayed against them. The horrors of slavery illustrate how every aspect of Black life was controlled under the exploitative dominance of white supremacy. Human beings were considered property and could be bought, sold, raped, and murdered; attempts to resist resulted in inhumane punishment not limited to the resister. It was not unusual for a child, husband, or wife to be sold as a means of control. The Jim Crow era installed legalized segregation and white superiority, as violence was painfully inflicted for the slightest infraction. The institutions of justice provided little relief. That protest occurred in the midst of these debilitating conditions makes its mere presence remarkable. Blacks rallied within repressive environments to create their own opportunities for advancement, survival, and, yes, protest. While victimized, they were determined to refute a victim's mentality. They built churches, schools, businesses, and homes as a unified statement of protest and self-determination. Many fought for the right to find inclusion as American citizens while others wanted to leave or form their own separate communities. Two things have been certain in the Black experience in America: It has been an experience of racist discrimination and terrorism, and it has been one of resistance.

This work is not a comprehensive effort to fill in the gaps in each ebb and flow of American history. It is instead an examination of influential protest movements by Black Americans through five time periods. American history is divided here into five historic time lines from the period of exploitation to the second decade of the twenty-first century. I have named each period with the rubric of a collective identity espoused by the majority of people of African descent during that period: African, Colored, Negro, Black, and African American, with a brief reference to Afro-American in section 4.

This work is unique in that there is no book that documents African American protest history from the beginning of the European invasion to the twenty-first century. Manuscripts with a similar focus are few, with seemingly none covering the period beyond the civil rights movement. Vincent Harding's excellent *There Is a River: The Black Struggle for Freedom in America* (1981) concluded at the end of the Civil War. August Meier and Elliott Rudwick's *From Plantation to Ghetto* was published in 1966. Louis E. Lomax's *The Negro Revolt* (1962) and Lerone Bennett Jr.'s *Confrontation: Black and White* (1965) concluded with the civil rights movement. Documentaries include Bennett's *Pioneers in Protest* (1968) and Joanne Grant's *Black Protest: History, Documents, and Analyses, 1916 to the Present* (1968). A few others offer similar analysis but are dated. This is the only work that extends from the sixteenth to the twenty-first century. Further, it is the only work using a formula timelining American history based on these five profiles.

Although the book covers the start of the African presence in what would become America through to modern times, it is not written in strict chronological order. As the material advances, so will the time line, but not every historical episode will be covered to the degree it might deserve. Section content is arranged by topics, often combining different time periods to give a fuller picture of its significance.

Section 1, "African Protest (1440–1775)," shows that Black protest has an African bloodline. From the start, the enslaved maintained an African label.

They not only preferred to be referred to as African; they *were* African. This section covers the period from contact with European traders in Africa to life in colonial America. It examines the fact that the first Africans came to America not as slaves but as a mixture of free men and indentured servants. The latter achieved autonomy, owned land, and controlled indentures. As the institution developed, rebellions throughout the Caribbean established independent, Maroon communities. Africans posed a hostile threat to slave-holders, as they were molded by a consciousness of what it meant to live free. Slavery slowly unfolded in the American landscape and produced the lasting scourge of white supremacy. This epoch bears witness to those who never lost hope. Across the Americas, insurrection occurred, intending to liberate and strike a blow against the institution of slavery. By this period's end, a different person evolved, as the enslaved African evolved into an enslaved American.

Protest movements during this period existed in the form of rebellions, litigation, and escapes. Slavery was not entrenched for the first African colonists, and once they gained their freedom from indentured servitude, they purchased land, worked farms, and raised families. They pushed back against efforts at a secondary status and sought to participate fully in society. They even controlled indentures and enslaved others. However, after legislation in the 1660s legalized slavery, a psyche of resistance created a system of protest that was at times subliminal and at times overt. Moments of resistance occurred daily, from the disobeying of orders to finding ways to slow down the regular order of plantation life. Direct and open defiance resulted in swift consequences, so when it did occur, often the results were fatal uprisings.

Section 2, "The Protest of the Enslaved: The Color Fight Back: 1776–1877," covers the War of Liberation (also known as the Revolutionary War) to post-Reconstruction. By 1750 the goal shifted, as the enslaved no longer desired to return to the land of their fathers but to acquire freedom in America. Most were born within the United States, never having set foot in the motherland. For the enslaved, the war to achieve independence from Great Britain was an opportunity for their liberation as well. Slavery birthed a double-minded American psyche, which cried out for independence from the British monarchy while holding Africans in chains.

For the first time, racial identity was debated with ideological profundity. For the previous generation, all were African without debate. But for this war generation, "African" as a title saw decreased usage by a people who defined themselves as Americans—Colored Americans. The term *Colored* helped define who they were—human beings made in the image of God. Being Colored was distinct from whiteness and a sign of pride and self-awareness. James Walker Hood, at the North Carolina constitutional convention, rejected the interjection of "Negro" as offensive and urged racial pride.[38]

Black protest reached an amazing height during this period of enslavement, as the banner of freedom waved vigorously between the two most significant wars in the nation's history. Both the War of Liberation (Revolutionary War) and the War to Free the Slaves (Civil War) produced a spirit of individual and organized rebellion in every region of the country. These two wars shaped the nation and embedded within Blacks a determination to challenge whites to live up to their creeds of liberty and the pursuit of happiness. The 1776 revolution witnessed Blacks fighting for both the Americans and the British, wherever freedom was to be granted. As a result, protest movements were sectional and differed according to the region of the country. In the South they were largely underground leading up to the War to Free the Slaves. The enslaved, in ways subtle and overt, mounted efforts to gain their freedom and end the institution. In the North, the abolitionist movement challenged slave legislation, escorted the enslaved as conductors of the Underground Railroad, and hid the enslaved in homes and churches. During the war, freed and enslaved men fought as soldiers, and women served as spies and nurses. Freedmen voted and held office during Reconstruction and passed progressive legislation granting equal access to public education for all children.

Section 3, "Protesting Reconstruction's Failures: Negroes in the New America: 1878–1954," covers almost two-thirds of the twentieth century, extending to the civil rights movement of the 1950s and 1960s. The term *Colored* was placed aside as *Negro* gained relevance. The former term, once viewed positively, came to represent inequality associated with white supremacy. Signs with the word *Colored* placed on doors and water fountains signified subservience. As mentioned above, *Negro* was in usage as far back as the 1830s, when a "Back to Africa" colonization convention urged the rejection of both *Colored* and *African* in favor of *Negro*. By the 1930s, organizations translated "Colored" into "Negro" and after 1940 few associations referred to themselves with the term *Colored*. *Negro* was the term of choice for Booker T. Washington, Marcus Garvey, and W. E. B. Du Bois. Frederick Douglass used "Colored" and "Negro" interchangeably. Reconstruction Senator Blanche Kelso Bruce stated defiantly, "I am a Negro, and proud of my race."[39] Some insisted on the capitalization of *Negro*. But *Negro* suffered from negative connotations as whites used it derogatively as a derivative of *neggah* and *n******. Roland A. Barton wrote in 1928 that "the word, 'Negro,' or 'n*****,' is a white man's word to make us feel inferior."[40] Earlier individuals from Philadelphia urged the usage of "Oppressed Americans," with little adoption.[41]

Once slavery ended and the period of Reconstruction died out, states in the South legalized segregation and Black inferiority through Jim Crow laws and policies. American apartheid was enforced by racial violence, especially lynching. Black protest converged to create institutions that directly confronted legalized discrimination. Schools, churches, businesses, and communities were constructed as a means to combat racism. Resources were combined to invest in improving the life and well-being of the community. Black intellectuals agitated as activists and engaged in the campaign for Black rights. Institutions of learning equipped the race with leaders trained to challenge and reform the system. By this period's end, war veterans again offered pivotal leadership for the upcoming civil rights movement, the culmination of all the protests emanating from the descendants of enslaved people who openly demonstrated for full citizenship rights. The Great Migration of this period changed the culture and racial demographic of the country as the largest migration of people in the history of the nation. And Black women played a prominent role in the fight against lynching, especially Ida B. Wells.

Section 4, "Black Protest (1955–1987)," covers the civil rights movement to the late 1980s. Even though the word *Negro* was a generally acceptable title in the 1930s, there arose strong opposition from more militant leaders like Adam Clayton Powell, who early on preferred *Black*. In the fifties and sixties, Malcolm X and Black Power adherents tendered a biting critique of the "so-called Negro." They provided articulations for the Black Power movements of the sixties and seventies. Malcolm X kindled the fiery linguistic transition from *Colored/Negro* to *Black/Afro-American* even as the integrationist rhetoric of Dr. King morphed into the radical pro-Black declarations of SNCC and Black Power organizations. The Black Power movement triggered a widespread rejection of *Negro*, as Stokely Carmichael, Charles Hamilton, and Whitney M. Young promoted a defiant label. Black power meant Black control, ownership, and governance over Black institutions. In its more moderate stance, it meant equal competition with white-controlled institutions. *Black* symbolized "self-determination, pride, self-respect, and participation and control of one's destiny and community affairs." It meant "group inclusion rather than individual access. . . . Black was associated with youth, unity, militancy, and pride, while Negro increasingly connoted middle age, complacency, and the status quo."[42] By 1968 the shift from *Negro* to *Black* was in full effect. National Black magazines, such as *Ebony*, dropped *Negro* and alternated between *Black* and *Afro-American*. By the seventies, the national press advanced the adoption of *Black* as appropriate terminology. A 1974 *Newsweek* polling of the Black public revealed a growing endorsement, as a majority looked favorably upon the usage of *Black*.[43] By 1980, 81 percent responded that they had no negative reaction to being referred to as *Black*.

The irony of this adoption was the fact that, for many, in previous generations, to be called *Black* was not viewed in a complimentary manner. One was a Negro, or even Colored, but *Black* reflected demeaning connotations of ugliness, evilness, and decadence. "You so Black" jokes and taunts directed at dark skin abounded. This period represented a new mind-set, a sense of being comfortable with one's complexion. Light-skinned elites among the middle class began to refer to themselves as a Black man or woman, rejecting earlier preference for the term *Negro*. This warming marked the first time that both groups of Blacks—those with lighter skin and those with darker—were comfortable with the skin they were in. Nina Simone sang to the Black students at the University of Mississippi, "To be young gifted and Black, oh what a lovely, precious dream. . . . It's where it's at." Black became normative for a people proud of their Black skin who tossed off all negative imaging inherited from a racist past. To refute individualism and self-hatred, popular slogans were repeated: "The blacker the berry, the sweeter the juice"; "Black is beautiful"; and James Brown's "Say it Loud! I'm Black and I'm Proud." Similar to earlier nuances contrasting *Colored* with *white*, the label *Black* offered a distinction from whiteness. Comparatively speaking, if the white race was comfortable with a color label, then so were Blacks. Bennett ruminated, "The word 'Negro' (was) an inaccurate epithet which perpetuates the master-slave mentality in the minds of both black and white Americans."[44]

The U.S. census participated in the debate. From 1790 until 2013, multiple attempts at classification occurred. It was not until 1970 that "Black" as a category would reappear, and the 1990 census contained the hybrid "Black, African Am., or Negro."[45] A 2010 controversy arose when "Negro" was listed for the last time. This year marked when census takers could choose more than one category.[46] In 2013, after "Negro" was eliminated from the annual American Community Survey, Nicholas Jones commented, "Few Black Americans still identify with being Negro and many view the term as offensive and outdated."[47]

Section 4 discusses the return of *Afro-American*. It was first introduced in the 1830s with limited popularity. Mostly in the naming of institutions, such as the *Baltimore Afro-American* (1892) newspaper and the National Afro-American League (1899).[48] It experienced the shortest shelf life of the names discussed here, falling rapidly into disuse. It was revived in the sixties as Malcolm X referred to people of African descent as Afro-Americans and founded the Organization of Afro-American Unity (OAAU) in 1964. After his death in 1965, few continued to refer to themselves as Afro-Americans.

The civil rights movement was the culmination of two centuries of Black protest. It used all the methods of previous movements in the form of marches, sit-ins, legislative lobbying, and direct resistance. Protesters paid a price as police responded with beatings, violence, and collaboration with the defenders of white supremacy. The movement forced the hands of presidents and Congress to desegregate the nation and provided political enfranchisement previously guaranteed by the Fourteenth Amendment but never fully enforced. The Black Power movement was the radical stepchild of the civil rights movement. Blacks who did not embrace Martin Luther King's nonviolent methodology advocated the right of self-defense. Malcolm X, the Black Panthers, and Deacons for Defense took up arms as a means to defend their communities and advance the destruction of Jim Crow segregation policies.

Section 5, "African American Protest: 1988–2020," presents *African American* as the dominant identity. This hybrid term resonates as a connection between Africa and America and is more expansive as an ethnic reference. At the 1969 Racism in Education Conference of the American Federation of Teachers, delegates unanimously called on all individuals, educators, and organizations to abandon the "slavery-imposed name" of "Negro" and adopt "African-American" or "Afro-American."[49] Widespread adoption was prompted by a 1988 push from Jesse Jackson. He was urged by Ramona Edelin, president of the National Urban Coalition, who said, "Calling ourselves African-American is the first step in the cultural offensive. Change here can change the world."[50] During a news conference that was reported in the *New York Times*, Jackson lobbied for *African-American* and the rejection of *Negro* and *Black*. "Just as we were called Colored, but were not that, and then Negro, but not that, to be called Black is just as baseless." His campaign met with a positive reception among African American opinion makers and eventual agreement by the national press. The *Times* opined,

> If Mr. Jackson is right and Blacks now prefer to be called African-Americans, it is a sign not just of their maturity but of the nation's success. In part because of Mr. Jackson's electoral success, Blacks may now feel comfortable enough in their standing as citizens to adopt the family surname: American. And their first name, African, conveys a pride in cultural heritage that all Americans cherish.[51]

Sociologist Tom W. Smith added, "The main goal of the switch was to give Blacks a cultural identification with their heritage and ancestral homeland. . . . Culture would then become a lever for improving the lot of Blacks. . . . Black was largely considered inadequate because it did not emphasize the cultural origins of Blacks."[52] Coming full circle, the reemerging desire to identify with Africa was evidenced by the wearing of African clothing, dashikis, and afros. Africanized rituals instilled in children a connection with their African heritage, with the holiday Kwanzaa being the longest lasting. While the last title adopted, *African American* experienced the most rapid ascendency. The *Washington Post* and the *Los Angeles Times* increased their usage of the term by fourfold within just six months. Black media outlets *Ebony* and *Jet* alternated between the two titles.

Nevertheless, *Black* was never completely forsaken and retains strong usage. Younger Blacks today prefer the title for many of the earlier reasons: it provides a greater sense of unity and represents racial pride. It was the term used to self-refer in African American homes and communities. Some utter, "We are not from Africa, I was born here in the U.S. I don't know anyone there, can't even say my ancestors are from there."[53] John H. McWhorter reflected in the *Los Angeles Times*,

> So, we will have a name for ourselves—and it should be Black. "Colored" and "Negro" had their good points but . . . we will let them lie. . . . Since the late 1980s, I have gone along with using "African American" for the same reason that we throw rice at a bride—because everybody else was doing it. But no more. From now on, in my writings on race I will be returning to the word I grew up with, which reminds me of my true self and my ancestors who worked here to help make my life possible: Black.[54]

Others reject *African American* for the opposite reason: that they were not born in Africa and prefer Black because it points to the Black experience, not just where you were born. Said Darien LaBeach, "I am Black, and within that, I am a Jamaican-born, African American man, but I call myself and identify as Black. . . . My blackness is the overarching umbrella of those different flavors of my identity."[55]

The term "people of color" (POC) promotes pan-racial unity among people of the African diaspora to represent a wider array of African descendancy for greater inclusion, especially for those of Caribbean ancestry. Records indicate that its usage dates back to the antebellum period, as "There grew up a class of free persons, which preferred terms such as 'Free People of Colour' and 'Coloured.'"[56] The 1807 ban on slave importation applied to "any Negro, mulatto, or person of colour." The Presbyterian Church (U.S.A.) voted during its 223rd General Assembly (2018) to drop the term "racial-ethnic" and replace it with "people of color." Children with parents from different races advocate for *biracial*.[57]

Black protest is a continuum that never ends and takes place on a multitude of plateaus as all around the country voices ring out in opposition to racial injustice. The demand for justice took to the streets as the Black Lives Matter movement grew into a global phenomenon in the 2010s. Modern protest takes the form of social media and other forms of technology. Out of the mold of Black protest arose other protest movements, including the women's and gay rights movements whose histories have origins in the white community.

As we move deeper into the twenty-first century, the question must be asked: What is the next manifestation of Black protest? For some, it is the opportunity to provide direct leadership in movements advocating for Black rights that whites will support and embrace. Another component is for whites to take the lead of Ibram X. Kendi and not simply proclaim, "I am not a racist" but work on being antiracist—working for the abolition of white supremacy. Black protest continues to evolve as the nation progresses and will adapt to new challenges as new coalitions form to transform the world into a more tolerant and loving place.

Section 1

The Age of Exploitation in the New World

African Protest: 1440–1775

The Negroes who came to America in the eighteenth century were strikingly different from those conditioned by one hundred years of bondage. . . . They did not feel inferior to white men and, what is more to the point, white men were not so sure that they were superior to them.[1]

—*Historian Lerone Bennett Jr.*

With race relations the way they are today at the beginning of the twenty-first century, one would think that there has always been racial tension between whites and Blacks. But before the mid-Atlantic slave trade, race was not a measuring stick for social standing. One's nationality, class, or caste defined one's ranking.[2] According to Lerone Bennett Jr., "Slavery, contrary to the general impression, did not spring from racism; racism sprang from slavery. The concept of race was a direct outgrowth of the slave trade. And it was deliberately invented by an exploiting group which needed a theology to maintain and defend privileges founded on naked force."[3]

For centuries an amazing lack of animosity existed between Europeans and Africans. The book *Forty Centuries: From the Pharaohs to Alfred the Great* declared, "The ancient Greeks copied Egyptian medicine and surgery and in many other fields of knowledge looked upon the Egyptian priests as their mentors."[4] The biblical story of Joseph demonstrates that nationality mattered more than race, as it was an abomination for an Egyptian to eat with a non-Egyptian. Joseph, a nationalized Egyptian, ate at the Egyptian table apart from his non-Egyptian, biological brothers.[5]

For three centuries, between 1440 and 1775, an African presence was established worldwide. Sailing vessels ventured from Iberia (Portugal and Spain) across the Atlantic to the western shores of Africa and back home again loaded with African cargo. African explorers migrated to the degree that by 1550, 10 percent of southern Iberia was of African descent. Between 1440 and 1640, as many as 400,000 Africans voluntarily relocated to Iberia. Portuguese sailors trafficked with African chieftains for commodities of gold, ivory, wax, peppers, grains, and, yes, human beings. Europeans and Africans lived, worked, worshiped, and fought together during this period of global interchange. There existed no distinction between the treatment of white and African enslaved persons. Africans were human beings who possessed intelligence and spirituality. They were protected by law, afforded church membership, gained freedom, married, and assimilated into society. Free and enslaved Africans labored as herders, shepherds, farmers, sailors, boatmen, artisans, domestics, stevedores, porters, construction workers, and street vendors. Moriscos, Moros, Moores, and berberiscos were Iberians of Muslim ancestry who could read and write Arabic.[6]

Africans who were forced onto American shores were of a different character and perspective than those bred into captivity. Their contribution, despite their captive state, was immediate and monumental. They were determined to maintain as many of the old ways as possible, and to pass traditions on to the next generation. Unfortunately, their heritage was stripped; it would not be found in the passing on of rituals but in a mental awareness that freedom was a birthright and worth fighting for.

PRECOLONIAL LIFE

Of the Africans who reached the United States, 90 percent came from Senegambia (Senegal, Gambia, Guinea-Bissau, Mali), the Upper Guinea Coast (Sierra Leone, Guinea), the Gold Coast (Ghana), the Bight of Biafra (eastern Nigeria, Cameroon), and west-central Africa (Angola, Congo, Democratic Republic of Congo, Gabon). Almost half of the arriving Africans came from two areas—Senegambia and west-central Africa.[7]

It was the European Age of Exploitation that radically altered race relations, benefiting European societies and detrimentally impacting nations populated by people of color. A new, lower form of caste distinction emerged based solely on race. The beginnings of what would become white supremacy furnished Western civilization with a justification for military and economic domination of non-European peoples. It altered the way nations interacted with one another, often no longer based on political alliances but on whiteness.

The opportunity for the rapid accumulation of colossal wealth led to the disintegration of global relations. Greed dictated foreign policy from this moment in human history in ways never before experienced. The annexation of lands and material resources enabled European nations to hoard the greatest accumulation of wealth and military might in human history. According to August Meier and Elliott Rudwick,

> The African slave trade and slavery were major factors in the quickening of European commerce, industry, and banking, and in the shift of economic power from the Mediterranean countries to northwestern Europe—all of which constituted the Commercial Revolution.[8]

Slave-produced wealth was first realized by Portugal, then Spain, followed by Holland, France, and England. Throughout industry, including the field of banking, profits were bolstered as the benefits of doing business with enslavers produced remarkable revenue. Banks offered investment and easily acquired loans to large plantation owners who in turn produced crops that augmented European markets.

Edward Baptist, writing almost fifty years later, came to the same conclusion: European and American wealth have as their economic foundation the exploitation and enslavement of human beings: "The returns from cotton monopoly powered the modernization of the rest of the American economy. . . . In fact, slavery's expansion shaped every crucial aspect of the economy and politics of the new nation." Throughout the 1800s, cotton production went from 1.4 million pounds to 2 *billion* pounds; from less than 30 pounds a day to over 100 pounds. Slave-picked cotton supplied the factories of Europe, especially England, and propelled the Industrial Revolution. It created businesses in the North as factories manufactured slave clothing and banks supplied loans for the purchase of slaves and land. The Bank of the United States had partnerships with southern planters granting credit and financial services: "Cheap slave-produced cotton fostered a virtuous cycle of investment capital, factory building, worker employment, consumer demand for goods and a secondary growth of workshops and businesses." By 1836, cotton played a role in the production of half the revenue of the United States economy.[9]

The Atlantic slave trade, between 1500 and 1860s, resulted in tens of millions of African men, women, and children being kidnapped and sold. Neither Africans nor Europeans were the first to engage in human slavery, as it had existed in various forms throughout human history. The enterprise would not have happened without major cooperation between African kings and European monarchs. Enslavement resulted from crime, debt, or capture. For four centuries, African hunters invaded the interior of West Africa to kidnap and sell millions of bodies to European traders. Reverend Peter Fontaine in 1757 noted, "The Negroes are enslaved by the Negroes themselves before they are purchased by the masters of the ships who bring them here."[10] Olaudah

Equiano recounted three people-stealers who climbed over his village wall to kidnap him and his sister. Once captured, half would perish during the months-long, hundred-mile journey to the African coast. The exchange in African bodies was so lucrative that nations fought wars for control of the nefarious trade.[11]

Africans who cooperated with whites had no awareness of the horrors to which they doomed their captives. Benjamin Quarles proposed that African chiefs traded captives, thinking that they obligated them to an African brand of enslavement. African slavery attached no stigma of inferiority, nor was personhood diminished to property. The enslaved in Africa served as household domestics and servants. There was little to prevent one from obtaining freedom and elevating status. Amongst the Ashanti, enslaved domestic servants could marry, own property, and were shielded from capital punishment. Benin custom provided liberation to all who could afford it. Those adopted lived as sons and daughters amongst the Dahomeans, Ashanti, and Ibo. Societal elevation to prominent positions was common in the Yoruba and Hausa kingdoms. Dahomean servants, sons of beloved enslaved wives, ascended to the throne.[12] Communal rights outweighed the interests of the individual; this eliminated the concept of personal property. Anyone could work land and harvest crops. For Africans, the concept of private ownership, of a person or land, was a surreal experience.[13]

The Portuguese established a three-hundred-mile "hunting ground," transforming the Gold Coast into a Slave Coast through a harvest of Black Gold. The Slave Coast ran three hundred miles along the western coastline from Senegal to Angola into the interior along the Senegal, Gambia, Volta, Niger, and Congo rivers. Ships floated downriver to frequent trading posts.[14] In 1611 the Dutch equipped a fort on the Gold Coast, and within four decades supplanted the Portuguese as the leaders of the slave trade. Fifty to sixty forts, factories, or barracoons south of Senegal were constructed as trading houses. Each factory held a thousand souls in secluded underground caverns to await the arrival of a ship. On the beach, a surgeon would poke and prod during a makeshift health inspection. A brand burned on the chest signified either Portuguese, Dutch, French, or English ownership.[15] Victims were exchanged for cowrie shells, cotton weaves, cloth, iron bars, sheets, firearms, gunpowder, brass rings, metal, and liquor. Each region bartered over a different commodity, with 150 different items negotiated.[16]

By the 1700s, fifty thousand humans were being transported annually across the oceans; by 1800, a hundred thousand were shipped each year.[17] According to August Meier, the number of captured Africans sent to the colonies of the British Empire is astronomical, with some estimates being as high as 15 million souls. Between the years 1680 and 1786, Great Britain was responsible for the purchase of 2,110,000 terrified captives and transported them to slave fields in North America and West Indian labor camps.[18] Each century the number grew exponentially. In the sixteenth century around 900,000 arrived. As many as 2,750,000 were brought over the following century and 7 million in the eighteenth and 4 million in the nineteenth. Near the end of the slave trade, estimates are as high as 15 million being transported from African shores.[19]

While American history is broadcast as having germinated from the English seeds of 1616, the African presence in the New World preceded Jamestown by a full century. As sixteenth-century Europeans sailed across the oceans, Africans were by their side. They were with the Portuguese, Spanish, Dutch, French, and British as sailors, scouts, pirates, free persons, and servants. African explorers Juan Garrido, Esteban, Jan Rodriques, Gaspar Yanga, Juan Bardales, Juan Garcia, and Juan Beltran traveled through present-day Mexico, Costa Rica, Honduras, Panama, Venezuela, Peru, Chile, Florida, Arizona, New Mexico, and Texas. When Christopher Columbus arrived in Hispaniola (now Cuba) in 1502, his crew included his African cabin boy, Diego el Negro; Alonzo Pietro navigated the Nina. Juan Garrido sailed with both Ponce de Leon and Hernan Cortez to Florida, Alabama, New Mexico, and California. In 1513 thirty Africans accompanied Vasco Nunez de Balboa across the Isthmus of Panama to the Pacific Ocean. Africans risked all with the Spanish conqueror Lucas Vasquez de Ayllon in 1526, roaming the waters of the Cape Fear River in North Carolina.[20] In 1532 African travelers trekked across the ocean onto Peruvian soil with Francisco Pizarro. Estevanico de Dorantes, also known as Esteban the Moor, hazarded into Arizona and New Mexico searching for El Dorado, the "Lost City of Gold." He was revered as a legend as the first nonindigenous person to venture into Arizona and New Mexico.[21] Between 1584 and 1590, Sir Francis Drake situated African settlers at a base on Roanoke Island in North Carolina.[22] When French Jesuit missionaries ventured as far north as Canada they were accompanied by Africans.[23] Over the centuries, gifted Africans such as York, Negro Abraham, Jean Baptiste Pointe du Sable, Ben Bruno, Edward Rose, George Bonga, and James P. Beckwourth served as explorers, scouts, and interpreters. The presence of Africans was so evident that it was said, "The first white man to meet an Indian in America was a Negro."[24] Or to put it more precisely, an African.

COLONIAL AMERICA

Although the landing of the first group of captive Africans in Jamestown, Virginia, in 1619 is traditionally considered the beginning of the institution of Black slavery in the North American colonies of England, the fact is that the category of slave was not yet clearly defined at that time. Nor were the Africans who arrived in the early period limited to or by that status. For several decades, indeed, Blacks in Virginia and elsewhere had a status within the laboring classes that varied from indentured apprentice and servant to free man and free woman; the nature of the quest for justice, the definition of the struggle for freedom, was also fluid.[25]

America developed out of a unique syncretism between the Old World and the New, as indigenous traditions and cultures amalgamated with those of Africa and Europe. Africans became Americanized, and America, Africanized, consolidated by the absorption of Native American life skills. The African diaspora was of tremendous benefit to Spanish and English colonies.[26]

In the latter part of the eighteenth century, the British, French, and Dutch overcame monopolies by the Portuguese and Spanish crowns to emerge as dominant trading nations. A triangular trade route transmuted African labor and American produce into European manufactured goods. Products were then sold in the colonies and the Caribbean. African labor enriched European countries, which controlled every aspect of this devil's triangle.

European American colonists reaped enormous benefits. Africans were forced to adapt to their new environs, and they quickly proved themselves skilled in spinning, carding wool, tanning, ranching, herding, shipbuilding, lumbering, ironworking, cooperage, distilling, blacksmithing, carpentry, and printing. They were capable seamen on fishing, whaling, and trading ships traveling the world. Some were physician apprentices and doctors.[27] According to Meier, the enslaved labored

> in the turpentine industry, in sawmills and quarries, in the coal and salt mines of Virginia, in the iron mines and furnaces of Virginia, Tennessee, and Kentucky. They labored as riverboat and deckhands, firemen, dock workers, and laborers constructing canals and railroads. They worked in the tobacco factories of Virginia, in textile mills from Virginia to Mississippi, in cotton presses, in tanneries, in shipyards, and laundries of many towns.[28]

Gambians arrived as expert cattle herders. African trappers worked alongside the French in the lower Mississippi in Biloxi. Angolans and Senegalese helped develop regions from Biloxi to Boston. Dutch speakers planted farms in lower Manhattan as Swedish and German speakers cultivated land in Pennsylvania and Delaware. Natives from Barbados transformed Salem, Massachusetts, and the Carolina Sea Islands.

Colonial Africans were treated not much differently than their white indentured counterparts. "The first black immigrants were not slaves, nor were the first white immigrants free."[29] Africans and white indentures began their journey in the New World as equal members of one community. Negro and white Americans confronted each other as "brothers, brothers-in-law, and fellow passengers on a journey into the unknown. For forty years or more, from 1619 to about 1660, Negro Americans accumulated property, participated in the public life of the community, and mingled and mated with whites on a basis of substantial equality."[30] At this point in history, race did not automatically make a white person free, nor an African enslaved. Africans imported into the Americas arrived as indentured servants to evolve into enslaved persons. In 1619 twenty Africans, seventeen men and three women, landed at Point Comfort (Hampton, Virginia) aboard *The White Lion*. Anthony (Antoney), Isabella, Pedro, William, Angela, Frances, Margaret, John Edward, and twelve others set foot in Jamestown. They came, maintaining the same status as whites, not as enslaved persons but as indentured servants. Their indenture could last four years or as long as seven. Anthony and Mary married in 1624 and gave birth to a son, William Tucker, on January 3, 1625. He was America's first child of African ancestry born in English North America and the first baptized.[31] The *New York Time*'s *1619 Project* celebrated the arrival of Africans as central to the founding of America:

> In August of 1619, a ship appeared on (the) horizon, near Point Comfort, a coastal port in the British colony of Virginia. It carried more than 20 enslaved Africans, who were sold to the colonists. America was not yet America, but this was the moment it began. No aspect of the country that would be formed here has been untouched by the 250 years of slavery that followed.[32]

By 1649 three hundred colonial Africans held virtually every right available to whites. Status was not equated with race but by the class distinction of being a free person or servant. Indentures, regardless of race, had more in common with one another, more so than poor whites and those who were wealthy. Whites and Africans of the same standing could comingle and unite their lives. They shared the same hopes and dreams of raising families and owning land. They worked, lived, loved, cohabited, ran away, married, raised children, and died together. Both became property owners with the right to sue, testify in court, and vote.[33] A handful held official posts. As property owners, they could own the rights of title for indentured servants, white and African. Anthony obtained his freedom and, in 1651, received 250 acres of land in Northampton County for importing five indentured servants. He was the first person to hold an African in perpetual captivity after winning a lawsuit against one of his indentures, John Castor, in 1654. Richard Johnson acquired one hundred acres upon the arrival of two white indentures.[34] Other African property owners included Benjamin Doyle (three hundred acres), John Harris (fifty acres), and Phillip Morgan (two hundred acres).[35] Six thousand white indentures outnumbered two thousand Africans in the year 1671. By the end of the century the African population mirrored the number of whites.[36]

But the relatively equal status of colonial whites and Africans was soon to change, as the need for more and more labor in the South led to a dramatic increase in the trafficking of human beings. Agricultural contributions gave impetus to the South's economic growth. The demand for cheap labor increased the trafficking of human beings. White indentures, deemed too expensive for the short-term commitments demanded, emerged as small farmers often at odds with large landowners. Profitable crops traveled on a southward trajectory, and the institution of slavery followed. As crops diversified, the type of labor required changed, which impacted the institution. The production of tobacco, rice, indigo, cotton, and sugar enriched the colonies. Planters grew tobacco in Virginia, Maryland, and North Carolina for the first marketable commodity.[37] South Carolina struggled to generate revenue until enslaved Africans made rice and indigo profitable. Rice transformed South Carolina into an economic powerhouse. Wealthy white immigrants from Barbados migrated to South Carolina escorted by enslaved men and women. In 1694 expert rice cultivators from Madagascar and the Rice Coast arrived. Bantu speakers introduced cultivation techniques superior to anything Europeans had devised.[38] Georgia's coastal region was equally suitable for rice, and Louisiana sugar produced wealth and prosperity.

But cotton was king and grew to be an economic juggernaut. The 1793 invention of the cotton gin significantly accelerated stagnant harvesting. The picking machinery of enslaved hands increased annual production to excessive heights. Field hands picking cotton in 1792 filled 13,000 bales. In twenty-five years, that number swelled to an exorbitant 461,000 bales and expanded to 2 million by 1840. In ten years, three out of every four enslaved men and women were engaged in the production of the crop.[39] Slave-harvested cotton enabled American mastery over the world's economy. The richest men in the world achieved wealth upon the backs of enslaved pickers. The European industrial age and America's banking system, shipping, and manufacturing industries rose to prominence upon the unpaid labor of enslaved men and women. American servitude was the engine powering the global economy, and it profited everyone but the enslaved.[40]

Colonial Protest

Enslaved Africans maintained the protest movement inherited from ancestors. From the moment of capture, Africans revealed themselves willing to die to resist captivity. It was one thing to keep a person enslaved who had been born into bondage; it was another to persuade one born in freedom to accept it docilely. They had a living memory of a homeland populated and ruled by people who looked like them. They had their own languages and cultures that no lash or brutal whippings could eliminate. This made first-generation enslaved Africans a relentless, constant threat. From the moment of captivity, escape was plotted in search of a way to return across the ocean. By the start of the War of Liberation,[41] the native-born enslaved population outnumbered those being shipped from across the ocean. Despite dwindling numbers, imported Africans comprised the majority of those who ran away. Dual motivations stemmed from a desire to regain liberty as well as nostalgia for homeland. They passed on to their children a fierce passion for freedom. The mother of Nat Turner, a native-born African, instilled in him a hatred that inspired his 1831 rebellion. Long after importation ended and the connection to Africa diminished, the spirit to rebel did not.

For the first-generation enslaved African, there was no question of who she was. She was not African American, Negro, or Colored, but an African in America. Those kidnapped retained a consciousness filled with self-worth that connected them through shared experiences. It was reinforced daily by facial and body scarring inscribed onto human flesh by fellow Africans during traditional rites of passage. This provided meaning in a world that attempted to strip a man of his masculinity and a woman of her femininity. They held onto languages and whispered words and phrases into young ears. Traditions and cultures were assimilated into their new reality, secretly passed on from one generation to the next. African traditions and rituals upheld the priority of the family and its sanctity as supreme. They may have been forcibly relocated to America, but they remained Africans.

FROM FREEDOM TO SLAVERY

There was no statutory recognition of slavery in Virginia until 1661. Steps in that direction had earlier been taken by modifying the definition of the condition of persons legally recognized as servants. Most of the Negroes brought into Virginia after 1640 had no indentures or contracts and could not look forward to freedom after a specified term of service. Some others that were brought in enjoyed the dubious distinction of having contracts providing that they were "servants for life" or "perpetual servants." This was the result of vigorous efforts, extending over a generation, to lengthen and renew terms of indenture so as to provide for continuous service.[42]

—*John Hope Franklin*, From Slavery to Freedom

Interracial relations in the colonies remained rather peaceful during the period from 1619 to 1660. There were opportunities for advancement for all who resided in European settlements, regardless of race. Both races felt that if one worked diligently, a decent life awaited. But change was coming that would doom one race to enslavement, and the other, to ownership. As indigenous lands were seized, there arose a shortage of hands to work the fields. The remedy appeared as judicial court rulings between 1640 and 1660 designated human beings as chattel property. In 1641 a court case was brought by an owner who claimed ownership of several enslaved children. The court ruled against him in favor of the parents, who maintained control over the lives of their children, for now. In 1656 a similar case decreed that the children of mulattos were servants while the children of Native Americans were free. In 1655 Elizabeth Key, a biracial woman, successfully sued for her freedom on the grounds that her father, Thomas Key, was a white Englishman and she was a baptized Christian. English Common Law, which was what then ruled the colonies, declared that the status of the father was the child's status. It was not until 1662 that Virginia fixed the child's status to that of the mother in order to keep biracial children fathered by white men in slavery. Between 1619 and 1661, because of these laws and the need for more and more labor, the lives of colonial Africans spiraled downward from indenture to permanent enslavement.[43]

Not only was the desire for wealth key in the disruption of race relations, but sexual jealousy also played a role in the emergence of racism. Procreation between whites and Africans birthed a disproportionate number of biracial children, mostly due to consensual relations between indentured African men and European women. White servants identified more so with Africans of their social caste with whom they labored and lived rather than wealthy planters with whom they shared race.[44] African men and white women, indentured and free, were routinely intimately involved and bore children. The sight of biracial children provoked feelings of discomfort for some whites. Such a mixture could prove to be an existential threat to developing theories of African inferiority and eventually threaten its moral justification. What were the sociological ramifications when a white woman fell in love with a Black man? If a white man loved an African woman, what status would the children have?

Rather than reexamine flawed assumptions, white male lawmakers introduced legislation to make illicit interracial relationships. Laws delegitimized Black-white relations and limited the rights of Africans. In the 1630s, colonial legislatures outlawed such cohabitations. White women faced severe penalties for consensual relationships with African men. A white man, Hugh Davis, was whipped "for defiling his body in lying with a Negro."[45] In 1662, Virginia became the first colony to pass laws against "intermingling" and "anti-amalgamation."[46] Pennsylvania, in 1726, prohibited marriage between Africans and whites. Reverend John Blacknall was fined fifty pounds in 1743 for marrying an interracial couple. Christian Finny, a white, female, indentured servant, had her term of indenture extended by two years for having two biracial children. These laws turned out to be ineffective as mixed marriages increased. By the start of the War of Liberation, most of the free people of color were biracial. North Carolina Supreme Court Justice William Gaston noted that most were the children of white women.[47]

A spiritual dilemma arose concerning the morality of Christian enslavers who participated in the nefarious trade. Religious faith was twisted to justify oppression. When it came to the relationship between Christians and the institution of slavery, it was "rice over righteousness," meaning that the labor needed to grow crops justified the means used. Economic greed sought a theological paradigm to underpin an emergent white supremacist worldview. The so-called "Curse of Ham" purported that the will of God commanded that the "Sons of Ham," Africans, serve as the servants of the white race.[48] Cain Hope Felder, in *Troubling Biblical Waters*, recorded that "the idea that the blackness of Africans was due to a curse, and thus reinforced and sanctioned enslaving Blacks, persisted into the seventeenth century."[49]

In the following decades, African humanity was securely locked in a box stamped "Slave." The year 1640 was the pivotal year in the transition from indentured servitude to perpetual enslavement. First, the race of the defendant compounded punishments in criminal cases, with Blacks facing harsher punishment. Also, the number of years served in indentured servitude was increased. Phase two was a sentence of lifetime enslavement. The capture of three runaway indentured servants resulted in two white men receiving four additional years while the African, John Punch, was made an enslaved person "for the time of his natural life."[50] The 1660s cemented the final phase and eliminated any chances for equality. Race forevermore set status—to be Black was to be enslaved while to be white was to be free. In 1662, as noted earlier, Virginia aligned the status of the child to that of the mother: "All children born in this colony shall be bond or free only according to the condition of the mother." This reversal of the 1641 ruling established a legacy of racial prejudice. In 1667, Virginia removed the last barrier to lifelong enslavement when baptism into Christianity no longer prevented permanent enslavement: "The conferring of baptisme doth not alter the condition of the person as to his bondage or freedome." The colonies of New Jersey, New York, Maryland, North Carolina, and South Carolina enacted similar legislation.[51]

Known more for its twentieth-century version, the concept of Jim Crow was introduced long before that harrowing period. Jim Crow, a period of legalized segregation, borrowed its name from a minstrel show jingle "Jump

Jim Crow." A white actor, Thomas "Daddy" Rice, painted in blackface, mimicked and belittled people of African descent as a form of white entertainment.[52] Jim Crow's social and legal policy of racial segregation designated separate water fountains, eating places, bathrooms, courtroom Bibles, and signs assigning usage for "Colored" and "White" people.[53] In the 1690s, the nation's first segregation laws were passed. Any manumitted man or woman (one set free from slavery) was given six months to vacate or be enslaved for an additional five years. In 1691 anyone freed in Virginia had to vacate the colony immediately. In 1705 enslaved Blacks were categorized as property and were forbidden to worship. Any apprehended off their plantation without a permission ticket could be punished. Any missing for over two months could be executed. They were barred from taverns after dark; race curfews were passed in Connecticut (1690), Massachusetts (1693), and Rhode Island (1703). New York limited gatherings to three slaves, and no more than twelve could attend a funeral. In 1713 South Carolina posted a Negro Watch with authority to stop, question, and detain any Africans after nine p.m. By 1715 North Carolina prohibited ownership of weapons by Blacks and withdrew their voting rights. In 1721 Delaware barred religious services and the bestowing of Christian names. In 1740 South Carolina's Negro Act authorized patrols, placed limits on gatherings, and outlawed literacy. In 1741 North Carolina legislators passed a series of similar regulations. Insurrectionists were executed, and emancipation required self-deportation within six months. South Carolina passed a freedman's poll tax and instituted status papers in 1760. Between 1753 and 1785, patrols, castration, badges, supervision, and curfews disrupted lives.

Thus, in just a few decades' time, the seeds of white supremacy were sown in the very ground that championed the right to "life, liberty, and the pursuit of happiness."

Section 2

The Protest of the Enslaved

The Colored Fight Back: 1776–1877

> Oppressed Americans! Who are they? Nonsense brethren! You are COLORED AMERICANS. Indians are RED AMERICANS, and the white people are WHITE AMERICANS, and you are as good as they, and they are no better than you.[1]
> —*The Rev. Samuel Cornish, Presbyterian minister*

Black protest in the one hundred years between 1776 and 1877 materialized in the resistance to slavery. It was a huge shackle around the necks of people of African descent, and it chained all, whether enslaved or free, white or Black. The enslaved were lifetime captives while freedmen and women were judged to be racially inferior. Whites were conflicted by a national creed professing universal freedom, but reality presented a limited freedom meant only for some. The enslaved engaged in protest to gain freedom by any means available: self-purchase, escape, or emancipation. Freedmen acted as coconspirators, assisting in private and public agitations. Northern men and women of color focused energy on racial equality in the face of discrimination and violence north of the border. To be Black in colonial America meant to live a life of constant protest.

This century bore witness to significant events that shaped the destiny of the United States. Two wars set the future course of the nation. The War of Liberation (Revolutionary War) occurred between 1776 and 1887 and the War to End Slavery (Civil War) between 1861 and 1865. Both were wars of independence. The first established a new nation; the latter liberated enslaved men and women from chattel slavery. Both impacted the country culturally, socially, politically, and economically.

The period between 1776 and 1865 was critical in the development of an American mind-set. The new nation founded on libertarian principles had to choose between its ideals and justifying an economic system based on enslavement. Not only did it choose exploitative wealth; it adopted an ideology of racial inferiority to validate forsaking the democratic principles it claimed to uphold. Race shaped the nation as deeply as any international and national political wrangling. White supremacy nurtured and matured. It empowered whites to believe that no matter whether you were rich or poor, newly arrived immigrant or second-generation American, you were better than anyone of African descent. Intrinsic worth was based on light skin color, which gave whites biological cohesion. Even those whites mired in poverty had a sense of superiority—at least you were not Black. The only worth for an African was measured by the revenue the white race received for their unpaid labor.

By 1776, a majority of the enslaved were born in the continental United States rather than kidnapped from Africa. This was the first generation to identify America as their homeland with no perceived connection to Africa other than skin pigmentation. It was the place of their parent's birth.[2] This affected the form and shape of resistance. This cognitive detachment from Africa culminated in a determination to achieve liberty and remain in the land of their birth. African-born parents and grandparents sought to maintain connection to cultural folklore and traditions, but emotional attachment dwindled. Historian Deborah Gray White wrote of this generation,

> They won't know Africa in the same way that their parents knew Africa. . . . The child also generally won't know freedom in the same way that a parent knew freedom. . . . Biblical names began to replace African ones. Escapes took different forms: newly transplanted Africans often fled in groups and established African-style "maroon" communities on the frontier, while American-born slaves usually escaped alone or in pairs.[3]

This generation no longer identified themselves as African but as Colored Americans. Freedmen associated the word *African* with bondage and felt no emotional connection. By 1835 the break was almost complete, as all desired a distinctiveness uniquely their own. Many asked, "If I am not white, then what or who am I?" They concluded that they were Colored, defined by who they were not. The white people they experienced were greedy, lustful, and cruelly inflicted a system of injustice. Colored set them apart from white people; Colored demonstrated a sense of self-awareness. It carried a more acceptable labeling despite the amount of skin melanin—light or dark, you were a person of color. It was an act of protest. This generation's protest was unique in that they fought against an institution, slavery, that had the enforcement and authority of the federal government. None of the branches of government were particularly friendly to overtures of liberation; instead, they passed and supported fugitive slave laws to appease Southerners. People of the African diaspora had to find local allies in a fight that was often regional and individualistic. It would take the Civil War to destroy slavery's hold. It was also a time of identity formation and nationality affirmation. Colored protest had the fewest resources and smallest revenue, and most of its combatants were in bondage. However, it also produced a tremendous sense of unity among those engaged in the fight, as both the enslaved and freed women and men listed emancipation as priority one for the race.

The agreement was not universal. Light-skinned, freed Blacks, counter to darker-skinned freedmen, voiced opposition to identification as Colored. Many were the birth children of African mothers and white planters and felt isolated from both. Their complexions more closely matched that of whites, and they sought to avoid the racist stereotypes directed at their dark-skinned brethren. The 1835 annual convention of the Colored People of America passed a resolution that urged "our people to abandon use of the word 'Colored,' when either speaking or writing concerning themselves; and especially to remove the title of African from their institutions, the marbles of churches, etc. . . ."[4] Both the resolution and the adoption of the terms *Anglo-African* and *Oppressed American* were ultimately rejected.

SLAVERY: BORN IN HELL

Slavery is the next thing to Hell.[5]
—*Harriet Tubman*

American slavery as an institution was unlike any economic or social system ever to exist in world history. It was far crueler and more punitive, unjust, and exploitative than European serfdom or African bondage. It was more complex in the social layers serving as its foundations, as differing realities for the same system existed depending on which region of the country it materialized. But at its core, it rested on the principle that one person had the absolute right to own another, could seize the benefits of his labor, and own her children. It created the unique determination that a human being could be reduced to property and could be discarded at the master's whim. The enslaved had no personhood or rights as residents or citizens of the United States. The legacy of slavery has been a continuation of the notion of Black inferiority. Black life is not valued or respected, as the Black Lives Matter slogan points out. This ingrained mind-set was witnessed in the 1857 ruling of Supreme Court Chief Justice Roger Taney that Blacks had "no rights a white man was bound to respect."[6] This is the curse American slavery has imposed on the United States, with impact on the global community.

Under this newly controlled and legislated period of slavery, nothing for the enslaved was as it had been: every aspect of life was regulated and tightly controlled. Families lived in daily fear of being sold away from one another. Individuals endured rape, dismemberment, sexual trafficking, solitary confinement, pedophilia, family separation, detention, and murder. The enslaved were commodities to their owners and subhuman to other whites. It was the worst possible situation a person could experience. Even those whose burden was not as arduous, due to biological lineage or position, desired to be free.

During this period, three classes of enslaved men and women existed throughout the institution of slavery. Field slaves worked in tobacco, rice, indigo, and cotton fields harvesting crops. House slaves provided domestic service to enslaver families. And large labor camps contained skilled laborers or artisans. They excelled as carpenters, blacksmiths, sawyers, coopers, leather workers, tanners, shoemakers, cloth workers, spinners, weavers, tailors, painters, brickmakers, and plasterers. Enslaved men living in northern states served as shipbuilders, printers, goldsmiths, silversmiths, cabinetmakers, ropemakers, fishers, whalers, butlers, and valets. Women operated as cooks, weavers, laundresses, and maids.[7] The most talented were rented out to farms, factories, or individuals for extra revenue. Some retained a portion of the money to buy freedom.

Living conditions were abysmal. Cabins were small and constructed of logs cemented with mud and sticks atop a dirt floor. One or two windows with flimsy shutters afforded minimum privacy, warmth, or security. Six to twelve persons, not all related, lived in a one- or two-room cabin. Food consisted of cornmeal, fat pork, coffee, lard, flour, and molasses, supplemented by greens, sweet potatoes, and garden vegetables. Men would work all day and hunt at night for rabbits, raccoons, and possums. Clothing was sewn together from feed sacks made out of osnaburg, a course, plain-weave fabric called "n***** cloth." Shoes would wear out before the year's end, leaving the person barefooted despite weather conditions.[8]

Such was the life of enslaved men, women, and children. Lives were controlled from sunup to sundown, from birth to death, with no guaranteed rights. In the words of Eugene D. Genovese, "Slavery stands convicted of inexpiable crimes against Black people . . . one of history's greatest crimes."[9]

Regardless, Black protest occurred. It was as varied as the institution. Protest continued despite the daily threat of punishment with brutal whippings delivered as messages to others that the consequences of rebellion were dire. The enslaved dared to resist both mental and physical bondage. Verbal refusals included creating a work environment where they refused to work and pretended to be unable to perform tasks. Direct protest included fighting overseers, running away, and planning rebellions. Each plantation owner was fully aware of the possibility of a slave insurrection and lived with a sense of foreboding. There existed a cycle of living dangerously each day. The enslaved desired freedom and dared to resist as much as was possible without endangering those they loved.

Stolen

Plantation owners regularly complained that enslaved persons stole as supplies diminished or went missing. The enslaved protested that owners had no right to criminalize taking crops by those who did the work. Any thievery they did, they believed, was secondary, and they accused masters of originating the art of theft. They dissected grievances as mere hypocrisy and used the very words and phrases of the oppressor as weapons against him. Appropriation of the fruit of their labor was not theft in their eyes but payment for unreciprocated toil. They were the ones who did all the work and had a right to share in the proceeds.

Slavery was the more significant criminal act, as they equated bondage with being pilfered. They challenged the veracity of the statements and charged whites with the theft of children, wives, husbands, mothers, fathers, uncles, and aunties. Nothing could rationalize family separations when children were sold. But the sale of children was the rule rather than the exception, as most were sold between the ages of five and ten. Advertised family units were often sold off one by one as young children sold for a cheaper price with greater financial returns. One-third of enslaved children experienced being a sale, either through their purchase, that of their parents, or coupled with their mother.[10] Nothing was a greater evil than the evils they endured. Every enslaved person lost loved ones never seen again. Stolen adults wound up with multiple families, depending on the number of times relocated. A silent, internalized protest was the only safe response to heartbreak as children, parents, siblings, and spouses were sold away.

The enslaved described their capture as theft from family and tribe. Enslaved person Shang Harris declared, "Dey talks a heap 'bout de n****** stealin'. Well, you know what was de fust stealin' done? Hit was in Africy, when de white folks stole de n******, jes' like you'd go get a drove o' hosses and sell 'em." Ann Parker complained, "My mammy, Junny, wuz a queen in Africa. Dey kidnaps her an' steals her 'way from her throne an' fetches her hyar ter Wake County [NC] in slavery." Hannah Crasson charged, "Dey stole [Granny Flora] frum Africa wid a red pocket handkerchief."[11]

Religious justification used by whites, including clergy, that slavery was God's will and intended for the enslaved's good was completely rejected by the enslaved. The enslaved ridiculed the use of Scripture, notably the Ten

Commandments, to embed in their psyche the command "Thou shall not steal." Their counterargument was that owners broke God's commandments and would be held responsible on judgment day.

Seasoned with Pain

No enslaved man or woman submitted to slavery willingly. Especially those who were born in freedom. Before they could be useful as human working machines, they had to have their consciousness altered, and for some, broken. This process was called "seasoning."

Before a man or woman would answer to the servant call, he or she had to be seasoned. Enslaved persons were not released to the plantation and trusted to perform labor subserviently without first being groomed. A tortuous method primed them for captivity, subverted the former self, and severed connections to a past life in preparation for enslavement.[12] Thomas Clarkson wrote in "An Essay of the Slavery and Commerce of the Human Species, Particularly the African,"

> It is conjectured, that if three in four survive what is called the seasoning, the bargain is highly favourable. This seasoning is said to expire when the two first years of their servitude are completed: It is the time which an African must take to be so accustomed to the colony, as to be able to endure the common labour of a plantation, and to be put into the gang. At the end of this period, the calculations become verified, twenty thousand of those, who are annually imported, dying before the seasoning is over.[13]

Captives in the United States were subjected to seasoning under the supervision of their new owners. An older enslaved man or woman would be assigned as a mentor to teach rules and prohibitions. Both were held accountable based on how quickly the new ward adjusted to life amongst the enslaved. American seasoning was in two versions. The first was a shorter version experienced upon arrival. A more extensive version awaited those in need of a more intense subduing. The most rebellious were imprisoned on work farms lorded over by cruel, sadistic overseers. The process groomed one for a life of submission to being poked and prodded publicly.

> The first generation of African-Americans, men made in the image of Cato, had to be mastered. The breaking of the slave, the destruction of the African as an individual—this was the first task before the pioneer white Americans. For slavery to succeed, it was necessary to annihilate the thinking processes of slaves. Naked power was not enough; the white man's power had to be internalized. The slave, in

other words, had to be robbed of his self-conception and self-respect. He had to become someone else or pretend he was someone else. . . . Equally harsh, and far crueler, was the mental violence, the wrenching of minds out of cerebral sockets and the crushing of bones of belief and habit.[14]

The gifted orator and abolitionist Frederick Douglass wrote in 1833 of his own experience with the crueler version of seasoning:

> Master Thomas at length said he would stand it no longer. I had lived with him nine months, during which time he had given me a number of severe whippings, all to no good purpose. He resolved to put me out, as he said, to be broken; and, for this purpose, he lent me for one year to a man named Edward Covey. . . . Mr. Covey had acquired a very high reputation for breaking young slaves . . . as a 'n*****-breaker.'. . . I lived with Mr. Covey one year. During the first six months of that year, scarce a week passed without his whipping me. I was seldom free from a sore back. My awkwardness was almost always his excuse for whipping me. We were worked fully up to the point of endurance.[15]

Those headed for the Caribbean or South or Latin America went through this same seasoning process. The remnants of a free mind had to be erased. It was imperative to break their spirits and remake them through a routine of inflicted pain, torture, and abuse. A freshly captured African made an insufferable enslaved person. He had to be reoriented from living for himself, the master of his own life, into an obedient, mindless zombie compliant to another's will.[16] Jamaica was a dreaded location, with an estimated 33 percent dying from the brutal seasoning process within the first year.[17]

Slave Name / Free Name

One of the first conditioning tools of the enslaver was to strip away all elements of one's past by imposing a new name, a slave name. Owners demanded that the child have a Christian or English name immediately after birth. A scene from the television mini-series *Roots*, written by Alex Haley, has Kunta Kinte beaten at a post until he accepted his new name, Toby.[18]

Names instill self-worth and help create one's identity. They give information on family and heritage. According to Ben L. Martin, "Names can be more than tags; they can convey powerful imagery. So naming—proposing, imposing, and accepting names—can be a political exercise."[19] Names are so vital that every culture puts forth naming traditions and rituals. In America infants inherit family names. African cultures named a child based on desired characteristics that would influence the child's destiny.

By first assigning a new name, the institution of slavery stripped not just one's name but any sense of individuality. The enslaved protested this erasure and created new traditions to pass on to daughters and sons. Enslaved communities kept alive African naming traditions secretly practiced and maintained by parents. West African cultural naming rituals occurred during the ninth month, when males received the name of a family member. Invoking this tradition challenged all attempts to reassign paternal legacy. Publicly the child was presented under an approved appellation while in private the newborn was gifted with an original name. A child could have two names, an African free name as well as an enslaved title. Several African derivatives were commonplace, such as Quaco, Quashee, Cuffee, and Phoebe.

A final act of defiance materialized in the rejection of names associated with enslavement. Upon manumission, they renamed themselves, retaining their first name and abandoning their owner's last name. Escapees to the North, where slavery was outlawed in most states by 1804, would celebrate upon arrival with a name change to symbolize a disassociation from the past. A new name represented psychological rebirth. A century later, the Nation of Islam (NOI) assumed a similar ideology and advocated that Blacks drop their last name, their slave name. Malcolm Little morphed into Malcolm X; Cassius Clay, into Muhammad Ali; Lew Alcindor, into Kareem Abdul-Jabbar; and LeRoi Jones, into Amiri Baraka. Similarly, Black parents, beginning in the late twentieth century, rejected labeling for their children by creating original names with phonetic spelling.

Sunup to Sundown

Formerly enslaved Henry James Trentham scornfully confessed, "Marster had four overseers on the place, and they drove us from sunup till sunset. Some of the women plowed barefooted most all the time, and had to carry that row and keep up with the men, and then do their cooking at night. We hated to see the sunrise in slavery time, 'cause it meant another hard day; but then we was glad to see it go down."[20]

Masters sought to squeeze out as much work as a single life would allow. The enslaved agonized under the demands of strenuous labor from the moment they were young children to when they were aged adults. Many labored six to seven days a week, depending on the degradation of the master's greed. Work did not stop due to weather, rain, snow, or sun. "[Enslaved persons] worked six days from sun to sun. Usual day began when the horn blow and stop when the horn blow. They get off just long enough to eat at noon. If they forcing wheat or other crops, they start to work long before day. Sometimes the men had to shuck corn till eleven and twelve o'clock at night."[21]

The life of a field slave was dreadfully agonizing. Their work in the field was set by the rising and setting of the sun, but they had additional chores such as feeding animals, repairing tools, and shucking corn, which meant they averaged sixteen hours of work a day. Women had to work as long and as hard as the men. All were underfed and poorly clothed. The annual distribution of clothing consisted of the men receiving two coarse cotton shirts, one or two pairs of woolen pants, maybe a set of poorly made shoes, and a woolen winter jacket. Women received a single dress, maybe two depending on the owner's whims. Even if the clothing wore into rags, it would not be replaced until the next distribution.[22]

The work of house slaves never ended as they were on call every hour of the day or night. They enjoyed fewer holiday breaks than field hands and assumed extra responsibilities for parties and celebrations. Even though they lived in relative comfort in the big house, they often slept in rooms just as bare as outdoor quarters, with little furniture or accessories. Some slept on the floor at the foot of the master's bed, or outside the door, to readily respond to the smallest whim. Former enslaved woman Elizabeth Sparks told Claude J. Anderson of the Federal Works Project, "I slept in my mistress's room, but I ain't slept in any bed. No sir! I slept on a carpet, an old rug, before the fireplace."[23] They were punished for the slightest infraction, such as a simple look perceived as defiance or sassing. Most house slaves were women who experienced savage beatings and sadistic treatment, as mistresses took their frustrations out on them, especially if their children bore a striking resemblance to her own. They were susceptible to rape by the master who would force on them sons, visiting males, neighbors, business acquaintances, and workers.

Everyone had to work; the start date for an enslaved child was as early as age five or seven. Joe Hugh of Zebulon, North Carolina, remembered that small children kept chickens out of the garden, swatted flies off the eating table, took water to the fields, collected kindling wood, and kept the yard clear of debris.[24] Sarah Louise Augustus recalled, "My first days of slavery was hard. I slept on a pallet on the floor of the cabin, and just as soon as I was able to work any at all, I was put to milking cows."[25] Robert Toatley described the atrocious practice of feeding enslaved children:

> You've seen pig troughs, side by side, in a big lot? After all the grown n****** eat and get out the way, scraps and everything eatable was put in them troughs. Sometimes buttermilk poured on the mess and sometimes potlicker. Then, the cook blowed a cow horn. Quick as lightning, a passel of fifty or sixty little n****** run out the plum bushes, from under the sheds and houses, and from everywhere. Each

one take his place and souse his hands in the mixture and eat just like
you see pigs shoving around slop troughs.[26]

To make this horrific life bearable, the enslaved negotiated for minor
incentives. Sundays were almost always off, with some parts of the day on
Saturday. Special holidays assigned time off on Good Friday, Easter, and
the Fourth of July. Christmas anticipated a break in the rigorous schedule,
enhanced by special privileges of travel and visitation to other plantations or
the closest city. Infrequently gifts were exchanged between families, with a
few owners distributing presents.[27] But for the most part, holidays were only
a brief respite.

Enslaved persons protested by doing everything in their power to slow
down work. There was a compromise between the enslaved and the master. "The masters held the upper hand, but the slaves set limits as best they
could."[28] Historians Raymond A. and Alice Bauer labeled it "indirect aggression" through the use of organized strikes as groups and individuals. Malingering, feigning illness or disability, property destruction, faking ignorance,
not showing up, and running away were a regular part of the life experience
of the enslaved.[29] Even the most passive would be silent, even when they had
knowledge of another's resistance. Certain men and women were known for
their belligerent behavior and were a threat to any who sought to dominate
them. Not even the threat of being sold down South softened the attitudes of
the most resolute. While most did not outwardly resist on a daily basis, the
inner motivation to protest was a constant.

Colorism

An African American proverb goes like this: "If you're light, you're all right!
If you're brown, stick around! If you're Black, get back!"[30] There are few
areas in the African American experience in which color prejudice has not
been present. The lighter your skin, the better your situation could prove to
be. During slavery, it was no guarantee of a less harsh experience, but it did
not hurt—especially if the plantation owner was one's father. This favorit-
ism was present in Black-white relations and affected relationships within the
race, both positively and negatively. Favored light-skin offspring most often
aligned themselves alongside their darker brethren and assisted in a variety of
ways. But in some regions, they looked askance upon their darker brothers
and sisters and mirrored the bigotries of white society. In the 1890s, "color-
phobia" was a term originated by Black leadership. Your value was based on
the darkness or lightness of your skin and could impact your ability to advance
socially, politically, and economically.[31]

Owners openly discriminated against both men and women based on how dark or light their skin hue. Preferential treatment and jobs were reserved for those with skin tones closest to white. Social status was affected as light-skinned Blacks were considered smarter and more suited for certain positions, especially working in physical proximity to whites.[32] Bettye Collier-Thomas and James Turner referred to the "value of color," where lighter skin granted the perception that one was intelligent and endowed with leadership capabilities: "The historical data support the observation that all too often the offspring of miscegenation on the plantation were more likely to have been manumitted, given property, some money and provisions for education, all of which accrued to them a distinct social advantage over others that continued after slavery."[33]

Passing as white has been a frequent occurrence throughout African American history. Any light-skinned runaway could pass him- or herself off as having only European ancestors. If a white-skinned person managed to escape far from home, it was possible to pass for white. Men would shave their hair to prevent hair texture from betraying them. In 1822 two of Sallie Hemings's children by Thomas Jefferson, Beverly and Harriet Hemings, walked away from Monticello to live as white, and "neither their connection to Monticello nor the 'African blood' was ever discovered." Once liberated, some chose to live openly as a person of color; others would integrate into white society and never reveal their racial identity.[34]

Color animosity has been constant throughout American history. Norfolk native William Coker remembered, not too fondly, skin prejudice within his community:

> First grade. The very first day, the teacher placed you in what was to be your permanent seat. All of the little fair-skinned, curly-haired girls and boys were placed on the first, second, then maybe some of them in the third row, according to how well they dressed and their skin complexion. There were no dark-skinned children on those three rows. . . . A little girl named Rosa, with black velvet skin and coarse, long black hair sat for eight years in the last row, in the seat closest to the door. She was almost voiceless.[35]

Colorism continues to this day and was even evident at the height of the aforementioned Kaepernick controversy. On iHeartRadio, former New England Patriots cornerback Rodney Harrison openly challenged Kaepernick's right to kneel on behalf of African Americans on the premise that he was not African American; therefore he could not understand racism. "I tell you this, I'm a black man. And Colin Kaepernick—he's not black. He cannot understand what I face and what other young black men and black people face, or people of color face, on an every single (day). . . . You know, I don't think he faces those type of things that we face on a daily basis." Kaepernick is indeed Black, the son of a white mother and Black father. When he was corrected, Harrison apologized on Twitter. "I should not have called Colin Kaepernick's race into question during this morning's radio interview. It was a mistake and I apologize. Last point I want people to know. I never even knew he was mixed."[36] Patrick Mahomes, the Super Bowl–winning quarterback who is also biracial, has had to defend his blackness. He addressed the issue in 2020 in *GQ* magazine: "I've seen how people, on Twitter, have tweeted and said, 'Oh, you're not full Black.' But I've always just had the confidence and believed in who I am. And I've known that I'm Black. And I'm proud to be Black. And I'm proud to have a white mom too. I'm just proud of who I am. And I've always had that confidence in myself."[37]

Owner-Father

It was no secret that enslavers raped enslaved women under their dominance; one need only witness the frequent presence of biracial children on small farms and large plantations alike. Enslaved adults knew firsthand the fathers of these children, while whites refused to acknowledge the obvious. An owner could have two families on the same manor. One lived in the main house with him while the other resided in the quarters, with no recognition of the relationship between the two. Mary Boykin Chesnutt wrote in her diary, "Like the patriarchs of old, our men live all in one house with their wives and their concubines; and the mulattoes one sees in every family partly resemble the white children. Any lady is ready to tell you who is the father of all the mulatto children in everybody's household but her own. Those, she seems to think, drop from the clouds."[38]

Enslaved children were often utilized as the primary caretaker for a white half brother or half sister and made responsible for their well-being. Ellen Craft was the daughter of her owner whose mother worked as a domestic in the Big House. At the age of eleven she was given to her white sister, Eliza, as a wedding gift.[39] Formerly enslaved W. L. Bost said,

> Plenty of the colored women have children by the white men. She know better than to not do what he say. Didn't have much of that until the men from South Carolina come up here and settle and bring slaves. Then they take them very same children what have they own blood and make slaves out of them. If the Missus find out, she raise revolution. But she hardly find out. The white men not going to tell and the n***** women were always afraid to. So they jes go on hopin' that thing won't be that way always.[40]

An enslaved woman and her children could gain independence out of a relationship with an owner who fathered her children. Children could be emancipated in adulthood or at their father's death. In 1851, owner Samuel I. Cabell wrote four wills containing the following statements:

> My woman, Mary Barnes, together with all her children, I do hereby give their freedom to take effect immediately at my death. . . . In the event of sudden demise, this instrument of writing is intended to show or make known that Mary Barnes and all her children—namely, Elizabeth, Sam, Lucy, Mary, Jane, Sidney, Ann, Soula, Eunice, Alice, Marina, Braxton and an infant not named, are and always have been free, as I have every right to believe they are my children. I want and it is my will that they shall be educated out of all the moneys, bonds, debts due me; land, stocks, farming utensils and household to be equally divided between them.[41]

While some encounters ended favorably, most did not. Heartrending is the response of many white fathers toward their children. Few were acknowledged, and there were severe consequences for any who dared speak publicly of this well-known secret. Children were informed by their mothers about their fathers but warned never to approach them in a familial manner. Candis Goodwin revealed in 1937, "Course all the time they know and I know, too, that Massa Williams was my pappy. I tell you something else. Got a brother living right on this here street. But it ain't knowed round here. It would ruin him. 'Course he's white."[42] Few children by enslaved women were emancipated at the moment of their birth by a father. Most remained enslaved, and many were sold by their own fathers. Isiah Jefferies confided, "I is what is known as a outside child. . . . I lived on the de Jefferies plantation, below Wilkinsville in Cherokee County. My father was Henry Jefferies. My mother was Jane Jefferies. . . . She was sold in slavery to Henry Jefferies."[43] White wives demonstrated extreme denial and tried to ignore their stepchildren or treated them severely. Savilla Burrell observed, "Old Marsel was de daddy of some mulatto chillun. De 'lations wid de mothers of dese chillun is what give so much grief to Mistress. De neighbors would talk 'bout it and he would sell all dem chillun away from dey mothers to a trader. My Mistress would cry 'bout dat."[44]

This reprehensible behavior wasn't limited to owners of the enslaved but to those who bought and sold them as well. Edward Ball revealed the misdeeds of trader Isaac Franklin as told to him by a descendant, Kenneth Thompson: "Bad habits concerning sex were rampant among some of those men. You know they took advantage of the black women, and there were no repercussions there. I read, in many places, that slave traders had sex with the women they bought and sold."[45]

The Fancy Trade

Sex played a significant role in the longevity of slavery. Enslaved women were sold for the sexual pleasures of white men from one region of the country to the next. Black women were viewed not only through an economic lens but though one of sexual exploitation by rape, child breeding, sexual leasing, human trafficking, prostitution, and sexual violence. Women were considered property with which white men could do anything they desired. "Fancy girls" or "fancy maids" were sold to participate in what was called the "fancy trade," which forced female mulattoes to live as mistresses, known as "mulatresses." Eugene Genovese revealed that certain cities possessed markets where women were sold for this purpose, with Louisville and New Orleans chief among them. He estimated that an attractive woman might sell for as much as $5,000 while a talented blacksmith would only gather $2,500.[46] The slave trader, Isaac Franklin, communicated through letters the price of his human commodities: "The fancy girl, from Charlattsvilla (Charlottesville), will you send her out or shall I charge you $1100 for her . . . I could have sold as many more if we had of had the right kind, men from 8 to 900 dollars, field women large and likely from 6 to 650 dollars . . . a great demand for 'fancy maid(s)' and a price of $900 for a 'Yellow Girl (Charlott).'"[47] Antebellum historians have not dealt adequately with this damning piece of Americana, as it places a blemish that is extremely difficult to remove.

Formerly enslaved Jacob Manson stated,

> Marster would not have any white overseers. He had n***** foremen. Ha! ha! He liked some of de n***** 'omans too good to have any udder white man playin' aroun' 'em. . . . He had his sweethearts 'mong his slave women. I ain't no man for tellin false stories. I tells de truth an dat is de truth. At dat time it was a hard job to find a marster that didn't have women 'mong his slaves. Dat wus a general thing 'mong de slave owners.[48]

Historian Tiye A. Gordon described "fancy girls" as women with African and white blood yet a near-white appearance. Dark-skinned females, however, were not exempt from sexual trafficking. Gordon writes, "The Fancy Trade was a clandestine prostitution ring . . . the buying and selling of mixed-race female slaves for the primary purposes of private prostitution and coerced concubinage . . . where the rape of Black women could be bought and sold."[49]

Edward E. Baptist dealt extensively with this topic in *The Half Has Never Been Told* and wrote about the pervasiveness of sex as an enticement. He powerfully documented sex as a prime influence in the conscious and unconscious motivations in the purchase of enslaved bodies. It is without debate that enslaved women were procured as nonconsensual mistresses, concubines, and prostitutes. Especially desirable were lighter-skinned women, often the children of white fathers who sold them, regardless of the nefarious designs of those paying.[50] Lerone Bennett analyzed a horrid interpretation:

> Beyond that was the obvious fascination of black skin for white men and women. The master opened his eyes on a soft black mother surrogate whoever afterwards held him in the lap of a monstrous and forbidden dream . . . and later, of course, it was this woman's daughter or, in many cases what turned out to be the same thing, his father's daughter, who initiated him into the mysteries of love.[51]

Collier-Thomas agreed: "In some cases, the value of the slave, as property, increased if the admixture produced a person of unique beauty. For comely female slaves, it could mean a life of concubinage, as they were frequently bought for that purpose."[52]

Formerly enslaved Mattie Curtis of North Carolina charged that not only did fathers sell their daughters but also participated in incestuous relationships: "Mr. Mordicia had his yaller gals in one quarter ter dereselves an' dese gals belong ter de Mordicia men, dere friends an' de overseers. When a baby wus born in dat quarter dey'd sen' hit over ter de black quarter at birth. Dey do say dat some of dese gal babies got grown an' atter goin' back ter de yaller quarter had more chilluns fer her own daddy or brother."[53]

The Breeding Machine

At the nation's founding, there was more direct opposition to the slave trade than there was against the institution of slavery itself, as the former was deemed more insufferable. The United States Constitution makes no direct mention of the words "slave" or "slavery" even though certain provisions allude to it. When ratified in 1787, article 1, section 9, clause 1, outlawed the importation of African slaves. As a compromise to southern states, the ban would be delayed for twenty years.[54] Long before the 1808 importation ban took effect, enslavers invested in the breeding and sale of human beings as an industry. The United States became the first nation to birth human children as a commodity of commerce. With the importation ban in place, enslavers realized early that birth rates could produce an accumulation in numbers and result in a net profit. The U.S. population increased as a result of biological breeding methods as 700,000 slaves in 1790 ballooned into four million by 1860. Virginia, Maryland, and North and South Carolina mass-produced captives, who were sold to the territories of Mississippi, Alabama, Arkansas, Texas, and Louisiana.

Slave breeding cast America onto the world's economic stage. Prior financial profit paled in comparison to the wealth gained from the birthing and sale of people by "natural increase." Throughout southern history, "breeding farms" harvested a human crop.[55] A charge issued during the 1787 Constitutional Convention alleged that the idea of prohibiting the importation of African slaves was to inflate their worth in southern colonies. In his 1792 budget, Thomas Jefferson formulated that each year his worth increased by 4 percent based on the birth rate of his enslaved population. He bragged to George Washington that Virginia's wealth increased through the birth and sale of children.[56] Virginia exported almost 300,000 human beings to other states between 1830 and 1860. Maryland was a secondary exporter, closely followed by the Carolinas, Kentucky, Tennessee, Missouri, and Georgia. Breeding was approved by every owner, regardless of race. The Black slave breeder William Ellison was notorious for breeding in South Carolina.[57] Samuel Hairston and his family were the South's largest breeders of human chattel. They controlled forty-five plantations defiling ten thousand slaves in Virginia, North Carolina, and Mississippi.[58]

Planters matched couples based on reproductive capability and forced young adults to procreate. According to the *Atlanta Black Star*, "Each enslaved male was expected to get 12 females pregnant a year. For five years, men were used for breeding. Owners demanded that females start having children at age 13. By 20, enslaved women were expected to have birthed four to five children. Women who birthed a child regularly were referred to as 'good breeders.'"[59] Certain men would be set aside as studs and loaned for pay to impregnate females on other farms. Rarely would they be informed about their children or allowed to establish bonds. The *Slave Narratives* identified an enslaved man named Burt as having produced more than two hundred offspring. Elige Davison confessed, "I been marry once before freedom, with home wedding. Massa, he bring some more women to see me. He wouldn't let me have just one woman. I have about fifteen and I don't know how many chillum. Some over a hundred, I's sure."[60]

As an incentive, promises were made to liberate an enslaved female once she bore fifteen children. This promise was rarely kept. When a woman had a child, minimum rewards were received. Barren women were punished. Her marriage would be dissolved, and she could be coupled with another man or see her husband attached to another woman. Formerly enslaved Thomas Hall registered his regret:

> Gettin' married an' having a family was a joke in the days of slavery, as the main thing in allowing any form of matrimony among the slaves was to raise more slaves in the same sense and for the same purpose as stock raisers raise horses and mules, that is, for work. A woman who could produce fast was in great demand and would bring a good price of the auction block in Richmond, Va., Charleston, S.C., and other places.[61]

Enslaved men and women were not willing accompanists in this wretched scheme and resisted forced sexual relations and involuntary marriage. They defied orders to cooperate in conception in every manner possible. Women would secretly practice birth control, refuse to engage in sex with male breeders, and were willing to withstand the consequences of beatings and being sold away. The enslaved, especially women, despised males who willingly participated in this ritual of sin. But despite this resistance, the practice endured until the mid-1860s and the war's end.

The Whipping Post

Punishment was a constant torment of slavery. Masters adhered to a belief that slaves would not work unless motivated by corporal punishment. Edward E. Baptist wrote descriptively on "torture for profit" as an instrument of the "whipping machine." Extreme cruelty motivated human fingers to do the impossible in order to increase production to higher and higher levels. Under the threat of torture, the enslaved trained their left hands to work independently of the right to increase prodigiously the amount of cotton collected. The master refuted any notions that enslaved labor was not as productive as free labor and concluded that slave-picked cotton contributed greatly to the industrial revolution in Europe and America's economic fortunes. All this was made possible by sadistic torture. Willis Cozart chillingly stated, "I'se seed n****** beat till de blood run, an' I'se seed plenty more wid big scars, from whuppin's but dey wuz de bad ones. You wuz whupped 'cordin' ter de deed yo' done in dem days. A moderate whuppin' wuz thirty-nine or forty lashes an' a real whuppin' wuz a even hundred; most folks can't stand a real whuppin'."[62]

The only way to escape a whipping was greater efficiency. Though there were less-extreme forms of punishment—the withholding of weekend passes, the denial of time off on weekends or travel privileges[63]—overseers professionalized sadistic measures to increase productivity. This was achieved through the infliction of savage whippings, floggings, and even dismemberment when production goals were not met, and often even when they were. Beatings were carried out with a lash, whip, or cat-o'-nine-tails on the back of a victim secured to a pole or tree—the whipping post. To intensify the pain, some were "bucked," with hands and feet tightly tied, with a stick slid between the elbows and knees to immobilize the victim. A typical punishment was thirty-nine lashes, one hundred in severe cases, by the owner, overseer, driver, or planter's wife.[64] Jacob Mason declared, "We worked all day and some of the night, and a slave who made a week, even after doing that, was lucky if he got off without getting a beating. We got mighty bad treatment, and I just want to tell you, a n***** didn't stand as much show there as a dog did. They whipped for most any little trifle. They whipped me, so they said, just to help me got a quicker gait."[65]

Pregnant women were not exempt from beatings, forced to lay on the ground face down, with a hole dug to hold their extended belly.[66] Paddles with holes induced blisters that were then basted with salt, pepper, or vinegar to intensify the pain. Family members would ease the agony by applying grease or lard to wounds once safely back in the cabin. Dismemberment was common. Ears were clipped or completely lopped off; toes, fingers, hands, and feet would be sawed off. Shackles and leg irons with dangling heavy metal balls cut into the flesh, causing severe swelling. Metal necklaces adorned with bells sounded an alarm in times of flight. If an enslaved person tried to run away, ankle tendons could be severed.

Slave patrollers hunted down runaways and ushered them back, often in worse shape than before they ran. Henry James Trentham described the lockup:

> Dere wus a jail on de place for to put slaves in. . . . Slaves wus put dere for punishment. I seed lots of slaves whupped by de overseers. . . . Some of de slaves run away. When dey wus caught dey wus whupped and put in de stocks in de jail. Some of de slaves dat run away never did come back. De overseers tole us dey got killed reason dey never come back. De patterollers [patrollers] come round ever now an' den an' if you wus off de plantation an' had no pass dey tore you up wid de lash.[67]

The Auction Block

The worst experience the enslaved endured was the separation of families, as children, parents, and siblings were sold on the auction block. It was not unusual to witness a coffle of chained slaves walking solemnly, guarded by traders and patrollers. Men, women, and children would parade to the town square in a march of agony and dismay. Any site could hold an auction—an open space, or a building with advertisements painted on its front. At times sales occurred on a simple, stage-like platform; other times, on merely a small, square box as buyers inspected these human commodities. W. L. Bost remembered,

> The auctioneer he stand off at a distance and cry 'em off as they stand on the block. I can hear his voice as long as I live. If the one they going to sell was a young Negro man this is what he say: "Now gentlemen and fellow-citizens here is a big black buck Negro. He's stout as a mule. Good for any kin' o' work an' he never gives any trouble. How much am I offered for him?" And then the sale would commence, and the n***** would be sold to the highest bidder. If they put up a young

n***** woman the auctioneer would cry out: 'Here's a young n***** wench, how much am I offered for her?' The poor thing stand on the block a-shiverin' and a-shakin' nearly froze to death. When they sold, many of the pore mothers beg the speculators to sell 'em with their husbands, but the speculator only take what he want. So maybe the pore thing never see her husban' agin.[68]

Grief was the immediate reaction when a family was separated. It drove parents to acts of desperation. No amount of desperate pleading, bargaining, or promises stopped a child's sale. Savilla Burrell stated, "They sell one of Mother's chillun once, and when she take on and cry about it, Marster say, 'Stop that sniffing there if you don't want to get a whipping.' She grieve and cry at night about it."[69] Most were never seen again, and it was a despair every enslaved person endured at some moment in life. Even in their later years they would remember the moment when they fell asleep in their mother's arms, only to wake up to find her forever gone. Elige Davison reflected,

> When you gather a bunch of cattle to sell they calves, how the calves and cows will bawl, that the way the slaves was then. They didn't know nothing about they kinfolks. Most chillun didn't know who they pappy was, and some they mammy, 'cause they taken away from the mammy when she wean them, and sell or trade the chillum to someone else, so they wouldn't get attached to they mammy or pappy.[70]

Extremely traumatizing was the examination by potential buyers. Intrusive hands and fingers violated every inch of skin. Crevices too private for public exposure were debased at a buyer's whim. Initially branded by captors, the new owner would rebrand using a red-hot iron, such as those used to burn marks onto cattle hides. Historian Edward Ball described the scrutiny: "Buyers looked at the people, took them inside, made them undress, studied their teeth, told them to dance, asked them about their work, and most importantly, looked at their backs."[71] Anyone with a scarred back was considered problematic, as scars indicated resistance despite brutal punishment. It was extremely rare to see a bare back absent of whip marks as embroidered scars whiplashed the spines of both men and women.

Any circumstance that affected the enslaver's household affected slave families. Children were shipped away as a dowry for a daughter's wedding. They were sold to settle debts, fulfill a will, or deliver punishment for disobedient behavior. The recurrent reason for a sale was debt settlement. Creditors received payment through the sale or confiscation of enslaved men and women. Owners with a large number of enslaved persons would sell one or two to purchase land or increase their money in hand. Enslavers practiced deceit to the enslaved, other whites, and even themselves. There was little that shamed the hearts of greed-driven owners, but many desired the appearance of being benevolent and swore that they did not separate families. Even those who resisted separating families relented, as it was easier to market an individual than find a buyer for an entire family. Auction records reveal that individual sales dominated most transactions. Once a child reached the age of five, there arose the danger that he could be sold at any time.[72]

The quickest threat to maintain order was that of being sold, to be "put into an owner's pocket." Sarah Debro said, "One day Grandpappy sassed Miss Polly White, and she told him that if he didn't behave hisself that she would put him in her pocket. Grandpappy was a big man, and I ask him how Miss Polly could do that. He said that she meant that she would sell him, then put the money in her pocket. He never did sass Miss Polly no more."[73]

Even in these conditions, there were acts of individual protest. Henry "Box" Brown escaped by mailing himself in a box from Richmond to Philadelphia. What prompted his act was the selling of his pregnant wife and three children. He lamented in 1849, "My agony was now complete, she with whom I had traveled the journey of life in chains . . . and the dear little pledges god had given us I could see plainly must now be separated from me forever, and I must continue, desolate and alone, to drag my chains through the world."[74]

Black Death

Death was a constant in the life of the enslaved. The average life span of an enslaved person was forty years. Poor nutrition, in combination with inhumane treatment, depleted the body's ability to fight off disease and injury. Many were simply worked to death. One out of every four infants died at birth. New mothers were seldom allowed maternal leave and were forced into hard labor in the field as soon as a day after their child's delivery. Mothers carried their newborns to the field and set them under a tree. Henry Bibb recalled, "The mothers have no time to take care of them—and they are often found dead in the field and in the quarter for want of the care of their mothers." Formerly enslaved Bob Jones mourned, "Durin' de course of our married life we had five chilluns but only one of dem lived ter be named, dat wus Hyacinth, an' he died 'fore he wus a month old. Edna [his wife] died too, six years ago, an' lef' me ter de mercies of de worl'. All my brudders an' sisters dead, my parents dead, my chilluns dead, an' my wife dead."[75]

When an enslaved person died, seldom was there anything resembling a funeral. According to Elijah Green, the body was buried at night, as the farmer refused to lose any portion of a day's work. On one plantation, the body was sandwiched between two boards painted black with shoe polish.[76] According to formerly enslaved Mary Reynolds,

When a n***** died, they let his folks come out the fields to see him afore he died. They buried him the same day—take a big plank and bust it with a ax in the middle 'nuf to bend it back, and put the dead n***** in betwixt it. They'd cart him down to the graveyard on the place and not bury him deep 'nuf that buzzards wouldn't come circlin' round. N****** mourn now, but in them days they wasn't no time for mournin.[77]

Georgia Baker remembered that "when a n***** died dem days, dey jus' put his body in a box and buried it."[78]

The enslaved's worth to the enslaver continued even after death. Historian Daina Ramey Berry, in *The Price for Their Pound of Flesh*, meticulously estimated financial value based on age, gender, region, and period in which they lived. A monetary price was set upon the enslaved before they were born, reevaluated from infancy to adulthood. Even death reaped financial benefits for the owner,[79] as insurance policies were secured in case of premature death.

There were other attempts to capitalize on the death of the enslaved. Bodies were purchased, legally and illegally, by medical schools to perform autopsies. Grave diggers dug up bodies for dissection. Doctors advertised in newspapers their willingness to pay above-market prices for the sick and elderly.

SLAVE PROTEST: BY LAND OR BY SEA

Mr. Woodward refers to Nat Turner's revolt as the "bloodiest" in our history. In this he is wrong, again; the uprisings in South Carolina, 1739–1740, in Louisiana, 1794–1796, and in Louisiana in 1811 caused greater loss of life than did Turner's. Of course, slave conspiracies—as those led by Gabriel in 1800 and by Vesey in 1822—involved hundreds, perhaps thousands, of rebels—and were bloody enough if one takes into account the lives of the rebels. The decade 1850–1860 also witnessed slave unrest and outbreaks more widespread than Turner's, though even the latter did shake Virginia to its foundations.[80]

*—Historian Herbert Aptheker responding to historian
C. Vann Woodward in a 1988 debate over the
number and frequency of slave uprisings*

Between 1509 and 1865, more than 250 land rebellions and almost 500 ship mutinies occurred. American slavery was an unimaginable abomination that stimulated hatred and a fierce aspiration for retribution. The enslaved realized that the institution was so entrenched—not just as an economic institution but also as part of the mental psyche of whites—that only total obliteration would eliminate it. The experience of slavery centered around violence; therefore, violence was justified as a viable option to obtain liberation. In the mind of the enslaved, violence was the only weapon capable of destroying the institution.[81] Insurrectionists concluded that it had to be obliterated through wholesale destruction. White supremacy had such a hold that only total eradication of the structures maintaining it would have any real effect. Whites who benefited from the institution had to be greeted with the same devastation they inflicted on the enslaved.

Insurrectionist Denmark Vesey's instructions were clear that the rebels would set fires, "and for every servant in the yards to be ready with axes, knives, and clubs, to kill every (white) man as he came out when the bells rang."[82] In 1770, Henry Ormond was ambushed by five of his enslaved persons. As he begged for his life, a young female replied as they strangled him to death that, since he had no mercy on them, they would have none on him.[83] There was a clandestine contract to meet violence with violence agreed on long before the uprising leader John Brown's death statement that "the crimes of this guilty land will never be purged away, but with blood."[84] One enslaved man pledged an oath that "'he would be damned if he did not kill his master, if he ever struck him again.' Another was ecstatic as he dug his master's grave: 'I have killed him at last.'" Women were no less docile, and one remarked in court, "'If she, the witness, were a man, she would murder her master.' Another woman was frank. 'If old mistress did not leave her alone and quit calling her a bitch and a strumpet, she would take an iron and split her brains out.'"[85]

Antebellum slavery existed in an environment grounded in subterfuge. Both master and slave were equally engaged in a dance of deception as each maintained a relationship of mutual distrust, deceit, and loathing. It was in the owner's interest to promote, and even believe, the image of the happy, contented, fun-loving enslaved whose only joy in life was to serve him. It was in the enslaved's interest to convey that she was not a threat while concealing genuine hatred.[86] The result was a combustible powder keg, liable to be lit by the smallest spark. Owners reacted with forcefulness to the smallest act of insubordination out of fear of being perceived as not in absolute control. The enslaved responded with a determination to deliver justice, inflicting the same level of injury.[87]

From the moment of capture, extreme caution had to be taken as resistance was an everyday occurrence.[88] The enslaved were aware that their relationship with whites was entirely economic and thus were knowledgeable of their financial worth. They knew that there were limits to a master's retribution, for a disabled individual decreased profitability. In the 1942 article "Day to Day Resistance to Slavery," Alice Bauer and Raymond Bauer revealed that the enslaved were very aware that their labor only benefited the master and that it was in their benefit to resist in every way possible. They defined their resistance as "indirect aggression"—the slaves as a group made a general policy of not letting the master get the upper hand.[89]

The constant fear of insurrection terrified whites. As much as the enslaved person lived in fear of punishment or sale, the master lived in constant apprehension of men and women plotting liberation. Historian David Robertson, in his biography of Denmark Vesey, disclosed, "To white residents, and some visitors, Charleston in the late eighteenth and early nineteenth centuries was a city of remarkable charm and beauty. But the fear behind these racial ordinances signifies that the white charm was like a grin frozen in the face of an anticipated horror . . . the fear was of a ferocious black revolt."[90] They realized that rebellion, as a contagion, quickly spread once one person was infected. Enslavers were keenly aware that the potential for resistance existed frequently in the thoughts of the enslaved. Fear resided in the heart of every owner never to slip into complacency, or a fatal blow might be struck by those living under the same roof.[91] A poor white couple shared the following:

> Where I used to live [Alabama] I remember when I was a boy . . . folks was dreadful frightened about the n******. I remember they built pens in the woods where they could hide, and Christmas time they went and got into the pens, fraid the n****** was risin'. . . . I remember the same time where we was in South Carolina we had all our things put up in bags so we could tote 'em, if we heard they was coming' our way.[92]

Daily sabotage sought to interrupt stability and cause disruption in the system. Constant actions of covert and overt defiance were common in the incidents of everyday living. Few worked to full capacity, knowing that the maximum productivity from one day's work would become the minimum required the next day. Those who did not meet an overseer's expectations were cruelly punished. Work strikes were to prevent ill-treatment and challenge unattainable goals. Techniques involved work stoppage, malingering, feigning illness, tool breakage, slowdowns, arriving at the wrong workplace, showing up with the wrong tools, pretending inability or knowledge, or even feigned stupidity. During planting season, seedlings would be trampled, wrongly rooted, or hoed over; supplies would be wasted or mysteriously disappear. Livestock would wander off through unlocked gates with valuable work time lost during the search. Resistance manifested itself despite the possibility of undeserved punishment, family separation, and unreasonable labor demands. Running away happened frequently. Some strayed for a short period as a defense against unjust treatment; others departed intending never to return. The typical runaway was a young, male field hand between twenty and thirty-five years of age. Africans and boat pilots were the most likely to flee, as they had both means and navigational knowledge. Escapes were planned and assisted by others who supplied food and information. Those born enslaved generally ran alone while newly arrived Africans escaped in groups of kin and tribe. Fall and spring were the favored seasons to run, as work increased, and the weather was suitable for traveling long distances without having to seek shelter from the elements.[93]

For those who stayed, resistance never ceased. Fire and poison were subtle yet ingenious tools, as the source of either was extremely difficult to diagnose. The threat of poison was always present, since slaves were responsible for the preparation of food.[94] Elijah Green revealed that an enslaved couple, Harry and Janie, were hanged in Charleston after they poisoned the family's breakfast after enduring a beating.[95] Fire was the greatest weapon in the hands of rebels, as tacticians used it as a diversionary trick to generate panic. Denmark Vesey and his coconspirators would repeat to one another, "Nothing could be done without fire."[96] The initial fire would be their owner's home, followed by the torching of entire towns. Grandiose schemes that were never carried out included the entire incineration of the cities of New York, Richmond, Charleston, and New Orleans. Once a fire started, it was difficult to extinguish as flames leaped from one wooden building to the next. Early American cities obsoletely fought fires by forming a bucket brigade as one line passed buckets of water to douse the burning structure as the other line passed the bucket back to the water's source. When New York's Governor Clark's house burned, his enslaved man Patrick replied that he wished that the governor was inside as the blaze consumed the house. In that same incident, another named Cuffee poured any water from buckets passed to him on the ground as he laughed and danced.[97]

It is remarkable that intimate details concerning insurrections were muted so successfully. Newspapers would not print stories of rebellions, and planters seldom discussed uprisings among themselves, especially in the presence of the enslaved. Owners universally agreed that it was in the institution's best interest to squelch any information of uprisings. It was also in the interest of their own survival not to allow successful forays to be widely known, lest they inspire others. Only in the most extreme circumstance was there public discussion. Nat Turner's uprising, August 5–11, 1831, in Southampton County, Virginia, had monumental shock value due to the high number of white casualties, around sixty. There was severe retaliation. As we will later see, while it is the most infamous, it did not have the highest death count, nor did it contain the largest number of rebels.

On every island where slavery existed, insurrection ensued. On almost every Caribbean island—including Cuba, Puerto Rico, Martinique, Antigua, Barbados, Jamaica, St. Vincent, the Virgin Islands, and Haiti—there was vehement revolution. Ten years after Christopher Columbus arrived there on his first stop in the Americas, Hispaniola (what is now Haiti and the Dominican Republic) was the location of a 1502 event where the governor accused angrily that "the Negroes encouraged the Indians to rebellion." It was more likely of mutual agreement as these two dark-skinned peoples united in revolt against white colonizers. It was said that "the Indians escaped first and then, since they knew the forest, they came back and liberated the Africans."[98] A 1522 insurrection on the island was a merger between indigenous people and Africans on a sugar plantation owned by the son of Christopher Columbus, Admiral Don Diego Colon. Africans escaped high into the mountains or trekked down into an island's interior to found New Afrikan communities. By 1542 Maroons, Black fugitives who banded together, posed a formidable threat to Spaniards who dared venture into their territory. They were fearless and defiant. They named their settlements *Disturb Me If You Dare* and *Try Me If You Be Men*. Maroon songs resonated with defiance: "Black man rejoice / White man won't come here / And if he does / The Devil will take him off."[99] They were so formidable that the governor of Jamaica granted autonomy under the condition that they desist in raiding towns and seizing livestock. He reached the same compromise with three other settlements of self-emancipated Africans.[100]

The Haitian Revolution of 1791 was the only successful overthrow in the hemisphere that resulted in an independent, Black-led island nation. Haiti (Saint-Domingue) was the world's first Black republic and the second colony, following the United States, to liberate itself from a European colonial power. Of more considerable significance, it birthed the first modern nation to abolish slavery, decades before the United States. Haiti assumed that it would have a diplomatic connection with the United States, as both uniquely experienced self-liberation and traditional democratic values.[101] Toussaint Louverture remarked, "It is not a liberty of circumstance, conceded to us alone, that we wish; it is the adoption absolute of the principle that no man, born red, black or white, can be the property of his fellow man."[102] Haitian independence had an immediate impact on the United States. Between 1791 and 1804, Haitians battled Napoleon's French army. Napoleon needed revenue to finance this and other wars and was thus compelled to sell the Louisiana Territory to the United States for the meager price of $15 million. The new territory doubled the terrain of the new nation.[103] Thus the Haitian Revolution unintentionally helped establish the United States as an economic powerhouse. The new territory, and in particular New Orleans, bolstered the nation's economy through slave labor. The sugar economy caused the swiftest accumulation of wealth the world had ever seen. In an ironic twist, the rebellion that destroyed slavery in Haiti accelerated its spread in the United States.[104]

It also had a powerful impact on the American enslaved. Haiti was on the lips of both Black and whites as the spirit of rebellion instilled both white fear and Black hope that it would happen on American shores. President Thomas Jefferson, a slaveholder, was a particular adversary to the new Black nation. By 1806, he cut off trade with the new republic, an act that did irreparable damage to the country's economy. The island nation presented such intimidation to American slavery that the United States did not formally recognize Haitian independence until 1862, almost sixty years after liberation. Black rebels took inspiration from the liberation achieved in Haiti and desired to accomplish the same for themselves. Haitians migrated into the country and told stories of valiant battles defeating better-equipped white armies by a people determined to throw off the shackles of slavery. Black leaders remembered and cherished the Haitian success as Frederick Douglass referred to Toussaint Louverture as "the noble liberator and law-giver of his brave and dauntless people."[105]

Spanish-owned Florida rose to the equivalent of the biblical promised land of milk and honey for the enslaved.[106] The original rail of the Underground Railroad ran not north but south, away from the southern British colonies. In 1687 the Spanish governor of Florida declared that any male slave of the British colonies who escaped southward would be emancipated if he swore loyalty to Spain, received Catholic baptism, and served in the militia for three years. As the news spread, bondsmen from the Carolinas and Georgia waded into St. Marys River and emerged on the other side liberated. Vast multitudes, assisted by Native Americans, ventured through dangerous terrain as the British publicly executed any they captured. As more and more journeyed south, a succession of Spanish governors refused all colonial demands to expel refugees. For almost two centuries, between 1600 and 1800, Black communities sprouted in the swamplands and marshes south of plantations as freed men and women established America's first free territories. Future president Andrew Jackson referred to Spanish-controlled Florida as "a perpetual harbor for our slaves."[107]

The 1687 establishment of St. Augustine in Florida made it both America's earliest city and the first territory established by people of African descent. Fort Mose, just north of the town, became the first permanent, self-governing settlement of African peoples in 1726. Thirty-eight armed men controlled the fort, wherein twenty families lived, comprised of sixty wives and children. This fort accomplished Spanish authorities' hopes as it became the first line of defense between Spanish Florida and British America. In 1738 a Mandinga warrior named Francisco Menende, an escapee from South Carolina, was commissioned as the fort's captain. He was the first Black officer to command Black soldiers in what was to become the United States. Between 1739 and 1840, the fort's soldiers effectively fought military campaigns against colonists from the Carolinas and Georgia and counteracted their attempts to repatriate them. During one attack on Fort Mose, African and Native American people repelled and killed seventy-five British soldiers.

Florida resulted in a coalition between people of African descent and Native Americans. In the eighteenth century, a union of tribes who spoke a variety of Muskogean languages took the name Seminole, a Crow word meaning "separatist" or "runaway." Escaped slaves merged with villages and became known as the Black Seminoles, Black Maroons, or Seminole freedmen. Danger threatened as a series of wars were initiated by their northern enemies who desired both land and fugitives. Between 1812 and 1858, three Seminole Wars were fought between the Seminole nation and the United States. The Seminoles inflicted defeat and embarrassment as well as great financial cost and the lost lives of soldiers as they successfully fought off the American government's attempts to seize property and freed men and women.

Slave-Ship Mutinies

Africans did not succumb to a life of enslavement without a struggle; this struggle continued from the moment of capture on land to aboard the ship. Benjamin Quarles wrote,

> The most serious danger by far was that of slave mutiny, and elaborate precautions were taken to prevent uprisings. Daily searches of the slave quarters were made, and sentinels were posted at the gun room day and night. But the captain and his understaffed crew were not always able to control their cargo of blacks. So numerous were slave insurrections on the high seas that few shipowners failed to take out "revolt insurance."[108]

Estimates are that one in every dozen ships experienced a mutiny. These ships included the *Brotherhood* or *Constant Mary, Robert, Africa, Hope, Don Carlos, Danish Patientia, Eagle, Le Courrier de Bourbon, Prince of Orange, Charleston, Scipio, Jackson, Sally, Nancy, Creole, Narborough, Claire, Amistad,* and many, many others.[109]

Historians rarely comment on the ship experience, rationalizing that docile captives were paralyzed by shock and trauma. The focus on capture in Africa and plantation life in combination with a lack of information on ship life led to the assumption that ship voyages were uneventful.[110] *If We Must Die* author Eric Robert Taylor disagreed, as he documented 493 ship mutinies between 1509 and 1865. He revealed that the number of mutinies was suppressed, as it was in the interest of ship captains and owners to keep them well-guarded secrets. Taylor disclosed that "slaves were rebellious, and people knew and accepted it as an inevitable consequence of the slave trade. . . . Shipboard revolts were not at all uncommon but in fact plagued slave traders every step of the way throughout the long history of the trade."[111]

From the moment a step was taken onboard, Africans scanned for opportunities to take control and sail to an African port. From the moment the wrist chains were unlocked, calculations were devised to overpower the crew.[112] Beginning around seven in the morning, eight hours were spent on deck, with the captives provided food and forced to exercise, usually dancing under threat. In his diary, one captain wrote, "They are fed twice a day, at 10 in the morning, and 4 in the evening, which is the time they are aptest to mutiny, being all upon deck."[113] The ship was most at risk while anchored in view of the home shore. They knew that if they seized control before sails were hoisted, they stood a greater chance of making it back home, and thus fought with even greater ferocity. One captain commented, "When our slaves are aboard, we shackle the men two and two, while we lie in port, and in sight of their own country, for 'tis then they attempt to make their escape and mutiny."[114]

Onboard, the men and women were separated, the latter being placed on deck in the stern. The men would be chained below for up to sixteen hours. The ship was packed using one of two methods, both inhuman and life-threatening. The first method was to pack the ship to capacity, which resulted in a higher number of deaths but assured an arrival with more survivors. Loose packing involved fewer bodies and lower mortality but with less revenue. "Most eighteenth-century slave ships had two decks with the 'tween-deck space reserved for slaves. In a Newport slaver, the average height between decks was three feet ten inches."[115] Men were housed for months in the cramped, dank, and dark crevices layered with biological waste: saliva, urine, excrement, and vomit. The air was so thick with dampness from the human exhaust that breathing was laborious and the stench overwhelmed the senses.[116] Alexander Falconbridge, a ship's surgeon, wrote,

> The hardships and inconveniences suffered by the negroes during the passage, are scarcely to be enumerated or conceived . . . the exclusion of the fresh air is among the most intolerable . . . the fresh air being excluded, the negroes' rooms very soon grow intolerable hot. The confined air, rendered noxious by the effluvia exhaled from the bodies, and by being repeatedly breathed, soon produces fevers and fluexes, which generally carries off great numbers of them . . . the floor of the rooms, was so covered with blood and mucus which had proceeded from them inconsequence of the flux (i.e., dysentery), that it resembled a slaughter-house.[117]

Crewing was a risky venture throughout the sixty- to ninety-day oceanic voyage. It was hazardous work for any crew disreputable enough to be in the business of transporting human cargo. Twenty-five to thirty crewmen were opposed by 300 to 700 rebellious captives. The crew watched for signs of rebellion, as those who relaxed paid with their lives. Ship captains attempted to purchase no more than twenty-five Africans from the same tribe to inhibit communication and limit cooperation. Captain William Snelgrave would buy or hire a bilingual African to serve as interpreter, linguist, broker, and spy.[118] Betrayals occurred when linguists or frightened prisoners relayed plans for mutiny to the captain.

Most attempts at mutiny were unsuccessful due to the crew's superior fire-power, having access to guns, cannons, swords, knives, spears, and other weapons. The captives exploited any material item to their advantage, for any blunt object could be transformed into a weapon. A hand-sized piece of metal, a standard block of wood, or a simple nail could be used to open a lock or stab a crew member in the eye. Successful attempts were often ultimately prevented due to a lack of nautical know-how and an unfamiliarity with ship instruments, including sailing the ship itself. Surviving crew members had to be trusted under the threat of death to sail the rebels home. They rarely did, steering the ships instead to American or Caribbean shores.

Despite efforts to prevent mutinies, attempts occurred quite frequently. Minor skirmishes were quickly put down and forgotten, but some resulted in the ship's capture. The *Clair*, harbored near Cape Coast Castle on the Gold Coast, was overthrown, and the crew forced to abandon the ship in 1729. The following year, ninety-six Africans commandeered the *Little George* and returned to the African coast, where they escaped onto the shore. In 1769, a fight erupted onboard the *Nancy* between the crew and the 132 captives. The fighting grew so fierce that the sounds of gunfire attracted the attention of locals. When they canoed to the ship and discovered the commotion, they joined the fight and subdued the crew. After the enslaved were liberated, the ship was destroyed. The *Narborough* mutiny resulted in the death of members of the crew; survivors were forced to sail the boat back to Bonny on the African continent.[119] In 1839, the Spanish ship *Amistad* was seized and redirected to Africa. Two surviving crew members deceptively rerouted it to Long Island, New York, where authorities arrested the insurgents. In November of 1841, the American ship *Creole* was commandeered by 135 Africans who mutinied and rerouted it to the Bahamas, where they secured freedom.[120]

The 1766 *Meermin* mutiny was a three-week affair that began when the naïve chief merchant convinced the captain that the Malagasy tribesmen were no threat and should help crew the ship. They were allowed to clean their weapons secured as souvenirs. They responded by killing the chief merchant and subduing the captain as they took over the ship. They were betrayed by crewmen who sailed them to a white port in southern Africa, where the mutiny leaders were imprisoned, and the rest, sold. The December 1804 *Tryal* insurrection was the inspiration for the Herman Melville story *Benito Cereno*. This successful overthrow demonstrated the complexities of navigating a ship to one's desired destination. Despite death threats, the sailors pretended to sail to Senegal until a suspicious American ship captain boarded to inspect the situation. The insurrectionist leader, Mure, walked closely beside the captain, who identified him as the "Captain of the slaves." The American attempted to speak privately in Spanish, but Mure and the others were fluent and closely listened to all conversations. The deception was discovered, several Africans were slaughtered, and the survivors were returned to slavery.[121] The 1797 *Loango* mutiny resulted in the death of all but five crewmen. The Africans were unable to navigate the ship and sailed aimlessly for forty-two days. When the slave ship *Thomas* pulled up alongside, they overpowered that crew and then controlled both ships. But after a month of floating without food and supplies, they turned to the rum onboard and were quickly subdued by the surviving crew members.

One unexpected consequence could lead to the deaths of all on board. Fires could be deadly and lead to an explosive end. In 1735 the captives defeated the crew aboard the *Dolphin*. Seeking weaponry, they broke into the powder room where weapons and ammunition were stored. Unfortunately, an explosion was sparked and resulted in the deaths of all aboard. In 1759, local villagers intervened to stage a rebellion aboard a docked ship. They wounded the captain, who fired his pistol into a stockpile of ammunition, killing every soul on board.[122] A few insurrections led to unexplained mysteries. In the waters of Newport, Rhode Island, in 1785, a drifting "ghost ship" was discovered without a single person on board nor any indication of what had happened.

Women played an important role in mutinies as capable accomplices. To the crew, they were less of a threat and were given restricted movement about the deck—not out of compassion, but to be readily accessible for immoral urges on the part of the captain and crew, as rape was commonplace. The crew would sexually abuse any woman as a supplement to low salaries and long voyages. But ravaged bodies did not break the spirit, and women proved to be essential allies for the men held below.[123] They cast attentive eyes and listening ears for valuable information on the best moment to attack. They smuggled weapons and tools to aid in liberating limbs bound by chains. Samuel Waldo, a Boston ship owner, wrote in 1734 to his ship's captain, "For your own safety as well as mine, you'll have the needful guard over your slaves, and put not too much confidence in the women nor children lest they happen to be instrumental to your being surprised which might be fatal."[124] During the previously mentioned *Loango* attack, two women smuggled weapons from an unlocked weapons chest to the men and assisted in taking over the ship. In 1721 a woman aboard the *Robert* was publicly executed for aiding an insurrection. Historian Harvey Wish wrote, "The insurrection itself was a desperate struggle waged with the courage of despair. . . . Captain Harding . . . hanged a woman leader by her thumbs, whipping and slashing her with knives."[125]

Youth did their part, as well. Captain John Newton, who found acclaim as the writer of the hymn "Amazing Grace," was first a slave-ship captain. Onboard his ship, he discovered a plan and searched the interior hull to find discarded chains, clubs, and stones. Two youth confessed beneath torturous thumbscrews.

Land Insurrections

Over 250 major land insurrections are known to have occurred in the history of the United States. Some were in partnership with indigenous people, but most were of African origin.[126] Owners had the onerous burden of keeping a watchful eye on rebellious Africans but also had to watch indigenous people and white indentures, who were often coconspirators. Owners stifled any information on the rebelliousness of enslaved victims and achieved remarkable success—few white Americans, then and now, had any real idea of their frequency. To discourage similar acts, the number of rebels slaughtered was widely publicized while the stories of murdered whites were suppressed. Trials were absurdities of justice, as testimony was acquired through torture and resulted in public executions. Captured rebels were immediately executed, with their heads posted on fence posts or pikes until they rotted away. Regardless of the deadly price paid for revolts, they continued to occur regularly. Despite the efforts to suppress news of these insurrections, word spread from plantation to plantation and across state lines through an informal communication network of enslaved family members who kept alive the memories of martyrs who sacrificed their lives.

A few rebels alone could light a spark, inspiring others to join a fight. The aim of these revolts was not merely destruction on individual plantations; insurrectionists envisioned a movement to destroy the institution of slavery. This hope was recorded in the vision of those captured in 1811 in German Town, Louisiana, the Stono River March, and the uprising of Denmark Vesey. From 1663 to 1861, the enslaved rebelled in Virginia, North Carolina, Kentucky, Illinois, Missouri, Alabama, Georgia, and North Carolina. Captain John Brown was an abolitionist who left Kansas to hatch a plot to capture the armory in Harper's Ferry, Virginia, and arm slaves for a war of liberation. Such were the intentions of John Anthony Copeland, Lewis Sheridan Leary, Dangerfield Newby, Shields Green, and Osborne Perry Anderson when they joined John Brown's raid to arm slaves in 1859. Brown did not originate the dream of igniting the enslaved to liberate themselves. For over a century, this goal existed in the minds of enslaved men and women who believed that others would join once the fight started.

In 1708, New York City had the densest slave population of all the colonies and experienced a greater number of revolts than any region outside the South. As an entry point, it was rivaled only by Charleston, South Carolina, as a slave harbor. Nearly two thousand Africans walked onshore daily from as many as eleven ships. Wall Street was first the home of a slave market long before it was a financial market. The enslaved in New York restlessly awaited the first opportunity to strike. On Long Island, a 1708 revolt resulted in the deaths of seven slaveholders and four enslaved men. Authorities put to death four enslaved rebels; three men were hanged, and a woman was burned alive. On April 6, 1712, New York City experienced the most destructive slave insurrection of any of the colonies. Gold Coast warriors, allied with Native Americans, vowed to destroy any white person they could apprehend. Armed with guns, swords, knives, and axes, twenty-three men set fire to several homes and put to death nine whites. This fearsome atmosphere so electrified the white population that mass hysteria led to persecution. In 1741, a series of secret meetings revealed a plot to burn the city to the ground, murder whites, and appoint an enslaved man, Caesar, as governor. A series of ten fires erupted, some part of a rebellion, others incidental. Regardless, the blazes caused a wild panic as the cry "The Negroes are rising!" was heard in every neighborhood. The resulting fright erupted in conspiracy trials followed by torture and deaths. Many of the accused were innocents caught up in the hysteria. One hundred twenty-two enslaved men and twenty white accomplices were arrested and executed. Years later, in Albany, several similar attempts were thwarted, including an insurrection where buildings were razed and set afire.[127]

Virginia rebellions were active in 1663, 1687, 1709, 1710, 1722, 1723, and 1730. In 1663, whites rebelled with enslaved Africans in Gloucester County. Hoping to stifle violence, the colony ended importing Africans, holding them responsible for the spirit of insurrection so dominant in the region.[128] Patrols were instigated in 1726 to fashion the appearance of control over the enslaved. Patrollers were vicious, quick to punish, and on duty throughout the night and day. They failed to prevent massive escapes two years later. Enslaved people on plantations along the banks of the James River escaped into the protection of surrounding forests. They attempted to re-create a semblance of their former life by constructing a village and electing an unnamed prince as leader. Bounty hunters put fire to their village, killed the prince, and re-enslaved the survivors. In 1792, nine hundred slaves collected muskets, spears, and clubs before being discovered. Eight years later, Gabriel Prosser of Henrico County visualized the capture of Richmond and seizure of the governor with an army of a thousand soldiers. His rebellion was foiled by an act of God as a tumultuous rainstorm delayed the insurrection, resulting in acts of betrayal. Enslaved people led by Nat Turner rebelled in August 1831 with intentions to liberate all the enslaved within the area and kill any whites they encountered. Turner gained fame and infamy after his 1831 revolt. The son of an African mother, he was instilled with a religious fervor and a desire to be free. Sensing a call from God, he became a slave preacher. He was convinced that the only way to eradicate slavery's evil was in the annihilation of slaveholders. His vision was to march, destroy homes, murder whites, and harbor every enslaved person who desired to be free. On August 22, 1831, he shed the blood of over fifty whites and inspired John Brown's 1859 raid on Harper's Ferry, which shared the intent to arm the enslaved.[129] Turner's rebellion had deadly implications, however. It was the largest massacre of whites, even considering those insurrections with far more enslaved participants. Blacks paid a tremendous price, as fifty-six were publicly executed, and another hundred, most of whom had nothing to do with the rebellion, were murdered by local militias.[130] There were long-term consequences, too, as this revolt crushed any sense of white invincibility and defeated the notion that the enslaved were passively content with their captivity. Punishments against individuals for the slightest infractions became much more brutal. State governments responded with a white-lash of repressive legislation, with laws restricting every aspect of the life of the enslaved. Local policies established local patrols with the authority to detain, punish, and kill those suspected of running away or planning to rebel. North Carolina went so far as to make illegal preaching by any Blacks, slave or free.

North Carolina proved to be an ideal location for runaways for whom Spanish-owned Florida was out of reach. The Great Dismal Swamp wilderness, as a natural border, proved to be an ideal haven. By the end of the eighteenth century, two thousand formerly enslaved constructed fifty encampments where land was cultivated, crops grown, and livestock raised. Inhabitants developed reputations as fearless defenders against any who dared venture too close. Outside of Wilmington, a politically independent and economically thriving community was led by the "General of the Swamps." His formidable raiding parties foraged for supplies and invaded white settlements. A fierce battle resulted in the general's death, along with five of his men and a white compatriot. His followers continued to raid throughout the War to End Slavery.[131] In July 1775, armed patrols deterred an uprising in Beaufort County with orders to shoot armed slaves encountered off site. Two white coconspirators were apprehended along with forty men of color. Swirling insurrection rumors in 1792 led to the establishment of a nightly watch to unearth hidden plans to incinerate towns. In 1798 Bertie County city leaders arrested three men organizing 150 men. Even without their leaders, the rebels attacked and fought a band of patrollers. In April of 1794, Quillo strategized in Granville County to murder any who dared to prevent the establishment of a settlement. An elaborate 1802 communication network carried insurrectionist information up and down the banks of the Roanoke River. A discovered letter revealed the names of conspirators with a set date of June 10. The ringleader, Bob, was the trusted enslaved man of U.S. Senator David Stone. Caesar, Moses, and Dave recruited Tuscarora Indians and impoverished whites, promising that those as far away as Richmond would join their cause. In another episode, an enslaved preacher, Dr. Joe, conspired with Tom Copper, a white abolitionist, to resist. Arrested and placed on trial, Copper daringly raided the Elizabeth City jail in a failed rescue attempt. While acquitted, Dr. Joe was ordered to stop preaching; a hundred slaves were arrested, with two sentenced to death by hanging.[132]

South Carolina was particularly explosive. The African population maintained a disproportionate 20-to-1 majority over whites in the rice regions. Rebellions were so frequent that Georgian planters complained that geographic proximity to South Carolina generated overwhelming trepidation among whites. Angolans feared as warriors with vast military experience naturally assumed leadership. Charleston emerged as a trade headquarters and thus contained the highest concentration of enslaved men and women in the colonies.[133] Actions in South Carolina included the following:

- In 1739, fourteen slaves burned several Charleston plantations to the ground. Just short of a century before Nat Turner's uprising, the Stono Rebellion was the bloodiest uprising of the eighteenth century and the largest revolt before the War of Liberation. On Sunday, September 9, 1739, Jemmy (Cato) and twenty Angolans rebelled, intending to flee to Ft. Mose in Florida. As they marched southward, their numbers accelerated to a hundred combatants who murdered forty whites and burned every plantation as they triumphantly shouted, "Liberty." They were just twenty miles from the state border when colonial militia attacked. The final death toll of the skirmish included sixty-nine rebels and twenty-three white colonists dying at each other's hands.[134]
- The General Assembly of South Carolina prioritized resistance to the uprisings. Colonial Legislators passed the 1740 Negro Slave Act to outlaw all small gatherings. This also abolished the importation of Africans for the next ten years in order to cut down on more potential revolts.
- Legislative action did not quell actions, though. In June, an accusation of the planning of an insurrection led to fifty rebels being hanged by the Ashley River outside of Charleston. Assembly records read, "An insurrection of our slaves in which many of the inhabitants were murdered in a barbarous and cruel manner; and that no sooner quelled than another projected in Charles Town, and a third lately in the very heart of the Settlements, but happily discovered in time enough to be prevented."[135]
- A 1797 plot caused the deaths of four Charleston men charged with planning to burn down the entire city. A later attempt to annihilate the town by arson and kill every white person was also deterred.

- In 1822, Denmark Vesey, inspired by the Haitian Revolution, planned the most highly organized and complex revolt on American soil. He convinced thousands to stockpile weapons in a warehouse for an entire year. He meticulously contrived to kill every white person excepting Quakers, Methodists, and poor white women who were not enslavers. Inclement weather and betrayal resulted in his arrest and the execution of thirty-five leaders.
- Dead but not forgotten, an 1829 Vesey-inspired conflict scorched eighty-five Charleston buildings to complete what Vesey started.[136]

In Georgia, as whites expressed outrage over the 1765 Stamp Act, a British requirement that the colonies purchase embossed British paper, the enslaved escaped to nearby swamps. Within four years, they constructed twenty-one houses, harvested rice crops, and constructed a protective fortification to deter invasion. Captains Cudjoe and Lewis commanded a troop of one hundred referred to as "the King of England's Soldiers." War veterans did more than remain hidden in the swamp as they went inland to raid plantations and attack Georgian militias. In 1787, a specially trained regiment was dispatched to destroy the settlement and capture all residents. After a heated battle, the rebels escaped into the swamp interior. When ordered, British troops refused to follow them into the swamps and vacated the region. Georgia and South Carolina authorities conspired and dispatched assassins who murdered Captain Lewis, placing his head on a pike. This outrage did not have the desired intention as rebel troops launched revenge attacks on neighboring whites.

Louisiana was a hotbed of sedition, with the enslaved outnumbering whites by a 3-to-1 ratio. In 1795 a failed rebellion in Point Coupee cost the lives of twenty-five insurrectionists. In 1811, the same Point Coupee region was the site of the most massive, most elaborately planned overthrow in the nation with ambitions to free every slave in the state and establish New Orleans as a city of Jubilee, a Black Republic. The German Coast Uprising occurred on January 8 when thirty men began a premeditated rampage by burning plantations and murdering enslavers. The first victim was to be the owner of the group's leader, Haitian-born Charles Deslondes, but he escaped by jumping out of a window, abandoning his son to be murdered. Over the next three days, a few dozen grew into five hundred insurrectionists "from 50 different nations with 50 different languages,"[137] on a fixed march to New Orleans, located thirty miles away, chanting "Freedom or Death." After a two-day battle, the rebels were subdued. Retaliatory executions sought to intimidate future revolutionaries. Severed heads, placed on pikes along the Mississippi River for sixty miles, served as grim threats. More than seventy-five enslaved men and women plus white planters died.[138]

Texas lived in a continuous state of apprehension. In the year 1860, fourteen north Texas cities lived under the constant threat of arson as Africans and indentured whites cast their lot together. When they received news that the Union Army was coming, enslaved men and women in Adams County made plans to rebel. It was one of their children who unwittingly revealed the conspiracy to local whites, resulting in forty participants' executions.

Slavery generated an atmosphere of violence and hostility wherever it existed. A vicious cycle was created wherein the harsher the suppression, the greater the resistance. The succession of land rebellions created a mood of high alert on the part of whites, who became more and more suspicious of the enslaved and sought to limit their ability to congregate and move freely. The enslaved never gave up on their willingness to consider rebellion, even attempts that offered little chance of success. Their desire to be free overwhelmed caution and self-preservation. Thoughts on their part for self-liberation and the chance for self-determination motivated their actions. Parents never gave up on the notion that their efforts might provide a different reality for their children.

Land rebellions were a constant from the start of slavery to the end. Even the most severe slave owner lived with a sense that it could happen at any moment. The impact of these land rebellions was a nation that denied its basic premises of integrity and truth. The South was constantly confronted with a false sense of aristocracy and respectful hospitality served up by those held in chains. Rebellions wiped away the veneer of deceit and forced the truth to the surface, a truth that was only dealt with through the issuing of blood.

Suicide, Mutilations, and Infanticide

It is difficult to comprehend the lengths an enslaved person would pursue to free herself. When faced with few viable options, she would sometimes resort to self-mutilation, suicide, or matricide. Suicide was a common option, and slaveholders went to great lengths to prevent it. Historian Joanne Grant notes, "Planters had much trouble with slaves fresh from Africa, the new slaves committing suicide in great numbers."[139] Africans not born into the institution would opt for death—seen as a return home and reunion with ancestors and family. Ship captives would frequently jump into shark-infested waters. Safety nets were placed along the ships' sides to catch those who flung themselves overboard.[140] One hundred jumped overboard from the *Prince of Orange* in 1737.[141] At the Georgian Sea Islands at Ebo Landing, witnesses described a procession of seventy-five suicide walkers from Igboland (Nigeria), who stoically strode to a watery death in 1803. Adults would perform impossible acts of defiance, including swallowing their tongues to self-asphyxiate. The ingestion of poison was frequent while others showed tremendous resolve by walking into the wintery elements to die by exposure. Desperate men and women would mutilate their bodies to prevent being sold, escape the hardship of labor, or deter rape. Ennis, a carpenter, used an ax to cut off one hand and sever fingers on the other.[142]

Even more heartbreaking to grasp, parents would murder their children, both privately and in the presence of owners. They justified their actions by saying that they would rather set them free in death than have them live in the bowels of misery. Some mothers would murder their children immediately after birth. Mothers were especially sensitive to the plight of females bound to a future filled with unspeakable sexual perversions and abuses. A New York enslaved mother buried her living infant in a wig box. Another abandoned her newborn babe to perish during a frighteningly cold winter day in 1741. A couple in Covington, Kentucky, agreed "by mutual agreement to 'send the souls of their children to Heaven rather than have them descend to the hell of slavery,' and then both parents committed suicide."[143] A planter's wife retorted of her disfigured slave Sylva, "She has been the mother of thirteen children, every one of who she has destroyed with her own hands, in their infancy, rather than have them suffer slavery."[144] Margaret Garner, husband Robert, and three children escaped across the frozen Ohio River, but when cornered by patrollers, she murdered her daughter Mary with a butcher knife and slashed the two boys across the neck. On a riverboat carrying the survivors back into Kentucky and slavery, she dropped her infant daughter Sicilia into the river.[145]

ENSLAVED RELIGION

Us n****** never have chance to go to Sunday school and church. The white folks feared for n****** to get any religion and education, but I reckon something inside just told us about God that there was a better place hereafter. We would sneak off and have prayer meeting. Sometimes the pattyrollers catch us and beat us good, but that didn't keep us from trying. [146]
—*Formerly enslaved man W. L. Bost*

Religion played a significant role in the resistance of the enslaved. Belief in the supernatural power of a God of justice, whether through a Christian or Islamic lens, engendered hope. African slaves initially retained a multitude of traditional African religions, including Islam. Over time, African traditional religions merged with Islam and Christianity into a hybrid belief system. Obeah men, who were conjurers, used charms, potions, soul transference, animal rituals, and nature ceremonies to empower. In North Carolina, conjurer John Koonering wore a costume of rags, animal skins, horns, and bells as he danced and sang while others played musical instruments called "gumba boxes." Funerals incorporated ecstatic grief expressions as adherents combined a ring shout with call-and-response. As African Christianity matured, these elements assimilated into structured worship services.[147]

Albert J. Raboteau, in *Slave Religion*, coined the term "invisible institution"[148] as a descriptor of enslaved worship, largely forbidden by owners and done in secrecy. The white church required a structured litany in an ecclesial setting. The oppressed had to conform to a restricting worship style alongside a racist theology. Sermons proclaimed white supremacy to a people sitting in pews segregated by race. They sat stoically in church, awaiting the moment they could worship unencumbered in the open spaces of nearby woods. This outside venue provided adequate room for religious expression typically frowned on within the confines of a sanctuary. They were free to dance the ring shout and respond verbally to messages of justice. They recited biblical stories trusting that the same God who liberated the Israelites would deliver them. For the moment, they were free.

Songs of faith helped ease the burden of repetitive manual labor and helped to increase solidarity. Singing in the fields emerged as a means of taking one's mind off of backbreaking work. The songs were relatively simple, consisting of only one or two lines, which made them easy to learn and share. The lyrics were simple yet spoke to the hardships of life while serving as a source of inspiration and protest. W. E. B. Du Bois interpreted spirituals as "the articulate message of the slave to the world"[149] to express their innermost feelings and desires.

The Christianity of the enslaved developed as a theology of liberation. This theology of freedom overwhelmed the system of slavery's subservient teaching. It critiqued the heretical doctrines of the enslaver's church and exposed its failings. It juxtaposed the life of Jesus with the racist behavior of white Christians: "Do not do as they do, for they do not practice what they teach."[150] Mattie Curtis bore witness to this hypocrisy:

> Preacher Whitfield, bein' a preacher, wus supposed to be good, but he ain't half fed ner clothed his slaves an' he whupped 'em bad. I'se seen him whup my mammy wid all de clothes offen her back. He'd buck her down on a barrel an' beat de blood outen her. Dar wus some difference in his beatin' from de neighbors. De folks round dar 'ud whip in de back yard, but Marse Whitfield 'ud have de barrel carried in his parlor fer de beatin'.[151]

Her testimony was seconded by Elias Thomas in his criticism of a Christian plantation owner: "I also saw ole man William Crump, a owner, whip a man and some children. He waited till Sunday morning to whip his slaves. He would git ready to go to church, have his horse hitched up to the buggy, and then call his slaves out and whip them before he left for church. He generally whipped about five children every Sunday morning."[152]

Slave preachers played an important role in the lives of the oppressed. Plantations would allow them to preach to the enslaved under certain conditions, mostly in the presence of whites. Some could read and write, but all were knowledgeable of the Bible. They were allowed relative freedom until rebellion occurred, and then their movements were suppressed, often with good reason as religion played a role in resistance. After Nat Turner, states outlawed preaching by Blacks to anyone, slave or free. They contextualized messages to match the moment: one for when the owner was present and another for when he was absent, radically different from one other. The enslaved were keenly aware that whites took them to church to teach them how to be compliant, obedient serfs. Sermons were of a nature to focus on passages that projected love and having a peaceful nature. Slaves were treated in a subordinate manner. They either had to sit in the back of the church, outside, or in a balcony.

Long before the twentieth-century theologian James Cone penned *Black Theology & Black Power*,[153] the enslaved critiqued America's slaveholding church as an abomination before a God of justice. The enslaved summoned a God who was on the side of the oppressed. Although many were illiterate, they memorized biblical verses and stories that instilled hope for a day of Jubilee when all the captives would be set free.[154] They discerned that God did not sanction enslavement and rejoiced in a God who had much more to say than "Slaves, be obedient to your masters."[155] One plantation owner growled that becoming Christians only made his captives worse. A South Carolinian recalled her enslaved mother's story that an overseer came to the cabins and instructed them to pray for the South as it was losing the war with the North: "Grandmother said they knew what was going on; they knew if the North won they would have a little more freedom . . . but she said her mother and father said, 'We must pray out loud for the South to win, but in our hearts we must pray that the North will win.'"[156]

They rejected sermonizing that contradicted the reality of their experience. Gayraud Wilmore, in *Black Religion and Black Radicalism*, recited the report by C. C. Jones when he preached to a slave congregation in Georgia:

> I was preaching to a large congregation on the Epistle to Philemon, and when I . . . condemned the practice of running away, one-half of my audience deliberately rose up and walked off with themselves; and those who remained looked anything but satisfied with the preacher or his doctrine. After dismission, there was no small stir among them; some solemnly declared that there was no such Epistle in the Bible; others, that it was not the Gospel; others, that I preached to please the masters; others, that they did not care if they never heard me preach again.[157]

From the 1730s to the 1800s, a robust religious revival swept the nation, the Great Awakening (c. 1730–1755) and the Second Great Awakening (c. 1790–1840). Methodist circuit riders and autonomous Baptist ministers preached at massive outdoor gatherings. The Great Awakening played a significant role in the Christianization of enslaved Africans to whom the messages appealed, and they flocked to the services. Traveling evangelists preached of a personal God who cared for the individual and was intimately involved in ordinary people's daily affairs. Faith involved a personal commitment to God, conversion, and spiritual renewal. Although sermons rarely addressed slavery, messages of individual freedom resonated.

The contributions of the enslaved to the Great Awakening have rarely been noted other than to view them as subjects of the revivalists. But the ability to worship unfettered interjected into the Awakening a jubilant manner to ecstatically express faith. Poor whites took notice and modeled their responses to the stresses of poverty in a similar fashion. Their contribution was the manifestation of the egalitarian equality voiced by preachers such as Jonathan Edwards and George Whitefield, who were not abolitionists but slave owners.

The enslaved modeled how to treat others with respect and dignity. They not only received the message of salvation but conveyed one as well as enslaved men and women went forth as preachers and leaders in the evangelical movement. The teaching of a "priesthood of all believers" enabled them to assume the mantle of preaching. While Presbyterians and Anglicans mandated education to preach, Methodists and Baptists had no preventive requirements. (This legacy can be seen today in the different number of Blacks in both sets of traditions.) Richard Allen, once converted, proselytized his master, who later sold him his freedom. By the end of the eighteenth century, free and enslaved preachers boosted conversion of the enslaved to an African Christianity. The Second Great Awakening of the early 1800s took the movement from the open field onto plantations with a message for both the enslaved and enslavers.

One of the benefits of being a person of faith was that it helped the enslaved deal with captivity. A theology of liberation promised a day of deliverance from slavery and punishment for their tormentors. The enslaved fused Christianity with beliefs from their traditional African religions, and their faith was enhanced by a belief in the spirit world and an emotional passion for worship. They found strength in the Bible and interpreted its teachings to fit their situation. Preachers memorized verses and passages, and some, almost the entire Bible.

From this moment in Black history, religious faith will be a major component in Black life. Descendants will refer to the faith of the slaves as inspiration during trying times, with writers making mention of this in poetry and prose. Although not nearly as intense as in the African context, faith in connection with the ancestors remains a part of the Black religious mind-set and is finding greater receptivity in the twenty-first century, as couples jump the broom and pour libations at weddings. Faith is central to every protest movement for Black Americans and essential to every aspect of life.

THE WAR OF LIBERATION: 1775–1783

> Slaves would fight for a freedom that actually had very little to do with Britain's hold on the Americas. They were considered important beyond their ability to work in the fields. Some found a purpose in fighting alongside men who had long considered them nothing more than property to be battered and bartered. . . . Many white Americans feared that Dunmore's proclamation would spark a full-scale insurrection among the slaves. For many free Blacks who considered themselves patriots, and for some whites as well, Dunmore's clever chess move underscored the contradiction of racial enslavement within the patriot cause and made them seek to broaden the bounds of the budding revolution. But for many others, including the army's new Virginia born commander (George Washington), the specter of a slave with a gun in his hand was beyond terrifying.[158]

For enslaved Americans, the war between the colonies and Great Britain was hoped to be a war of liberation (1775–1783), not just for a rebellious colony but also for enslaved people. The cry of "Liberty or Death" saturated the provinces; the enslaved listened attentively to perceive just how penetrating was this talk of liberation. Slaves recognized the irony that patriots who fought for freedom denied it to others in all thirteen colonies. War was an opportunity to see how all-inclusive the words of the Declaration of Independence would prove to be. While Jefferson initially denounced the trade as "execrable commerce . . . assemblage of horrors," a "cruel war against human nature itself, violating its most sacred rights of life & liberties,"[159] southern delegates wanted independence for white men only and deleted any mention of slavery from the Constitution.

For the enslaved, patriotic utterances were more than just war slogans but words to live and die by. They were keenly aware that pious talk was not intended for Africans. Nevertheless, they appropriated the same language and applied it to their situation. Both Black and white leaders debated and waited for the right moment. They vowed that there would be no partial application of freedom; if any were to be free, all must be free. The coming war ignited a hope that liberty could extend to all, even those held in bondage. They reasoned that to obtain it, they must be willing to participate in the conflict. The war was an optimal opportunity, and they were ready to fight on the side of a slave nation if it meant the smallest chance for their liberty. Most desired to fight for the land in which they were born but would sign up for the side promising emancipation. They would fight for country or against it.[160]

Initially, both the British and the colonists refused to recruit Black soldiers. The colonists were fearful to arm slaves out of a concern weapons would eventually point in their direction. Slave owner General George Washington issued an executive order that forbade enlistment on July 9, 1775. He did this despite prior service of such soldiers in southern and northern colonial militias during the French and Indian War. Their numbers in the Massachusetts army and navy were so prolific that the enslaved population shrunk massively in the colony.[161] Washington faced pressure to reverse course from Black soldiers who made no effort to hide their displeasure.[162] He had observed their courage and willingness to fight during the Battle of Bunker Hill, and his army was saved on two occasions by Black soldiers. On August 30, 1776, Colonel John Glover's sailors, with a "number of Negroes," evacuated Washington's entire army of 20,000 across the East River as they faced annihilation by 32,000 British soldiers. This same integrated navy ferried Washington across the Delaware River with Prince Whipple, a Black soldier, at his side (as depicted in the famous Emmanuel Leutze painting). An unnamed slave saved Washington's cousin's life, Lieutenant Colonel William Washington, during the Battle of Cowpens in 1781. Despite all this, the future first president of the new country allowed those already in the army to remain but barred new recruits.[163]

The British blinked first and realized the valuable contribution slaves could make in the war. In 1775 Virginia's royal governor, Lord Dunmore, issued an order promising freedom to all who would fight for the crown: "I do hereby further declare all indented servants, Negroes, or others, free that are able and willing to bear arms, that join His Majesty's Troops."[164] He realized that he could replenish his ranks while depleting potential soldiers from a Continental Army badly in need of them. The British judged rightly as thousands fled plantations to sign up for his "Ethiopian Regiment." South Carolina lost one-fourth of her population and posted patrols to round up fugitives. Seven thousand fled Georgia while many went south to Spanish Florida and Indian territory. Virginian Landon Carter complained bitterly, "Moses, my son's man, Joe, Billy, Postillion, John, Mulatto Peter, Tom, Panticover, Manuel and Lancaster San, ran away, to be sure, to Ld Dunmore."[165] In 1781, the British army invaded Washington's Potomac plantation and absconded with eighteen slaves, including Harry Washington, who joined the "Black Pioneers." Thomas Jefferson lost twenty-two in a similar raid.[166]

The Continental Congress, noticing this trend, altered course in May of 1775 and permitted recruitment. Washington reversed his previous order on December 31, 1775. The response was immediate. Within weeks, five thousand enslaved men signed their signatures or marks, including Jefferson Liberty, Jube Freeman, and Dick Freedom. By 1777, slaves were promised emancipation in return for military service by every state except South Carolina. Owners escaped mandatory service and sent proxies to serve in their stead. In 1778, Rhode Island freed those who had served in an all-Black battalion throughout the war's duration and paid reparations to owners whose bondsmen enlisted. Southern states initially only recruited freedmen. This did not prevent desertions, as thousands escaped to join the fight. The losses were astounding. In 1778 alone, Virginia lost 30,000 enslaved men. Between 1775 and 1783, South Carolina enlisted 25,000 as Georgia lost 15,000, or 75 percent. In eight years of war, over 100,000 enslaved men fled American plantations to join the battle.

Black soldiers became a significant part of the Continental Army. According to the U.S. *Army Military History* Web page, one French officer estimated that as much as a quarter of the army was of color. In New England and Virginia, they served in almost every unit; Rhode Island, Connecticut, and New Jersey had the highest percentages.[167] They fought alongside white soldiers at Concord, Fort Ticonderoga, Trenton, Yorktown, Lexington, Bunker Hill, Great Bridge, and White Plains. The 1st Rhode Island Regiment received high commendations as "the most neatly dressed, the best under arms, and the most precise in its maneuvers."[168] Historian Henry Wiencek wrote that "this Rhode Island unit, mostly Black, would be hand-picked by Washington and Lafayette to carry out the most important assignment of the climactic battle of the Revolution—the assault that ended the war."[169]

Black soldiers served alongside white soldiers in the infantry and artillery, with a handful in the cavalry and a disproportionately high percentage in the navy as sailors and pilots. Their positions included foragers, drummers, musicians, spies, wagoners, valets, waiters, sailors, gunners, cooks, artisans, and commissaries. They cleared roads, constructed fortifications, loaded weapons and ammunition, and managed the horses. Most were registered not by their names but as "A Negro Man" who was a "private." They connected being a soldier with being free and took new names to reflect their status, such as Pomp Liberty, Dick Freedom, Jupiter Free, and Jeffery Liberty.

Peter Salem (Salem Poor), Prince Whipple, Primus Hall, Phoebe Fraunces, Prince Estabrook, Prime, Jack Sisson, Louis Cook, James, Barzillai Lew, James Armistead Lafayette, and Pomp Blackman received recommendations for bravery in battle. Bunker Hill veterans Seymour Burr and Titus Coburn fought alongside Peter Salem, who shot the British commander, Major John

Pitcairn. Salem fought so fiercely that fourteen officers signed a letter of commendation saying that he "behaved like an experienced officer," as well as a "brave and gallant soldier."[170] Jack Sisson assisted in the capture of British General Richard Prescott. Louis Cook, commissioned as a lieutenant colonel, became America's first Black military officer on June 15, 1779. He served under Washington during the French and Indian War and the Revolutionary War. William Flora, in the Battle of Great Bridge, December 1775, fired relentlessly to cover retreating soldiers. Prince Whipple and Oliver Cromwell of Burlington, New Jersey, crossed the Delaware River with Washington. Cromwell fought at the battles of Trenton, Yorktown, Princeton, and Brandywine. Washington signed his discharge papers and awarded him a badge of merit for six years of duty. Lemuel Haynes served as a Massachusetts and Vermont minuteman; he fought at the battles of Fort Ticonderoga and the siege of Boston. He penned the essay "Liberty Further Extended," arguing that the freedom he and others fought for should be extended to all. Caesar, the pilot of the *Patriot*, captured an enemy brig carrying supplies, a feat Robert Smalls would later duplicate in the War to End Slavery. A pilot, Minny, was one of two boat pilots killed in combat.[171]

Several demonstrated extraordinary ability as spies. Perhaps the most famous spy in all of the Continental Army was the legendary James Armistead Lafayette of Virginia. He was a double spy who pretended to serve General Cornwallis as he dispatched valuable information through a Black network to colonial headquarters. His namesake and mentor, Lafayette, assisted him in receiving his freedom and a $40 annual military pension. Phoebe Fraunces saved the life of George Washington in her father's tavern, Black Sam. When she learned of a plan to poison the general, she informed Washington, and the traitor was hanged. On the other side, Boston King escaped to join the British in Charleston, May 1780, to serve as a courier and spy for Cornwallis.

After the war, Virginia liberated 150 sailors for their service. Prime, a New Jersey man, escaped from his loyalist master, served, and was emancipated. Joseph Ranger served nine years in the American navy and received 100 acres of land plus a $96 annual pension.[172] Agrippa Hull fought at Valley Forge, the Battle at Monmouth Courthouse, and was present at the surrender of British General John Burgoyne. He was in almost every major campaign, including Cowpens, Eutaw Springs, Ninety-Six, Guilford Courthouse, and the Siege of Charleston. He died in 1848 as the largest Black landowner in Stockbridge, Massachusetts. James Forten, a free man, enlisted at age fifteen and was captured aboard the *Royal Louis*. When offered freedom if he joined the British Army, he refused. "No, I'm a prisoner for my country," he said, "and I'll never prove a traitor to her interests."[173] He served seven months as a prisoner of war. Once the war was over, he accrued wealth as a sailmaker and financier of the Underground Railroad.

William "Billy" Lee served as Washington's body servant, butler, and valet. He was with him at Yorktown and Valley Forge, for all eight years of the war and the First Continental Congress. When Washington died, his will stipulated that his 125 slaves receive freedom at his wife, Martha's, death. Lee, considered to have been Washington's best friend and confidant, was freed at the will's reading. Crispus Attucks gained fame as the first martyr of the American Revolution. He was buried in Boston's Granary Burying Ground with annual remembrances, a statue, and a Memorial Day celebration.

The war could have been the beginning of the end of slavery. Washington and his officers were radicalized. After the army was integrated, the dignity and bravery of the Black soldiers challenged racist notions. Wiencek quoted an army officer who said that "the Continental Army was creating 'a foundation for the Abolition of Slavery in America.'" According to Wiencek,

> The war was a powerful solvent; it eroded even the adamant foundations of slavery. . . . In Congress and in the camps, there was talk that the time had come to give slaves freedom if they would serve. The movement toward emancipation became so powerful that the leaders of that time, including influential officers in Washington's headquarters, could see the outlines of a new order taking shape.[174]

Both sides promised to slave-soldiers that if they survived the war, they would be forever free. By the war's end, a remarkable number did gain freedom, but British leaders were far more faithful than Americans to the promise of manumission. Huddled with defeated British forces in Manhattan, foreboding fear existed among two thousand enslaved persons that they would be handed over to Americans and reenslaved. Commander Sir Guy Carleton refused to turn his back on his Black soldiers, who had served the British crown so admirably. He sailed away with over three thousand. Six thousand boarded British ships in Charleston; three thousand in New York; four thousand in the port of Savannah. Thousands went south to Spanish Florida, and others, to the West Indies.[175] The final result was not perfect. Soldiers that accompanied the British to Nova Scotia were assured liberty and a farm. It was not to be. Within four years, they were starving. Some ended up reenslaved in the Caribbean.[176]

The Americans both kept and broke promises. Some enslaved soldiers were freed, but significant numbers were repatriated with their former owners. After the British defeat at Yorktown, Washington ordered the recapture of British slave-soldiers. American military leaders placed guards on the beach to prevent escape, and Americans demanded their return from British regiments. Washington presented the demand in person. Even colonists who sent stand-ins attempted to reinstate many to their former status. War veteran James Roberts bitterly lamented, "Honor, justice, and the hope of being set free with my wife and four little ones prompted me to return home. I was soon after separated from my wife and children and sold for $1,500. And now will commence the statement of my wages. For all my fighting and suffering in the Revolutionary War for the liberty of this ungrateful, illiberal country to me and my race."[177] In North Carolina, William Kitchen refused to free Ned Griffen, his enslaved replacement. Griffen appealed to the North Carolina General Assembly, which not only honored the promise but granted him the right to vote in perpetuity.

THE UNFINISHED REVOLUTION

George Washington won the Revolutionary War with an army that was more integrated than any American military force until the Vietnam War. . . . The United States owed its liberty in significant measure to Black troops. Here is the mystery of the era written in blood: in the face of the known heroism of these black troops, how is it that the Revolution preserved slavery? George Washington, the slaveholder who led the war for liberty, personifies that paradox.[178]

Despite the hope and sacrifices that many had made, the war that birthed American independence failed to achieve the same for the enslaved. As far as whites were concerned, the country remained the same, now just without the control of the British. But for enslaved men and women, everything had changed. If the country could be liberated, so could they. A revolutionary renaissance sought to bring to completion the unfinished revolution. The war imprinted a belief that freedom was a right not just for white colonists but for all. The public refrain of "Liberty or Death" energized freedmen who redefined themselves as deprived citizens and dishonored native sons. Always more radical than their white allies, men of color became even more so as they embraced being African *and* American.

Northern whites were ideologically affected, with heated debates attempting to interpret the war's significance for the future direction of the new country. For some, the war delegitimized slavery. Abigail Adams, the wife of John Adams and the mother of John Quincy Adams, wrote to her husband,

"I wish most sincerely there was not a single slave in the province; it always appeared a most iniquitous scheme to me [to] fight ourselves for what we are daily robbing and plundering from those who have as good a right to freedom as we have."[179] The Marquis de Lafayette was instrumental in planting the seed of doubt in the mind of George Washington concerning the legitimacy of slavery. He urged the general to begin the march toward emancipation by freeing his own slaves, but it was an act Washington was not yet ready to perform. Lafayette was never able to come to emotional or mental grips with the existence of slavery in the "land of the free and the home of the brave." He wrote, "I would never have drawn my sword in the cause of America, if I could have conceived that thereby I was founding a land of slavery."[180] An emancipation movement grew as former colonies legislated in favor of abolition of slavery. As early as 1652, Rhode Island passed the first antislavery statute, but it lacked enforcement. The Continental Congress voted on April 6, 1776, to end slave importation by 1808, but this did not extend to a ban on slavery itself.[181] In 1777, Vermont abolished slavery, followed by New Hampshire and Pennsylvania in 1780. The Pennsylvania General Assembly concluded that the promises of the revolution would extend to every American. Black children born in the state from that day forward would be free at age twenty-eight. Massachusetts outlawed slavery and declared that all men were born free, intentionally quoting Jefferson's original antislavery statement. Connecticut and Rhode Island voted in 1784 for gradual emancipation, followed by New Jersey in 1804. This synergy led to antislavery societies that grew in strength and effort each decade.[182]

Northern men of color displayed a vibrant voice with a new strategic vision and accelerated their protest efforts. Unity replaced individualism as resources were combined for collective benefit. Between 1780 and 1830, a convention movement brought together the brightest minds for the greatest articulation of debunking slavery in the nation's history. Conventions, organizations, churches, and the press served as advocacy agencies. The fight for liberty was not yet over. It was on a journey to a fuller understanding of its meaning.

THE ABOLITIONIST MOVEMENT

The loss of the South as a recruiting ground for abolitionists coincided with the acquisition of a new element, greater in ardor than the lost component if somewhat below it in formal education and social rank. This new element was the Negro. . . . Negro participants, fittingly enough perhaps, formed a more integral component

of the abolitionist crusade than of any other major reform in
America. . . . At one of their meetings a typical resolution, such as
the following by former slave William Wells Brown, might brand
the United States as a willful liar, a shameless hypocrite, and the
deadliest enemy of the human race.[183]

The abolitionist movement was one of the most definitive protest movements in the history of the world. It served as a lead-up to the War to End
Slavery and was a predecessor to the civil rights movement. From 1774 to
1865, abolitionists relentlessly campaigned for eradication of the institution
of slavery. The first effort was the Pennsylvania Society for Abolition (1774),
followed by the Society for Promoting the Manumission of Slaves (1785), and
the American Anti-Slavery Society (1833). Although concentrated on ending
slavery, organizations did not have as a goal the elimination of white supremacy. They were, therefore, reticent to recruit men of color. But freed men and
women were determined to engage and difficult to ignore. They worked in
a variety of ways to end southern slavery while combating white supremacy
in the North. Participants were a mixture, but the majority were formerly
enslaved. Some purchased freedom; others escaped or were emancipated.
Disproportionately they were the children of enslaved mothers and white
fathers. A smaller number were born due to liaisons between free African
women and white men, or they were the children of white women and African
men. Some could trace their genealogy back to the 1780s, an aftermath of the
Revolutionary War. Few disassociated themselves from the plight of brothers
and sisters in bondage, and they worked diligently to end the institution.[184]

Prominent Black abolitionists included Frederick Douglass, Harriet Tubman, Sojourner Truth, David Walker, Henry Highland Garnet, William
Wells Brown, Octavius Catto, Charlotte Forten Grimke, Francis Grimke,
Frances Ellen Watkins Harper, James and Sarah Forten, Josiah Henson, and
William Still.[185] Black abolitionists were an exceptional assortment of women
and men who made it their life's goal to overthrow slave autocracy. This fearless collection of men and women compelled the nation to reassess the meaning of democratic principles. Their primary tool was the spoken word from
"pulpit, pamphlet, and press." Demonstrations in northern cities consisted of
marches, public meetings, and antislavery conventions. Ardent New Yorkers
sued slaveholders in the courts. Militant abolitionists, such as David Walker
and Henry Highland Garnet, called for warfare. Abolitionists orchestrated
techniques used during the civil rights movement:

The abolitionists pioneered in the use of nonviolent direct action.
Abolitionists, like contemporary rebels, held mass meetings, sang
freedom songs, and staged sit-ins and freedom rides. They marched,

demonstrated, and picketed. They were often in jail, where they sang freedom songs at all hours of the night and day . . . their main aim was "to blister the conscience" of the good, the silent, and the indifferent. Their targets were the American government, the church, the business establishment—everyone. . . . With missionary zeal, abolitionists waged "a holy war."[186]

Abolitionists Frederick Douglass, Sojourner Truth, Harriet Tubman, and Maria Miller W. Stewart spent lifetimes in the struggle and volunteered great energy to female suffrage, as well. James Forten, William Watkins, and Robert Purvis led a "Free Produce" campaign and refused to purchase food commodities harvested by slave labor. Today's free-trade campaigns mirror their actions. In 1850 a published letter by former slave and tailor Henry Weeden recited his refusal to repair a U.S. marshal's coat: "With me, principle first. Money afterwards. Though a poor man I crave the patronage of no being that would volunteer his services to arrest a fugitive slave or that would hang 100 n*****s for 25 cents each."[187]

Their greatest impact was when the formerly enslaved exposed the tortures of slavery. Theodore Wright, James Forten, Robert Purvis, and Charles Lenox Remond appeared as the early spokespersons for the movement. While passionate, they were never enslaved and could not speak firsthand of what it meant to live as a slave. It was the voices of the enslaved that proved extremely compelling as they recounted firsthand the ghastliness of daily existence. Their testimony exerted immeasurable influence as the face and voice of those in chains. Abolitionist propagandists swayed the hearts and minds of all who listened as they recounted unending abuse: the agony of families broken apart, children snatched from flailing arms, and harrowing escapes eluding those seeking their reenslavement. Frederick Douglass, Sojourner Truth, Henry Bibb, Josiah Henson, David Ruggles, Charles Ray, William Still, Henry "Box" Brown, Charles L. Remond, and Harriet Tubman were highly effective in bringing to northern sensibilities the miseries of enslavement. They refuted the proslavery narrative that victims were well fed, adequately clothed, and decently treated. Their stories moved audiences to heartbreak and induced higher sensitivity and empathy. Through public speeches and Sunday sermons, their oration expounded firsthand slave evils and popularized the movement.[188]

They expanded their reach and illustrated on the printed page the depths of slavery. They published in books and newspapers stories of terrorism. Autobiographies cataloged vulgar revulsions long before *Uncle Tom's Cabin* (1852). Ottobah Cugoano (1787), Venture Smith (1798), Mary Prince (1831), Frederick Douglass (1845), and Henry "Box" Brown (1849) published firsthand testimonies of those who had "felt the lash" and "worn the shoe."

Afterward, William C. Nell (1855), Charles Ball (1858), William Craft, and Louis Hughes (1897) continued to tell their stories in their own voices. Mary Prince confided in her autobiography, "I was made quite a pet of by Miss Betsey, and loved her very much. She used to lead me about by the hand, and call me her little n*****. This was the happiest period of my life, for I was too young to understand rightly my condition as a slave, and too thoughtless and full of spirits to look forward to the days of toil and sorrow."[189] Sarah Parker Remond and Harriett Jacobs graphically detailed sexual abuses inflicted on enslaved women by white men.

Early in the movement, abolitionists sought a unified front but differed regarding strategy. The earliest white abolitionists, mostly Quakers as well as William Lloyd Garrison, advocated for propaganda, moral persuasion, and passive resistance. They held at bay any calls for bloodshed. Black abolitionists, out of respect for Garrison, whom they revered, initially restrained efforts, but with impatience. They held no such illusions about the power of persuasion. They advocated for direct action, fugitive assistance, interventions to stop repatriations, insurrection, social equality, and full citizenship rights. They criticized the hypocrisy of whites who loathed slavery but were silent on equality. They would not compromise in their opposition to slavery and deportation. They opposed any who suggested that the final solution would be the removal of people of color from American shores, and they criticized white abolitionists who supported this colonization movement, a policy advocating the return of people of African descent to the continent of Africa.

Dissension among most whites eased with the passage of three devastatingly destructive laws: the Fugitive Slave Act of 1850, the Kansas-Nebraska Act (1854), and the Dred Scott Supreme Court ruling (1857). The 1854 Kansas-Nebraska Act gave the authority to each territory to decide whether it would allow slavery or prohibit it. It repealed the Missouri Compromise, which limited slavery north of latitude 36.30. The Dred Scott decision denied the Scotts their freedom despite the fact that they had been taken to a state where slavery was outlawed. Chief Justice Roger Taney decreed that the Scotts were not citizens and had no right to sue. By 1857 abolitionism had transformed itself into a more radical movement triggered by the 1850 Fugitive Act. The 1850 law was not the first fugitive legislation. Similar statutes passed in 1643, 1705, and 1793. The 1643 law mandated immediate return. In 1705, New York, Virginia, and Maryland assigned rewards for slaves fleeing into Canada. Southern states inserted a Fugitive Slave Clause into the 1787 Constitutional Convention, which denied sanctuary for those who escaped. The 1793 law gave masters the authority to pursue escapees into free territory and return with captives.

The Fugitive Slave Law of 1850, the "man-stealing law" or "the Blood-hound Bill," combined the worst components of prior legislation and intensified defiance. It outlawed assistance and compelled citizens to help recapture escaped slaves. Magistrates were incentivized by a $10 payment for those returned and a $5 fee for all released.[190] Bounty hunters and slave catchers could, and did, claim any person of African descent as a fugitive. Solomon Northrup, author of *Twelve Years a Slave*, was kidnapped and enslaved for over a decade. A false arrest detained Richard Allen until friends intervened.

Rather than serving as a deterrent, these laws increased activism as outrage metamorphosed into resistance. Northerners, Black and white, responded with amplified defiance. Many saw no other recourse but to physically interfere to prevent reenslavement. Peaceful agitation gave way to direct action by those initially hesitant but who for the first time contemplated violence. Influenced by their Black counterparts, northern white abolitionists reevaluated the efficacy of physical resistance in the face of aggressive proslavery legislation. Northern states passed "personal liberty" laws requiring a hearing before a judge before extradition.

Recapture was no longer met with passivity, as growing numbers of whites and freed men and women intervened to rescue captured runaways. Chaotic confrontations erupted between hundreds, at times thousands, when information surfaced of an apprehension. In 1837, interventions prevented repatriations in Boston, Philadelphia, and New York. David Ruggles sued owners and personally escorted fugitives hidden aboard a ship. In Syracuse, New York, arrestee Jerry McHenry was rescued from authorities on October 4, 1851. Five thousand angry Bostonians attempted to rescue Anthony Burns when he was arrested in Boston in 1854. The 1851 Christiana Riot served as a warning that war was imminent. In Christiana, Pennsylvania, William and Eliza Parker hid secured escapees in their home. Later, Frederick Douglass absconded with the couple and escorted them to Canada.

THE UNDERGROUND RAILROAD (UGRR)

The Underground Railroad is one of American history's mysterious creations. It eventually adopted such terms as "conductors," "stations," "routes," "cargoes," "packages," and "passengers" as suitable for its work even though it had no literal association with railroading; and "underground" was a fitting, and tantalizing, way to describe its activities, which were clandestine and illegal, best carried out away from the bright light of public examination. As a formal term, it refers to the movement of African-American slaves escaping out of the South and to allies who assisted them in their search for freedom. Sharing nothing more than language and imagery with the steam technology of the day, the Underground Railroad is one of history's finest symbols of the struggle against oppression.[191]

The Underground Railroad (UGRR) materialized as the action wing of the abolitionist movement. Members relocated thousands of fleeing enslaved people. From 1786 to 1865, over 200,000 men, women, and children escaped slavery via the UGRR. Sixty thousand fled after the 1850 Fugitive Slave Law passed. The railroad was a human replication of a roadway routed along trails, rivers, back roads, tunnels, and paths from the South to the northern United States, and even beyond into Canada. A series of homes, barns, churches, dens, and caves housed the escapees and their "conductors" along the treacherous journey.[192] Northern destinations included Philadelphia, Wilmington, Baltimore, and New York. The railway west directed escapees to Topeka, Kansas; Cairo/Springfield, Illinois; and Chicago.[193] Michigan contained a popular UGRR route through Vandalia, Raisin Township, Schoolcraft, Battle Creek, Marshall, Niles, Adrian, and Detroit. Of the estimated 45,000 Michigan escapees, over 1,500 frequented the home of Dr. Nathan and Pamela Thomas.[194]

During the 1790s, Isaac T. Hopper surfaced as the lead organizer of this escape network. Throughout the 1820s, the invisible railway ran from the slave state of North Carolina to the free state of Indiana. In the 1830s New York was the most viable escape route into Canada. The British Methodist Episcopal church (BME), the oldest Black church in St. Catharines, was an important Canadian depot. Passengers traveled across the river from Buffalo, New York, to Fort Erie by way of a secret ferry.[195] David Ruggles and Isaac Hopper facilitated the New York City route and assisted in six thousand escapes, including that of Frederick Douglass.[196] Philadelphia's William Still served as the meticulous "Father of the Underground Railroad." He painstakingly chronicled intimate details assisting a hundred fugitives, including his brother. Josiah Henson conducted 118 fugitives and wrote the book *The Life of Josiah Henson*. His story was the inspiration for Harriet Beecher Stowe's *Uncle Tom's Cabin*.[197]

Throughout the eighteenth and nineteenth centuries, conductors escorted thousands and equipped temporary stations to hide runaways. They were journalists, wagoners, educators, doctors, poets, businessmen, newspaper editors, authors, laborers, domestics, coachmen, cooks, orators, and ministers.

They were extremely passionate and took formidable risks. Vigilance committees delivered food, clothing, and shelter in New York, Boston, and Philadelphia. The New York Vigilance Committee, started in the 1830s, helped to resettle refugees.

Most were people of color and operated with meticulous planning from start to finish. Mistakes could be costly, as imprisonment, torture, murder, and enslavement faced all caught. Escape had to be at the right moment, on the most suitable day, under proper weather conditions. Fugitives had to traverse hundreds of miles without detection or raising suspicion. Winter flights were hazardous as the bitter cold slowed travel and endangered life. The journey could take months. Nature provided clues for foot travelers traveling by the invisible railway. During daylight hours, a northern route was followed by walking midway between the rising eastern sun and its westward trajectory. At night the faithful North Star sparkled the path to freedom. Moss on the cooler side of a tree trunk pointed north.[198] Water provided nourishment and quickened travel. Many married male abolitionists had wives who were just as involved, if not as recognized. Sarah Parker Remond was a member of the Salem Female Anti-Slavery Society and gave abolitionist speeches at the age of sixteen. She successfully sued the city of Boston for $500 when she was assaulted for rejecting segregated seating at the Boston Howard Athenaeum. Mary Ann Shadd, raised by abolitionist parents, provided shelter in her home. She used her 1883 law degree from Howard University to provide legal services.

Few could be trusted on the trek through unfamiliar and hostile territory filled with patrollers and bounty hunters. Every conceivable ploy exploited disguises, falsified papers, and elaborate plots. Waterways shipped refugees aboard boats, ships, canoes, ferries, and rafts. They hid runaways in homes, churches, caves, and dens. Passengers were smuggled underneath false wagon bottoms, under floors, and behind walls. Charlotte Giles and Harriett Eglin disguised themselves as veiled mourners adorned in black traveling to a funeral. The married couple William and Ellen Craft masqueraded as a sickly master and slave attendant. Henry "Box" Brown and Joseph Johnson were sealed inside boxes and shipped to Philadelphia. Brown arrived successfully on his first attempt whereas Johnson was apprehended in Wilmington, Delaware, but succeeded on his second attempt aboard a steamship.[199]

Unfortunately, for every successful trip on the railroad there was a heartbreaking story of capture. Seventy-seven enslaved families set sail aboard *The Pearl* as it sailed down the Potomac River from Washington, DC, to the coast. Vicious winds forced the schooner to dock on the Chesapeake. Thirty-five slavecatchers boarded the ship and discovered the stowaways.

THE PROPHET, THE EVANGELIST, AND MOSES

The Lord has made me a sign unto this nation, an' I go round a'testifyin', an' showin' their sins agin my people. My name was Isabella; but when I left the house of bondage, I left everything behind. I wa'n't goin' to keep nothin' of Egypt on me, so I went to the Lord an' asked him to give me a new name. An' the Lord gave me Sojourner, because I was to travel up and down the land, showin' the people their sins, an' being a sign unto them. Afterward, I told the Lord I wanted another name, cause everybody else had two names; and the Lord gave me Truth, because I was to declare the Truth to the people.[200]

—*Sojourner Truth*

This epoch in American history introduced within one generation three remarkable individuals. Few periods in American history have witnessed a trio endued with the personality and character traits possessed by Sojourner Truth, Frederick Douglass, and Harriet Tubman. Though they were not the only ones, they deserve special places of honor in the chronicles of freedom fighters. They shared surprising similarities in background. All were born into an institution that enslaved them, yet they managed to escape with their humanity intact. Douglass and Tubman ran away; Truth confided that she and her daughter "walked away." Douglass and Tubman were born four years and miles apart in eastern Maryland; Truth was their senior by two decades. Each escorted fugitives escaping the South. All were suffragettes and fought alongside white women demanding a woman's right to vote. Tubman spent nights in Douglass's home. All were people of faith.

Sojourner Truth (c. 1797–1883) was a true evangelist. Everything she did was in obedience to the call of God as an agent of justice and love. She proclaimed God's unconditional love for her race and equally for her gender.[201] Her advocacy on behalf of four million enslaved men and women was relentless. This remarkable woman, gifted with the ability to articulate the complications of American race relations, used the vernacular of plain, everyday speech. She spoke in a Dutch accent—she grew up with a Dutch family in New York and spoke only Dutch until age nine—yet with a captivating resonance. She cast a spell over those within the sound of her voice and inspired any seeking discernment. She spoke in a straightforward manner about what it was like to suffer as an enslaved person and be hounded as a woman. She never allowed anyone to disrespect her humanity, gender, or femininity. In an 1851 speech that became one of her signature moments, she refuted one man's rhetoric who argued that white women should be protected by asking,

"Ain't I a woman?" She swept aside his argument persuasively, stating that she had to work harder than any man simply because she was an enslaved woman. She did not mince words or try to win political points, appointments, or friends. She demanded racial justice and equality for women.[202]

Frederick Douglass (1818–1895) was a prophet. He was, perhaps excluding the Rev. Dr. Martin Luther King Jr., the singular most-impactful African American in the history of the United States. Born into slavery, he rose to be the principal spokesperson for the abolitionist movement, his race, and social justice advocates. He displayed an assortment of talents as a lay preacher, newspaper editor, presidential advisor, abolitionist, Underground Railroad conductor, vice-presidential candidate, orator, political appointee, bank manager, and Haitian ambassador. Oration was his greatest gift, and his timeless speeches are known for the inspiration of his words and powerful discourse. He was a gifted singer who often intertwined his lectures with spirituals to stir up the audience's passions. He toured Europe to wide acclaim and generated contributions for his newspaper and the abolitionist movement. During his life, he was the most recognizable American in the world and in great demand up to the moment of his death. He died in his home as he was preparing for a speaking engagement at the age of seventy-seven.[203]

Harriet Tubman (1822–1913) was the Moses of her people, an UGRR conductor who rescued hundreds from the land of bondage to the promised land. She cast aside her slave name and recast herself after her mother, whose first name was Harriet. Like Moses, she seemed to have a direct line of communication with God, speaking and listening to a divine voice that guided her. She was a Christian, scout, UGRR conductor, army recruiter, laundress, nurse, abolitionist, military commandant, spy, cook, guide, suffragist, philanthropist, and caregiver. Despite being hunted by bounty hunters, she ventured south to lead slaves hundreds of miles. She never learned to read or write and relied on a photographic memory. For a decade, she facilitated at least nineteen rescues, absconding with a small army of men, women, and children. Famously, she "never lost a passenger." She led a detachment of Union soldiers through waters lined with explosives to rescue seven hundred men, women, and children. Throughout life, she struggled financially to meet her needs yet opened her home to family, orphans, and the elderly.[204]

The prophet, the evangelist, and Moses dedicated their lives to the service of others. They sacrificed by answering a divine call from a God they knew personally as a God of justice. A God who cared for "the least of these," and sent three deliverers to challenge America to live out the full truth of what it claimed to be. In 1868 Tubman requested that Douglass write a statement of support for her upcoming biography. Douglass responded,

You ask for what you do not need when you call upon me for a word of commendation. I need such words from you far more than you can need them from me, especially where your superior labors and devotion to the cause of the lately enslaved of our land are known as I know them. . . . I know of no one who has willingly encountered more perils and hardships to serve our enslaved people than you have. Much that you have done would seem improbable to those who do not know you as I know you. It is to me a great pleasure and a great privilege to bear testimony for your character and your works, and to say to those to whom you may come, that I regard you in every way truthful and trustworthy. Your friend, Frederick Douglass.[205]

THE WAR TO END SLAVERY

No matter where I fight, I only wish to spend what I have, and fight as long as I can, if only my boy may stand in the street equal to a white boy when the war is over.[206]
—*A Black volunteer in the Civil War*

For Black Americans, the 1861 onset of the Civil War represented the eve of a long-awaited day of Jubilee. No Americans more eagerly anticipated the call to war, and no demographic was more willing to fight. It was the moment they'd waited for their entire lives. For northern civilians, it was a "white man's war," to be fought by and amongst whites. It had nothing to do with slavery. For Black Americans, it was "The War to End Slavery." Above all others, this was a war the Black man wanted to fight. Frederick Douglass went on a tour promoting "the freeing of the slaves as a war measure and, secondly, the use of slaves and free Negroes in an army of liberation."[207] Historian David W. Blight wrote, "By 1863 the war to save the Union had irrevocably become as well the war to free the slaves, and black soldiers came to symbolize their people's struggle for freedom, a recognition of their humanity, the rights of citizenship, and a sense of belonging in a new nation."[208]

Ironically, as in previous war efforts, the country's leadership reverted to the old and failed stereotype that men of color would not fight. President Lincoln was not predisposed to conscription, as he feared it would alienate border states who remained in the Union. His admitted goal was to preserve the Union and if that could be achieved "without freeing any slave I would do it, and if I could save it by freeing all the slaves I would do it; and if I could save it by freeing some and leaving others alone I would also do that."[209] Freedmen and the enslaved defined the war as an opportunity to free "all the slaves." They ridiculed the southern states' rights argument of a war against northern aggression. The Charleston, South Carolina, newspaper the

Mercury conceded this point on Jan. 13, 1865: "It was on account of encroachments upon the institution of slavery . . . that South Carolina seceded from that Union. It is not at this late day, after the loss of thirty thousand of her best and bravest men in battle, that she will suffer it to be bartered away."[210]

While government and military leaders debated, freedmen and the enslaved acted. Movement emerged from the bottom up rather than descending from the highest levels of government. They lobbied local officials and the White House to recruit men of color. Frederick Douglass was relentlessly issuing statements to the press and engaging in political confrontations.[211] The enslaved escaped in massive numbers to Union lines. Those who remained sabotaged plantation operations. Historian Robert Engs declared, "The slaves freed themselves."[212]

Brigadier General Benjamin Butler, the commander of the Union's Fort Monroe, took in three Virginia fugitives on May 23, 1961. He stated that he would detain the Negroes as "contraband of war."[213] Unwittingly, he established future military policy by his designation of "contraband." Congress picked up the labeling and passed the 1861 First Confiscation Act, declaring that any property, including slaves, used in insurrection against the United States, the president can seize and confiscate for the benefit of the Union.[214] The enslaved could now be wrested from the Confederacy into service for the Union. The 1862 Second Confiscation Act emancipated any enslaved persons who reached Union lines. On July 17, 1862, the Militia Act authorized the enlistment of Black men as laborers and soldiers. The Emancipation Proclamation, issued on January 1, 1863, declared free all enslaved persons in areas in rebellion against the Union. Lincoln's Emancipation Proclamation declared that "such persons of suitable condition will be received into the armed service of the United States."[215]

Ironically, the first northern regiment of Black soldiers was from the heart of Dixie. General Ben Butler redirected the Louisiana Native Guards into the first unit in May 1863. Captains and lieutenants of their hue led these former confederates. In October 1862, General James Lane led the 1st Kansas Colored Regiment into battle at Island Mound, Missouri, the first time soldiers of color would fight for the Union. One reporter wrote, "It is useless to talk anymore about Negro courage. The men fought like tigers, each and every one of them, and the main difficulty was to hold them well in hand. Saddle and mount is the word."[216]

Union General David Hunter, an abolitionist, formed the first Black regiment from the ground up, the 1st South Carolina Colored Infantry, before the Militia Act and Emancipation Proclamation were issued. He assumed authority he did not have when he declared free all slaves within the states of South Carolina, Georgia, and Florida. He ordered his men to enlist all able-bodied Black men. Lincoln revoked his orders and refused the soldiers weapons, uniforms, or compensation after four months of training. Nevertheless, the precedent had been set. By the end of 1863, twenty regiments stood ready, with thirty additional units established within the year. On January 26, 1864, the 54th Massachusetts Infantry emerged with two sons of Frederick Douglass, Charles and Lewis, commissioned as sergeant majors. On June 30, 1863, the Federal Government introduced the United States Colored Troops (USCT) and placed existing regiments under the War Department.[217]

Frederick Douglass announced that once an enslaved man buttoned up a soldier's jacket, he was no longer enslaved; he was now a free man. The Bureau of Colored Troops estimated that the former enslaved comprised three-fifths of troops of Black regiments in every branch. They served as soldiers, sailors, laborers, cooks, teamsters, and stevedores. One hundred twenty infantry regiments, twelve regiments of heavy artillery, ten batteries of light artillery, and seven cavalry regiments fought in forty-one large battles and 449 lesser engagements. They were pivotal in conquering Petersburg, Wilmington, Charleston, and Richmond. Prior to Lee's surrender, 40 percent of the soldiers surrounding Richmond were from the USCT. Of the 28,000 soldiers stationed along the Mississippi River, 18,000 were of color.[218]

The U.S. Navy enlisted 18,000 sailors as firemen, stewards, coal heavers, and boat pilots. Fifteen percent of all navy ships were crewed by men of color, and some comprised 90 percent of the crew. Of twenty-five Medal of Honor recipients, eight were sailors. Seaman Robert Sweeney was awarded twice (1881 and 1883). It is unclear if Sergeant William Carney (54th Massachusetts Regiment) or seaman Robert Black (naval battle on December 25, 1863) received the first medal. Robert Smalls captured a Confederate ship anchored in the Charleston harbor on May 13, 1862, and navigated it to Union lines. Fifteen slaves escaped aboard the ship and crewed the vessel.

Black nurses bandaged casualities back to health and comforted the dying. They accompanied soldiers into enemy territory, provided instruction in reading and writing, and established schools. Twelve served in the U.S. Navy.

Both sides underestimated the resolve and determination that men of color possessed. The War Department instituted a double standard by paying lower wages of $10 a month compared to the $13 white soldiers received. The 54th Massachusetts refused the governor's proposal to compensate for the difference. In solidarity, white officers refused pay. The policy was reversed, and pay retroactively reimbursed. The Confederacy publicized that any Black soldier apprehended in battle would be reenslaved as a fugitive slave. If outfitted in a Union uniform, he would be executed, even under the banner of surrender. White soldiers would be held as prisoners of war. Congress responded immediately with countermeasures declaring that for every soldier reinstated to slavery, a corresponding number of Confederate prisoners would be sentenced to hard labor. During the Fort Pillow Massacre on April 12, 1864, in Tennessee, three hundred surrendering Black Union soldiers were shot or bayoneted to death by over two thousand Confederate soldiers under the command of Major General Nathan Bedford Forrest. The slaughter inspired Black soldiers bent on revenge. On September 29, 1864, outside of Richmond at New Market Heights, General Butler rallied the 4th and 6th U.S. Colored Troops under the cry "Remember Fort Pillow." The Union Army responded by refusing prisoner exchanges.[219]

There were limited moves in the Confederacy to utilize the manpower in such abundance throughout the South. As early as March 2, 1861, Louisiana newspapers reported that volunteers formed the 1st and 2nd Louisiana regiments. In June 1861, Tennessee became the first state legislature, on either side, to authorize the recruitment of "all free male persons of color between the ages of fifteen and fifty." States gathered recruits from Tennessee, Louisiana, and Alabama. South Carolina owner William Ellison offered fifty-three of his enslaved men to fight against the Yanks. In August 1861, Black soldiers commanded howitzer batteries at New Market Bridge, Virginia, and Lynchburg and were with Lee in Richmond and Petersburg. By 1864, desperation forced the Confederacy to reconsider its rejection of soldiers of color. In February 1865, Robert E. Lee wrote of the necessity of arming slaves: "We must decide whether slavery shall be extinguished by our enemies and the slaves be used against us or use them ourselves."[220] On March 13, 1865, the Confederate Congress passed legislation but did not guarantee to free any who served. "Nothing in this act shall be construed to authorize a change in the relation which the said slaves shall bear toward their owners."[221] This move killed any motivation to fight for the Confederacy. To complicate loyalties, those Black men in Confederate grey were not viewed well by fellow Black men and women. They were whipped and demeaned and had mud thrown onto their uniforms. Enslaved men and women cursed them as complicit in their own captivity. Jefferson Davis biographer Edward Pollard indicated that Black Confederate soldiers were looked on with distaste and hatred: "The mass of their colored brethren looked on (them) with unenvious eyes."[222] War veteran Thomas Hughes wrote in 1904 that the soldiers "appeared to regard themselves as isolated or out of place, as if engaged in a work not exactly in accord with their notions of self-interest."[223]

The Confederates were correct in their assessment that arming enslaved men was a dangerous endeavor. Once you made an enslaved man a soldier, the soldier would not be complacent as an enslaved person. Resistance was an instinctive response to bondage, and it was likely the enslaved would liberate themselves, and others, with weapons of war. If somehow the South managed to fight the Union to a stalemate, it would have only been a matter of time before military-trained guerillas instigated covert hostilities.

Throughout slavery, whites underestimated the enemy in their ranks. Racial arrogance assumed that house servants remained loyal confidants to the secrets whispered in the Big House. Many enslaved stood squarely on the side of the Union and were a reliable source of military intelligence. Feigning nonattentiveness, they listened closely to the affairs of war discussed while they performed household chores. Illiterates perfected the ability to retain information with detailed specificity, an invaluable talent in espionage.[224] Those who were literate absorbed newspapers and military communiques and then divulged the information to field hands, who passed it on to Union troops. President John Adams observed, "The [N]egroes have a wonderful art of communicating intelligence among themselves; it will run several hundreds of miles in a week or fortnight (two weeks)."[225] Mary Elizabeth Bowser, a Black maid in the Confederate White House under Jefferson Davis, served as a Union spy. She and Elizabeth Van Lew operated an espionage network in Richmond on behalf of the Union Army. They lifted valuable information on military maneuvers and battle plans. Literate, she possessed photographic recall and memorized exposed dispatches. Van Lew wrote, "Most generally our reliable news is gathered from Negroes, and they certainly show wisdom, discretion, and prudence, which is wonderful." She described Mary as a "maid, of more than usual intelligence." In 1865 Bowser was forced to flee and attempted one final act of sabotage, to burn down the Confederate White House. She managed to escape but the fire was put out.[226] In 1861 William A. Jackson, Jefferson Davis's house servant and coachman, escaped to the Union camp stationed at Fredericksburg, Virginia. His details about Confederate supply routes and military strategy proved to be so vital they were cabled directly to Washington. Major General Irvin McDowell mentioned Jackson in a letter to Secretary of War Edwin Stanton praising his information on Confederate war operations.[227]

Of the almost 200,000 Black men who served the Union cause, 90,000 had escaped from the Confederacy, 45,000 came from border states, and the remainder were from the North. The 68,178 United States Colored soldiers who died in the war endured the highest percentage of casualties of any race.[228] Historian James M. McPherson wrote that "weighed in the scale of the Civil War, these 190,000 black soldiers and sailors tipped the balance in favor of Union victory."[229] President Lincoln attributed the Union victory in no small degree to their bravery. He confided in 1864 that without their sacrifice, "we would be compelled to abandon the war in three weeks."[230]

The war changed everything for both races and impacted every region of the country. Blacks came out with great expectations. They had nothing to lose and everything to gain. They wanted land, political rights, and economic gains. They felt that they had earned these rights not as a debt for slavery but because they helped win the war, suffering great casualities in the process. They were willing to do anything to find their way in the world and produce a better world for their children than the one they had experienced.

THE RECONSTRUCTION DECADE

A century and a half after it began, Reconstruction remains one of the most pivotal moments in American history, with enduring relevance to the world we now inhabit. Even if we are unaware of it, Reconstruction is part of our lives in the early 21st century. . . . The definition of American citizenship and the rights citizens should enjoy. . . . The victims of unequal treatment; the proper response to episodes of terrorism—all these are Reconstruction questions. . . . One cannot understand American history or modern American society and politics without knowing something about Reconstruction.[231]

Lerone Bennett Jr. estimated that "for ten years in these United States, for one hundred and twenty months, America tried democracy."[232] Congress responded to the assassination of President Abraham Lincoln on April 15, 1865, by inaugurating the Reconstruction Era (1866–1877). It was a time of incredible hope for the emancipated, hope that not only had emancipation arrived but with it the rights of citizenship. For the first time, people of African descent were acknowledged as American citizens. With the passage of the Thirteenth (December 18, 1865), Fourteenth (July 28, 1868), and Fifteenth (March 30, 1870) Amendments, slavery was eradicated, citizenship granted, and enfranchisement secured. The formerly enslaved could legally marry, which validated their coupling, and their status as parents established that of their children. America was on its way to being America—if only for a decade.

People of African descent quickly took advantage of the newly available political opportunities. They voted and won state and national elections. They were appointed to governmental positions and educated others on their rights, amazing accomplishments for people just years removed from slavery. Working with white Republicans, they drafted some of the most progressive state constitutions in the country's history, which benefited the impoverished of every race. Bondage, indentured servitude, and debtor's prisons were made illegal. Women gained the rights of property ownership as well as rights within divorce proceedings. Public education was ensured regardless of race or caste. Louisiana, Mississippi, and South Carolina integrated their school systems.[233]

Political and social improvements upgraded the lives of citizens of every hue. If Reconstruction had been allowed to run its course, ills plaguing the country would have been rectified, and the future of the nation, redirected.

Between 1866 and 1875, the Reconstruction Congress proved itself to be the most racially progressive in U.S. history. Initially, out of a vengeful response to Lincoln's assassination, it forced accountability onto the South for the devastation of the war. It halted President Andrew Johnson's mediocre plan for reentry of Confederate states. Five civil rights statutes necessitated that state constitutions protect freed men and women. The Freedmen's Bureau Act of 1865, the Civil Rights Act of 1866, the Civil Rights Act of 1870, the Civil Rights Act of 1871, and the Civil Rights Act of 1875 afforded rights the Constitution failed to provide.

Congressional actions were of benefit to citizens of African descent. On March 3, 1865, Congress launched the Bureau of Freedmen, Refugees, and Abandoned Lands (Freedmen's Bureau). It was tasked to feed millions of hungry people, construct hospitals and orphanages, and allot "not more than forty acres" of land to former slaves. Courts deliberated over the arrest and prosecution of those participating in acts of terrorism. By August, it distributed to 100,000 hungry men, women, and children cornmeal mush and saltwater. On April 9, 1866, the Civil Rights Act strengthened citizenship rights as a safeguard against the restrictive Black Codes passed by southern states. A Second Freedmen's Bureau Bill empowered federal agents to intervene to prevent violence. On March 2, 1867, the first Reconstruction Act divided the South into five military districts under the jurisdiction of generals, instituted biracial constitutional conventions, and ensured the right to vote. Southern states had to ratify the Fourteenth Amendment before readmittance into the Union. On July 11, 1870, the Naturalization Act made people of African descent citizens of the country in which they were born. Congress addressed disenfranchisement in the North with the passage of the Second Enforcement Act (February 28, 1871). Northern cities with 20,000 residents had to ensure that local and state elections were fair. The 1875 Civil Rights Act outlawed discrimination in public accommodations in railroads, hotels, restaurants, inns, theaters, public conveyances, and amusement parks. The 1865 Freedman's Saving and Trust Bank, Freedman's Bank, operated thirty-seven branches in seventeen states and Washington, DC. Seventy-two thousand depositors invested $3,000,000 of their hard-earned dollars. Frederick Douglass served as the bank's president until it closed in 1874.

The new citizens responded with enthusiastic participation in the world of politics. A day after the passage of the Fifteenth Amendment, Thomas Mundy Peterson became the first person of color to vote in Perth Amboy, New Jersey. Highly effective organizers traveled throughout the South and registered voters, who became a powerful force in local and state elections. Black conventions held in Alexandria, Raleigh, and Charleston called on state constitutional conventions to fulfill congressional requirements. Over 735,000 registered voters accounted for one-third of state convention delegates. Thirteen hundred Black mayors, prosecuting attorneys, sheriffs, justices of the peace, and superintendents of education were appointed. Two thousand public officials were elected in South Carolina and Louisiana. In the former, Black state legislators held 87 of the 127 seats. Jonathan J. Wright sat on the state supreme court, and Francis L. Cardozo served as secretary of state. Sixteen members of Congress included two senators and fourteen members of the U.S. House of Representatives. Their ranks included seven lawyers, three ministers, one banker, one publisher, two schoolteachers, three college presidents, Union Army veterans, and a host of former slaves.

In 1870 Joseph Hayne Rainey (SC) was elected to the U.S. House of Representatives as the first man of color to serve. In 1875 John Adams Hyman (NC) became the first HOR member from his state. In Mississippi, Hiram Revels (1870) became the first African American in the Senate, ironically and fittingly occupying the seat vacated by Jefferson Davis. Blanche K. Bruce (1874) was the first African American elected to a full six-year term. He was the only senator to have experienced slavery firsthand. Representative Roy Lynch served as Speaker of the House. Mississippi, Louisiana, and South Carolina elected Black lieutenant governors, and P. B. S. Pinchback occupied the governor's seat in Louisiana. In 1872, white woman Victoria Woodhull was nominated by the National Radical Reformers as the first female presidential candidate. Her running mate, Frederick Douglass, was the first African American vice-presidential candidate. George Henry White from North Carolina was the last Black man to serve in Congress in the nineteenth century. After he declined to run for another term in 1901, it would be 1929 before another African American served in Congress, 1972 before another was elected from a former Confederate state, and 1992 before another was elected from North Carolina.

Reconstruction Presidents: Johnson, Grant, Hayes, and Garfield

Despite the achievements made in the Reconstruction period, after Lincoln's death came a period without strong presidential leadership. The country needed resolute presidential leadership with a vision to unite the country, but not at the expense of the formerly enslaved. What it received were four presidents who mostly lacked the moral courage to withstand the political backlash to Reconstruction from white supremacy.

President Andrew Johnson (1865–1869) was an ardent racist who considered people of color an inferior race residing in a country to which they did not belong. This career politician was the worst possible successor to Lincoln. He was stubborn, racist, and incompetent. In 1868, he was impeached by the House of Representatives and did not run for a second term.

President Ulysses S. Grant (1869–1877) was the stoic hero general of the war. He desired to defend freed men and women, but like Lincoln he was slow to act, fearing political reprisal for promoting egalitarian policies. He spoke forthrightly about the rights of the former slaves and endorsed the Third Force Act against the recently formed Ku Klux Klan. He dispatched federal troops into the South to defend people of color but at times responded too slowly, resulting in massacres in Louisiana and South Carolina. His actions did not match his convictions when needed most.[234]

Rutherford Birchard Hayes (1877–1881) became the nineteenth president under a cloud that would lead to the end of Radical Reconstruction. The 1876 presidential election between Democrat Samuel J. Tilden and Republican Hayes ended in a contentious stalemate. An electoral commission in 1877 reached a compromise—Hayes would become president under the condition that he withdraw federal troops from the South. Hayes was incredibly naïve in his conviction that the South would respect freed persons' rights. He lacked the capacity to measure accurately southern vitriol.[235] This compromise would usher in a reign of terror that lasted a hundred years.

President James A. Garfield (March 4, 1881–September 19, 1881) became the second president to fall prey to an assassin's bullet. He was shot by a former supporter angry that he did not receive a desired appointment. Historians do not generally list Garfield in connection with Reconstruction. His short-termed presidency, all of six months, has been listed out of what might have been. Coming into his presidency, he believed stronger than any of his predecessors, including Lincoln, in equality. A profoundly religious man, he thought that the War to End Slavery was punishment from God for the sin of slavery. The criticism of him was that many of his statements were grounded in paternalism. However, no politician uttered stronger public endorsements of equality, and it shall forever be unknown the benefit that might have been received from his presidency.

After only a decade, Reconstruction was over and with it the racial progress achieved to that point in history. A period of severe repression followed that completely wiped away the advances for which people had struggled for so long. Four presidents who could have made a difference in helping the country heal from a devastating war came and went. One, Johnson, saw the country moving forward while holding people of color back. Hayes misinterpreted the anger of southern whites and the apathy of northern whites. Grant was sympathetic to the cause of racial justice but rendered impotent by political compromises and internal corruption by his cabinet. Garfield never had a chance to act on his convictions. Four presidents at the most pivotal moment since the signing of the Declaration of Independence failed to provide the leadership needed to reshape the nation, or rather, to shape the nation into the image it has always held of itself. Lincoln's death provided the motivation for Congress to act and fall in line with resolute leadership. What was lacking was a clear vision and a determination to see it through. And because of that, the nation would revert to a stage of racial oppression that would take a century and a civil rights movement to set back on course.

SLAVERY'S CHILD: WHITE SUPREMACY

Slavery wus a bad thing an' freedom, of de kin' we got wid nothin to live on wus bad. Two snakes full of pisen. One lyin' wid his head pintin' north, de other wid his head pintin' south. Dere names wus slavery an' freedom. De snake called slavery lay wid his head pinted south an' de snake called freedom lay wid his head pinted north. Both bit de n*****, an' dey wus both bad.[236]
    —*Formerly enslaved woman Patsy Mitchner from North Carolina*

As soon as the war ended, defeated Southerners released all of their hatred, anger, and misplaced vengeance upon four million formerly enslaved people. The War of Northern Aggression became a perverted War of Repression. Whites refused to embrace a worldview in which people of color were treated equally. Self-deception convinced them that the war had been fought to protect their homeland and uphold a state's right for self-determination. They neglected to acknowledge that they fought the war for the right to own human beings as property and profit from their exploitation. In their minds, the destruction of their way of life was everyone's fault but their own. An irrational fear of retribution assumed that white supremacy would be replaced by Black supremacy, and equilibrium could only be achieved at their expense. Whites wanted their country and way of life back. Not only was there a desire to regain political power but to reconstruct a racist society grounded in white supremacy. There was a festering anger directed at the formerly enslaved over the loss of white society and the destruction of property. Internally, they vowed that slavery had ended, but Blacks would never be politically, economically, or socially their equals.[237]

Between 1890 and 1908, white supremacy surfaced as a political weapon enforced by violence. Mississippi enacted the first Black Code on November 24,

1865: An Act to Confer Civil Rights on Freedmen. Alabama, South Carolina, Louisiana, Florida, North Carolina, Texas, Tennessee, and Kentucky passed similar laws. Rather than confer rights, the codes eliminated vocational choices and disenfranchised voters of color. Interracial marriage, possession of firearms, liquor, the right to vote, jury participation, and property ownership were made illegal for men and women of color. Though the federal government passed laws to overrule many of the Black Codes, severe backlash assaulting the freedom of Black men and women had commenced.

Race Massacres

In the lead-up to war, the decade of the 1860s was extremely violent as hundreds were brutally massacred. In 1863, New York City erupted in the Draft Race Riot. Poor whites were incensed when President Lincoln initiated a mandatory draft to offset dwindling military recruitment. On Saturday, July 11, the date of the draft's onset, hundreds destroyed the provost marshal's office and targeted people of color. For four consecutive days, arson destroyed buildings, homes, and the Colored Orphan Asylum. The blood of one thousand spilled onto city streets accompanied by five million dollars of property damage.[238]

On May 1–3, 1865, southern whites, angry over the war's loss, made Memphis, Tennessee, a dangerous place for anyone acting in the pursuit of social, economic, and political justice. Black federal soldiers patrolled city streets with authority to maintain the peace and arrest violators. Confrontation erupted when two wagons collided and two police officers attempted to arrest the Black man. A shooting led to one officer's death and wounding of the other. Black soldiers had weapons confiscated and were ordered to remain in the barracks. Confederate veterans, Irish immigrants, businessmen, policemen, and firefighters took to the streets to murder, rape, and damage property. It was dangerous to be Black on the streets as the mob assailed innocents. Seventy-five men, women, and children were assaulted; forty Black men and two whites were murdered. Criminals raped five women and destroyed ninety-one homes, four churches, and eight schools. A hundred persons were robbed, and there was $120,000 of destruction to federal property. Congressional hearings resulted in the passage of a civil rights bill and the Fourteenth Amendment.[239] An 1866 Freedmen's Bureau investigation on the Memphis Race Riot reported,

> The remote cause of the riot as it appears to us is a bitterness of feeling which has always existed between the low whites & blacks, both of whom have long advanced rival claims for superiority, both being as degraded as human beings can possibly be. . . . These causes combined produced a state of feeling between whites and blacks, which

would require only the slightest provocation to bring about an open rupture.[240]

Louisiana endured substantial viciousness as the war was refought between veterans of both armies. On July 30, 1866, Black veterans and white Republicans convened a constitutional convention to draft laws to overturn the state's discriminatory Black Codes. As two hundred delegates met inside a hall, a thousand Confederate veterans bombarded the building with a swarm of bullets. Delegates who surrendered were gunned down, holding a white flag of surrender. Police arrived on the scene and joined in the slaughter. When federal troops arrived, they discovered one hundred casualties, with thirty killed; twenty-seven were Black, and three, white.[241] On August 25–29, in Coushatta, Louisiana, the White League murdered twenty men of color and six whites. An 1874 siege occurred in Vicksburg, Mississippi, where three hundred died. In Hamburg, South Carolina, the Black militia refused to turn over weapons; seven men were murdered; six were of color, and one was white.

In Camilla, Georgia, a dozen men died on September 19, 1868, due to efforts to suppress their vote. Nine days later, whites in Opelousas, Louisiana, went on a murder rampage and killed at least fifty and as many as two-hundred-plus men and women. The following year a campaign against streetcar segregation erupted into disruption as both races attacked the other. Savannah, Georgia, experienced bloodshed.[242] Hamburg, South Carolina, the site of an earlier conflict, experienced an even larger incident on July 4, 1876. The Republican governor raised an all-Black militia to combat violence across the state. Eighty-four soldiers were stationed in Hamburg when hundreds of Red Shirts, a violent white supremacist militia, surrounded the armory and attacked. A firefight ensued, and seven men of color were murdered in cold blood with no repercussions against their killers.[243]

Vote and Die

In Meridian, Mississippi, in 1871, a racially diverse crowd of Republicans held elected office. Three Black politicians were arrested under the fabricated charge of making provocative speeches. During their trial, an altercation occurred; a gun was fired; and the judge was murdered. A riot grew into a coup as Republicans were forced out of office. Thirty blacks were killed.[244]

In 1872 a disputed gubernatorial election in Louisiana occurred as both political parties claimed victory and installed their candidates. White mobs declared the Democratic candidate victorious and murdered two hundred members of the Black militia and numerous civilians. Many were killed while surrendering or after being tortured. President Grant declared the

Republican, William P. Kellogg, the winner. Refusing to accept the decision of the president, thousands marched into New Orleans and installed Democratic candidate John McEnery as governor. For three days, they held the statehouse, capitol building, and military arsenal under their control. Learning of the approach of federal troops, they vacated the city.

The year 1874 was a disastrous one for the overthrow of legally elected officials. Throughout the South, racist groups such as the White League, White Line, and Red Shirts united to assassinate Black and Republican officeholders. On November 3, 1874, the White League murdered voters and forced elected officials from office. Over a thousand voters were forcibly disenfranchised in Barbour County, Eufaula, and Spring Hill, Mississippi. Elected Republicans were forcibly evicted from office with seven hundred votes destroyed or not counted. In both places, Democrats won every election.

The 1874 Vicksburg Massacre occurred when Democratic paramilitary units went on a ten-day killing spree. In Mississippi, every Black elected official, including sheriff Peter Crosby, was forced to resign at gunpoint. Crosby would not go away as ordered and organized Union veterans to counterattack. The much larger Democratic force overpowered his forces and killed three hundred men on the streets of Vicksburg, Mississippi. This event inspired similar actions as southern states approved similar plans. According to August Meier, a mass hysteria seized the southern white population based upon an unrealistic fear that Blacks would gain political, social, and economic power and oppress the population. "The great wave of riots of 1874–76 accompanied the white Democratic drive to 'redeem' the South of Radical Republican control, and the turn-of-the-century outbreaks were designed to deprive Blacks of the limited political rights they still enjoyed. Whites viewed these events as such sharp wrenches of the social order that they sometimes referred to a riot as a 'rebellion' or a 'race revolution,' demonstrating, as contemporaries put it, 'the determination of leading white citizens to liberate the city from Black tyranny.' Almost any attempt of Negroes to realize their hope for a racially egalitarian society could call forth violent repression from whites."[245]

Section 3

Protesting Reconstruction's Failures

Negroes in the New America: 1878–1954

No group has attracted more attention or has had its role more misrepresented by contemporaries and by prosperity than Southern Negroes during radical reconstruction. The period has been described as one of Negro rule, as one of gross perfidy with the Negro as the central figure, since the reins of misgovernment were supposedly held by Black militiamen. Negroes were not in control of the state governments at any time anywhere in the South. They held public office and, at times, played important parts in the public life of their respective states. But it would be stretching a point to say that their roles were dominant, and it would be hopelessly distorting the picture to suggest that they ruled the South.[1]
—*John Hope Franlkine*, Reconstruction after the Civil War

The Negro protest movement had to readjust and evolve to confront the new reality of life without the evil of slavery, but it was a life filled with new, more life-threatening dangers. Protest energies did not dissipate, as slavery's end did not mean an existence without brutality or injustice. Any hopes for assistance from the federal government waned after Reconstruction ended and the South was quickly reassimilated into the Union. It was given authority to deal with the Black race as it deemed most appropriate. Blacks faced a region that blamed them for the war and sought to reinstate white supremacy through domestic and legislative terrorism. Blacks quickly realized that freedom in the South meant social, political, and economic domination. They created an overground railroad as millions migrated from southern killing fields to western and northern regions of the country. A landless, illiterate people protested by combining their meager resources to construct churches, schools, and businesses. These institutional foundations were instrumental in the fight against white supremacy. This generation of protesters paved the way for the coming civil rights movement as they challenged racism and created the means by which to combat it.

African American historian Rayford Logan described the years between 1877 and 1901 as the "nadir of American race relations," the lowest point to be an African American in the United States of America. He argued for 1901 being the pinnacle of racial violence. John Hope Franklin and others argued for a later date around 1923. Between 1900 and 1965, resistance manifested itself in a wide variety of ways. Jim Crow was in full effect as the nation erupted in insurgences. Blacks responded with a determination to withstand the discriminatory blows by creating institutes of self-help. Defiance emerged as schools, churches, and mutual aid societies blossomed. Voluntary migration out of the South to escape persecution led to all-Black towns.

Of the five identities in this book, the label *Negro* had the dubious distinction of not originating within the Black community. With origins in Spanish and Portuguese, it was in common usage amongst whites. Black intellectuals were ambivalent about its usage, going back and forth between rejecting and embracing it. Collier-Thomas and Turner wrote,

> By 1915 support for Negro as a universal term emanated from three distinct sources. There were those who argued that Negro was anthropologically and ethnologically correct. Anthropologist Johann Blumenbach listed Negro among his five species of human beings. Others reasoned that Negro was the most commonly used term, and finally, some felt the term was legally correct, since most states legislated that anyone with a trace of "Negro blood" was Negro.[2]

The *Baltimore Afro-American* newspaper's November 1912 edition stated the following:

> The statutes of Kentucky, Maryland, Mississippi, North Carolina, Tennessee, and Texas assert that "a person of color" is one who is descended from a Negro to the third generation, inclusive, though one ancestor in each generation may have been white. According to the law of Alabama, one is "a person of color" who has had any Negro blood in his ancestry for five generations. . . . In Arkansas, "persons of color" include all who have a visible and distinct admixture of African blood. . . . Thus it would seem that a Negro in one state is not always a Negro in another.[3]

As early as 1882, leaders advocated for usage of *Negro* over the term *Colored* as it symbolized militancy, assertiveness, and defiant pride. Senator Blanche K. Bruce stalwartly barked, "I am a Negro and proud of my race." Frederick Douglass made constant reference to the term, and Booker T. Washington advocated substituting it in place of *Black*, *Colored*, or *Afro-American*. A Negro adoption movement was led by W. E. B. Du Bois and Marcus Garvey. By 1919, the Negro Year Book confirmed that "there is an increasing use of the word 'Negro' and a decreasing use of the word Colored and Afro-American to designate us as a people. The result is that the word Negro is, more and more, acquiring a dignity that it did not have in the past."[4]

Newly formed institutions embraced it as a name: American Negro Academy (1897), National Negro Business League (1900), United Negro Improvement Association (1914), Association for the Study of Negro Life and History (1926), and National Council of Negro Women (1935). Carter G. Woodson championed Negro History Week. By the early twentieth century, the term was normalized through wide acceptance and usage. Martin Luther King Jr. and other civil rights leaders projected themselves as part of the Negro race. A coalition of intellectuals, organizations, and the Black press campaigned for its capitalization. On March 7, 1930, the *New York Times* weighed in: "In our 'style book' 'Negro' is now added to the list of words to be capitalized. It is not merely a typographical change; it is an act of recognition of racial self-respect for those who have been for generations in 'the lower case.'"[5] In 2020, it updated that decision to capitalize the "b" in Black.[6]

THE NORTHERN BETRAYAL OF THE NEGRO

Lincoln got the praise for freeing us, but did he do it? He give us freedom without giving us any chance to live to ourselves, and we still had to depend on the southern white man for work, food and clothing, and he held us through our necessity and want in a state of servitude but little better than slavery. Lincoln done but little for the Negro race and from living standpoint nothing. White folks are not going to do nothing for Negroes except keep them down.[7]
    —*Formerly enslaved man Thomas Hall*

The compromise of 1877, sending Hayes to the presidency and federal troops back north, removed the last remaining obstacle to southern intimidation. Thus, the election on the centennial of the Declaration of Independence removed any chance for a lasting and complete democracy. After a decade of Reconstruction, white Northerners were weary of southern complaints that the presence of federal troops was an unnecessary burden borne by the white man. Alliance within the white race overcame any war grievances. The North reverberated with theories of corruption under "the Black Sea of Negroism," repeating a bogus cry of "Emancipate the whites." Both harbored

long-standing racist stereotypes of a childlike race better left to the control
of whites closest in proximity. There was widespread agreement that Southerners should handle the former bondsmen in the manner they deemed most
appropriate. Northern businessmen lustfully surveyed the South for investment and industrialization.[8]

Southerners reacted to Black activism with political suppression and cultural
dominance. Former owners feared that servants would become masters, for the
shackles had been removed, and this new man no longer acted subserviently.
The former bondsmen had no intention of working without proper compensation. They refused to be treated in a deferential manner or to beg for a mere
scrap of dignity. The South, however, realized that it didn't need a return to
slavery; it could restore a social order based on racial constrictions. For all who
refused to acquiesce quietly, violence ensued. Starting in 1877, thirty-five Black
officeholders were murdered. The more public the atrocity, the more effective
the warning; this would be the fate of any who dared to forget their place in
southern society. The South's version of Reconstruction resulted in a period of
violent repression that lasted until the civil rights movement.

DOMESTIC TERRORISM

> On the very day that (President) Hayes delivered his acceptance
> speech, the town of Hamburg, South Carolina, was the scene of a
> bloody riot. Another race riot occurred at nearby Ellenton, Sep-
> tember 15–20. Many Southerners and some Northerners justi-
> fied the resort to force as the only means by which the whites
> could obtain redress for the wrongs which, they alleged, had been
> inflicted upon them by a Negro majority. But Grant's attorney-
> general, Taft, wrote Hayes on September 12 that "it is a fixed and
> desperate purpose of the Democratic party in the South that the
> Negroes shall not vote, and murder is a common means of intimi-
> dation to prevent them."[9]

America has always been a dangerous, terror-plagued nation for people of
color. There is no period in the nation's history not filled with repression per-
petrated toward people of African descent. While the South has a reputation
for racial hostility, viciousness in the North occurred early and often in the
decades before the war. Between 1830 and 1850, rioting erupted in Rhode
Island, New York, Philadelphia, Pittsburgh, Cincinnati, and other cities.
Whites attacked Blacks for no reason other than the color of their skin. In situation after situation, a perceived incident of offense would justify a response so
violent that children would be murdered without remorse or hesitation.

In Providence, Rhode Island, the townships of Snowtown and Hardscrabble were inhabited by families of color. In 1824 and 1831, white mobs burned down the homes of residents for minor encroachments. The state's 1784 law mandated the gradual emancipation of all slaves, and by 1820 there existed a Black population of a thousand. Mostly concentrated in Hardscrabble, they were independent and proud. In 1824 an argument between two men, one white and one Black, erupted over who would surrender the sidewalk for the other to pass. Later that day, angry whites invaded Hardscrabble and burned down the homes of seven families and did significant damage to four others as a crowd of whites cheered. In September of 1831, in Snowtown, a saloon brawl resulted in a white man being shot by a Black resident. For four days, a white mob of a thousand laid waste to homes. After a raucous crowd refused to disperse, the militia fired and killed four whites.[10] An 1841 confrontation in Cincinnati resulted in gunfire as both sides fired at each other. Whites gained an advantage when a small cannon fired upon their adversaries. During two days of rioting, the police refused to intervene.[11]

The Ku Klux Klan was the greatest perpetrator of racial violence. In 1866, former Confederate general Nathan Bedford Forrest, of the Fort Pillow Massacre, created a Tennessee social club. First known as the Invisible Empire of the South, it developed as individual guerilla cells comprised of poor whites, former Confederates, and plantation elites. Between 1869 and 1871, this group, which became known as the KKK, operated a military campaign enforcing white supremacy. It inflicted brutal castigation and targeted white Republican carpetbaggers, southern scalawags, and persons of color engaged in economic or political empowerment. Its weapons were nighttime raids, intimidation, and heinous murder. Members disguised themselves in long, white hooded robes topped by horns yet were often recognized by long-term residents. Formerly enslaved Robert Toatley wrote,

> Soon things got wrong and de devil took a hand in de mess. Out of it come to de top, de carpet bag, de scalawags and then de Ku Klux. Night rider come by and drap something at your door and say: "I'll just leave you something for dinner." Then ride off in a gallop. When you open de sack, what you reckon in dere? Liable to be one thing, liable to be another. One time it was six n***** heads dat was left at de door.[12]

A primary goal of the Klan was to eliminate the growing political and economic capability of freed men and women. It was a life-threatening endeavor to endorse Reconstruction's work or run for office on the Republican ticket. The Democratic Party worked in conjunction with the Klan to undermine elections and suppress the nonwhite vote in areas where whites constituted the minority. A secondary goal was the elimination of business efforts of men of color. Burnt crosses and shattered windows from drive-by shootings accompanied nighttime abductions. Murders in broad daylight scared witnesses too terrified to testify. Regularly churches and schools were burned and bombed. Terrorists committed almost 3,500 lynchings between 1865 and 1900.

The Klan was not the only fanatical organization involved in clandestine activities. Historian Rayford W. Logan penned this period as a "new civil war" as "regulators, Jayhawkers, the Black Horse Cavalry, the Knights of the White Camellia, the Constitutional Union Guards, the Pale Faces, the White Brotherhood, the Council of Safety, the '76 Association, the Rifle Clubs of South Carolina, and above all, the Ku-Klux Klan terrorized, maimed and killed a large number of Negroes."[13]

The cruelties of hate magnified tenfold as beatings, murders, rapes, kidnappings, and torture became a part of southern reality. It is difficult to convey accurately the virulent, racist hatred normalized as a part of life in America's southland. False charges of the rape of white women by men of color justified lynching. Motives for murder included reading a newspaper or book, having the wrong job, or having a sexual partner of another race. The whip was reintroduced as an instrument of torture on any who refused to work for inferior wages. Noted historian of the Jim Crow era, Richard Wormser noted with grisly detail the atrocities committed against Black bodies. Decapitations, mutilations, and tortuous acts were rather commonplace. Colonel Samuel Thomas observed, "To kill a Negro they do not feel murder: to debauch a Negro woman they do not consider (rape); to take the property away from a Negro they do not consider robbery."[14]

Lynching

Lynching in America massacred thousands of men and women. The act of lynching had consequences beyond the individual atrocity and served as a threat to an entire race. Murders by extrajudicial hordes were a weapon of fear to control, intimidate, and dominate. The Equal Justice Initiative (EJI) reported the following in *Lynching in America: Confronting the Legacy of Racial Terror*:

> During the period between the Civil War and World War II, thousands of African Americans were lynched in the United States. Lynchings were violent and public acts of torture that traumatized black people throughout the country and were largely tolerated by state and federal officials. These lynchings were terrorism. . . . Indeed, some public spectacle lynchings were attended by the entire white community and conducted as celebratory acts of racial control and domination.[15]

Music producer Quincy Jones recalled being on tour in the 1940s in Texas: "In the middle of the city there's this small church and there was a rope with a black dummy hanging off of the steeple. This was everyday stuff then. You know you just better be careful."[16]

The Tuskegee Institute documented the lynchings of 3,438 men and women between 1882 and 1951. Lynchings happened across the South and beyond, including Alabama, Arkansas, Florida, Georgia, Illinois, Indiana, Kansas, Kentucky, Louisiana, Maryland, Mississippi, Missouri, Ohio, Oklahoma, North Carolina, South Carolina, Tennessee, Texas, Virginia, and West Virginia. Lynch mobs seized any occasion to murder in a carnival-like atmosphere. Notices sent out beforehand attracted huge crowds. Ten thousand witnessed the lynching of Jesse Washington on May 15, 1916, in Waco, Texas. Ell Persons was murdered before a crowd of five thousand on May 22, 1917, in Memphis, Tennessee.[17]

Black activists initiated an antilynching campaign from the 1890s to the 1930s. A political push lobbied legislators to criminalize the act by passing antilynching legislation. Throughout the 1920s, each proposed bill failed to exit committee. The Dyer Anti-Lynching Bill was the only legislation voted on by the Senate, but it failed as well. (As late as 2020, Senator Rand Paul blocked then-senator Kamala Harris's antilynching bill, which was cosponsored by Senators Cory Booker and Tim Scott. In a hundred years, Congress has failed to make lynching a federal crime.)

African American women were pivotal leaders. They contributed to the NAACP's lobbying efforts, publicized lynching horrors, and were tireless fund-raisers. The groundbreaking journalist Ida B. Wells's work "A Red Record: Tabulated Statistics and Alleged Causes of Lynching in the United States in 1892, 1893, 1894" equated lynching with white supremacy. Her document "Southern Horrors: Lynch Law in All Its Phases" was the first to link consensual sexual relations between Black men and white women as the flame igniting racist hatred: "In our own land and under our own flag, the writer can give day and detail of one thousand men, women, and children who during the last six years were put to death without trial before any tribunal on earth. Humiliating indeed, but altogether unanswerable, was the reply of the French press to our protest (over the conviction of Captain Dreyfus): 'Stop your lynchings at home before you send your protests abroad.'"[18]

For the NAACP, the antilynching crusade was a central focus. Outside the national office in New York City hung a banner on ill-omened days that said, "A Man Was Lynched Yesterday." On July 28, 1917, a silent march paraded down Fifth Avenue in New York City. The NAACP pressed marchers to advance silently through the streets in opposition to lynching and for an end to white supremacy. An NAACP flyer urged people to participate, asking, "Why do we march?" along with the following answer:

We march because by the Grace of God and the force of truth, the dangerous, hampering walls of prejudice and inhuman injustices must fall. We march because we want to make impossible a repetition of Waco, Memphis, and East St. Louis by rousing the conscience of the country and bring the murderers of our brothers, sisters, and innocent children to justice. We march because we deem it a crime to be silent in the face of such barbaric acts.[19]

Dressed in white apparel, women were accompanied by husbands and children on a Saturday morning, maintaining a stoic solemnity of dignity and poise. Their upright posture demonstrated that they were not bent over in submission, but neither would they demean themselves or place the lives of their children in jeopardy. Ten thousand protested with their feet that day in the nation's largest city.[20] Their example would become a global model for future marches and a precursor to those during the civil rights movement. James Weldon Johnson wrote in his 1938 autobiography *Along This Way*, "The streets of New York have witnessed many strange sites, but I judge, never one stranger than this; among the watchers were those with tears in their eyes."[21]

Coup d'État American Style

The Jim Crow era of racial segregation resulted in an overlooked anomaly in American history, the overthrow of local governments. The French phrase *coup d'état* is defined as a "blow against the state." The United States heralds itself for the peaceful transition of political power, but several elected governments were overthrown by the barrel of a gun.

In 1883 in Danville, Virginia, the Black public enjoyed a majority on the city council. It enacted cross-racial hires in the persons of four police officers and every justice of the peace. On election night, a coup culminated in the murder of four elected officials, voter suppression, and a stolen election.[22]

Wilmington, North Carolina, had a growing Black middle class and emerging electorate. Two thousand whites attacked the only Black newspaper in the state on November 10, 1898. Editor Alexander Manly repudiated charges of rape against a man of color, printing that the sex was consensual. A mob retaliated by destroying his printing press and threatening the editor's life. Between fifteen and sixty residents were murdered; elected Republicans were ousted; and former Confederates were inserted into their position. The federal government ignored calls to intervene and reestablish elected officials.[23] A report read, "By sundown, Manly's newspaper had been torched, as many as 60 people had been murdered, and the local government that was elected two days prior had been overthrown and replaced by white supremacists. For all the violent moments in United States history, the mob's gruesome attack was unique: It was the only coup d'état ever to take place on American soil."[24] "Pitchfork" Ben Tillman of South Carolina was quoted as saying, "We have scratched our heads to find out how we could eliminate the last one of them; we stuffed ballot boxes. We shot them. We are not ashamed of it."[25]

When terror did not achieve results, political leaders relied on legislation. In 1890 Mississippi stripped voting rights through a series of constitutional amendments. South Carolina followed suit in 1895. Between 1898 and 1903, Alabama, Louisiana, Virginia, and North Carolina produced identical legislation. Oklahoma and Georgia passed similar laws in 1907 and 1908. These laws were in the form of poll taxes, grandfather clauses, literacy tests, and property ownership requirements. While generally grouped with the rest, a grandfather clause granted voting rights to those who possessed the right before 1867. It was a guarantee that whites who could not meet other qualifications could vote. As long as any ancestor had voted, so could his white descendant. Allowing only whites to vote in primaries ensured winning the race, as the only candidates were conservative Democrats. By 1915 the disenfranchisement of almost every southern and northern man of color was complete.[26] But rather than producing disillusionment, it incentivized people of color to increase political actions.

Church Burnings

Throughout African American history, the Black church has been one of, and in many communities, *the* key institution providing spiritual and societal empowerment for the Black community. Carter G. Woodson maintained that "Black history and Black church history intersect[ed] at so many points as to be virtually identical."[27] E. Franklin Frazier defined it as "a nation within a nation."[28] C. Eric Lincoln proposed that the Black church's impact goes far beyond the Black community. Churches served as places of worship, vigilance committees, mutual-aid societies, underground railroad stations, community centers, activist headquarters, educational academies, distribution centers, and strategy-planning quarters.[29]

Racist oppression sought to suppress not only the individual but also the Black church, the informal headquarters of Black protest. Suppression was demonstrated through violence, and specifically arson. It is astounding to read how many church histories record a fire during some time in their story. Churches were a common target for burning or destruction by bombing as an attack on the congregation and the entire Black community. There was a Black-church boom after 1865 that was met with arson and terrorism lasting into the twentieth century. During the civil rights movement there was violence targeting church buildings at the rate of one church a week, according to civil rights historian Taylor Branch. During Freedom Summer in 1964, a church was set afire every other day in Mississippi.[30] According to Michele M. SimmsParris, between 1957 and 1963 hundreds of churches were burned and bombed in Alabama, Mississippi, Tennessee, Arkansas, and Georgia.[31]

This means of attack against the Black community did not end with the civil rights movement. Between 1995 and 1996, 145 Black churches were burned; within twenty-one months a total of 230 buildings were torched.[32] Between January 1995 and February 1996, a larger number of Black churches were burned than in the previous five years. In 1995 President Clinton created the National Arson Task Force to study remedies to prevent such attacks. The task force investigated 827 church burnings and bombings. Every five days a church burned.[33] The first report specified that in less than three years, 429 worship sanctuaries were burned or bombed. The numbers dropped to 209 in 1997 and were down to 166 the next year.[34] During the first six months of 2015 seven Black churches were destroyed by fire. The U.S. Historic Trust placed Black churches on its "most endangered" list.[35]

SLAVES TO SHARECROPPERS TO CONVICTS

This was the beginning of the Senator's convict camp. These men were prisoners who had been leased by the Senator from the State of Georgia at about $200 each per year, the State agreeing to pay for guards and physicians, for necessary inspection, for inquests, all rewards for escaped convicts, the cost of litigation and all of the incidental camp expenses. . . . A Georgia peon camp is hell itself![36]
    —*An anonymous free laborer working at a convict camp in 1900*

When slavery ended, oppression did not cease but evolved into more virulent acts of cruelty. White supremacy did permanent and lasting damage to the American psyche. Monetary value was attached to an enslaved person, and in a bizarre manner gave limited protection to the enslaved. The lives of freed men and women carried no financial value. A free Black person was considered worthless.

The Civil War demolished the South's economy. In return for past labor, former slaves received no compensation, land, tools, crops, nor work animals. The South created a system of sharecropping and land tenancy during the first decade after the Civil War that tied both Blacks and whites to the land deep into the 1930s. Planters and their former slaves both wanted the same thing: to own and work farmland. Out of desperation to feed their families, Blacks labored in the only labor vineyards available, sharecropping. It was an economic system of legalized larceny with little benefit for those who did all the work, while landowning whites received the bulk, if not all, of the profit. The planters created an economic system wherein they had control of the means of production as the owners of land and equipment. They scripted the language on contracts that were unfavorable for those desperate enough to sign. It was a credit system with accumulating interest. Laborers were provided the use of farmable land, seeds, fertilizer, tools, and the use of a mule. By the end of the season the worker was indebted, as expenses were greater than earnings. Many were confined to pay off outstanding debts before they could seek other means of employment. For Blacks, sharecropping was only a step above slavery.[37]

Michelle Alexander's book *The New Jim Crow* exposed social and economic exploitation utilizing the criminal justice system. The convict lease system was a racialized penal system manifested in a twofold division: the prison farm and the chain gang. Thousands were enslaved, not under the control of an individual but under the authority of the state. Southern states exploited a loophole in the Thirteenth Amendment that permitted enslavement through penal punishment. The Black Codes legislated the arrest of so-called vagrants throughout the South and assessed fines for vagrancy, unemployment, loitering, or lack of ID or proof of work. Those convicted could work off their charges by being loaned to unscrupulous business owners. A leasing corporation assigned them to work sites including mines, railroads, and, yes, plantations. The pay was so minimal that it would take years to eliminate the smallest fine, which accumulated the longer it went unpaid. Breaking a contract caused an extension on the length of imprisonment. This new manifestation of slavery swept up women and children and herded thousands into debtors' prisons. For the first time in the nation's history, American prisons contained more African Americans than whites.[38]

In the early 1900s, the state penal system again evolved with the introduction of the chain gang. In 1908 Georgia's prison reform received national acclaim as it converted its convict lease system into a chain gang to repair roads and highways. Thousands of men, no longer slaves hoeing on the plantation, were now prisoners working roads. The federal government promoted this system as a means to improve the South's economy and provide badly needed road repair. The Peachtree State misrepresented its elimination of the leasing system while in reality merely shifting locations. Politicians ballyhooed, "Bad boys make good roads." White progressives identified the idea as prison reform, rationalizing that inmates could spend time away from the constraints of a prison cell. Conservatives applauded the free labor and the replenishing of state budgets. The *Mississippi Encyclopedia* said the following about the South:

[It was] bankrupt in the wake of the Civil War and faced with the difficult task of rebuilding and sustaining an infrastructure. Mississippi and other state governments turned to a familiar expedient to fund their penal institutions. In the late 1860s many southern prisons began leasing convicts to plantations and industries bereft of the cheap labor formerly supplied by slaves. As the majority of inmates were African American, this new form of compulsory labor helped to bridge the gap between the Black Codes and Jim Crow as a form of social control that embodied the common racial hierarchies in the South. [39]

Prisoners lived in excruciating conditions and remained chained throughout their incarceration. An enslaved person had financial worth whereas a convict had none, and replacements were abundantly available for little to no cost. They were shackled throughout the day and restrained at night with metal restraints linked from one ankle to the next. A bathroom to relieve oneself was a hole cut into the floor. Food was of the worst quality and barely consumable. A white overseer stood watch with a rifle in hand as prisoners labored from sunup to sundown, and he would not hesitate to shoot any who dared attempt to escape. There was brutal punishment for the defiant. Prisoners staked to the ground had molasses poured over their bodies to attract insects. They endured being locked in a sweatbox for days in hundred-degree temperatures. Bodies were racked and stretched as unbreakable cables slowly pulled limbs apart. They were tortured for the smallest infraction with no consequences for a guard who shot or killed a prisoner.

One would think that morality would end this barbarity, but it was racist sympathy that stopped the abuse. The Great Depression resulted in a growth in the incarceration rates of white men, which prompted sympathetic outrage over these inhumane conditions. By 1940 road gangs significantly dwindled, and by 1960 the practice had practically disappeared. But in 1995, Governor Forrest James revived it in the Alabama Limestone Correctional Facility. He proclaimed with racist justification that it made Alabama safer as prisoners were too coddled watching television and lifting weights. Arizona, Florida, Iowa, Massachusetts, and Wisconsin followed suit, with women and juveniles now included.

THE OLD JIM CROW

Summarizing the matter in the large, segregation is ill-advised because: 1. It is unjust. 2. It invites other unjust measures. 3. It will not be productive of good, because practically every thoughtful

Negro resents its injustice and doubts it sincerity. Any race adjustment based on injustice finally defeats itself. The Civil War is the best illustration of what results where it is attempted to make wrong right or seem to be right. 4. It is unnecessary. 5. It is inconsistent. The Negro is segregated from his white neighbor, white businessmen are not prevented from doing business in Negro neighborhoods. 6. There has been no case of segregation of Negroes in the United States that has not widened the breach between the two races. Wherever a form of segregation exists it will be found that it has been administered in such a way as to embitter the Negro and harm more or less the white man. That the Negro does not express this constant sense of wrong is no proof that he does not feel it.[40]

—Booker T. Washington in 1915, a month before his death

The turning of the calendar to the twentieth century symbolically represented hope that a new century would usher in a racial reformation. This century produced momentous developments in the African American drama. Between 1916 and 1964, two migrations, prompted by two world wars and economic opportunity, changed the demographic makeup of the country and the fortunes of an entire race. According to the Economic History Association,

> The nineteenth century was a time of radical transformation in the political and legal status of African Americans. Blacks were freed from slavery and began to enjoy greater rights as citizens. . . . They had become much less concentrated in the South, in rural places, and in farming jobs and had entered better blue-collar jobs and the white-collar sector. They were nearly twice as likely to own their own homes at the end of the century as in 1900, and their rates of school attendance at all ages had risen sharply. Even after this century of change, though, African Americans were still relatively disadvantaged in terms of education, labor market success, and homeownership.[41]

But this progress did not come without a high price. The hundred years following Reconstruction initiated a backlash that faded any hope that had emerged from emancipation. Domestic terrorism, political disenfranchisement, and economic bondage created an environment one level above slavery. The Black Codes, *Plessy v. Ferguson*, and Jim Crow legalized segregation in education, transportation, and residential living.[42] Legalized hatred materialized as the law of the land unrestricted by federal protection. Southern states devolved into two societies, separate and unequal, one Black, one white.

Across the South, every aspect of society was separated by race under laws enacted after Reconstruction. Bathrooms, movie theaters, parks, schools, and buses stipulated that Blacks could not sit or ride next to whites. It was a tool of white supremacy that taught whites that they were superior to Black people and were destined for governance and power. The most appalling aspect was that people of color had to be subservient to whites at all times and in all places, public and private. America was unapologetic for its minimization of Black humanity. It was considered demeaning for a white person to think of a Black man or woman as an equal.

Each decade in the early 1900s witnessed more strident restrictions enforced by the power of the federal and state governments. Not limited to southern norms, Jim Crow was initially instigated in the North. Northern racism propped up a wall of hatred amid extreme persecution. Political disenfranchisement existed throughout New England. Oregon and Illinois heavily penalized internal migration, and Black neighborhoods suffered under impoverished living conditions and low-paying jobs.[43] Boston declared that "Colored people are not allowed to ride in this omnibus." New York assigned which streetcars people of color could ride. Philadelphia Blacks could only sit on the front row of seats. None could ride in the interior of a stagecoach but were assigned to the worst, most decrepit railroad cars. Steamboat transportation was limited to the outside deck, regardless of the season or weather conditions.[44]

It was, however, the South where persecution dominated. As early as 1816, New Orleans passed a stringent law legislating segregated seating in all areas of public accommodation. In South Carolina, Charleston and Savannah prohibited free Blacks from entering public parks. Baltimore, Charleston, and New Orleans regulated jails and poorhouses into separate quarters. The 1870s and 1880s partitioned public schools, followed by railroads in the 1880s and 1890s. Regulations prohibited proximity in waiting rooms, restaurants, buses, trains, elevators, entrances, colleges, hospitals, water fountains, trolley cars, ticket windows, sidewalks, movies, circuses, jails, prisons, swimming pools, sports, orphanages, asylums, phone booths, schools, public transportation, and use of courtroom Bibles. Blacks were excluded from the best paying jobs and denied employment in entire industries and trades.[45] Richard Wormser wrote,

> Blacks had to address white people as Mr., Mrs., or "Mizz," "Boss," or "Captain" while they, in turn, were called by their first name, or by terms used to indicate social inferiority—"boy," "auntie," or "uncle.". . . They had to give way to whites on a sidewalk, remove their hats as a sign of respect to whites, and enter a white person's house by the back door. Whites, on the other hand, could enter a

Black person's home without knocking, sit without being asked, keep their hats on, and address people in a disrespectful manner.[46]

Mob actions struck fear in the hearts of any who dared step out of line, Black or white.

Each decade witnessed a new onslaught of Jim Crow legislation and discriminatory public policy. The Supreme Court impaired civil rights by adverse rulings that eradicated political rights. The 1873 *Slaughter-House* case ruled without logic or reason that the Fourteenth Amendment prevented states, not individuals, from discriminating. It essentially allowed states to pass laws that removed all federal prosecution of individuals who violated the rights of people of color, leading to the persecution and murder of countless men and women of African descent. The following day it ruled in *Bradwell v. Illinois* against Myra Bradwell and denied her admission to the Illinois bar. In March 1876, *U.S. v. Cruikshank* invalidated congressional intervention under the Enforcement Act of 1870. In the 1880 *Virginia v. Rives* case, it ruled that forbidding men of color from juries did not nullify their right to serve. This precedent eliminated the presence of Blacks from juries, making a trial by one's peers practically impossible. On October 16, 1883, the Supreme Court limited Congress's authority under the Fourteenth Amendment to prohibit discrimination on public accommodations, railroads, and hotels. In 1890 the Mississippi state constitution disenfranchised nearly all its Black voters. It was followed in quick succession by Alabama, Georgia, Louisiana, North Carolina, Oklahoma, South Carolina, and Virginia. In 1896, there were 130,334 Black voters in the state of Louisiana; by 1908, there were only 1,342, or 1 percent.

On May 18, 1896, the monumental *Plessy v. Ferguson* decision instituted the "separate but equal" doctrine and legalized segregation nationwide. It stated plainly that "if one race be inferior to the other socially, the constitution of the United States cannot put them upon the same plane." An avalanche of discriminatory legislation landed on the books in the form of grandfather clauses, literacy clauses, poll taxes, and others that eliminated the ability of Blacks to vote. On April 25, 1898, in *Williams v. Mississippi*, the court refused to declare the voter suppression components of Mississippi's state constitution unconstitutional. These rulings nullified the constitutional amendment gains of Reconstruction and handcuffed federal intervention.

American apartheid was established throughout the country, legalized by the Supreme Court, and enforced by violence. By 1914 southern states and northern cities instituted separation laws. The North reintroduced features of previous segregation regulations. In the United States, Jim Crow remained entrenched until the 1960s, when the civil rights movement successfully challenged its legality.

BOOKER T. AND W. E. B.

Easily the most striking thing in the history of the American Negro since 1876 is the ascendancy of Mr. Booker T. Washington. . . . His programme of industrial education, conciliation of the South, and submission and silence as to civil and political rights, was not wholly original. . . . But Mr. Washington first indissolubly linked these things; he put enthusiasm, unlimited energy, and perfect faith into his programme, and changed it from a by-path into a veritable Way of Life. And the tale of the methods by which he did this is a fascinating study of human life. It startled the nation to hear a Negro advocating such a programme after many decades of bitter complaint; it startled and won the applause of the South, it interested and won the admiration of the North; and after a confused murmur of protest, it silenced if it did not convert the Negroes themselves.[47]
— *W. E. B. Du Bois*, The Souls of Black Folk

W. E. B. Du Bois and Booker T. Washington were the most influential Black leaders in the late nineteenth and early- to mid-twentieth centuries. Their strategies for social and economic progress were as different as their lives, and it was as if they were created to be adversaries. Washington was born enslaved in Virginia; Du Bois was born free in Massachusetts. Washington worked his way through the historically Black Hampton Institute; Du Bois was the sixth man of color to attend Harvard. Washington stressed work; Du Bois, intellect. Washington promoted the gradual receipt of civil rights; Du Bois demanded immediate human and civil rights.

Booker T. Washington (1856–1915) rose to become the most recognized and influential Black leader of his day. His self-help philosophy appealed to white political and economic leaders, and his September 18, 1895, Atlanta Cotton Exposition Speech catapulted him as the anointed spokesman for his race. He stressed hard work and an accommodationist attitude as a remedy for racism. His philosophy pursued an end to hostility through accepting second-class status. Washington advised the wealthiest philanthropists in the world as Andrew Carnegie, John D. Rockefeller, George Eastman, and William Howard Taft sought his advice. Washington's political influence was referred to as the Tuskegee Machine, and it ruthlessly weighed who received financial funding based on their favor or disfavor.[48]

William Edward B. Du Bois (1868–1963) was perhaps the most prolific academic in the country's history. He was an intellect, scholar, reformer, integrationist, sociologist, historian, writer, Pan Africanist, and émigré. His voice spoke in every justice movement from the 1890s to the 1950s. Almost single-handedly, he memorialized in print Black life and history. His book *The Souls of Black Folk* (1903) correctly argued that "the problem of the 20th century is the problem of the color-line—the relation of the darker to the lighter races of men in Asia and Africa, in America and the islands of the sea. . . . The history of the American Negro is the history of this strife. . . . He simply wishes to make it possible for a man to be both a Negro and an American."[49] It is required reading for those seeking to understand race in America.

Du Bois promoted what he called a Talented Tenth collection of educated Blacks for political leadership. He was a race man and a progressive advocate for women's rights and the first to promote a pan-African connection between Africa and American Blacks.[50] He wrote in *Souls*, "One ever feels his twoness—an American, a Negro; two souls, two thoughts, two unreconciled strivings; two warring ideals in one dark body, whose strength alone keeps it from being torn asunder." [51] However, Du Bois overestimated the impact of a "Talented Tenth." He struggled with charges of elitism and, despite his brilliance, he was never able to mobilize a movement or establish himself as a leader of others. He reflected that he loathed "the essential demagoguery of personal leadership."[52] He charged the NAACP with elitism and abandoned his work with the organization.

Both men were to have a deep and abiding influence on the Black heart and mind. While they presented two radically different approaches to Black advancement, most Blacks chose to follow the adherence of both. Jobs were limited to domestic work in the North and agricultural labor in the South; nevertheless, their aspirations were high, especially for their children. Many cast their buckets down where they were but out of necessity, not choice. They had no intentions of similar limitations placed on their children's futures. Washington refused to accept the depth and viciousness of white supremacy.[53] Rather than applauding Black entrepreneurship, local whites felt threatened and reacted in retribution. The Black masses understood this as they fled the South. Contrary to Washington's council, they desired the right to vote and hold office and would have readily done so if a peaceful opportunity had been available. They wanted every opportunity for their children, especially education, to become doctors, lawyers, teachers, and politicians. Benjamin Quarles accused Washington of being an accomplice to murder: "He destroyed the Negro's ability to protect himself at an hour when he needed protection most. . . . Down went millions of buckets and up they came—filled with blood."[54] Quarles contended that Washington disarmed Black citizens by urging passivity when direct action was required. Acquiescence disarmed a people with few weapons to fight against violent racial discrimination.

If these two titans had secretly formed a partnership, they would have been a formidable team. To do so would have ensured a more comprehensive platform of self-help and advocacy. On one occasion, these political opponents were to coalesce with another of Washington's archrivals, William Monroe Trotter, against the movie *The Birth of a Nation*. The film, directed by D. W. Griffith, glorified the violence of the KKK and portrayed Blacks as incompetent villains. When the film came to Boston, Trotter arranged a protest that gathered thousands outside the movie theater and resulted in his arrest and imprisonment. One participant reflected, "I look over the vast crowd of Negro men and women, and the thought came to me, this is a united people. And though in the minority now, they are going to win. All the Black leaders coming together, Washington, Du Bois, Trotter, forgetting their differences. Ten million Negroes would be united. A nation would really be born."[55]

NEGRO INSTITUTIONS

We have reduced the illiteracy of the race at least 45 percent. We have written and published nearly 500 books. We have nearly 800 newspapers, three of which are dailies. We have now in practice over 2,000 lawyers, and a corresponding number of doctors. We have accumulated over $12,000,000 worth of school property and about $40,000,000 worth of church property. We have about 140,000 farms and homes, valued in the neighborhood of $750,000,000, and personal property valued about $170,000,000. We have raised about $11,000,000 for educational purposes, and the property per-capita for every colored man, woman, and child in the United States is estimated at $75. We are operating successfully several banks, commercial enterprises among our people in the Southland, including one silk mill and one cotton factory. We have 32,000 teachers in the schools of the country; we have built, with the aid of our friends, about 20,000 churches, and support 7 colleges, 17 academies, 50 high schools, 5 law schools, 5 medical schools, and 25 theological seminaries. We have over 600,000 acres of land in the South alone. The cotton produced, mainly by black labor, has increased from 4,669,770 bales in 1860 to 11,235,000 in 1899. All this was done under the most adverse circumstances.[56]

—*North Carolina Congressman George White's
final speech in Congress in 1901*

During post-Reconstruction, Black men and women realized that they were on their own. The federal government sought to solidify an alliance with southern whites while withdrawing from the rights of freed men and women. Any hopes of a transformed America dissipated as the federal government turned a blind eye and enabled the spread of white supremacy. In response, Blacks banded together to form self-help societies in every region of the country.

The fight for educational and political rights was advanced by fraternal clubs, mutual aid societies, vigilance clubs, and Black-owned newspapers. Editors and publishers used the printed word to broadcast a positive image and celebratory stories. Nonprofits rallied the masses behind campaigns. Public commemorations celebrated events, created holidays, and were accompanied by lobbying for civil rights and judicial remedy.

The Negro Church

After the War to End Slavery, the Black Christian church was no longer the "invisible institution" hindered by paternalist and domineering oversight. The church of the African diaspora was a vibrant, living institution. It was the first Black institution under their control that was applied as an instrument of protest and worship. It served as a multipurpose resource in every area of life as it constructed schools, businesses, and empowerment centers. Its leaders moved beyond sanctuary aisles to advocate in the hallways of legislative power. They finally achieved the independence to worship and the means by which to organize.

W. E. B. Du Bois wrote in *The Negro Church*,

> The African church is the oldest Negro organization, dating in part from Africa itself, and here Negroes have had the most liberty and experience.... The Negro Church is the only social institution of the Negroes which started in the African forest and survived slavery; under the leadership of priest or medicine man, afterward of the Christian pastor, the Church preserved in itself the remnants of African tribal life and became after emancipation the center of Negro social life. So that today the Negro population of the United States is virtually divided into church congregations which are the real units of race life.[57]

Clerical leadership played an irreplaceable role in the totality of Black life. Ministers preached on Sunday and during the week partook in politics, business, and education. Du Bois wrote a compelling essay on Black clergy in *The Souls of Black Folk*, eulogizing influential ministers such as Henry McNeal Turner and his grandfather Alexander Crummell. Women constituted the majority of congregants and served in leadership roles as evangelists, exhorters, and lay ministers.

Early Baptists and Methodists were the most successful in attracting significant interest and commitment from Blacks. Itinerant white preachers were a varied assortment and not attached to a local congregation but responded to all who came to hear them preach. Some accepted any who professed faith and accepted congregational integration. A few Black ministers pastored either white or mixed-race congregations. The Louisiana Baptist Association held in membership one Black minister who served a term as moderator. Two interracial Methodist congregations existed in Baltimore in the latter half of the 1780s. This persisted until the 1790s when racist attitudes dampened interactions. Presbyterians adhered to a policy that their presbytery and synod meetings would, regardless of race, accept commissioners from Black congregations with all the rights and privileges of white commissioners.[58]

The first Black denomination, the African Methodist Episcopal Church, originated through dissatisfaction with the United Methodist Church. Despite moderate acceptance by the Methodist and Baptist churches, Christian denominations were unable to resist racist norms. White churches would allow free persons of color to join but severely limited their participation, regulated their seating, and denied them opportunities for leadership. White supremacy manifested itself the moment one stepped across the threshold as the only seats available were in the balcony, "galleries, n***** pews, and African corners."[59] Segregation was present in Sunday school classes, the sacrament of Holy Communion, and baptisms. Africans made a deliberate decision not to abandon their faith in Christ Jesus as savior; rather, they left white churches to start their own, either within established denominations or entirely new ones.

Richard Allen converted during the Great Awakening and convinced his owner to allow him to purchase his freedom. He relocated to Philadelphia, where he preached and started a prayer meeting in the mostly white St. George's Methodist Church. He and Absalom Jones rejected the racist hypocrisy of the Methodist Church by walking out in 1787. They founded the Free African Society as a nondenominational mutual aid organization to provide resources and support to the Black community. In 1794 Mt. Bethel, "Mother Bethel," led to the founding of the African Methodist Episcopal Church in 1816 in Philadelphia, known as "Freedom Church."[60] It was the first interstate organization created by people of color, and it germinated churches in New York, New Jersey, Delaware, and Maryland.[61] Others sprouted as the African Methodist Episcopal Zion Church (1821), the Colored/Christian Methodist Church (1870), the National Baptist Convention U.S.A. (1895), and the Progressive National Baptist Convention (1961). In North Carolina, the Baptist and AME Zion churches contained the largest Black membership, totaling 80 percent of all churchgoers. Others with significant numbers were the African Methodist Church, the Colored Methodist Episcopal Church, and the northern-based United Presbyterian Church's Black appendages in the South (Catawba Unit, Yadkin Presbytery, and Cape Fear Presbytery).

While there was not the same burst of denominational nativity, individual congregations did sprout in the South. By 1859, an estimated 468,000 Christians of color lived below the Mason-Dixon Line. The first church was the Silver Bluff Baptist Church located in Beech Island, South Carolina. Other congregations included the African Baptist Church (Mobile, Alabama), "Bluestone" Church (Mecklenburg, Virginia, 1758), Springfield Baptist Church (Augusta, Georgia), and the First African Baptist Church (Savannah, Georgia). By 1900, the formerly enslaved constructed Baptist, Methodist, Presbyterian, Episcopal, and Congregational congregations across the southern landscape. The Congress of National Black Churches was formed in 1978 by the seven largest Black denominations.[62]

In the nineteenth century, the United Presbyterian Church trained a disproportionate number of Black clergymen who served as pastors, abolitionists, Underground Railroad conductors, newspaper publishers/editors, educators, authors, missionaries, orators, and political leaders. John Chavis, David Walker, William W. Catto and son Octavius, Daniel A. Payne, John Gloucester, Samuel Cornish, Francis James Grimke, Charlotte Forten Grimke, Theodore S. Wright, Charles Gardner, Henry Highland Garnet, James W. C. Pennington, and William Drew Robeson I (the father of Paul Robeson) had Presbyterian roots.[63] The denomination ordained the Rev. John Chavis as their first ordained man of color in 1800. He pastored a white congregation in North Carolina until the state legislature made his actions illegal following the Nat Turner rebellion. Other states responded in kind and placed limitations on Black preachers. William Henry Sheppard, referred to as the Black Livingstone, was a missionary, minister, anthropologist, photographer, big-game hunter, art collector, and humanitarian. Commissioned as a missionary to the Belgium Congo in 1890, he was instrumental in displacing Belgium's colonial, dictatorially brutal rule.[64]

The 1906 Azusa Street Revival in Los Angeles spawned by Rev. William J. Seymour caused a second spiritual awakening. Revival services in this corner church developed into the worldwide phenomenon of Pentecostalism. From April 9, 1906, a three-year revival took place with laying on of hands resulting in miracles of healing. Seymour preached of a Pentecostal bestowal of the Holy Spirit through speaking in tongues. Those in attendance included Asians, Native Americans, Latinos, whites, Blacks, immigrants, native born, rich, and poor. Their integrated services called for a renewal of the spirit to live simple, noncontaminated lives without sin, coffee, or jewelry. As word of what was happening in Los Angeles spread, so did its influence, inspiring evangelists to spread the gospel. A newsletter, *The Apostolic Faith*, published 40,000 copies weekly. Pentecostal denominations label the awakening at 312 Azusa Street as the origin and birth of the modern Pentecostal movement.

The Negro Academy

Education has been, after the right to vote, the most sought-after prize for African Americans. One could say that the vote was the preferred channel to acquire quality education. It is difficult to rank one above the other as both were vital for a people's subsistence long denied. Before legalized literacy, the African diaspora seized any opportunity to learn to read and write. They understood that the academic prohibition was grounded in keeping them impotent and stagnant. Nothing was as prohibited or would ensure as severe a punishment as being able to read a book or write one's name. Once acquired, education was a powerful weapon in the fight against white supremacy and a tool to challenge theories of inferiority. It was highly valued, for it allowed children to have a future different than the present hell their parents inhabited. On February 22, 1869, educator M. A. Parker, of Raleigh, North Carolina, remarked,

> It is surprising to me to see the amount of suffering which many of the people endure for the sake of sending their children to school. . . . We are anxious to have the children "get on" in their books, and do not seem to feel impatient if they lack comforts themselves. A pile of books is seen in almost every cabin, though there be no furniture except a poor bed, a table and two or three broken chairs.[65]

Whenever a Black neighborhood started, the first public building constructed was a church, followed by a school. In the North, early steps created educational opportunities for children and adults. The Free African School, founded in New York City in 1787, was the nation's first school for Black children. By 1834 six additional schools were constructed by white sponsors. By the end of the century, people of color were the lead benefactors. In 1797 Black parents opened a private school in the home of Prince Hall. It took three years for a public school for Black students to open. In 1807 the African Benevolent Society reopened a Newport, Rhode Island, school. In Philadelphia, ministers created hybrid church-schools in their buildings. Bethel AME Church instituted the Society of Free People of Color for Promoting the Instruction and School Education of Children of African Descent.[66] A second academy opened in 1820 with five hundred students; within ten years four others were formed.

Boston began with a segregated public school but by 1855 had integrated its public-school system, the first in the nation. Philadelphia established its first school in 1822 and by 1850 established eight more. By 1870, the Freedmen's Bureau, in partnership with churches, established 4,500 schools and twenty-four colleges/universities with 9,000 teachers. Seven years later, 250,000 students were under the tutelage of 30,000 teachers. In 1872, Maryland required each local board of education to build a Black school. Blacks in Frederick had a thriving population with a grocery store, barbershops, beauty salons, restaurants, clothing stores, doctor's offices, bars, several churches, and later a hospital. Two churches, Quinn Chapel and Asbury Methodist Episcopal on West All Saints Street, each housed a school. In 1917, the South Bentz Street School was constructed, followed by a Black school in 1920. The latter became Lincoln High School and was the only such institution in Frederick for thirty-five years.[67]

As expected, Black education in the South moved much slower. White opposition hampered efforts to achieve public education for Black children, but not completely. Despite preventive legislation, small schools opened in several states. By the 1800s, efforts by freed men and women individually and collectively were having an impact. In Charleston, the Brown Fellowship Society and the Minor Society promoted public education. In 1829 a graduate of the latter opened a new school. Baltimore and Washington were enclaves for the operation of several schools. As elsewhere, churches were instrumental in the establishment of learning institutions.[68] In Florida, Fessenden Academy provided a world-class education for young Blacks. Students from the Caribbean, Africa, and all across the United States attended.[69]

Women were exceptional in leading the way for education of a people denied its benefits. In 1861, Mary S. Peake founded the first all-Black school in Hampton, Virginia. She taught both enslaved and free Blacks. Susie King Taylor served with the First South Carolina Volunteers as a nurse and a teacher in an unpaid role for all four years of the war. She dressed wounds and taught children and soldiers to read and write. She wrote the only book on Black nurses during the war: *Reminiscences of My Life in Camp*, in which she disclosed the following:

> After I had been on St. Simon's about three days, Commodore Goldsborough heard of me, and came to Gaston Bluff to see me . . . and wished me to take charge of a school for the children on the island. I told him I would gladly do so, if I could have some books. He said I should have them, and in a week or two I received two large boxes of books and testaments from the North. I had about forty children to teach, besides a number of adults who came to me nights, all of them so eager to learn to read, to read above anything else.[70]

Educators Mary McLeod Bethune, Nannie Helen Burroughs, and Charlotte Hawkins Brown were "The Three Bs." Mentor Lucy Craft Laney made it the "Three Bs Plus One." Individually they were highly accomplished women; collectively, they were a force of nature. They left a legacy of achievement few have matched. Their academic institutions substituted for the country's failure to educate its Black citizens. Lucy Craft Laney founded Haines Institute for

Industrial and Normal Education. Mary McLeod Bethune educated students at Bethune-Cookman. Nannie Helen Burroughs educated females at the National Training School for Women and Girls in Washington, DC. Charlotte Hawkins Brown opened the doors of Palmer Institute outside of Greensboro, North Carolina. They championed each other and shared strategies on fund-raising and networking. Each advanced a teaching triangle. Brown focused on education, religion, and deeds; Bethune had the three Hs: "the Head, the Heart, and the Hand." Burroughs articulated the three Bs: "the Book, the Bible, and the Broom." Nannie Helen Burroughs summed up their collective agenda: "If in our homes there is implanted in the hearts of our children, of our young men and of our young women, the thought they are what they are, not by environment, but of themselves, this effort to teach a lesson of inferiority will be futile."[71] Their goals were the same—empowerment and uplift of Black people through the training of the mind. All served out of strong religious convictions and believed that female leadership was a vital component. If women succeeded, everyone did.

A formerly enslaved people, penniless, generated an incredible amount of revenue to fund local educational efforts. South Carolinians contributed almost $17,000 after emancipation. Christian denominations established colleges and universities by purchasing land, hiring staff, and constructing buildings. Between 1865 and 1881, universities were established around the South in Raleigh (Raleigh Institute/Shaw University), Jefferson City (Fisk University), Nashville (Fisk), Atlanta (Augusta Theological Institute/Morehouse College and Atlanta Baptist Female Seminary/Spelman Seminary), Washington, DC (Howard University), Harper's Ferry (Storer College), Hampton (Hampton Normal and Agricultural Institute/Hampton Institute/University), and Tuskegee (Tuskegee Normal and Industrial Institute). Adult education evolved from vocational training into law, medicine, architecture, and general education. From these efforts, communities established debating clubs, fire companies, militia companies, and temperance clubs. All of this ensured elevation through the procurement of a comprehensive education.

Negro Business

Every professional business pursuit was obstructed for people of the African diaspora during this period. Nonwhites were judged as unintelligent and lacking in discipline to handle the rigors of entrepreneurial leadership. Men and women who dared to acquire wealth were accused of being uppity, "bourgeois Negroes" who were a threat to white livelihood and integrity. Despite overwhelming odds, in the years following 1865, freed men and women demonstrated amazing capacity in the construction of churches, schools, banks, businesses, homes, and towns. Economic viability enhanced political influence and the power to affect social change.

Creative entrepreneurs became titans of industry and acquired millions. Shomari Wills wrote in *Black Fortunes,*

> Early in our country's history, African Americans who achieved wealth were often attacked, demonized, or swindled out of their money by those who knew the Jim Crow court system would offer no redress to a black person. In their first decades of existence, the black elite survived assassination attempts, lynchings, frivolous lawsuits, and criminal cases meant to destroy or delegitimize their wealth.[72]

Beverly Bunch-Lyons wrote,

> During the postbellum era, those with an entrepreneurial spirit operated their businesses selling food, used clothing and furniture, and hand-made crafts. Others were involved in businesses such as journalism, hairdressing, shoemaking, and tailoring. Emancipation provided the opportunity for African Americans to expand their business ventures into other areas including the undertaking business, but only rarely did it provide the opportunity to expand one's client base outside of the black population.[73]

They crafted businesses as

> barbers, hackmen, draymen, owners of livery stables . . . blacksmiths, grocers, fashionable tailors, restaurateurs and caters, proprietors of coal and lumber yards, and occasionally hotel owners . . . shoemaking and building trades . . . carpenters, tailors and dressmakers, brickmakers, shoemakers and bootmakers, and cabinetmakers. . . . In 1850 New Orleans free Blacks numbered one architect, five jewelers, four physicians, eleven music teachers, and fifty-two merchants, exhibiting an even greater occupational diversity than in Charleston.[74]

Paul Cuffee was a successful eighteenth-century sea captain and businessman who hired all-Black crews. "Free Frank" McWorter's success as a saltpeter manufacturer enabled him to purchase the freedom of sixteen members of his family and to charter the town of New Philadelphia, Illinois. James Forten amassed a fortune as a Philadelphia sailmaker employing a crew of forty employees, both Black and white. Thomas Day, a North Carolina furniture maker, hired workers of both races in his factory. Stephen Smith owned a lumberyard and coal business in 1822 and financed abolitionist endeavors. Jeremiah Hamilton, Wall Street's first Black millionaire, was worth $2 million when he died in 1875, $250 million in today's dollars. Maggie Lena

Walker was the first woman, Black or white, to charter a bank, the St. Luke Penny Savings Bank in Richmond, Virginia.[75]

James Porter, William Coleman, and Joseph Randolph started the first Black insurance company, the Afro-American Insurance Company, in 1810. Aaron McDuffie Moore, John Merrick, and Charles Clinton Spaulding co-founded the North Carolina Mutual Life Insurance Company, in 1898, the largest African American life insurance company in Durham, North Carolina, "America's Black Wall Street."[76] Alonzo Herndon and Samuel Wilson Ruth-erford achieved similar success with the Atlanta Life Insurance Company (1905)[77] and the National Benefit Insurance Company in Washington, DC. Frederick Douglass Patterson owned and operated a vehicle manufacturing plant, C. R. Patterson & Son Carriage Company of Greenfield, Ohio. It was renamed the Greenfield Bus Body Company and manufactured the Patterson-Greenfield car. The company, started by his father, C. R. Patterson, produced twenty-eight different horse-drawn carriages including buggies, buckboards, phaetons, and surreys. His fifty employees made five hundred carriages annu-ally. A financial donor for the civil rights movement, A. G. Gaston was worth $130 million at his death. Black millionaires existed in the industries of soft drinks (J. Bruce Llewellyn), computer information management (Joshua I. Smith), real estate (Herman J. Russell), cable industry (Don Barden), and the steel industry (David Bing). During the 1980s, Reginald F. Lewis made the Lewis Company (TLC) into the world's largest Black-owned company.[78]

Black scholars celebrated their accomplishments yet cited criticism. E. Franklin Frazier, in *Black Bourgeoisie*, charged the Black middle class with an elitism infected by color psychosis. He alleged that wealthy individuals established communities separated by skin tone, wealth, and class:

> They are rejected by the white world, and this rejection has created considerable self-hatred . . . since they do not truly identify them-selves with Negroes . . . the members of the black bourgeoisie in the United States seem to be in the process of becoming NOBODY. . . . Because of its struggle to gain acceptance by whites, the black bour-geoisie has failed to play the role of a responsible elite in the Negro community.[79]

He charged light-skinned Blacks as colorists who despised their darker-skinned counterparts. William B. Gatewood, in *Aristocrats of Color: The Black Elite, 1880–1920*, agreed with Frazier in his critique of successful light-skinned Blacks. According to his calculations, they inherited a contagion of pigment snobbishness from whites and disconnected themselves from mem-bers of their race. They created their own Black Codes based on lineage, skin hue, manners, and education demanding subservience to a "colored aristocracy."[80] The biracial descendants of undertaker Edwin G. "Captain" Harleston (1854–1931) and his formerly enslaved partner Kate Wilson successfully separated themselves from darker-skinned people of color. As they acquired education and wealth, they increased the separation between themselves and the wider community.[81]

While these charges cannot be completely dismissed, Black bourgeoisie's overall history presented a mixed legacy. There was color separation, yet it is illegitimate to charge Black elites as isolationists living a fairy-tale existence. No matter how much wealth families acquired, they were still Black, quarantined from interaction. Their opportunities were just as limited as those of people with darker pigmentation. Many were race men and women proudly committed to the fight. Many could have passed for white but refused to refute their heritage, stood alongside Black brothers and sisters, and sacrificed much. Shomari Wills challenged the universality of Frazier's sentiment. He chronicled the lives of six millionaires in *Black Fortunes: The Story of the First Six African Americans Who Survived Slavery and Became Millionaires*. Mary Ellen Pleasant, Robert Reed Church, O. W. Gurley, Hannah Elias, Annie Minerva Turnbo, and Madam C. J. Walker were wealthy, generous, and philanthropic: "Much of their money these first Black millionaires devoted to helping advance racial equality."[82] In Miami, E. W. F. Stirrup was the wealthiest businessman in Coconut Grove, owning land from Munroe County to Fort Pierce. The street where his home sits bears his name: Charles Street.[83] Alonzo Herndon and his wives Adrienne and Jessie, the wealthiest Black family in Atlanta, donated generously to charity, church, and Atlanta University. To construct their fifteen-bedroom mansion, they hired formerly enslaved men rather than educated contractors. Their son, Norris, donated land to Morris Brown College, the NAACP, employee scholarships, and cash bail for arrested civil rights demonstrators. He signed ownership of the family barbershop over to his employees.[84] Elizabeth Downing Taylor researched the philanthropy of Daniel Murry and the Washington, DC, middle class. Mark Whitaker wrote of the Black elite of Pittsburgh and their multifaceted business empire. Holdings included the *Pittsburgh Courier* and two Negro League baseball teams. A host of gifted jazz musicians were residents including Billy Strayhorn, Billy Eckstine, Earl Hines, Mary Lou Williams, and Erroll Garner.[85]

Mutual Aid Societies

One of the more practical steps was the formation of mutual aid societies. There was a consensus that for struggling families to find relief from the ravages of white supremacy, resources would have to be pooled. Many believed that if the race demonstrated morality, thrift, and industry, it would gain white acceptance. Booker T. Washington echoed this ideology, which existed long before he broadcast it onto the national stage.

Church members from local congregations assembled northern and southern support agencies. Members paid monthly dues of one shilling for education, insurance coverage, and job training. It placed a stipulation that one's plight was not self-inflicted or caused by reckless impulsivity. There was an abundant supply of applicants for both membership and aid.

The Free African Society in Philadelphia, April 12, 1787, was put together under the leadership of Richard Allen and Absalom Jones. Chapters grew to a hundred branches averaging seventy-five members. The Philadelphia Library Company of Colored Persons, Phoenix Society of New York City, Coachman's Benevolent, and Humane Mechanics produced reading libraries, schools, and ethics classes.[86]

Slave owners' mistrust of these societies inhibited but did not prevent southern groups from forming. Baltimore emerged as the center, with thirty associations averaging dozens of members in 1835. In Charleston, separate organizations formed in 1790 and 1791. The first, the Brown Fellowship Society, was an exclusive club reserved for light-skinned Blacks. Those excluded formed the Free Dark Men of Color, whose level of activity equaled their predecessor. Pressure from suspicious whites, who feared that they might assist slaves to rebel, curtailed the abilities of these groups. The Brown Society acquiesced by making a public declaration that they would not participate in insurrection.[87]

Secret fraternal orders formed with a similar purpose. Prince Hall, a war veteran, minister, and Free African Society member, put forth the first order of Colored Masons in Boston in 1787. In 1797, he joined Absalom Jones, Richard Allen, and James Forten to plant masonic roots in Philadelphia. A lodge was in Providence, Rhode Island, and by 1825, lodges existed in Washington, DC; Louisville; and New Orleans. In 1843, Peter Ogden formed the Negro Odd Fellows in New York. Groups called the Galilean Fishermen, Nazarites, Samaritans, and Seven Wise Men were concentrated in Baltimore.[88]

Advocacy Conventions and Organizations

"By the force of our demands, our determination and our numbers, we shall splinter the segregated South into a thousand pieces and put them back together in the image of God and democracy."[89] Those words were uttered by the great civil rights leader, politician, and icon John Lewis. Throughout Black history, collective efforts created organizations to confront institutionalized racism. Black men and women, jointly and separately, formed associations against systemic racism. This began well before the civil rights movement of the 1950s and 1960s. From 1780 to 1830, the movement to unify led to the establishment of churches, newspapers, and annual conventions. From the 1830s to the 1870s, a convention movement strategized annually as ministers, publishers, lawyers, physicians, businessmen, editors, academics, and politicians participated in collective advocacy. A twofold strategy advocated for pertinent issues. These were the earliest endorsers of the self-help ideology later advocated by Booker T. Washington. They stressed education, school construction, moral character, and wealth accumulation. Vocational training schools helped students acquire business acumen.[90]

Each decade of the antebellum period generated a different policy platform against white supremacy. In the 1830s, moral persuasion attempted to sway the hearts and minds of whites against the vileness of slavery and toward a commitment to its elimination. The goal of the 1840s was the acquisition of political power to influence the passage of antislavery legislation. In the 1850s, an awareness movement advocated self-reliance, unity, economic growth, and emigration, both domestically and internationally. During the 1860s, southern state conventions promoted an accommodationist paradigm calling for education, morality, and entrepreneurship. The 1870s prioritized the rights of local citizens for improved working conditions for the first time. Middle-class convention leaders were not aligned with the masses' primary interests for land, education, and the vote. Elites were often separatist and did not associate with any not considered their peers. They did not socialize nor seek counsel even in matters of mutual concern to the race.

During the week of June 6–11, 1831, delegates from New York, Pennsylvania, Delaware, Maryland, and Virginia gathered to discern the way forward. During the meeting held in Philadelphia's Bethel Church, Richard Allen was elected president. Over the next year, delegates encouraged white Americans to join them. This reversal in leadership caught liberal whites unprepared, as they previously were the ones doing the inviting and were not necessarily open-minded when it came to Black leadership. An open letter, "Address to the Nation," declared opposition to slavery, support for African repatriation, and training academies. It called for a reconsideration of the Fourth of July from a day of patriotic celebration to a day of mourning, lament, and prayer over the nation's failure to live up to its egalitarian values.

Unique to the convention movement was the gathering of the formerly enslaved in summits. For half a century following emancipation in 1863, they gathered in cities for mutual endorsement and advocacy. A common refrain was "to reflect on the past and act on the future." They were among the first to press for reparations, petitioning the federal government for freedman pensions. They were critical of the criminal justice system and pushed for pardons for married prisoners. In 1915, a pension association for formerly enslaved persons, the National Ex-Slave Mutual Relief, Bounty and Pension Association of the United States, filed a $68 million lawsuit, *Johnson v. McAdoo*, against the federal government. These estimated damages were from tax revenue from the production of cotton between 1862 and 1868. The claim was denied by the DC Court of Appeals, and the Supreme Court upheld the lower court's decision. Callie House, a former enslaved woman from Nashville, Tennessee, rose to leadership in the reparation effort. She successfully rallied thousands who supported her efforts. To silence her, the government indicted her on the charge of mail fraud and sentenced her to a year in jail.[91]

In July 1905, twenty-nine Black opponents of Booker T. Washington, including William Monroe Trotter and W. E. B. Du Bois, traveled to Niagara Falls, Canada, to discuss ways to diminish Washington's power and influence. The Niagara movement was unique in that Blacks established it to challenge one of their own. The principles behind Niagara were in direct opposition to Washington's accommodationist philosophy. A progressive platform promoted voting rights, health care, educational facilities, and adequate housing. The Niagara movement's Declaration of Principles (1905) announced, "We refuse to allow the impression to remain that the Negro-American assents to inferiority, is submissive under oppression and apologetic before insults. Through helplessness we may submit, but the voice of protest of ten million Americans must never cease to assail the ears of their fellows, so long as America is unjust."[92] The Niagara movement sent a powerful message to the country. It stood apart from other Black organizations for its robust, unequivocal demand for equal rights. It unapologetically demanded economic and educational opportunities as well as suffrage for Black men and women.

As the Niagara movement grew to 170 members in thirty-four states by 1906, it encountered difficulties. Internal ruptures would not heal. Du Bois supported the inclusion of women; Trotter did not. The rift gave way to the creation of the National Association for the Advancement of Colored People (NAACP).[93] The NAACP, established in 1909 in New York City, echoed Niagara's goals. Its purpose was the fulfillment of the Thirteenth, Fourteenth, and Fifteenth Amendments. The Constitution was a paper promise in the face of overwhelming political, economic, educational, and social discrimination. Founding members included W. E. B. Du Bois, Ida Wells-Barnett, Archibald Grimke, Mary Church Terrell, and white progressives Mary White Ovington, Henry Moskowitz, William English Walling, and Oswald Garrison Villard. William Monroe Trotter refused to attend due to the inclusion of women. By 1910 a national office, located in New York City, operated with a board and president. Du Bois was the only Black on the executive level and served as the director of publications and research.

That same year he birthed the literary magazine *The Crisis*, which demonstrated remarkable sustainability and impact. The first legal victory for the NAACP came in 1915 when it challenged the constitutionality of so-called grandfather clauses, laws written to deny Blacks the right to vote. In *Guinn v. the United States*, the U.S. Supreme Court agreed. The NAACP voiced opposition to the racist film *The Birth of a Nation*, which defamed Reconstruction and applauded the KKK. Its successful call for a 1917 silent march in New York City helped cement the NAACP as the pivotal organization for Black rights in America. It advocated for the federal government to indict perpetrators of lynching. By 1919, the NAACP had 90,000 members and more than 300 branches.

What is now the National Urban League was birthed in New York City on September 29, 1910, by Ruth Standish Baldwin and Dr. George Edmund Haynes as the Committee on Urban Conditions Among Negroes. It merged with the Committee for the Improvement of Industrial Conditions Among Negroes in New York (1906) and the National League for the Protection of Colored Women (1905). It emerged as the National League on Urban Conditions Among Negroes to improve living conditions and provide economic empowerment. It researched employment, housing, educational, as well as health and sanitation opportunities. Its staff coached southern migrants and trained social workers. Both the NAACP and National Urban League were integrated, with whites serving in critical leadership roles.

In 1914 Marcus Garvey founded the Universal Negro Improvement Association (UNIA) in Jamaica. It was the largest organization created for and by Black Americans, with hundreds of thousands of members. He was the first prominent leader to equate blackness with positivity, strength, and beauty. He promoted racial pride, economic self-sufficiency, and an independent Black nation. His movement gained prominence when he relocated to New York City in 1916. He corresponded with Booker T. Washington and embarked upon a thirty-eight-city speaking tour. His "Declaration of Rights of the Negro Peoples of the World" was ratified at a UNIA convention at Madison Square Garden in 1920. "We have no animus against the white man. All that we have as a race desired is a place in the sun. . . If sixty million Anglo-Saxons can have a place in the sun, . . . if sixty million Japanese can have a place in the sun, if seven million Belgians can have a place in the sun, I cannot see why. . . four-hundred-million Black folks cannot. . . If you believe that Africa should be one vast empire, controlled by the Negro, then arise,"[94] he said. Blacks joined the UNIA, attended his rallies, and contributed sizable donations. He perfected his entrepreneurial skills to build the Black Star Line shipping company and the Negro Factories Corporation; the latter operated grocery stores, a restaurant, laundry, moving company, and publishing house. In 1923, the U.S. government arrested him and convicted him of mail fraud. After Garvey served a two-year jail sentence, President Calvin Coolidge issued a pardon and deported him. He died in London in 1940.[95]

A. Philip Randolph was the founder of the Brotherhood of Sleeping Car Porters and the Negro American Labor Council (NALC). He excelled on two fronts: as a leader in union organizing and as a powerful political influencer. Long before Martin Luther King Jr. came on the scene, Randolph was a power player with the ability to mobilize his base quickly and effectively. The Sleeping Car Porters provided opportunities for advancement and pay on behalf of the men who worked for the railroad. It was the first African American union incorporated into the American Federation of Labor (AFL). It forced negotiations and a settlement with the Pullman Company on behalf of Black porters.

Randolph was also instrumental in planning the 1963 March on Washington, with the leverage that he had met success after earlier threats to hold two similar marches. He called them both off, but only after his demands were accepted. As early as 1941, he called for a march on Washington against the shortage of prominent positions for Blacks in the national defense industry. He called off a march protesting military discrimination after President Franklin Roosevelt signed Executive Order 8802, creating the Fair Employment Practices Commission, which investigated charges of multinational tyranny. Executive Order 9981, signed by President Harry S. Truman, ordered the desegregation of the armed forces in 1948. Randolph later wrote, "Equality is the heart and essence of democracy, freedom, and justice, equality of opportunity in industry, in labor unions, schools and colleges, government, politics, and before the law. There must be no dual standards of justice, no dual rights, privileges, duties, or responsibilities of citizenship. No dual forms of freedom."[96]

The National Council of Negro Women (NCNW) was founded on December 5, 1935, by a coalition of twenty-eight of the most notable Black women's organizations. Mary McLeod Bethune served as founder and president until 1949. She envisioned a federation working together to improve conditions nationally and internationally. The NCNW focused on information gathering, networking, and sponsoring educational programs. In 1949 Bethune was succeeded by Dorothy Boulding Ferebee and by Vivian Carter Mason in 1953. Under the latter's leadership, the NCNW embraced cooperation between white women and women of color. In 1957, Dorothy Irene Height was appointed the fourth president and rose to become one of the principal architects of the emerging civil rights movement. With the passage of the Civil Rights and Voting Rights Acts in 1964 and 1965, the NCNW shifted its focus to economic issues. After receiving tax-exempt nonprofit status in 1966, it trained Black women for service, helped low-income women in job training, addressed the problems surrounding youth, and initiated efforts to help poverty-stricken Black farmers in the South. Height remembered the impact Mary McLeod Bethune had on her when they first met. "I remember how she made her fingers into a fist to illustrate for the women the significance of working together to eliminate injustice. 'The freedom gates are half ajar,' she said, 'We must pry them fully open.'"[97]

Today the NAACP, the National Urban League, and the National Council of Negro Women continue in the fight for freedom, recognition, and opportunity. Each in their respective work continues to fulfill their stated missions of fighting for political rights, improving Black life, and equipping female leadership for the advancement of Black people. At its 2020 convention, the National Council of Negro Women rededicated itself to its mission "to advance opportunities and the quality of life for African American women, their families and communities."[98] The *Baltimore Sun* determined in 1995,

> Still, the need for both organizations remains. For instance, the Republican majority in Congress has said it will eliminate or drastically reduce federal funding to Urban League programs. And states with conservative governors and legislators—the number of those states increased after last November's [1994] elections—have traditionally been hostile to efforts to empower the disenfranchised. The Urban League—and the poor, the powerless, and the disenfranchised that the Urban League serves—will need someone lobbying on its behalf in Washington and in state capitals across the country. Who will it turn to? Who provided that function in the past? Why, the NAACP. It is not yet time to let that venerable organization die.[99]

The Negro Press

With the publication of the first colonial newspaper in 1690, printed papers reflected the racial prejudices of the times. Most contained unflattering articles about people of African descent and openly endorsed racist theories. Antebellum newspapers posted rewards for runaways combined with stories of criminality. Frustration over the absence of an impartial and unbiased media motivated an infiltration into print. *Freedom's Journal*, the first Black newspaper, was published March 16, 1827, in New York City by Rev. Samuel E. Cornish and John B. Russwurm. The first issue proclaimed, "We wish to plead our own cause. Too long have others spoken for us."[100] By 1861, twenty-four periodicals served as a communication agency for those of African descent.[101]

The Negro press (or Black press) performed a dual role. It served as a purveyor of news and as an instrument advocating for social change. For over two centuries, it confronted the evils of enslavement, racism, and white supremacy. It served as a communiqué for an aggrieved community barred from mainstream journalistic channels. Black-owned newspapers and magazines projected a realistic depiction of Black life and culture. Publications disseminated a positive image to the rest of the world. *Ebony* publisher John H. Johnson stated in 1975, "*Ebony* was founded to provide positive images for Blacks in a world of negative images and non-images. It was founded to project all dimensions of the Black personality in a world saturated with stereotypes. . . . Few magazines dealt with Blacks as human beings with human needs. Fewer magazines with the whole spectrum of Black life."[102]

Newspapers not only reported the news but implemented campaigns for social change. Owners, editors, and reporters were social activists as much as journalists. The most blatant call for equality materialized from editors who radicalized the printed word in a manner previously unseen. It was not until 1831 before white abolitionist papers, such as the *Liberator*, used a similar methodology. They were hugely successful in rewriting the narrative and were considered a threat to white supremacy. Papers were destroyed to prevent distribution; owners were refused financing, received death threats, and saw their presses demolished. T. Thomas Fortune sunk his entire life into his work, lost his home, and suffered alcoholism and depression. Frederick Douglass took out a second mortgage to finance his paper. Fire believed to be arson destroyed his home and twelve volumes of his paper. Ida B. Wells self-financed her presses only to have all her equipment destroyed and death threats made against her that forced her out of Memphis. Southern legislatures made possessing such newspapers illegal, and distributors had their weeklies confiscated. A communal network enabled companies to survive. Ministers and Pullman porters circulated bundles to ministers for allocation to church members, a relationship between the Black press and the church that still exists. Pullman porters would deposit bunches at various locations along their stops for distribution within local communities.

According to Carl Senna's *The Black Press and the Struggle for Civil Rights*, in 1940, just four papers carried an astronomical distribution of 274,954 subscribers. By 1947, newspapers were in the hands of 627,405 readers. Senna wrote that by 1948, there were "56 college campus publications, 100 religious and special interest periodicals, and 169 black newspapers—4 with regional editions and a total combined circulation of 4 million."[103] In 1859, the *Anglo-African American* magazine was published, the first Black-focused magazine, and by 1990, twenty-five similar magazines existed.

Black papers were a useful tool in the racial challenge. Following each other's lead, they advocated for the integration of three pivotal institutions: the military, business, and baseball. Posted headlines encouraged readers to be economically strategic where they spent their hard-earned dollars through the "Don't Shop Where You Can't Work" and "Buy Black" campaigns. The *Pittsburgh Courier* pushed for military integration just two months after Pearl Harbor (Feb. 7, 1942). The "Double V Campaign"—"Victory at Home, Victory Abroad"—was a national effort to desegregate jobs in the war industry. To ensure baseball's integration, papers reported daily on Jackie Robinson and pushed his success before a hungry public, hoping it was just the beginning for an integrated America.

Negro Directories

An offshoot of the work of the Black press was the publication of information directories for the use of the Black population. A precursor of the telephone book, these lists dispensed intelligence for travelers navigating dangerous and unfamiliar territories.[104] Diane Nash was an organizer for the Nashville Student Movement and the Freedom Riders. She reminisced, "Because I grew up in Chicago, I didn't have an emotional relationship to segregation. I understood the facts and stories, but there was not an emotional relationship. When I went south and saw the signs that said, 'white' and 'colored,' and I actually could not drink out of that water fountain or go to that ladies' room, I had a real emotional reaction. . . . I really resented that. I was outraged."[105]

There were approximately two dozen such directories that existed from 1835 to 1966. The first one was created to provide New York abolitionists the names of slave traders and bounty hunters. The second listed Chicago businesses that catered to people of color. The last guided a nationwide audience traveling around the country. Freedom rider Diane Nash remembered that "travel in the segregated South for black people was humiliating. The very fact that there were separate facilities was to say to black people and white people that blacks were so subhuman and so inferior that we could not even use the public facilities that white people used."[106]

The New York Committee of Vigilance, under the penmanship of David Ruggles, published the 1835 *Slaveholder's Directory*. Vigilance committees provided safety for escaped fugitives from the South. Those in pursuit posed a grave danger to the life and liberty of the self-liberated. This directory took the unusual step not of listing safe havens, which could be compromised, but rather of counterattacking by posting personal information. They printed the names and addresses of police, judges, and New York City officials engaged in the repatriation of enslaved people.

D. A. Bethea guided travelers to places that welcomed them with his 1905 *Colored People's Blue Book and Business Directory of Chicago, Illinois*. The 140-page booklet, sold to Black travelers and residents of Chicago, directed customers to businesses of color. Its table of contents listed churches, secret societies, secular societies, women's clubs, newspapers, the Chicago Amateur Musical Club (C.A.M.C.), and a classified business directory. Subcategories included Knights of Pythias, Grand Army of the Republic, funeral homes, physicians, lawyers, nurses, architects, artists, barbers, bakeries, baths, bands/orchestras, painters, photographers, music, restaurants, tailors, and undertakers. Other Chicago directories included *Black's Blue Book: Directory of Chicago's Active Colored People and Guide to Their Activities* (1917) by Ford S. Black and *Scott's Blue Book: A Classified Business and Service Directory*, printed in the 1940s.[107]

Cities with similar directories included Akron, Ohio; Atlanta; Baltimore; Boston; Buffalo, New York; Cairo and Carbondale, Illinois; Chicago; Cincinnati; Dallas; Denver; Des Moines, Iowa; Detroit; Memphis; Muskogee, Oklahoma; New York City; Oklahoma City; Pittsburgh; St. Louis; and Washington, DC.[108]

To be a Black traveler was a precarious endangerment if one did not know where to stop to resupply. Black travelers needed information about where to shop, eat, sleep, or get gas, especially in southern states. Mahalia Jackson gave a first-person description of the difficulties she faced:

> From Virginia to Florida it was a nightmare. There was no place for us to eat or sleep on the main highways. Restaurants wouldn't serve us. Teen-age girls who were serving as car hops would come bouncing out to the car and stop dead when they saw we were Negroes, spin around without a word and walk away. Some gasoline stations didn't want to sell us gas and oil. Some told us that no rest rooms were available. The looks of anger at the sight of us colored folks sitting in a nice car were frightening to see.[109]

The *Negro Motorist Green-Book*, published between 1936 and 1966, maneuvered travelers to safe locations for lodging, food, gas, and friendly accommodations. Harlem postal worker Victor Hugo Green first concentrated on New York listings but later expanded nationwide. The directory was mandatory to endure long-distance car travel and revered for its pertinent information. Its listings included hotels, taverns, garages, night clubs, restaurants, service stations, automotive repair shops, tourist homes, roadhouses, barbershops, beauty parlors, campgrounds, and amusement parks. The 2018 movie *The*

Green Book served as a reminder of the hostility one could face for simply visiting with out-of-town family, even if one were a famous musician.

THE GREAT MIGRATIONS

Scholars have identified 13 distinct migrations that "formed and transformed African America," according to the Schomburg Center for Research in Black Culture, a division of the New York Public Library. Some are well known. The transatlantic and domestic slave trades are the largest of the migrations and also the only ones that were involuntary. The Great Migration of the 20th century—the movement of blacks from the rural South to the cities of the North—is also a touchstone of popular history. Others are less often discussed: Haitian immigration to the United States in the late 1700s and early 1800s; the movement of free African-Americans to the North in the 1840s; and immigration from Africa and the Caribbean since the 1970s. The voluntary migrations demonstrate independence and a willingness to make choices for a better life—what scholars call agency. "That's action. That's taking your life in your hands." "That's the very definition of agency."[110]

Migration has always been a critical protest tool used by masses of people around the world. The migrations of the African diaspora are amongst the greatest movements of people in human history. Throughout U.S. history inferiority was the mantle placed on America's dark children. They attempted to remove it by relocating to safer regions. Those who stayed to protect children and families bore that sacrifice in the hope that one day life would be equitable. The first migrations were involuntary, as captives marched from the interior of Africa to the coast. Some of the same marched in a coffle, a group of slaves tied together, deep into the lower South of what would become the United States. The nineteenth century witnessed voluntary migrations, as a myriad of millions resisted with their feet. Although acting individually, they were part of a collective movement to take control and alter their situation. Those who transported everything they owned to an unfamiliar place followed a siren call of a promise for a better life. They were part of a seminal movement transpiring in many places at the same moment for relief from oppression.

The southwest movement of the enslaved (from 1830 to 1860) energized the country's expansion and economic growth. The 1808 ending of the slave trade completely revolutionized the inhuman repletion of the enslaved as Africans were no longer shipped into the country. Upper southern states supplied the lower states with enslaved men, women, and children, who were marched to locations "down South." Families were torn apart as daughters and sons were seized from parents' gripping fingers; husbands and wives were dragged away from the only life they had known. This forced resettlement was twenty times larger than the more infamous Indian removal campaigns of the 1830s. No other North American migration, forced or voluntary, lasted longer and resettled more people before 1900. Enslaved people endured a three-month, thousand-mile trek from the tobacco South to the cotton South. Coffles walked from Maryland, Virginia, the Carolinas, and Georgia southward to Florida, Alabama, Mississippi, Louisiana, Arkansas, and Texas. The trading companies Franklin & Armfield and Bolton, Dickens, & Company transformed New Orleans into the country's largest market for enslaved people, occupied by fifty "people-selling companies." Virginia alone forcibly resettled 450,000 enslaved men, women, and children as Maryland, the Carolinas, Kentucky, Tennessee, Missouri, and Georgia followed suit.[111]

Edward Ball labeled the "Slave Trail of Tears" as "the great missing migration—a thousand-mile-long river of people, all of them black, reaching from Virginia to Louisiana. During the 50 years before the War to End Slavery, about a million enslaved people moved from the Upper South—Virginia, Maryland, Kentucky—to the Deep South—Louisiana, Mississippi, Alabama. They were made to go, deported, you could say, having been sold."[112]

Slave traders hired as slave trading agents and auctioneers received 2.5 cents per sale. Cities built prisons for the storage of human cargo awaiting sale.[113] Averaging twenty-five miles daily, the enslaved persons walked in a coffle of chained men bound from one neck to the next, linked by a rope confining women and children. Guards consisted of armed white men on horseback trailed by supply wagons. Marchers numbered from twenty to the hundreds. An 1834 cluster contained three hundred enslaved men, women, and children valued at $140,000. Most were young men and boys between the ages of twelve and twenty-four. Once separated from parents and siblings, most never saw or heard from their family members again. An enslaved woman, Josephine Smith, witnessed a caravan headed to New Orleans: "It was in August, and the sun was bearing down hot when the slaves and their drivers leave the shade. They walk for a little piece, and this woman fall out. She dies there 'side of the road, and right there they buries her, cussing, they tells me, about losing money on her."[114]

Emigration

Native-born Africans longed for family reunification in the land of their birth through an emigration movement. In Massachusetts, petitioners lobbied the assembly for the right "to transport ourselves to some part of the Coast of Africa, where we propose a settlement." In 1788, the Negro Union of Newport, Rhode Island, urged men of color to emigrate back to Africa. In 1795 negotiators urged Governor Zachary Macauley for permission to resettle in Sierra Leone. Wealthy shipowner Paul Cuffee transported thirty men and women to Freetown, South Africa, in 1815. Richard Allen initially favored voluntary migration to the island nation of Haiti. In August 1824, a total of 200 sailed to the island. By 1825 between 6,000 and 12,000 left the United States for life in the Caribbean. Life proved too difficult, and 2,000 returned to America.[115]

For whites, the eighteenth-century colonization movement proposed colonizing Africa with dispossessed Africans from the United States. This led to the creation of the American Colonization Society in 1817. There were several reasons for this: Large groups of whites refused to believe that the two races could coexist without warfare. Abolitionists, while opposed to the institution of slavery, held onto theories of inferiority and incompatibility. Another reason was the growing number of freed men and women, who posed a problem as they pressed not only for slavery's abolition but also for racial equality. They were more radical in strategy and confronted abolitionists on their racism. As a result, Congress negotiated in 1822 for the creation of Liberia, on the west coast of Africa, as a relocation site. In 1852, 8,000 boarded ships; 3,600 were formerly enslaved persons accompanied by 2,800 freedmen.[116]

Most men and women of African descent rejected both movements and chose to stay in America. They realized that colonization was simply an effort to be rid of their presence. They linked colonization and slavery as twin sisters. An 1831 New York convention of free Black citizens declared, "This is our home, and this is our country. Beneath its soil lie the bones of our fathers; for it, some of them fought, bled, and died. Here we were born; and here we will die."[117] Abolitionist Robert Purvis stated the sentiment of most: "A few may go, but the colored people as a mass will not leave the land of their birth."[118]

Migrations

An immediate and unforeseen consequence of the war was the response of the enslaved to the presence of federal troops rampaging throughout the South. Wherever Union troops set up camp, hundreds of the self-liberated would miraculously appear. Their arrival caused an unforeseen crisis for the army. What to do with the thousands of able-bodied men and women standing at their tent door? To return them to southern plantations meant replenishing lost labor. Neither Congress nor President Lincoln was eager to alienate border states with slaves of their own. No policy was set early in the war.

The enslaved were not willing to sit idly by awaiting a decision. They forced the Union's hand by abandoning plantations and farms by the thousands to gather outside Union campsites. During the war between 500,000 and 700,000 escaped, costing the southern economy half a billion dollars in revenue and supplies.[119] Congress passed the Confiscation Act permitting the enslaved to be used as "contraband of war" to aid the Union Army. Once the policy of seizing slave contraband was adopted, the freedmen were invaluable in protecting the nation's capital as laborers girding up the city's fortifications. Despite being exploited, underpaid, or unpaid, they continued to labor in the war effort. Throughout the South, crops went unharvested, livestock neglected, and homes abandoned because of a severe worker shortage in fields, factories, and mines. Those who remained on plantations did their part for the fight and demonstrated insubordination by doubling down on the proven tactics of breaking tools, work slowdowns, and outright defiance.

A smaller migration involved former slaves vacating rural areas for the safety of southern cities. In the 1830s, enslaved men and women in urban centers decreased due to their forced movement to rural, agricultural regions to exploit their labor. After the war, the newly emancipated invaded cities in significant numbers, as millions left farms and villages for the South's largest cities. Rural communities were extremely hostile. City incentives included security, refuge, employment, and family reunification. Within one generation a people who had been mostly rural migrated to southern metropolitan areas. People mainly accustomed to agriculture and equipped with farm skills pushed their way into southern factories. Throughout the South between 1865 and 1870, so many deserted the rural areas that the ten largest southern cities doubled in population.[120] In North Carolina, the vast majority of Blacks, 80 percent, lived in urban areas by 1920.[121]

Cities in both the North and South saw increases in the number of persons entering city boundaries. Sixty thousand resided in metropolitan areas in 1790; within seventy years, there were half a million. Cities that benefited from their presence included New York, Boston, Philadelphia, Cincinnati, Washington, Baltimore, Charleston, Mobile, and New Orleans. There were high concentrations in North Carolina, Virginia, Maryland, and the Virginia tidewater region. Their numbers increased due to two factors: natural birthrate and migration.

Between 1521 and 1821, 200,000 people of color relocated to the western portions of the United States and Central Mexico in a westward migration. In 1862, President Lincoln signed the Homestead Act and granted ownership of public lands occupied for five years. This was an unprecedented opportunity for land ownership and wealth creation. A rumor spread that the federal government set aside the entire state of Kansas for freed men and women, which influenced settlers to move into Morris and Graham counties in Kansas. The *Topeka Colored Citizen* newspaper ran an ad advocating for westward migration: "Our advice . . . to the people of the South, Come West, Come to Kansas. . . . It is better to starve to death in Kansas than be shot and killed in the South."[122] In 1874, Benjamin "Pap" Singleton, an escaped Tennessee slave, enticed thousands to migrate to Kansas through the creation of his Edgefield Real Estate and Homestead Association. He circulated a widely read circular titled "The Advantage of Living in a Free State." Between 1874 and 1890, ten thousand journeyed to the Sunflower State. The starting point was Independence, Missouri, where Hiram Young, a former slave, acquired wealth as a manufacturer of wagons and oxen yokes. By 1860 he sold over 800 wagons and 50,000 yokes annually to those venturing into the western territory.[123]

"Exodusters" participated in the Exodus of 1879 as thousands of southern Blacks emigrated westward. Oklahoma Territory caught the Exodusters' attention when the federal government arrogated the land set aside for the Comanche and Cheyenne and redirected it to homesteaders. Black Americans took advantage of the famous April 22, 1889, "run" for land claims with a mind-set to establish towns and settlements absent from racist interference.[124] Sarah and Edwin P. McCabe founded Langston City, named for Virginia congressman John Mercer Langston, a supporter of migration who pledged money for a town college. They advertised in their newspaper, the *Langston City Herald*, for buyers to relocate to Kansas from Arkansas, Texas, Louisiana, Missouri, and Tennessee. The newspaper ad read, "Langston City is a Negro City, and we are proud of that fact. Her city officers are all colored. Her teachers are colored. Her public schools furnish thorough educational advantages to nearly two hundred colored children."[125] By 1891, two hundred people lived in a thriving farming industry of business owners, a doctor, minister, and schoolteacher. In 1900, Black land ownership peaked at 1.5 million acres valued at $11 million.

Isabel Wilkerson, in *The Warmth of Other Suns: The Epic Story of America's Great Migration*, wrote poetically,

> Over the decades, perhaps the wrong questions have been asked about the Great Migration. Perhaps it is not a question of whether the migrants brought good or ill to the cities they fled to or were pushed or pulled to their destinations, but a question of how they summoned the courage to leave in the first place or how they found the will to press beyond the forces against them and the faith in a country that had rejected them for so long.[126]

The years between World War I (1914–1918) and the onset of the Great Depression (1929) were economically bountiful for the United States, as jobs were plentiful in northern cities. In 1915 and 1916, natural disasters in the South decreased the number of jobs available while a reduction in European migrants increased opportunities for meaningful employment in the North. Southern oppression, in combination with northern opportunity, stirred something deep in the spirit of southern Blacks. Ecological influencers, including a boll weevil infestation and destructive weather patterns, doomed work in cotton fields. Northern companies sent recruiters deep into the South to entice Black workers to migrate. The *Chicago Defender* newspaper single-handedly influenced thousands to relocate. Southern white-owned businesses reacted to the loss of cheap labor by banning Black newspapers that echoed the migratory call. Between 1915 and 1930, Black Southerners relocated to northern and southern cities as well as the West. Between 1915 and 1920, 500,000 to 1 million relocated to the North plus another 700,000 to 1 million westward. Northern cities provided economic opportunity as well as a perception of less hostility. New York City's Harlem became ground zero as whites moved out and people of color moved in. Within three square miles in Manhattan, 175,000 people transformed the neighborhood into the epicenter of the African diaspora.

Unfortunately, for every opportunity, there was a downside. Inadequate housing facilities and intense job competition infuriated European immigrants who resented their presence and demanded segregated living units. The new migrants felt isolated in impoverished communities and received lower wages. Tensions erupted when deadly race massacres exploded in Springfield, Illinois; Rosewood, Florida; New York City; Los Angeles; Detroit; and Greenwood, Oklahoma.

Between 1940 and 1960, World War II triggered another wave of migration from rural to urban areas, from southern locations to northern and western destinations. Five million Black Americans departed the South following the United States' entry into WWII in 1941. By 1960, 40 percent of Black Americans resided in the northern and western sections of the country, with three-quarters listed as city dwellers for the first time in American history. Years of discrimination caused a weariness in the land of their birth. A major incentive was the lure of well-paying defense industry jobs in shipyards and aircraft factories on the West Coast. During the 1940s, 443,000 migrated to California, Oregon, and Washington, as each state grew in diversity by 33 percent. California benefited the most as 338,000 migrated to its shores. Oklahoma, on the other hand, lost 23,300 residents due to a history of hatred. From 1950 to 1980, the Black population in America's urban centers increased from 6.1 million to 15.3 million. Isabel Wilkerson wrote,

> The Great Migration is often described as a jobs-driven, World War I movement, despite decades of demographic evidence and

real-world indicators that it not only continued well into the 1960s but gathered steam with each decade, not ending until the social, political, and economic reasons for the Migration began truly to be addressed in the South in the dragged-out, belated response to the Civil Rights Act of 1964.[127]

Demographics held steady until the early twenty-first century, when a reverse migration emerged emanating from the North back to where it all began, the South. Generations born in northern enclaves answered an unspoken command to return to their African ancestors' foster home.[128] Black flight reduced Chicago's population by 180,000 as Atlanta replaced it as the city with the second-largest African American populace, second only to New York City. Detroit, Chicago, New Orleans, and New York each decreased by 100,000. Los Angeles lost almost 55,000 city residents to Atlanta and other southern cities. William Frey said that the reversal "began as a trickle in the 1970s, increased in the 1990s, and turned into a virtual evacuation in the first decade of the 2000s."[129] Frey, a Brookings Institution demographer, disclosed in his book *Diversity Explosion: How New Racial Demographics Are Remaking America*, that those packing their bags were young, college-educated men and women of the African diaspora partnering with baby boomers. This reversal that began in the 1970s gained momentum in the 1990s, and the flood gates burst open by the start of the twenty-first century.[130]

Wilkerson challenged whether this reversal is on the scale of the original migrations and deserving of the title "Great." She stated that many who relocated discovered that the "New South" retains many of the old "isms" though they were not as apparent as in the days of blatant racism.[131] Louis Lomax summarized the 1966 Watts rebellion and the conditions numerous Black men and women endured after migrating. "The tragedy of Watts is not that the Negroes burned it down but that the white community plans to build it back just like before without assessing the real needs and without addressing themselves to their solution. Negroes in Watts have a pathology of failure—they failed in the South and failed to find the promised land in Los Angeles."[132]

This migration reversal has a chance of reshaping the South from the land of Dixie and racial oppression into a more racially tolerant society. Politically, the impact is being felt in southern districts once viewed politically as red (Republican) that have flipped to blue (Democrat) due to the Black vote. In 2020, Democratic presidential candidate Joe Biden won the state of Georgia due to the work of Black women, particularly Stacey Abrams, registering numerous Black voters, something considered almost impossible as recently as the 2016 presidential election. Migration has increased the number of young, college-trained African Americans in a region where academic qualifications for high-end jobs are not always equal between whites and Blacks. It will likely increase the number of Black-owned businesses as many who are relocating come with a wide background of operating and owning their own businesses. The Black family will benefit, for those who fled left family members who are welcoming their relatives' children home with open arms. For a people who are family oriented yet whose ancestral stories only go back a few generations, the emotional lift could be life changing.

THE NEGRO WEST

> For African Americans even more was riding on their march west. They carried a greater need, a heavier burden, and paid a higher price. More than Europeans, pioneers of color pined for a home of their own, a place to educate children, protect women and nail down elusive dreams. More than others who rode in from afar, black women needed community respect and the law's shielding arm. Black men needed a land where a man's job and worth were judged by his skill, not his skin color.[133]

While there are many periods in the American story where the presence and contributions of people of African descent have been erased from the annals of history, one of the most notable is in the story of the American West. Out west, people of African descent had one of the highest demographic percentages of any region. As many as 25 percent of those living west of the Mississippi were of African descent prior to 1865. By the *Smithsonian*'s estimate, one in every four cowboys had African ancestry.[134] By 1825, 25 percent of all Texans were of African ancestry. By 1860, it had risen to over 30 percent, with the census reporting 182,566 enslaved people. The word most associated with the West, *cowboy*, has a racial connotation. A white worker was called a cowhand; Blacks were called cowboys.[135]

Overall there was less animosity in the Old West due to large swaths of land, fewer people, and greater distances between them. Your life could depend on the man riding next to you, and in a shootout, his color took on less relevance than survival. There was a higher level of respect and equality unknown to many Black Americans living in other regions. But discrimination did exist, and it increased as the war approached. Towns barred Blacks from eating in restaurants or staying in certain hotels. Indiana barred Black immigration in 1813; Ohio placed a five-hundred-dollar penalty on any who wanted to reside. Indiana, Nebraska, New Mexico, Utah, Washington, and Oregon disenfranchised or barred entry entirely by 1860. When Oregon became a state in 1857, it appeared as the only free state that excluded anyone of African descent by a provision in its constitution. Indiana, Illinois, Michigan, and Iowa not only prohibited interracial marriage but dissolved all that existed.[136]

With the onset of the War to End Slavery, white ranchers who left plantations to enlist in the military entrusted them to the management of those they enslaved. Having acquired the skills needed to run a ranch, they proved more than capable. When owners returned, they retained these cowboys to ensure the same level of productivity, but this time for pay. They led cattle drives to the rail stations in Kansas, Colorado, and Missouri, where livestock shipped to the North earned ten times the amount paid in Texas. All-Black crews populated several Texas ranches.[137]

Black men and women performed every task and lived every experience of the wild, wild West. They herded cattle, fought rustlers, and served as cooks, lawmen, domestics, bronco busters, laundry owners, ranchers, Pony Express riders, and outlaws. Names of celebrity status include Matthew "Bones" Hooks, Daniel Webster Wallace, Nat "Deadwood Dick" Love, Johana July, Henrietta "Aunt Rittie" Williams Foster, Bass Reeves, "Stagecoach Mary" Fields, James Beckwourth, Cranford "Cherokee Bill" Goldsby, Bill Pickett, George Washington, John and Mary Jones, Greenbury Logan, and Aunt Clara Brown. These alone occupied a litany of professions as stagecoach drivers, explorers, builders of towns, rodeo stars, ranch hands, lawmen, business operators, bandits, philanthropists, and Underground Railroad conductors. William Robinson and George Monroe rode for the Pony Express in California. Robinson's route was Stockton, California, while Monroe, the more famous of the two, covered the entire state. His wagon entertained visiting dignitaries such as William T. Sherman and presidents Rutherford B. Hayes and Ulysses S. Grant. The station in Yosemite National Park, Fort Monroe, carries his name.

Blacks functioned on both sides of the law as bandits and lawmen. Sheriff Willie Kennard operated in Yankee Hill, Colorado, in 1874 and brought to justice the notorious Barney Casewit. He was Colorado's first Black lawman, a corporal in the 7th Illinois Rifles Company, and an instructor at Montrose Training Camp. The life of deputy marshal Bass Reeves contained the stories of legends. He arrested over three thousand fugitives and killed fourteen in the line of duty. Accusations of cultural appropriation charged that the television series *The Lone Ranger* was based on his life. His biographer Art T. Burton, who wrote *Black Gun, Silver Star: The Life and Legend of Frontier Marshal Bass Reeves*, sees too many similarities for Bass not to be credited.[138]

Since the beginning of European exploitation, there developed what could be defined as a natural bond between Native Americans and Blacks. They became allies in opposition to white racism to prevent the seizure of Indian lands and the enslavement of African peoples. Some of the earliest encounters record a fascination with Black pigmentation on the part of indigenous peoples, who touched the skin to see if the dark color would rub off. Starving European exploration parties were rescued by Native Americans due to the presence of Blacks who were deemed to be medicine men. Blacks proved to be of great value as negotiators between Native Americans and whites. The enslaved man York was vital to Lewis and Clark's 1803 expedition due to his ability to learn languages quickly and assimilate into Native culture. His efforts accounted for the expedition's completion due to York's ability to form relationships with tribes they encountered. Jim Beckwourth lived with the Blackfoot, Crow, and Snake Indians and was a leader in the Crow tribe for six years.

Native Americans banded with African escapees, welcomed them into villages, and refused to return them to slavery, even after demands were made by enslavers. From the earliest slave uprisings, especially in the Northeast, collaborations between indigenous and African people were formed. The infamous Trail of Tears march contained 1,600 Black Cherokees. This forced caravan of 100,000 Native Americans from the southeastern United States between 1830 and 1850 was implemented by the United States government under its Indian removal policy. The Florida-based Seminoles bloodline was infused with Black blood as the two races intertwined into one. Whites attempted to create division between the races as Native warriors were hired to capture runaways. Black veterans were ushered into the Buffalo Soldiers of the Ninth and Tenth Cavalry units, each containing a thousand men. Their job was to monitor the frontier, which meant they fought against Native American people (Cheyenne, Comanche, Kiowa, Apache, Ute, and Sioux) on behalf of the U.S. government. Some estimates state that a majority of Blacks living have traces of Native American DNA.[139] Historian William Loren Katz, in *Black Indians*, listed several prominent Blacks with Native American ancestry, including Crispus Attucks, Paul Cuffee, Frederick Douglass, and Langston Hughes.[140] There is a shortage of acknowledgment of the role played by each race in the other's story of survival in American history. In many cases, their stories are intertwined, filled with narratives of struggle, success, and defeat.

NEGRO TOWNS AND COMMUNITIES

There are, for instance, among the colored people of the town [Durham, NC] fifteen grocery stores, eight barber shops, seven meat and fish dealers, two drug stores, a shoe store, a haberdashery, and an undertaking establishment. . . . This differs only in degree from a number of towns; but . . . in Durham a black man may get up in the morning from a mattress made by black men, in a house which a black man built out of lumber which black men cut and planed; he may put on a suit which he bought at a colored haberdashery and socks knit at a colored mill; he may cook victuals from a colored grocery on a stove which black men fashioned; he may earn his living working for colored men, be sick in a colored hospital, and buried from a colored church; and the Negro insurance society will pay his widow enough to keep his children in a colored school. This is surely progress.[141]

—W. E. B. Du Bois, writing in 1912

The greatest postslavery threat Blacks faced was the ongoing persecution at the hands of whites—by individuals, mobs, and the government. In a survival mode, they realized that the safest location was as far away from white people as possible. At every opportunity, they established towns and independent communities and filled them with churches, farms, businesses, banks, newspapers, schools, and colleges. Norman L. Crockett's research revealed that "the black-town idea reached its peak in the fifty years after the Civil War . . . . at least sixty black communities were settled between 1865 and 1915."[142] The Historic Black Towns and Settlements Alliance (HBTSA)[143] lists an astounding 1,200 Black settlements, enclaves, and towns and credits Booker T. Washington as playing a major role in their establishment.

Settlements ranged in size from a few hundred to thousands, and they stretched from Maine to Florida and Alabama to California, in nineteen states.[144] Oklahoma was the destination state in the massive construction of fifty Black towns and settlements. Between 1865 and 1920 Oklahoma towns included Clearview, Langston, and Boley, the largest.[145] The Greenwood District of Tulsa, founded by O. W. Gurley, contained churches, banks, fraternal clubs, a train depot, post office, power plant, and telephone company and covered forty city blocks.[146] Nicodemus, Kansas, was advertised as "the Largest Colored Colony in America. All Colored People that want to go to Kansas, on September 5th, 1877, can do so for $5.00." Three hundred Black Kentuckians left for Kansas that same year.[147] By 1880, 316 residents resided there.

The first Black towns predated the Civil War. In 1836, Frank McWorter, formerly enslaved in Kentucky, was the first Black man to found and register a town: New Philadelphia, Illinois. His 160 acres of farmland became a settling location for Blacks to purchase their own homes. Using proceeds from the sale of land and produce, he purchased sixteen family members from slavery.[148] In 1865 Princeville, North Carolina became the first municipality in the nation to be incorporated by Black Americans. The newly emancipated established Freedom Hill or Liberty Hill. The town was renamed for Turner Prince, a prominent and influential carpenter.[149]

In mid-seventeenth-century New York City, free Blacks owned farms that spread over 130 acres in Washington Square Park. Between 1825 and 1857, Seneca Village's 264 residents were Manhattan's first Black neighborhood, with dozens of homes and three churches (the First African Methodist Episcopal Zion Church, founded in 1853), a school (Colored School No. 3), and several cemeteries. In 1857, the New York State legislature seized the land under eminent domain to construct Central Park. From the 1830s to the 1860s, Manhattan's first Black settlement possessed the land underneath what is now Wall Street. Bedford-Stuyvesant in Brooklyn was the second-largest area for Blacks before the War to End Slavery. Henry C. Thompson sold to James Weeks, both formerly enslaved persons, land for a Black settlement named Weeksville. The district contained schools, churches, an orphanage, a senior center, and a newspaper, *The Freedman's Torchlight*. Congressman George Henry White was a lawyer, banker, real estate contractor, school principal, state legislator, and the only Black district attorney in the country. He constructed the still-existing town of Whitesboro near Cape May, New Jersey.[150]

In 1863 the federal government built Freedman's Village on the grounds of the Custis and Robert E. Lee estate, the south end of Arlington National Cemetery. By the end of the war, 40,000 fugitive slaves relocated to Washington, DC, in southern Anacostia. In the 1890s, North Brentwood was incorporated as a Black municipality located on Holladay Avenue (Rhode Island Avenue). The metro area included several Black towns and communities in Maryland, including Prince George's County, Maryland, which included Glenarden, Lincoln, Chapel Hill, Rossville, Ridgely, and North Brentwood. On Oct. 6, 1871, Sugarland had three founders: William Taylor, Patrick Hebron Jr., and John H. Diggs. This trio contracted with George W. Dawson, formerly enslaved, to purchase land for a church at the cost of $25. The deed dictated that property be the site of a church, school, and "burial site for people of African descent." Sugarland got its name under the claim that "the women (t)here were as sweet as sugar."[151] In 1908, Lincoln was a sanctuary for wealthy Blacks who wanted a nature-themed exit from city restrictiveness. Glenarden began in 1910 when W. R. Smith purchased and developed vacant land into fifty-one houses, a post office, a two-room schoolhouse, St. Joseph's Catholic Church, barbershops, two restaurants, and a dry-cleaning station.

In Virginia, John Henry Pinkard cultivated eighteen acres into Pinkard's Court in Roanoke County.[152] Durham, North Carolina, was one of a few cities known as "Black Wall Street," according to W. E. B. Du Bois and Booker T. Washington. The western portion of Franklin Street in Chapel Hill, North Carolina, contained a barbershop, a tailor, restaurants, a movie theater, two churches, and a funeral home in the decade between 1920 and 1930.[153] Georgia locations included Pleasant Hill in Macon, Hancock Avenue in Athens, and Auburn Avenue in Atlanta. *The Atlanta Journal and Constitution* referred to Auburn as "the richest Negro street in the world."[154]

In 1870, Rosewood, Florida, was established, and, by 1915, it had three hundred residents. In 1884, Rossville was built by Augustus Ross. Eatonville was incorporated in 1887 and was the hometown of writer Zora Neale Hurston, where her father served as mayor.[155] As the Flagler railroad moved southward, it led to the creation of towns, reserving the northwest quadrant for Black citizens. Coconut Grove in Miami contained the "first Black community on the South Florida mainland (the 1880s). Odd Fellows Hall, which served as a community center and library, Macedonia Baptist Church . . . and the A.M.E. Methodist Church, which housed the community's first school."[156] Today the northwest sections of North Palm Beach, Palm Beach, and Fort Lauderdale have historic Black communities. Colored Town (today Overtown) came into being in Miami-Dade, Florida, when the city was incorporated (1896). It was known as the Harlem of the South. D. A. Dorsey purchased an island in Miami in Biscayne Bay for local Blacks. He maintained ownership until the 1930s depression.[157]

In Alabama, Hobson City existed as a haven for Blacks, controlled by Black residents. In 1887, Isaiah Montgomery purchased land from Joseph Davis, the brother of Jefferson Davis, to establish churches, banks, schools, stores, and a post office in Mound Bayou, Mississippi. His son, Isaiah, established the town of Mound Bayou, complete with a post office, six churches, a bank, public and private schools, and a newspaper, *The Demonstrator*.

Shankleville (1867) and Kendleton (1870) were among the first of several towns in Texas populated by Black residents. Thousands purchased land and built homes along the Buffalo Bayou outside Houston in Freedmen's Town. For sixty years, churches, schools, stores, theaters, and entertainment hubs were a source of life and vitality there. By the 1920s, it was affectionately known as Little Harlem.

From 1875 to 1900, the Consolidated Coal Company recruited migrants from Virginia and West Virginia to venture to Iowa. Buxton, Iowa, was "a black man's town" populated by five thousand, with two justices of the peace and two deputy sheriffs. In 1911, Blackdom, New Mexico, was the state's first all-Black settlement. It soon grew to three hundred residents with a post office, blacksmith shop, businesses, a hotel, and the Blackdom Baptist Church, which also served as a schoolhouse.

In 1908, the California Colony and Home Promoting Association was the state's first all-Black township. U.S. Army Lt. Colonel Allen Allensworth located it thirty miles north of Bakersfield. By 1914, this town housed a school system, its own judicial system, and a hotel on the Santa Fe rail line. It is today Colonel Allensworth State Historic Park.

The Destruction of Negro Towns and Communities

For over a century, Blacks built these towns and filled them with homes, churches, and businesses; for over a century, whites destroyed them and confiscated the property. Between 1917 and 1923 mob terror devasted neighborhoods and towns in order to disrupt Black economic advance. Twenty-six episodes of mob violence displaced victims throughout the country. Racial hatred, economic jealousy, and evil intent led to destruction and flight as entire towns were burned to the ground and thousands murdered. Newspapers labeled the obliteration as race riots or race wars rather than the unprovoked brutal massacre of innocents. Land was seized in Florida, Georgia, New York, Oklahoma, Kansas, Texas, and elsewhere. Destroyed towns included Ocoee, Florida (1920); Greenwood/Tulsa, Oklahoma (1921); Rosewood, Florida (1923); and neighborhoods in New York City (1863), Atlanta (1906), East St. Louis (1917), Chicago (1919), Washington, DC (1919), and Knoxville (1919).[158] As noted in an earlier chapter, the 1863 New York City draft riots destroyed the High Points District of Manhattan. New York's first district settled by freedmen was located at the intersection of Anthony, Cross, Orange, and Little Water. Wall Street currently resides there.

By the first decade of the twentieth century, Blacks in Atlanta experienced life in a prosperous middle-class atmosphere. Home to the millionaire insurance magnate Alonzo Herndon, the 35,000 Black residents set themselves apart from working-class whites and Blacks, who experienced tension over jobs. In 1906, two newspaper editors, Hoke Smith and Clark Howell, were deadlocked in a gubernatorial election. Rather than alienate white voters by courting the Black vote, each resorted to a campaign of false accusations, accusing Black men of the rape of white women and forgetting their secondary place in society. On September 22, 10,000 white men rampaged Brownsville, Georgia; they attacked businesses and streetcars and killed innocent men—with estimates as low as twenty-five and as high as forty. When Black men armed themselves in self-defense, the militia confiscated their weapons and arrested 250 Black men as fighting continued. Recovery from the destruction to Brownsville took decades before economic viability would return. W. E. B. Du Bois chronicled the event in a poem titled "The Litany of Atlanta."[159]

On July 29, 1910, a white mob rampaged through Slocum, Texas, and murdered between twenty-two and two hundred. Multiple bodies were buried or decomposed in the woods. Many were shot in the back as they ran, hoping to escape the mayhem. Not one white person was killed. The rioters seized property and possessions. Sheriff William H. Black reported,

> Men were going about killing Negroes as fast as they could find them, and so far as I was able to ascertain, without any real cause. These Negroes have done no wrong that I could discover. There was just a

hotheaded gang hunting them down and killing them. I don't know
how many were in the mob, but I think there must have been 200 or
300. . . . They hunted the Negroes down like sheep.[160]

In 1917, Blacks in East St. Louis were hunted down and brutally murdered
and tortured in a maddening three-day rampage. Reporter Carlos F. Hurd
gave graphic details on the unprovoked destruction of lives. One victim had
a heavy stone dropped on his neck as he lay wounded. Another was stoned
biblical style and hanged twice. White women laughed as they assaulted Black
women, refusing to relent despite cries asking "for mercy."[161]

In Ocoee, Florida, whites rioted when Black leaders and landowners dared
to vote despite threats of retaliation. On November 2, 1920, election day,
landowners July Perry and Moses Norman cast their ballots. Norman was
beaten, and Perry was murdered with a sign attached to his lynched body that
read, "This is what we do to n***** that vote." Five hundred residents were
driven away, between six and sixty killed, two dozen homes, two churches,
and a lodge burned, and all lands were confiscated. A 1926 deed in the courthouse recorded that Armstrong Hightower's father sold fifty-two of his sixty
acres for $10. Survivor Hightower described the cleansing by saying, "That's
the night the devil got loose in Ocoee."[162]

In 1923, in Rosewood, Florida, on New Year's Day, a white woman
claimed that a Black man sexually assaulted her. Bands of white men, supposedly searching for the alleged suspect, murdered or wounded any unlucky victim unfortunate enough to cross their path. White friends intervened to save
Rosewood survivors, but the town was destroyed, and property, confiscated.
Only two buildings survived the carnage, not one resident ever returned, nor
was anyone ever charged with the heinous crimes committed.

Greenwood, Oklahoma, located adjacent to Tulsa, had 10,000 residents.
Along with Durham and Atlanta, Greenwood was considered a "Black Wall
Street" with thirty grocery stores, hotels, restaurants, theaters, and transportation services. On May 31, 1921, resentful whites spread false rumors that
a white woman had been assaulted, burned the town of thirty-five acres, and
routed the residents. A total of 1,250 homes were destroyed, and as many as
300 lives lost. The police and National Guard arrested scores of Blacks but no
whites. Several guardsmen joined the rioters. White mobs prevented firemen
from attempting to put out homes on fire.[163]

Sundown Towns

Towns that once had Black residents today have none. Formerly racially
diverse regions are now all white. James W. Loewen, in his book *Sundown
Towns*, exposed that between 1890 and 1968 white Americans established

Sundown, Sunset, or Grey Towns exclusively for white people. In his 2009 paper he described it as "A town or county with very few African American households decade after decade, or with a sharp drop in African American populations between two censuses, is a sundown town. . . Credible sources must confirm that whites expelled African Americans, or took steps to keep them from moving in."[164]

Beginning around 1890, whites transformed integrated regions into districts "for whites only." Expulsions happened throughout the South, threatening any person of color who allowed the sun to set while they were within city boundaries. Towns would brazenly display a sign posted at the edge of city limits: "N*****, don't let the sun go down on you!" Blacks were forcibly expelled and threatened to return at their own peril. When local whites dared to intervene, they stared down the barrel of a shotgun or were murdered. Prohibitions targeted Blacks, Jews, Chinese, and Native Americans. Ordinances barred people of color from renting or owning property within town, city, or county limits. Territories "cleansed" in this way ranged from individual towns to surrounding counties.[165]

Elliot Jaspin labeled these acts "racial cleansing." He surveyed census records and listed areas with a sudden decrease in diversity. The evidence was startling; a town would record Black residents one year, only to report the following year a complete disappearance from the rolls. He described a newspaper headline that read, "Missouri Mob's Work, Kills Three Negroes, Burns Their Homes and Drives Every Negro Out of Pierce City."[166]

American suburbs, ranging in size from a few hundred to tens of thousands, originated as sundown towns. In 1912, 1,100 Blacks living in Forsyth County, Georgia, were driven out by Klan violence.[167] Regions with similar histories included Washington County (Indiana, 1964); Comanche County (Texas, 1886); Polk County (Tennessee, 1894); Lawrence County (Missouri, 1901); Marshall County (Kentucky, 1908); Boone County (Arkansas, 1905 and 1909); Unicoi County (Tennessee, 1918); Laurel and Whitley Counties (Kentucky, 1919); Vermillion County (Indiana, 1923); Mitchell County (North Carolina, 1923); and Sharp County (Arkansas, 1906).

These were not just idle threats; those who stayed too long were threatened, with fatal consequences for some. Blacks warned one another before heading into certain localities to drive without stopping or slowing down. A teen who once took a bet to walk through one such town was never seen again.[168]

Red Summer of 1919

World War I ended in 1918, and 380,000 Black soldiers returned to what they hoped would be a different America. They had fought to make the world safe for democracy in anticipation of experiencing such democracy at home. What they discovered was a country engaged in a reign of terror, outraged over the sight of Black soldiers in uniform. White soldiers abandoned their former comrades and were instrumental in acts of violence against them. James Weldon Johnson termed 1919 "Red Summer." He wrote, "Men and women of my race were being mobbed, chased, dragged from streetcars, beaten and killed within the shadow of the dome of the Capitol, at the very front door of the White House."[169]

It was due to the efforts of returning soldiers that Black resistance took a turn. For the first time, men trained for combat and equipped with arms were in plentiful supply. When attacked, they fought back to defend families and fight off those primed for murder. Resistance was through three strategies: "armed self-defense, use of the Black press, and pressure on law enforcement and the courts."[170]

Commonly termed race riots, these attacks on Blacks are more accurately labeled race *massacres*. Between April and November 1919, the country bled from ninety-seven lynchings, massacres in three dozen cities, and thousands murdered. Thousands of armed white mobs, without provocation, openly murdered unarmed Black men and women. One Chicago reporter wrote that whites were "destroying the life of every discoverable Black man."[171] Police failed to stop the carnage, often joining in the murderous affairs. According to historian David F. Krugler, destruction devastated Charleston, South Carolina; Millen, Georgia; Vicksburg, Mississippi; Knoxville, Tennessee; Norfolk, Virginia; Annapolis, Maryland; Washington, DC; New London, Connecticut; Elaine and Bisbee, Arkansas; Syracuse, New York; Omaha, Nebraska; Longview and Houston, Texas; Gary, Indiana; Bogalusa, Louisiana; Chicago; and St. Louis.[172]

Washington, DC, saw one of the earliest conflicts. On July 19, whites murdered army veteran Randall Neal, angry at the sight of him in uniform. Black veterans coalesced to avenge his murder. Armed clashes made the city a war zone with bullets flying in both directions. The city endured the deaths of thirty Blacks and ten whites, with 150 wounded. Historian C. R. Gibbs shared an interview he had with an eyewitness: "[It was] not just blind race hatred, but resentment of social gains the Black community made just after World War I. When we embraced the capitalist aesthetic, folks lynched us. When we showed we were prosperous, people burned down stores on the premise we violated social codes and legal codes."[173]

In Millen, Georgia, on April 14, two white police officers and four Black men were killed, and churches were burned. In May, in Vicksburg, Mississippi, the sheriff watched as Lloyd Clay was shot, stabbed, and lynched. In Chicago in July, a week of mob violence left twenty-three Blacks and fifteen whites dead; 537 were injured, and 1,000 families were made homeless. It began after a young Black boy was pelted with rocks and drowned after he mistakenly swam across an invisible line in the Lake Michigan water separating white and Black swimmers. A Black crowd demanded the arrest of those who killed him. The police refused, and the violence ensued.[174]

In Knoxville, in August, the Tennessee National Guard was called in to stop a gun battle between a white lynch mob and residents of a Black neighborhood. The National Guard opened fire on the Black residents with a machine gun. Eyewitnesses testified that hundreds of bodies were dumped into the Tennessee River or buried in a mass grave. In September Omaha, Nebraska, was gruesome as Will Brown was killed, the courthouse set on fire, and the mayor almost lynched when he intervened.

Arkansas was a particularly bloody state, with well over a thousand murders that year. The Elaine Massacre in September was one of the worst, with estimates of hundreds of Blacks and five whites murdered. The cause was labor organizing by Black sharecroppers led by Robert Hill. Mobs deputized by Sheriff Frank Kitchens used Black bodies for target practice and burned homes and churches. Soldiers participated and shot victims at random. A murdered elderly women had her body dragged behind a vehicle. A total of 285 were arrested, and 122 of them were charged. The "Elaine Twelve," all Black union members, received the death penalty. The Supreme Court overturned the verdict in 1923.[175]

African American soldiers fought back in Washington, Chicago, South Carolina, and wherever riots occurred. Soldiers planned self-defense patrols to protect family, friends, and neighbors. In Bisbee, Arkansas, Buffalo Soldiers—Black regiments labeled such by Native Americans as a reference to their revered buffalo—clashed with police. In Washington, DC, soldiers surrounded Howard University and waited on rooftops with rifles.[176] A doctor in Longview, Texas, rallied others to protect a friend falsely accused. Veterans of the 370th Infantry Regiment, 93rd Division, marched down Chicago's South Side to defend civilians. Joe Etter died in his attempt to prevent the state militia from gunning down Knoxville residents. In Washington and Chicago, women defended neighbors and families. Carrie Johnson, alongside her father and weapon in hand, forced back a crowd attacking their home.[177]

The "Red Summer" was a history of terror compacted into eight months. But it was still just one year in a string of years filled with domestic terrorism. From the last quarter of the previous century until the 1960s, Black life was regularly filled with random acts of violence from every quarter. Daily humiliations, if confronted, could be a cause for violent retaliation. The mob actions would continue for most of a century. But they would not serve the intended purpose. Rather than causing Blacks to submit to white supremacy, they produced resistance. Blacks defended themselves and their communities against armed mobs. They established academic, societal, and fraternal institutions to build up the community. They banded together to construct resources that still exist today in the form of organizations such as the NAACP.

The combination of the Red Summer, the racism of the Woodrow Wilson administration, and overall discrimination provoked a response from the Black community to fight back on every front. The NAACP ramped up its efforts to address lynching and political disenfranchisement. World War I veterans fired back at white mobs intent on murder and destruction, saving lives by their defense. It stiffened the spines of whites who preferred not to see the level of intense racial hatred that was a by-product of white supremacy. Even the normally tepid President Wilson felt compelled to say to the nation that "the white race was the aggressor and that the stain cast upon everyone of the majority group and our land was the more sensible because our Negro troops are but just back from no little share in carrying our cause and our flag to victory."[178]

THE HARLEM RENAISSANCE

The attitude of America toward the Negro is as important a factor as the attitude of the Negro toward America. . . . We shall let the Negro speak for himself. . . . The mind of the Negro seems suddenly to have slipped from under the tyranny of social intimidation and to be shaking off the psychology of imitation and implied inferiority. . . . The American mind must reckon with a fundamentally changed Negro. . . . It will call for less charity but more justice; less help, but infinitely closer understanding.[179]

—*Alain Locke*

Between 1920 and 1940, one of the most dramatic artistic explosions in the history of the United States took place. The Harlem Renaissance was an action of artistic protest unlike any that contemporary society has experienced. Black art, long suppressed, proved that artistry could find expression on a Black canvas. The suppressed, creative energy of the race, held back for centuries, synergized in literature, music, theater, dance, drawing, painting, sculpture, printmaking, and photography. Each art form was an exploration of the Black experience. Artists were determined to be a bridge between the Black and white worlds and fought to gain full access to the opportunities available to every artist, regardless of race. Blacks must use every resource available to them and appreciate fully their African heritage, artistic creations, and cultural contributions not fully appreciated by white society. Blacks had an important message that needed to be heard if America was to be America.[180]

Writer and philosopher Alain LeRoy Locke, called the dean of the Harlem Renaissance, fostered a new cultural identity in the 1920s and 1930s. His 1925 anthology *The New Negro: An Interpretation* escalated Black art from obscurity to widespread appreciation. The Renaissance was labeled as the beginning of the New Negro Movement. Locke described it as a "spiritual coming of age" in which Blacks recognized their creative genius. He sought to eradicate racist stereotyping by reconceptualizing what it meant to be Black. Its goal was not just to reorient white opinion but also to redefine the race's perception of self as an inferior being producing mediocre art. Locke's challenge called for a reevaluation of heritage and the repair of broken intraracial relationships. It was governed by a higher level of artistic expression found only in the Black mind and not dictated by Victorian values. A greater sense of self-awareness was caused by eliminating elitist and racist influences.[181] Charles Johnson kicked off the renaissance with a dinner in March 1924 at Manhattan's Civic Club for Black poets and writers. He reflected that this was an opportunity for Blacks not only to display their artistic talents but to fight for social rights.[182]

During the First Great Migration, millions of talented men and women migrated north. By 1920, 300,000 African Americans had moved to Harlem, making New York City the renaissance's cultural center. Harlem materialized as the artistic capital because of an overabundance of talent and the chance to interact with creative peers. While Harlem was the center, it was a nationwide phenomenon with artwork germinating in all regions of the country.

Although viewed as a collective, exceptional individual artists excelled in the effort to eradicate racist caricatures and promote racial pride. Literary works by Gwendolyn Bennett, Arna Bontemps, Langston Hughes, Richard Wright, Jacob Lawrence, and Charles White described vividly the lives of Black people. Poets Langston Hughes, Gwendolyn Brooks, and Countee Cullen penned lines revealing the most profound thoughts and expressions of Black consciousness. Sculptors and painters molded Black beauty in clay and on canvas.

Artists of this generation created works instrumental in impacting the way art was expressed. Black music gave birth to a broad collection of offspring. In performances by Gertrude "Ma" Rainey, Bessie "Mother of the Blues" Smith, Louis Armstrong, James P. Johnson, Duke Ellington, and Josephine Baker, audiences not only heard but experienced something new, innovative, and emotionally satisfying. There were no limits uninvestigated as harmonic freedom eliminated boundaries and stressed creative expression. Continuous pulsating tempos, irregular rhythms, and tonal highs and lows entertained, bewildered, and enthralled. It generated a spirit of nonconstrained expression unlike any-thing by any previous culture. It was sexy, intoxicating, and seductive.

The Jazz Renaissance changed the way live music was performed. Louis Armstrong's impact continues to resonate as his rhythmic syncopation influ-enced both Black and white artists. Billie Holiday and Bessie Smith were renowned for their unique vocal sounds. Hazel Scott was a musical prod-igy at the age of three and the first Black person to host her own television show. She created the Hazel Scott sound, called "Jazzing up the Classics," by playing a classical piece at an increased tempo with syncopation with her left hand.[183] Sister Rosetta Tharpe, "The Godmother of Rock 'N' Roll," was a musical superstar in the 1940s and 1950s. Her guitar playing blended Delta blues, New Orleans jazz, and Black gospel. She was a forerunner to Prince and exerted a massive influence on Elvis Presley and other white rock and rollers. Bob Dylan called her a "powerful force of nature."

A dance renaissance ushered in the Charleston, Lindy Hop, jitterbug, shuf-fles, tap, and twist. Black dance styles were appropriated by white performers unwilling to acknowledge their debt. Fred Astaire performed in blackface in a warped homage to dance moves appropriated from Bill "Bojangles" Robin-son. There were selective opportunities for Black artists to appear in movies and on Broadway: *Shuffle Along* featured Josephine Baker; *The Little Colonel* displayed the talents of Bill "Bojangles" Robinson; *Porgy and Bess* starred John Bubbles and, later, Sammy Davis Jr. as Sportin' Life. "The First Negro Dance Recital in America" occurred in New York and featured Hemsley Winfield and Edna Guy. Black dancers and promoters included Katherine Dunham, Pearl Primus, Donald McKayle, Talley Beatty, Garth Fagan, Bill T. Jones, Joel Hall, Virginia Johnson, Robert Battle, Chuck Davies, and Alvin Ailey.[184] Pearl Primus was the first Black dancer to achieve international status, and Katherine Dunham ushered Black dance to the national stage. Black dance companies included the Chicago Negro Dance Group (1931) and the Alvin Ailey American Dance Theater (1958).

The Harlem Renaissance was a major protest against the idea of Black inferiority. The underlying motivation was the uplift of the Black race by rejecting the badge of inferiority placed on it by centuries of white supremacy. Alain Locke's thesis of racial uplift through artistic excellence was a constant thread throughout the period. The literary journal *Fire* produced creative works that helped trigger the explosion of Black creativity, demonstrating to the world that old stereotypical images were wrong. Although credited as last-ing only two decades, art continued to be produced well into the 1970s, and the Harlem Renaissance continues to be analyzed by critics into the twenty-first century. Its lasting influence is seen as the works of Langston Hughes and Zora Neale Hurston are being discovered and explored by a new generation of disciples. Black Americans for the first time made a claim to having a contribution to the world's cultural achievements.

THE NEGRO SOLDIER

I was an American soldier for 35 years. I was a Black American soldier. And I followed in a long tradition of Black men and women who have served this nation since long before the Revolutionary War. For so many years they served their nation without their nation ever serving them. They served because they believed in the promise of our democracy, they believed what the Declaration of Independence said. But for so many years they were denied the rights and privileges that other Americans enjoyed. Their story isn't well known. Their story was suppressed. Historians did not write about it well enough. But it's a wonderful story. It is the story of a group of Americans who never lost their love of this country, never lost their faith in what the Founding Fathers had promised them.[185]

—*Colin Powell*

Blacks have fought, bled, and died in almost every war America has waged. However, former fighting rigor was unable to defeat reoccurring racism no matter how admirably Black soldiers performed in the past. At each war's start, they had to prove themselves willing and able to fight. The lessons of military gallantry gained from previous wars were replaced by theories of inferiority and cowardice.

Presidents George Washington and Abraham Lincoln initially refused Black recruitment. For plantation owners, the idea of training and arming slaves was far more terrifying than enemy troops. A 1703 South Carolina law that allowed Negro soldiers to fight Native Americans was rebuffed by the following sentiment: "There must be great caution used, lest our slaves, when arm'd, become our masters."[186] The French and Indian War (King William's War) contained twenty-five Black militia companies from New York, Connecticut, and South Carolina. During the War of 1812, 247 soldiers fought in the 26th U.S. Infantry Regiment from Philadelphia. Paul Jennings, President James Madison's manservant, helped First Lady Dolley Madison evacuate the White House and, on the way out, retrieved the famous Gilbert Stuart portrait of George Washington. His memoirs became the first published remembrances of life in the White House: *A Colored Man's Reminiscences of James Madison*.[187]

Black soldiers also fought in the Battles of Lake Erie and New Orleans. An enslaved man named Joe fought in the Alamo. Wounded and captured by

Santa Anna's army, he escaped and returned to his homeplace in Alabama. In the end, Blacks were instrumental in winning both the Revolutionary War and the Civil War. After the Revolution, Black soldiers returned to a land freed from tyranny but not from African slavery. Despite the fact that almost 200,000 African Americans fought in the Civil War, a majority of the rights they gained from enlisting were systematically eliminated after the war.

For an institution painstakingly meticulous in record keeping, reports of valor were ignored or altered by the War Department. The ample evidence that Black soldiers had fought bravely in earlier wars was ignored or rigorously suppressed by military officers and government electors. Historian Robert B. Edgerton wrote in *Hidden Heroism*,

> Few Americans today appear to be aware that Black men, and sometimes women, fought in combat even before the Revolutionary War and have been intrepid warriors in all but one of this country's wars since then. . . . What is more, until quite recently there was a concerted effort by many, including highly placed military men and political leaders, to portray Black soldiers as fools and cowards. The accomplishments of Black Americans in military service not only played a pivotal role in Black history but deserves a place of respect in the history of all Americans.[188]

In each conflict, war-proven veterans and others had to reconvince the country's political and military leaders that their race would fight. Regardless, each time they joined the fight out of the hope that this time would be different.

Women in the Military

The desire to fight included women of African descent who were not willing to sit on the sidelines. Just as enslaved men fled the plantation during the Civil War for the refuge of a Union camp and enlisted, women did so as well. They, too, saw war as an opportunity for a better life in the future. While exempted from fighting, they bandaged wounds, washed uniforms, fed troops, and educated the illiterate. Some, hired by the government, remained on the plantation and harvested cotton for revenue. Both governments used Black nurses in Maryland, Virginia, and North Carolina. Ellen Campbell, Alice Kennedy, Sara Kinno, and Betsy Young served aboard the floating navy hospital *Red Rover*. William Cathey, who served in St. Louis, Missouri, with the 38th U.S. Infantry in 1866, was actually Cathey Williams, a woman who posed as a male soldier. She was the only known Black woman to serve in the army and the only female Buffalo Soldier. She wrote, "The regiment I joined wore the Zouave uniform and only two persons, a cousin and a particular friend, members of the regiment, knew that I was a woman. They never 'blowed' on me. They were partly the cause of my joining the Army. Another reason was I wanted to make my own living and not be dependent on relations or friends."[189]

During the Spanish-American War, Black nurses enlisted to combat outbreaks of yellow and typhoid fever in 1898. The surgeon general of the army falsely believed that they were immune from the disease and recruited thirty-two women, which soon grew to eighty. They patrolled the halls of Charity Hospital in New Orleans, Freedman's Hospital in Washington, DC, Provident Hospital in Chicago, and Massachusetts General in Boston.[190]

World War I provided limited opportunities for nurses of color to participate in the American war effort. The army finally relented and welcomed them into the nurse corps in 1918. Nurses who signed up through the American Red Cross and the Army Nurse Corps went to Camp Grant in Illinois and Camp Sherman in Ohio, where they cared for injured Black and German soldiers. Aileen Cole Stewart and seventeen others became the first full-time, active-duty women of color in the U.S. Army.[191]

On June 25, 1941, President Franklin D. Roosevelt's Executive Order 8802 created the Fair Employment Practices Commission to eradicate prejudice in the defense industry. The following year, the Women's Army Auxiliary Corps (WAAC) stipulated that 10 percent of the women be of color but serve in segregated units. In June 1943, Frances Payne Bolton, congresswoman from Ohio, introduced an amendment to the Nurse Training Bill to bar racial restrictions. The response was overwhelming as two thousand women enrolled in the Cadet Nurse Corps. Only at the war's end did the navy end discrimination in its women's reserve unit, WAVES (Women Accepted for Voluntary Emergency Service) on October 19, 1944. With the help of Dr. Mary McLeod Bethune, nurses Harriet Ida Pikens and Frances Willis entered military service on December 22, 1944. Phyllis Daley was the first commissioned navy nurse in 1945, leading the way for five hundred others to follow. The 824 enlisted women and 31 officers of the 6888th Central Postal battalion went first to England and then to France in segregated units. By the war's end, 6,520 functioned in the WAAC/WAC (Women's Army Corps). It took until 1948 for the air force to open its doors, yet it ended racial separation at a faster pace. In September 1949 the U.S. Marine Corps became the last to enlist women of color.[192]

Other Black women found different ways to serve the American cause. Josephine Baker, the world-famous entertainer and singer who resided in France, was a spy during World War II. While traveling across Europe, she gathered vital information and secretly passed it to the French military. She would pin information to her dress and write messages in invisible ink on her sheet music pages.

During the Korean and Vietnam Wars, Black women served in war zones. Chief Warrant Officer Doris Allen recalled, "Maybe 20,000 people are on that Wall in Washington D.C. because they didn't listen. And the reason I think they didn't listen, I still believe it today: black, WAC, intelligence, spec-7, and enlisted. Had I been—truth be told, had I been a blonde cutie, maybe they woulda, mighta listened. I doubt it. But if I had been a man, they would have listened, I believe. Had I been an officer, maybe they would have listened. But that's—being a woman, being black, being WAC, and those things."[193]

Coast Guard

To board a sailing ship in the nineteenth century was a daring enterprise. Sailors and passengers were lost at sea on a regular basis. The military established the U.S. Life-Saving Service (LSS) in 1871 as the precursor to the U.S. Coast Guard. Unlike the other areas of the military, Blacks had a long and varied history in the navy, with one fourth of the navy being Black during the Revolutionary War. Still, it was difficult to find life-saving stations that would allow Blacks to serve in all-white stations. There was a fierce determination on the part of former sailors to overcome discrimination and serve.

Richard Etheridge, a war veteran, was appointed the Pea Island Station's captain after the white crew was dismissed for negligence. Located along the coast of North Carolina, north of Cape Hatteras, it was the first station with a captain and crew of African descent. A new station was constructed when the one Etheridge staffed mysteriously burned down. They were one of the best-trained teams in the service as their captain rigorously drilled them in the procedures of rescuing distressed ships. Authors David Wright and David Zoby wrote,

> The reason for the segregation at Pea Island was simple: to put Black lifesavers into one station as a way to go on including them in the LSS (Life-Saving Service). Black surfmen numbered among the district's finest. . . . This is not to suggest that Richard Etheridge was hired merely because of the color of his skin. On the contrary, were he not the man he was, the Northern officials would not have been willing to risk upsetting the area's racial conventions to appoint him. They did not want just any black man. . . . No, Richard Etheridge stood out, not only among the black lifesavers but among all of the Outer Banks surfmen.[194]

The rocky coastline of North Carolina has been a ship destroyer, endangering any ship that dared to navigate too close to shore. In 1896 the schooner *E. S. Newman* crashed within the boundaries of the Pea Island station. An alert crewman spotted the distress signals even as a storm hid the ship's carcass from view. Unable to shoot a rescue rope, the men daringly swam out using a rescue line to usher every person onboard ashore, alive and well. The courageous rescue was recognized posthumously by the coast guard in 1996, with its highest award, the Gold Life-Saving Medal. Etheridge and his wife are buried on the grounds of the North Carolina Aquarium on Roanoke Island while a display inside the building illustrates the brave rescue.

World War I

World War I presented a paradoxical, bewildering process in American military history concerning the recruitment of men of African descent. In 1917, President Woodrow Wilson declared that "the world must be made safe for democracy," even as men and women of color wondered when America would be made safe for them. Ironically, as racism had previously barred their military service, it impacted enlistment in the opposite direction this time, as all-white draft boards rarely exempted Blacks from active service, even those with jobs and families.

Although 400,000 Blacks served during the war, only 43,000 were in combat units. They trained in segregated, ill-equipped bases with inadequate food and clothing. The army set them aside primarily as laborers and justified this racial prejudice by claiming that Blacks were either too inept or cowardly to fight. The U.S. Marine Corps would not allow any persons of color to enlist.[195]

Service in the American military was second-class, but life for the Black soldier was decidedly different for those assigned to duty in France. Despite urgings from the American military to treat Blacks as inferiors, the French army and civilians warmly embraced them. In an army memo titled "Secret Information concerning Black American Troops," French officers were warned not to accommodate them as it would offend white Americans. They were instructed to avoid intimacy; not to shake hands, eat, visit, or socialize with them; and not give them too much praise. The French rightly ignored this council and embraced the Black soldiers fighting on their soil. The first to arrive were four regiments of the 93rd Division, which included the 369th Infantry Regiment. To the French, they were known as the Men of Bronze; to the Germans, they were Harlem Hellfighters. The 369th comprised only one percent of the American troops in the country but occupied 20 percent of the front lines held by Americans. They were fearless and stood their ground for an incredible 191 consecutive days. They received 550 medals and were awarded the French Croix de Guerre 180 times, with many making the ultimate sacrifice of their lives. The French raised a granite monument as a memorial on the spot where they fought. (Invading Germans destroyed it in 1940.) Armed with grenades and a bolo knife, Private Henry Johnson, while on guard duty, single-handedly fought off over forty Germans. Bill "Bojan-gles" Robinson, the dancer, served in the trenches and performed with his band of brothers from the New York 15th Infantry.[196]

The American military awarded soldiers from the all-Black 92nd Division twenty-one Distinguished Service Crosses, more than were awarded to any of the white divisions fighting in the same area. The army withheld its highest honor and did not award a single Medal of Honor to any Black soldier dur-ing World War I. Commander Major Warner A. Ross recommended forty of his men for medals, but not one was granted.[197] The American-born pilot Eugene Jacques Bullard earned the name "Black Swallow of Death" as he flew for the French Foreign Legion with a 94 percent kill rate. He was awarded fifteen French combat medals, including the Croix de Guerre and the Legion d'honneur. When he attempted to fly for the United States, he was refused, so he joined the French underground as a spy. In 1994 he was posthumously commissioned as a second lieutenant in the U.S. Air Force.[198] Major Warner A. Ross of the all-Black 3rd Battalion of the 92nd Division's 365th Regiment said,

> In the battle line and out of the battle line, before the armistice and after the armistice, there was not a phase of military art of the awful game of war at which the battalion did not excel. At going over the top, attacking enemy positions, resisting raids and assaults, holding under heavy shell fire, enduring gas of all kinds, at patrolling no-man's land, at drill, on hard marches, in discipline and military cour-tesy, at conducting itself properly in camp or in French villages, and in general all around snappiness, it excelled in all.[199]

World War II

By the start of World War II, one would think that the military would have discarded the racist notion that men of African descent would not fight. Sadly, this was not the case. Veteran Allen Price shared the following:

> Seven of us went over, we was in England, tried to get into the para-troopers. We went to one, Screaming Eagles, we went in and the ser-geant asked us, "What do you want?" We said, "We understand you looking for paratroopers." He said, "You see anybody in this room your color?" We said, "No." He said, "Get the hell out!" We went over to the Rangers, tried to get in the Rangers, they wouldn't accept us. So what you going do? It's a hell of a thing. Yeah, we wanted to fight. What the hell we go to service for? To fight![200]

These men were prevented from serving by a Jim Crow mentality that infected every facet of military leadership. A draft with all-white draft boards refused to enlist eligible Black men, unlike in the previous war. Southern military leaders falsely testified that white troops would never fight alongside Blacks, undergirded by a fear that Black officers would command white soldiers. Those Black soldiers that were able to enlist were sent to democratize Germany in segregated units. Even blood was separated into white and Black pouches. Black Military Police officers stationed in the American South could not enter the same restaurants where their German prisoners were served without hesitation. Skepticism existed in Black minds whether they should send their sons and daughters to defend a country so enamored with white supremacy. There was less enthusiasm for this fight because fathers, grandfathers, and great-grandfathers who bled in previous wars saw little meaningful change. But other Black leaders believed that the 1940s presented a unique opportunity for progress and lobbied for recruitment.

When the United States entered the war in 1941, there were fewer than four thousand Black soldiers. By the war's end, 1.6 million served as infantrymen, pilots, tankers, medics, and officers in the army, navy, air force, marine corps, and coast guard. Most were denied access to combat units and 90 percent were relegated to service units in supply, maintenance, and transportation. The Red Ball Express carried a half-million tons of supplies to the First and Third Armies throughout France and was vital to the war effort. Dorie Miller, assigned the role of cook, was awarded the Navy Cross for shooting down Japanese planes that attacked U.S. battleships docked in Pearl Harbor on December 7, 1941. Almost two years later, on November 28, 1943, he was killed in battle during the Battle of Tarawa.

Despite attempts to deny them the opportunity to prove their bravery in combat, many did experience warfare. They fought in the Pacific in the all-Black divisions of the 92nd Buffalo Soldiers and 93rd Blue Helmets. Two thousand fought on D-Day in the First Army on the beaches of Omaha and Utah. The 327th Quartermaster Service Company and the 320th Anti-Aircraft Barrage Balloon Battalions protected vulnerable troops' beach landing from aerial attack. The 761st Tank Battalion, the Black Panthers, fought its way through France during the Battle of the Bulge under the command of General George Patton and his Third Army. They fought in Belgium, helped defeat the Nazis, and occupied Germany after the war.[201] In 183 days of combat, thirty towns in France, Belgium, and Germany were captured as the Black Panthers helped extricate Austria. Staff Sergeant Ruben Rivers received the Medal of Honor posthumously.

The army's first-ever Black fighter and bomber groups consisted of 1,100 trained pilots in the 332nd Fighter Group known as the Tuskegee Airmen. Colonel Benjamin O. Davis served as their commander. He led a 1,600-mile trek to Berlin, during which three Nazi planes were shot down and six others damaged. The Tuskegee Airmen flew 15,000 sorties between May 1943 and June 1945. They flew support missions over Anzio and escorted bombers over southern Italy. They destroyed 111 enemy aircraft in the air and another 150 on the ground. They bombed over six hundred trains and other moving vehicles. They sunk a destroyer along with forty additional sea craft. Sixty-six airmen lost their lives, but the unit never failed to protect escorted bombers. White bomber crews requested the escort of the Tuskegee Airmen, known as the Redtails.[202]

The navy escorts USS *Mason* (DE-529) and the USS *PC-1264* were crewed by Black sailors. In October 1944, the *Mason* led twenty ships to safety in England despite battering by a severe storm and 75-knot winds. *PC-1264* ensign Samuel L. Gravely Jr., on May 2, 1945, became the first Black officer and later the navy's first admiral.

Black Marines trained at Montford Point, fought in the Pacific, and engaged the Japanese in Guam and Saipan. They landed on Omaha Beach on June 6, 1944, D-Day, as the 84th Chemical Company shielded invading troops. The first Black paratroopers were the 555th Parachute Infantry Battalion, known as the Triple Nickles, in 1944. They were unique as a Black battalion, from the privates to the commanding officers. Seventeen of the twenty were college students or athletes who completed training and were awarded silver wings at Fort Benning, Georgia. Six graduated as officers. They served in more airborne units that any other paratroopers in military history. Because the war was nearly over by that point, they were deployed to Oregon as the first smoke jumpers in military history, fighting forest fires. They were also assigned the search for Japanese diversionary balloon bombs sent across the Pacific Ocean to American soil. They made 1,200 jumps and only lost one man, medic Malvin L. Brown on August 6, 1945. He was the first smoke jumper to die in the line of duty. In December 1947, the dissolved Triple Nickles were reinstated as a part of the 82nd Division. It was the first Black army unit integrated into an American combat division. Members later formed the 2nd Ranger Infantry Company during the Korean War. They made the first combat jump by a Ranger unit and were the first Black unit to land in Korea in March of 1951.

Although America in 1946 had not changed much when Black troops returned from combat, it did not deter soldiers determined to bring back home the rights they experienced overseas. For the first time, they had been treated as equals to white men, and many pledged to continue fighting for democracy in the place it mattered most, America. As a result, a host of veterans later became leaders in the civil rights movement. Medgar Evers, Amzie Moore, Hosea Williams, and Aaron Henry were among the World War II veterans who joined the NAACP in record numbers and established new chapters throughout the South. They fought for humane treatment in the South and economic justice in northern workplaces. They volunteered in

the 1963 March on Washington and did as much as anyone to integrate the
U.S. military. Their accomplishments are recognized in the National WWII
Museum in Washington, DC.

Maria Höhn wrote in *Military Times*,

> They fought in the Pacific, and they were part of the victorious army
> that liberated Europe from Nazi rule. Black soldiers were also part of
> the U.S. Army of occupation in Germany after the war. Still serving
> in strictly segregated units, they fought to democratize the Germans
> and expunge all forms of racism. It was that experience that convinced
> many of these veterans to continue their struggle for equality when
> they returned home to the U.S. They were to become the foot soldiers
> of the civil rights movement—a movement that changed the face of our
> nation and inspired millions of repressed people across the globe.[203]

In July of 1948, President Harry S. Truman signed Executive Order 9981 that
desegregated the armed forces. It would take three full years before the order
was implemented during the Korean War. For the first time, Black officers were
in command of white soldiers. Sergeant Cornelius Charlton asked to be relieved
of his administrative duties in order that he could join other soldiers in the fight.
He was the second African American to be awarded the Medal of Honor, posthumously recognized for his actions at the battle of Chio-Ri in 1951. His father
said at his funeral in West Virginia, "The death of my boy distinctly makes a liar
of those who said that the Negro will not fight for our country."[204]

The Vietnam War saw the full integration of Blacks into the U.S. military
for the first time since the days of the Revolution. The war took the lives
of 7,264 Blacks, and twenty received the Medal of Honor. *Time* magazine
wrote, "In the unpredictable search-and-destroy missions throughout the
central highlands. In the boot-swallowing, sniper-infested mangrove swamps
of the Mekong Delta, on the carrier decks and in the gun mounts of the 7th
fleet offshore, the American Negro is winning, indeed, has won, a Black badge
of courage that his nation must forever honor."[205] By the end of the Vietnam War segregation was permanently eradicated from all military branches.
Today, it is a distant memory, with the military receiving high marks for
equal opportunity, regardless of race.

THE SAME OL' DEAL

In 1935, the Works Progress Administration (WPA) employed
approximately 350,000 African Americans, about 15% of its total
workforce. The Federal Music and Theatre projects also supported black musicians and actors. The WPA made significant

contributions to the preservation of African American culture and history with the Federal Writers' Project. [206]

In 1936, Blacks maintained their loyalty to the Republican Party because it was the party of Abraham Lincoln. Up to that point, 75 percent voted Republican, but there were strongly heard complaints that it was no longer the party of Lincoln when it came to civil rights. President Franklin D. Roosevelt's New Deal enabled the switch to the Democratic Party, mainly due to the egalitarian nature of his wife, Eleanor Roosevelt, who partnered with Mary McLeod Bethune to advocate for Black rights.[207] Roosevelt's administration, by the standards of the day, was quite progressive. He was the first president to condemn lynching publicly. He appointed the first Black federal judge and brigadier general. He was responsible for hiring over 1 million Blacks and for the education of a similar number of children, as well as funding the works of countless artists. He was advised by a Black Cabinet or Black Brain Trust.[208] A. Philip Randolph forced the president to issue an executive order to eliminate discrimination in the defense industries by threatening to hold two marches on Washington.

But President Roosevelt failed miserably when it came to African American economic progress. His administration promoted home ownership, the foundation for economic advance to middle-class status, but only for whites. The New Deal's publicized intent was to boost the economy through infrastructure promotion and relief to millions of hungry and impoverished Americans. The inheritance of a family home is a fundamental manner in which middle-class families bequeath wealth. His support for American families would have had no more deserving recipients than African Americans, who suffered disproportionately from legislated poverty and crippling racism. However, the president gave in to racial politics as unions and southern congressmen pressured him to exclude Blacks from the millions of program dollars distributed.[209] Richard Rothstein, in *The Color of Law*, stated that the federal government devastated any chance African Americans had to improve their economic status through home ownership by denying them access to federal benefits. Countless families would have been removed from poverty without the racial exclusions. The result was increased isolation, with northern Black families relegated to ghettos.[210] Ira Katznelson's book, *When Affirmative Action Was White*, documented the efforts of the U.S. government to implement segregation throughout the country. The New Deal was the original affirmative action, designed to help whites escape poverty through federal subsidies and programs.[211] But the New Deal proved to be the same old deal for Blacks.

The National Recovery Administration (NRA) openly discriminated against Black workers; it withheld the best paying positions and paid lower wages. The Federal Housing Administration (FHA) secured for white families access to low-interest, no-down-payment loans but denied acceptance for Blacks seeking to move into white neighborhoods. The Agricultural Adjustment Administration (AAA), through its program of acreage reduction, eliminated the jobs of 100,000 Black men between 1933 and 1934. The Home Owners Loan Corporation and the National Labor Relations Act excluded agricultural and domestic workers. Blacks could not apply for assistance as union workers since most unions forbade them membership. The 1935 creation of Social Security excluded Blacks and Mexican Americans by barring agricultural, domestic, and railroad workers. This act eliminated 65 percent of American Blacks from benefits. Roosevelt's former executive director of his Economic-Security Committee confirmed that Southerners wanted total control over the distribution of resources to the elderly. They insisted that there be no oversight by the federal government through the refusal of funds due to discrimination directed towards Negroes.

Charles Lane explained that "Blacks did not move into overcrowded slums as a matter of group preference. Nor was private discrimination by white developers, banks, and homeowners' associations exclusively to blame, though it was certainly a key factor. Rather, the federal government used its expanding power to promote apartheid-like separation of whites and blacks in cities and towns across the country."[212] "Restrictive racial covenants," used by real estate agents, and redlining, practiced by banks, excluded Blacks from acquiring loans for home purchases. Rather than challenging these practices, New Deal agents denied loans to "inharmonious racial or nationality groups" considered bad investments that lowered white property values. Government constructed separated communities for defense workers even in neighborhoods adjacent to Blacks.[213] Tom Sugrue dissected the economic effects of exclusion in northern cities and notes that Blacks paid more for housing than whites.[214] In an interview he stated,

> In most of the north, unlike in the south, racially separate schools were not mandated by law. But school segregation was widespread in the north and can't simply be described by the misleading term "de facto." Many northern school districts maintained officially separate schools or cordoned off blacks in their own classrooms, or redrew school attendance zones when black families began to move in.[215]

Blacks confronted President Franklin on a regular basis for inclusion. By the time of his election, they had amassed a political network capable of penetrating even the highest office in the land, the presidency. Lobbying presidents had occurred since the days of Washington but never from the inside of an administration as through his Black cabinet. As a result, Blacks were able to access public assistance for the first time through housing units and relief checks. The downside was a lack of available jobs for which they could apply. The Great Migration concentrated Black voting strength in several northern districts and could sway an election one way or another. Mary McLeod Bethune, Robert C. Weaver, William L. Hastie, Ralph J. Bunche, and William Trent Jr. were race relation advisors to the administration. An NAACP campaign against John J. Parker's appointment to the Supreme Court was successful. Despite political gains, the fight was not yet won as Blacks soon realized that helping to decide elections did not mean producing legislation that would lead to meaningful change. The frustrations of the shortcomings of the New Deal were reflected in the national resistance to racial progress. But rather than give up, Blacks redirected their efforts toward economic empowerment and attempted to force industries to hire Black workers in positions previously denied to them.

Section 4

The Civil Rights and Black Power Movements

Black and Afro-American Protest: 1955–1987

After nearly eight years of verbal sparring through the media, two great African-American leaders, Martin Luther King, Jr., and Malcolm X, finally met for the first and only time in Washington, D.C., 26 March 1964. . . . The meeting of Martin and Malcolm has profound, symbolic meaning for the Black freedom movement. It was more than a meeting of two prominent leaders in the African-American community. It was a meeting of two great resistance traditions in African-American history, integrationism and nationalism. Together Martin, a Christian integrationist, and Malcolm, a Muslim nationalist, would have been a powerful force against racial injustice. When they were separated, their enemies were successful in pitting them against each other and thereby diluting the effectiveness of the Black freedom movement. Both Martin and Malcolm were acutely aware of the dangers of disunity among African-Americans. They frequently spoke out against it and urged African-Americans to forget their differences and to unite in a common struggle for justice and freedom.[1]
                    —*James Cone*, Malcolm & Martin & America

The Black/Afro-American protest generation created the most concentrated freedom movement in the country's history. It was the most radical movement yet, for even as it appropriated the tools of past efforts, old strategies were taken to a new level of confrontation. This generation's work produced a protest movement that swayed the American public. In contrast with the African and Colored movements, its total platform was a public one—to disrupt life in the country as a form of protest. Similar to past generations, once white terrorists discovered the identities of the leadership of this movement, its members paid dearly, often with their lives. But they were willing to risk arrest, brutal beatings, and domestic terrorism to effect change. This genera-tion embraced civil disobedience in order to sway public opinion and move politicians to action, and it demonstrated success by using the authority of the federal government to implement national change.

The civil rights movement was the most impactful human rights campaign in the history of the United States of America. It has been considered the second act of the first civil rights movement, the abolitionist movement of 1775–1865. The civil rights movement of the 1950s and 1960s was a con-tinuation of the struggle to eliminate centuries of white supremacy infused in American society. Its uniqueness was that in just two decades it achieved tangible results and served as the catalyst for dismantling public approval of racism. Victories in the courts, congressional legislation, and triumphs both nationally and locally were monumental achievements. But many paid a ter-rible price of destruction of property, time spent in jail, and loss of life. It comprises an epic story of heroes such as Rosa Parks, Martin Luther King Jr., Bayard Rustin, and John Lewis. It also has villains such as Sherriff Bull Con-ner and Governor George Wallace. It has a list of characters widely ranging from presidents of the United States to unknown childhood marchers. It is a story of perseverance and protest in the face of insurmountable odds. Yet because they would not give up, it is the story of change coming to America.

The brief, three-decade period between 1955 and 1987 resulted in an intense emotional and intellectual wrestling over Black identity. People of African descent struggled over how they would be defined. The controversy touched deep emotions as many, particularly young adults, were engaged in a cerebral search for self-definition, the nature of their relation to Africa, and what it meant to be Black in America. It signaled a shift in tactics: to mass protest, direct action, and violent and nonviolent confrontation. There was a shift in racial identity, too, as *Colored* was dropped for the then more radical use of the word *Negro*.

Huey Newton defined Black Power as "giving power to people who have not had power to determine their destiny."[2] With the civil rights movement at its height, many felt that it was not forceful enough to demand change or educate people toward a pro-Black mentality. No longer were they going to accept the white man's stereotypical labeling of Black people. They were Black people involved in a struggle to emancipate themselves. Black Power advo-cates attempted to separate themselves from so-called Negroes. They mili-tantly pressed newspapers and magazines to accept *Black* and *Afro-American* as proper titles and wrote letters critical of their usage of antiquated terminology.

Black mostly won out by the end of this time period, as individuals, and organizations, espoused the mantra of "Black and Proud." Institutions and publications renamed themselves. There was voiced opposition to the use of either *Colored* or *Negro*. The Racism in Education Conference of the American Federation of Teachers unanimously endorsed a resolution calling for the abandonment of the "slavery-imposed name (Negro) for the terms 'African American' or 'Afro-American.'"[3] The National Conference on Black Power passed a resolution to substitute *Black* for *Negro*. The *Negro Digest* became *Black World*, and *Negro History Week* emerged as *Black History Month*. The *New York Amsterdam News* announced that it would no longer use *Negro* in print as subscriber letters ran nine-to-one in favor of *Afro-American*. One wrote,

> We like the word because we are descendants of Africans and because we are Americans. There is a cringing from the word "Negro," especially by the young, because that name was imposed on us. . . . [They] link the word "Negro" with Uncle Tom. They seldom use the word "Negro." They used "Black" and "African." Some of them even object to the word "Afro-American," preferring the term "Afram."[4]

As with every period of transition, there was resistance from those who charged that white intellectuals were behind the promotion of the term *Black*. More periodicals were adopting its usage in print and advocating for the usage of *Black*, and the more radical members distrusted any strategies endorsed by the white community.

THE CIVIL RIGHTS MOVEMENT

The Civil Rights Movement in America began a long time ago. As early as the 17th century, Blacks and whites, slaves in Virginia and Quakers in Pennsylvania, protested the barbarity of slavery. Nat Turner, Sojourner Truth, Frederick Douglass, William Lloyd Garrison, John Brown, and Harriet Tubman are but a few of those who led the resistance to slavery before the Civil War. After the Civil War, another protracted battle began against slavery's legacy, racism and segregation. But for most Americans, the Civil Rights Movement began on May 17, 1954, when the Supreme Court handed down the Brown v. Board of Education of Topeka decision outlawing segregation in public schools. The Court unlocked the door, but the pressure applied by thousands of men and women in the movement pushed that door open wide enough to allow Blacks to walk through it toward this country's central prize: freedom.[5]

— *Julian Bond in the foreword for* Eyes on the Prize

Judicial and legislative victories reveal only one side of the real impact of the civil rights movement. It did not end discrimination but forever altered the consciousness of the nation. It exposed the immorality of white supremacy and the fallacy that it was religiously ordained or permissible in a democracy. This was the ideological synergy of earlier movements, including that of ancestors who attacked the hypocrisy of slavery in a free nation. Its most significant victory has been the steady, growing acknowledgment by whites that they can no longer view racism as a positive virtue in the United States of America, that it is indefensible and against everything the country stands for. While white supremacy continues to poison the systems of governance and economic institutions, many white Americans have rejected racism and white supremacy. In the United States today, even racists publicly deny they are racist.[6]

The success of this movement and its impact on the United States and the world cannot be denied. Though the movement did not achieve equality or eliminate white supremacy, it did force a greater awareness on the part of society of what it meant to live as a person of color in America. The country came face-to-face with its contradictions. The nation was set upon a different path in the realization and acknowledgment that (1) racism was America's original sin; (2) a debt was owed to the descendants of African slaves; and (3) America was still a promise unfulfilled.

School segregation was in full effect in the United States following the May 18, 1896, U.S. Supreme Court *Plessy v. Ferguson* ruling. "Separate but equal" was constitutional, according to the ruling, as long as states provided equal accommodations for both races. Then, in 1954's *Brown v. Board of Education*, the U.S. Supreme Court unanimously ruled that separation nullified equality and was therefore unconstitutional. This landmark ruling, applauded by Blacks, created in whites strong resistance. Seventeen states, eighteen school districts, and the District of Columbia initially continued these segregationist policies. But four years later, only seven states (Virginia, South Carolina, Georgia, Alabama, Florida, Mississippi, and Louisiana) remained separate. That number was reduced to three in 1961 as only South Carolina, Alabama, and Mississippi schools remained segregated. Brown was the first brick removed from the wall of injustice, with implications beyond academics. NAACP lead attorney Thurgood Marshall (later to be named to the Supreme Court) mounted a brilliant strategy, proving how Jim Crow laws hampered children.

The desegregation of the bus line in Montgomery, Alabama, in 1956 was another significant victory for the movement. For more than a year, the Black citizens of Montgomery refused to ride city buses. Their goal was not merely the right to sit in the front rows of a city bus but also to remove the stain of inferiority stamped on the foreheads of people of color. The system demanded acquiescence and a servile mentality, demonstrated through the public acknowledgment that white people were superior and Blacks inferior. The benefits of first-class citizenry could be denied, the system said, because Blacks were beneath the dignity of any self-respecting white man or woman. To be Black in America was to be without merit or any recognition of shared humanity. That was what the men and women of Montgomery walked to overcome; bus desegregation was secondary.

Protests targeting transportation had been pivotal in the fight for equality long before Montgomery. Historian Blair Kelley revealed that between 1900 and 1960, campaigns to desegregate public transportation occurred in twenty-five southern cities. Individuals leading or participating in such movements included Pauli Murray and Adelene McBean (1940); Adam Clayton Powell (1941); Jackie Robinson (1941); Irene Morgan (1944); Jo Ann Robinson (1946); Sarah Louise Keys (1952); the Rev. T. J. Jemison and the Baton Rouge Bus Boycott (1953); Aurelia Browder, Susie McDonald, Jeanette Reese, Claudette Colvin, and Mary Louise Smith (1955); and Wilhelmina Jakes and Carrie Patterson (1956).[7]

The strategy that sparked the civil rights movement did not begin in the twentieth century; it had been around since at least the seventeenth century. It always centered around the use of personal vehicles (carriages, hacks, horse-drawn taxis, drays, carts, and wagons) to transport boycotters. There was a wide range of pushback as transportation operators and public officials attempted to force compliance to local ordinances. A concern over financial deficits played a role, but mostly it was to force Blacks to submit to local ordinances and not disrupt the status quo. Massachusetts was a locale with regular occurrences, as some refused to abide by separated seating orders or refused to ride as a matter of principle. Determined individuals would ignore regulations and sit in sections reserved for whites. Abolitionist David Ruggles was a constant irritant as he regularly boarded and sat on seats reserved for "whites only." For his efforts, he was forcibly removed, and in 1841 he was physically assaulted by a ticket seller for his obstinance.

In 1842 Charles Lenox Remond testified before the Massachusetts House of Representatives that a white man's "social rights" should not interfere with a "Negro's civil rights." The legislature took action the following year and desegregated public transportation. Frederick Douglass was adamant in his refusal to abide by custom and was assaulted for his refusal to vacate trains and streetcars. Many complainants filed lawsuits. On July 16, 1854, Elizabeth Jennings Graham boarded a New York City bus only to be forcibly ejected by the conductor. She won her lawsuit and was awarded damages, but the court refused to outlaw the practice. In 1856 a judge ruled against a minister that the company's business was of greater importance than his rights as an individual and that integration would disrupt trade. An 1861 Philadelphia court ruled that a company was within its rights to use force in the ejection of riders of color committing violations.[8] The number of similar cases was great and contained some of the leading civil rights voices of their days:

- Ida B. Wells successfully sued and won damages ($500) from the Chesapeake and Ohio Railroad Company after being removed from a car. The Supreme Court of Tennessee reversed the decision under the justification that Wells caused the company "difficulty" when she refused to move.
- Sojourner Truth single-handedly integrated the streetcars of Washington, DC, after a successful lawsuit.
- In 1863, a succession of demonstrations in San Francisco by Charlotte Brown, William Bowen, and Mary Ellen Pleasant against the horse-pulled "whites only" streetcar company resulted in desegregation.
- In 1865 William Still led a successful campaign to force the Pennsylvania state legislature to outlaw segregation in railroad cars.
- In 1867 Octavius V. Catto successfully integrated Philadelphia's horse-drawn transportation system.
- In 1868, Kate Brown was arrested and physically harmed in Washington, DC, for failing to leave the (white) ladies' car.
- In 1870 a boycott desegregated Louisville, Kentucky's streetcar system after a series of "ride-ins" where Black passengers boarded Central Passenger Railroad Company's white-only cars. After filing a desegregation lawsuit, boycotters refused to ride during the winter months. On May 14, 1871, the company and city desegregated all vehicles.

The case of Homer Plessy had the greatest notoriety. After his 1892 ejection and arrest from the white-only section of a New Orleans rail car, shoemaker and public education activist Plessy went to court. The Supreme Court in 1896 ruled against him, establishing the "separate but equal" doctrine. A similar attempt before the court also failed when in 1910, attorney J. Alexander Chiles sued the Chesapeake and Ohio Railroad for illegally removing him from the white section within the "Colored Coach." Banker Maggie Lena Walker organized a successful crusade against the Virginia Passenger and Power Company, and within a year the company was out of business. In 1944 Irene A. Morgan was arrested in Saluda, Virginia, in violation of the bus segregation statute. When she refused to give up her seat to a white couple, the driver called the police, who arrested her. She remembered saying, "When I told them they were hurting my arms, one said, 'Wait till I get you to jail; I'll beat your head with a stick.'" She took her case to the Supreme Court, which struck down segregation in interstate travel on buses. But the South ignored the ruling, citing that state law had precedence over federal law. A Philadelphia newspaper ran a story with the headline "White Supremacy Reigns on Bus Despite New Law."[9]

Montgomery: In the Beginning

The Montgomery Bus Boycott (December 5, 1955–December 21, 1956) was a campaign wherein the Black residents of Montgomery, Alabama, refused to ride buses for 381 days. The initial spark was the arrest of Rosa Parks for refusing to give up her seat to a white passenger and move to the back of the bus. She described the incident quite simply: "He said, 'Why don't you stand up?' And I asked him, 'Why do you push us around?' He said, 'I do not know, but the law is the law and you're under arrest.'" That same year Montgomery attorney Fred Gray sued on behalf of four female plaintiffs: Aurelia Browder, Susie McDonald, Claudette Colvin, and Mary Louise Smith. The lawsuit argued that segregated seating on city buses violated equal protection under the law and was therefore unconstitutional. On June 5, 1956, the *Browder v. Gayle* ruling of the Supreme Court declared segregation on public buses unconstitutional, using *Brown v. Board of Education* as a legal precedent. The court declared, "In fact, we think that *Plessy v. Ferguson* has been implicitly, though not explicitly, overruled. . . . there is now no rational basis upon which the separate but equal doctrine can be validly applied to public carrier transportation."[10]

In 1961, the Congress of Racial Equality (CORE) sought the integration of interstate buses and terminals and organized college students and young adults in the Freedom Rides. Even though the Supreme Court had ruled segregation unconstitutional, little had changed. The strategy was controversial and split the movement's leadership. Martin Luther King Jr. emerged as the leader of the Southern Christian Leadership conference (SCLC) and the movement for civil rights. He was a young pastor in Montgomery, Alabama, at Dexter Avenue Baptist Church. He and other Black leaders in Montgomery led the successful desegregation effort, and King rose as the leader in the fight for Black rights in America. He endorsed the Freedom Rides but had private reservations about the tactic and never boarded any of the buses. Younger advocates, led by James Farmer, corralled twelve groups of riders to travel from Washington, DC, to Jackson, Mississippi.

On May 4, 1961, two buses left DC only to get as far as Virginia, where the riders were arrested. In Rock Hill, South Carolina, John Lewis, later an esteemed U.S. congressman, was battered and arrested. In Anniston, Alabama, on May 14, a bus was firebombed while police stood idly by. James Farmer remembered,

> Before the bus pulled out, however, members of the mob took their sharp instruments and slashed tires. The bus got to the outskirts of Anniston and the tires blew out and the bus ground to a halt. Members of the mob had boarded cars and followed the bus, and now with

the disabled bus standing there, the members of the mob surrounded it, held the door closed, and a member of the mob threw a firebomb into the bus, breaking a window to do so. Incidentally, there were some local policemen mingling with the mob, fraternizing with them while this was going on.

On May 17, 1961, a second bus was stopped outside of Birmingham and the riders were again arrested. The Interstate Commerce Commission (ICC) succumbed to the pressure and ruled segregation on interstate buses illegal.[11]

On April 12, 1963, the city newspaper in Birmingham, Alabama, published an open letter from eight white clergymen to King, who had recently been arrested for civil disobedience and was languishing in the city's jail. The eight called for patience and criticized King's actions as counterproductive. His response, known as "Letter from Birmingham Jail," remains one of his most powerful statements. "The judgment of God is upon the church as never before," he wrote. "If today's church does not recapture the sacrificial spirit of the early church, it will lose its authenticity, forfeit the loyalty of millions, and be dismissed as an irrelevant social club with no meaning for the twentieth century. Every day I meet young people whose disappointment with the church has turned into outright disgust."[12]

Reverend Dr. Edward V. Ramage, the pastor of First Presbyterian Church in Birmingham, Alabama, was one of the white pastors who had signed the open letter. When he read King's response, he was forever changed. According to the church's Web page,

> Dr. King's words had a strong effect on Dr. Ramage, who took the controversial step of declaring that FPC would be a church open to all of God's people, regardless of race. Though many members of [the] congregation were opposed to this idea, and he would eventually lose his job because of it, Dr. Ramage refused to back down, and his vision was ultimately affirmed by the Session. The prophetic nature of this call continues to shape our mission and ministry today.

At its 223rd General Assembly in St. Louis in 2018, the Presbyterian Church (U.S.A.) voted to begin the discernment process to place King's letter in its *Book of Confessions*.

The March on Washington

In 1963, a century after the Emancipation Proclamation, the life of the average Black American was marked by high unemployment, minimal wages, reduced mobility, and political disenfranchisement. The movement's leadership called for a national rally in Washington, DC. Talk of such a gathering was not new.

A. Philip Randolph canceled two threatened marches after political concessions, one from President Roosevelt and one from President Kennedy. But this march went forward. On August 28, 1963, the March on Washington for Jobs and Freedom demanded a comprehensive civil rights bill. On that day, a racially diverse crowd of 250,000 men, women, and children was electrified as speakers challenged America. The "I Have a Dream" speech by the Rev. Dr. Martin Luther King Jr. was a fitting climax to a day of peaceful protest. President Kennedy, skeptical before the Washington march, was extremely pleased and invited its leaders to the White House to discuss pending civil rights legislation. After the president was assassinated in November of that year, the March was credited with the passage of the Civil Rights Act of 1964 and the Voting Rights Act of 1965. After King was murdered on April 4, 1968, both houses of Congress passed the Fair Housing Act. President Johnson signed it into law as the last legislative achievement of the civil rights era.[13]

The "I Have a Dream" speech is closely associated with the March on Washington, but it has several versions. King gave a version in Rocky Mount, North Carolina, on November 27, 1962. There he spoke before 1,800 people in the Booker T. Washington High School gym. A recording of the speech was discovered in the local library by university professor Jason Miller. King told this audience,

> I have a dream that one day right here in Rocky Mount, the sons of former slaves and the sons of former slave owners will meet at the table of brotherhood, knowing that one God brought man to the face of the Earth. I have a dream tonight that one day my little daughter and my two sons will grow up in a world not conscious of the color of their skin, but only conscious of the fact that they are members of the human race.[14]

In Savannah, Georgia, Penn School on St. Helena Island was a regular retreat location for King and the movement. There he practiced and perfected the speech.[15]

A less recognized march, the Great Walk to Freedom, occurred in Detroit on June 23, 1963. Over 125,000 men and women, with King at the helm, marched to overcome racism in Detroit and the nation. King spoke at Cobo Arena and gave a shorter version of the "I Have a Dream" speech:

> I go back to the South not in despair . . . I go back believing that the new day is coming. And so this afternoon I have a dream. It is a dream deeply rooted in the American Dream. . . . I have a dream this afternoon that one day . . . right here in Detroit, Negroes will be able to buy a house, or rent a house, anywhere that their money will carry them, and they will be able to get a job. Yes, I have a dream this afternoon.[16]

Selma

In 1965, Alabama was rocked by a wave of highly publicized demonstrations. On March 7, six hundred demonstrators marched along Highway 80, intending to head from Selma to the state capital in Montgomery, fifty-four miles away. After crossing the Edmund Pettus Bridge, they were attacked by Alabama state troopers. Here's how John Lewis remembered the event:

> And we saw the state troopers and members of Sheriff Clark's posse on horseback. The troopers came toward us with billy clubs, tear gas, and bullwhips, trampling us with horses. I felt like it was the last demonstration, the last protest on my part, like I was going to take my last breath from the tear gas. I saw people rolling, heard people screaming and hollering. We couldn't go forward . . . so we were beaten back down the streets of Selma, back to the church.[17]

The attack, which was recorded by television news cameras, became known as Bloody Sunday.

The impact was immediate. Americans recoiled in horror as they watched the brutal beatings. On March 21, Martin Luther King Jr. led another march from Selma to Montgomery, in conjunction with demonstrations in eighty cities. A march that began with 3,300 marchers grew to more than 25,000 by the time they entered Montgomery four days later. In a televised address President Johnson challenged the nation to "overcome the crippling legacy of bigotry and injustice. . . . We Shall Overcome." Congress responded by passing the Voting Rights Act that August.[18]

But other marches led to different results. On June 6, 1966, James Meredith, the first Black student admitted to the University of Mississippi, set out on a solo March against Fear and Intimidation from Memphis, Tennessee, to Jackson, Mississippi. As he crossed the Mississippi state line, a bullet from a sniper's rifle stopped him, leaving him with serious injuries. King took up the march with SNCC leader Stokely Carmichael, who uttered the battle cry "Black Power." This was the beginning of a new and more radical part of the movement, as the younger generation of Blacks cried out, "What do you want? Black Power!"

Birth of the SCLC, SNCC, and CORE

Desiring to duplicate the success of the Montgomery Bus Boycott, movement leaders wanted to promote a nonviolent civil rights strategy. In 1957 the Southern Negro Leaders Conference on Transportation and Non-violent Integration came into being, electing King as its first president. Internal discussion associated the new organization with the Christian church, so the word *Christian* replaced *Negro*, creating the Southern Christian Leadership Conference (SCLC). King justified the decision at its initial conference: "This conference is called because we have no moral choice, before God, but to delve deeper into the struggle—and to do so with greter reliance on non-violence and with greater unity, coordination, sharing and Christian understanding."[19] It put forth a trinity of wants: white participation, resistance, and the recruitment of young radicals. A primary emphasis was the elimination of poverty through improved housing conditions and wage increase. It was the first body that openly encouraged whites to join in the cause of Black liberation.

Between 1961 and 1965, the SCLC was active in the movement's campaigns. Its first attempt to implement change in the desegregation of Albany, Georgia, met with failure. City officials refused to respond with brutality, which eliminated media coverage. Without outside pressure, the city also refused to respond to demands. The SCLC next targeted Birmingham, which was much more willing to respond with force. In 1963, Sheriff Eugene "Bull" Conner reacted to demonstrations with police dogs and fire hoses. With cameras rolling, all of America saw the brutality of southern racism as women were beaten with batons. SCLC cofounder Ralph Abernathy defiantly charged, "We are not afraid of the rain. We are not afraid of the water hoses. We are not afraid of the dogs. All of us have been sprinkled, poured, or baptized once before and we're willing to be baptized again, baptized by the city of Birmingham. . . . We will stick together."[20] President Kennedy, along with the entire nation, was repulsed and lobbied for the passage of what would become, after his death, the 1964 Civil Rights Act. The SCLC helped plan the 1963 March on Washington and in 1965 registered Black voters in Selma, Alabama. King's 1968 assassination dealt a near-fatal blow to the SCLC. His successor, Ralph Abernathy, could not generate the magnetism of King, and it lost much of its past prominence.

The Congress of Racial Equality (CORE) attracted young, vibrant leadership. CORE, created in 1942, became one of the most strategic arms of the civil rights movement. It played a pivotal role in the creation of Freedom Rides, Freedom Summer, and the 1963 March on Washington, and it significantly increased the number of field secretaries. On February 16, 1960, King, speaking at White Rock Baptist Church in Durham, North Carolina, attributed its effectiveness to "the fact that it was initiated, fed, and sustained by students."[21] James Farmer, co-founder of CORE, summarized its primary tactic as "advising your adversaries or the people in power just what you were going to do, when you were going to do it, and how you were going to do it, so that everything would be open and above board."[22]

The Student Nonviolent Coordinating Committee (SNCC) was the most radical of the civil rights organizations. SNCC's challenge was not just against the white power structure but contended with the movement's strat-egy as well. Young people were impatient with the slow pace of change and the movement's desire to avoid direct confrontation. They were the "shock troops of the revolution." They reoriented decision making from the bot-tom up rather than descending from the top brass. Leaders implemented Freedom Rides and voter-registration efforts and confronted King over com-promises made. In 1964 it assembled one thousand volunteers, mostly white college students, to infiltrate the state of Mississippi during Freedom Sum-mer. There they instituted Freedom Schools attended by both children and adults, with a strong focus on teaching Black history, civics, and African cul-ture. As the work increased, violence escalated in concurrence with decreased federal protection. That summer mobs in Mississippi destroyed thirty-seven churches and three dozen homes, and several businesses were bombed or set afire. Over one hundred volunteers were beaten and arrested. The bodies of Freedom Riders Andrew Goodman, James Chaney, and Michael Schwerner were discovered buried in a pile of dirt. The state of Mississippi condemned the civil rights workers while shielding those guilty of brutality, murder, and arson from prosecution.[23] It wasn't until 2005 that the state charged white supremacist Edgar Ray Killen with the killings. He was found guilty and died in prison in 2018.

Congress responded by passing the Voting Rights Bill of 1965. According to one historian,

> The Voting Rights Act of 1965 got its birth in Freedom Summer. It was signed in August of 1965, and one of the most important things it did was it abolished literacy tests, and it put voting in seven Southern states under federal supervision. And that above all else, the legacy of Freedom Summer, really, really changed American politics. By the end of 1965, 60 percent of Blacks in Mississippi were registered to vote.[24]

An outgrowth of the work of SNCC was the 1962 Council of Federated Orga-nizations (COFO), which supported Freedom Riders and increased voter reg-istration in Mississippi. SNCC energized it with new leadership, workers, and renewed purpose in Mississippi and Georgia. Fannie Lou Hamer and Carolyn Daniels proved invaluable. COFO registered 80,000 new voters in Freedom Registration.

In 1964, Fannie Lou Hamer, a field secretary for the SNCC, led a delega-tion called the Mississippi Freedom Democratic Party (MFDP) to the Demo-cratic Convention in Atlantic City, New Jersey, and challenged the seating of an all-white delegation. President Johnson lobbied the convention against the MFDP. They lost their bid and rejected the counteroffer of two delegates.

New Movements Emerge

In 1965 SNCC and the SCLC collaborated on the 54-mile march from Selma to Montgomery. After state troopers launched their vicious attack, tensions arose when the SNCC accused the SCLC of betrayal by negotiating a compromise with Alabama Governor George Wallace over the promise of a peaceful march, a compromise negotiated in their absence and without their opinion. The ruptured relationship led SNCC to commit to a new and more confrontational ideology of Black Power in 1966, a term coined by newly elected president Stokely Carmichael. It was first used by Richard Wright in his 1954 book *Black Power*, and later as a slogan by Carmichael. H. Rap Brown, even more radicalized than Carmichael, affirmed violence as intrinsic to the American way of life and a proper response to racism. Lowndes County, Alabama, was 80 percent Black, with not one being a registered voter. Carmichael and John Hulett created the Lowndes County Freedom Organization (LCFO) under the symbol of a black panther. This seed developed into the Black Panther Party for Self-Defense. (See pages 197–200 for further discussion of the Black Power movement.)

With the civil rights movement centered in the South, more radical leaders appeared in the North. Prominent among them was Malcolm X (1925–1965), born in Omaha, Nebraska, the son of a Baptist preacher. In prison he became a member of the Nation of Islam (NOI) under Elijah Muhammad. His voice was a strong one, denouncing racial violence and promoting the right of self-defense. He openly criticized King's leadership as illogical and suicidal in the face of mob hysteria. He articulated the anger of the masses and represented "Black manhood." For many Black Northerners, he was a more preferable leader than Martin Luther King Jr. in his stance endorsing the humanity of Black people and his rejection of nonviolent resistance. He grew disillusioned with the NOI and its leader Elijah Muhammad, and some in the NOI saw Malcolm X as a threat to Muhammad's leadership. He traveled throughout Africa, embracing Sunni Islam after completing the Hajj to Mecca. On return to the United States, he established the Organization of Afro-American Unity (OAAU) and made overtures to King to consider a working relationship. After repeated death threats he was assassinated in New York City in 1965 by members of the NOI.

To quote Juan Williams, "The Civil Rights Movement involved thousands of people, Black and white, young and old, who fought to make America live up to its promise of equality."[25] Between 1954 and 1965 the movement shocked, amazed, moved, and frightened the American public, especially white America. It was perhaps the bravest movement since the abolitionist movement hid enslaved men and women in the attics and basements of churches and homes at the risk of losing everything. The movement and its leaders were motivated by a desire to acquire the right of full citizenship; they demanded to be treated as human beings worthy of the right to vote. They simply wanted the rights due them and their children, without living under the threat of violence and intimidation. The change they were hoping for has been slow and incomplete in arriving, but through their efforts, change has come to America.

THE LEADERSHIP OF BLACK WOMEN

> I'd never related to the story of John Quincy Adams the way I did to that of Sojourner Truth, or been moved by Woodrow Wilson the way I was by Harriet Tubman. The struggles of Rosa Parks and Coretta Scott King were more familiar to me than those of Eleanor Roosevelt or Mamie Eisenhower. I carried their histories, along with those of my mother and grandmothers. None of these women could ever have imagined a life like the one I now had, but they'd trusted that their perseverance would yield something better, eventually, for someone like me. I wanted to show up in the world in a way that honored who they were.[26]
> —*Michelle Obama*, Becoming

In every movement for justice, the role of women has been unacknowledged, underrecognized, and underappreciated. They worked in hostile and racist environments as third-class citizens, bearing the burdens of sexism, racism, and classism. Black women put their lives on the line to the same degree as men, and many paid the ultimate price. The civil rights movement operated through the support of women who often put themselves second to the needs of their people. According to Gerda Lerner, in *Black Women in White America*,

> The Black woman's aim throughout her history in America has been for the survival of her family and of her race. . . . Black women, speaking with many voices and expressing many individual opinions, have been nearly unanimous in their insistence that their own emancipation cannot be separated from the emancipation of their men. Their liberation depends on the liberation of the race and the improvement of the life of the black community.[27]

Women faced discriminatory practices and contended with Black men who sought to subjugate, and at times, dominate their lives. The *Independent* newspaper printed the following moans of a southern domestic: "We poor Colored women wage-earners in the South are fighting a terrible battle. . . . On the one hand, we are assailed by white men, and, on the other hand, we are assailed by Black men, who should be our natural protectors."[28] The 1961 Freedom Riders, escorted from the Birmingham jail in the middle of the night, were abandoned on the road by Sheriff "Bull" Conner. They walked to the nearest home and were refused entry by an elderly man who answered the door. John Lewis recounted the incident: "We knocked on the door, said, 'We are the Freedom Riders. Please let us in.' He responded, 'Uh-uh, y'all can't come in here.'" Catherine Burks-Brooks remembered, "My mother had always told me that you need some help, then you try to talk to the lady of the house. And I said, 'Let's talk loud and wake up his wife.'" She came to the door and ushered them in, saying, "Y'all children, come on in."[29]

A major motivation for protest by Black women was the infliction of rape by white men who terrorized them without fear of reprisal. Slavery's finale was the continuance of rape by white men who did so without hesitation and without consequence. It was an instrument of terror intentionally inflicted to subdue the race, paralyze Black men into inaction, and minimize Black women. It was an act of double stigmatization. Black men were harmed psychologically by their inability to protect their mothers and wives; Black women had to live with the lifelong emotional and physical trauma of violence committed against them with little recourse. Rape was a crime committed by white men of every profession, both working-class and white-collar. Black women working as cooks and maids of middle-class families were viewed as prey. Women would be coerced in their employer's homes, while tending children in the park, anywhere they encountered white men. Walking alone down a dirt road could lead to a dangerous encounter. An anonymous nurse confided that she lost her job because she refused the advances of her "madam's husband." Her husband confronted the man, who then slapped him and had him arrested. In court the judge stated, "This court will never take the word of a n***** against the word of a white man." She testified that she was aware of fifty white men in her town who were raising two families; a white family in the "Big House" and a Black family in the "Little House."[30]

Protest actions preceding the civil rights movement targeted the incidence of rape in order to end its occurring across the South. Campaigns were launched through the 1950s and 1960s triggered by attacks on Black women. Author Danielle L. McGuire connected Black protest against rape with the birth of the civil rights movement. The 1944 rape of Recy Taylor in Abbeville, Alabama, and the follow-up investigation by NAACP activist Rosa Parks was a prime illustration of the resistance of Black women. The meeting between Recy Taylor and Rosa Parks led to the formation of the Committee for Equal Justice. With support from locals, Parks organized what the *Chicago Defender* described as the "strongest campaign for equal justice to be seen in a decade."[31]

Eleven years later this group became the Montgomery Improvement Association, responsible for the 1955 Montgomery bus boycott which birthed the civil rights movement. McGuire defined the movement's being nurtured by the continuing struggle to protect Black women from "sexualized violence and rape."[32] Mary Church Terrell spent her life as an advocate for gender equality—as a suffragist, activist, lecturer, and writer. She wrote in 1904,

> Throughout their entire period of bondage Colored women were debauched by their masters. From the day they were liberated to the present time, prepossessing young Colored girls have been considered the rightful prey of white gentlemen in the South, and they have been protected neither by public sentiment nor by law. . . . White men are neither punished for invading it, nor lynched for violating Colored women and girls.[33]

Her motto, "Lifting as We Climb," proclaimed her belief that the successful individual carried a responsibility to advance the race. Her amazing stamina enabled her to win the battle to desegregate Washington, DC's lunch counters.

From the first enslaved mother to today's sheroes, women have resisted victimization and labored to end violence and discrimination. Ida B. Wells publicly criticized the lynching of Black men on falsified charges of rape. This one-woman crusader and suffragist fought for justice through writing, lecturing, and organizing women. Ella Baker was a key figure in the formation of the Southern Christian Leadership Conference and helped establish the Student Nonviolent Coordinating Committee (SNCC) on the campus of Shaw University in Raleigh, North Carolina. Fannie Lou Hamer started the Mississippi Freedom Democratic Party and was instrumental in creating the 1971 National Women's Political Caucus. Her most famous phrase is "I am sick and tired of being sick and tired." She movingly testified before the Democratic National Convention in 1964, "I question America. Is this America? The land of the free and home of the brave? Where we have to sleep with our telephones off of the hook because our lives be threatened daily. Because we want to live as decent human beings in America."[34] Septima Poinsetta Clark, the "Mother of the Civil Rights Movement," crafted an innovative teaching paradigm that instructed illiterate adults to read, write, and count. Rosa Parks was the most widely recognized female personage in the movement for civil rights and revered as "the Mother of Freedom." Mahalia Jackson, widely respected for her decorum, grace, and intellect, was a spiritual powerhouse, and her voice renewed Dr. King's spirit.

There are more noteworthy Black women throughout American history than can be recounted. Special recognition is deserved for the women, mothers, daughters, aunts, nieces, and friends who fought an unending battle for the well-being of their children and men. Mothers who, by their spiritual and moral strength, inspired their daughters to resist. Women who endured Jim Crow, lynchings, rapes, fires, and bullets. Women who taught others how to survive and overcome.

YOUTH LEADERSHIP

We had on the first day over 500 students in front of Fisk University Chapel, to be transported downtown to the first Baptist Church, to be organized into small groups to go down to sit in at the lunch counters. We went into the five-and-tens—Woolworth, Kresge's, McClellan's—because these stores were known all across the South and for the most part all across the country. We took our seats in a very orderly, peaceful fashion. The students were dressed like they were on their way to church or going to a big social affair. They had their books, and we stayed there at the lunch counter, studying and preparing our homework, because we were denied service. The managers ordered that the lunch counters be closed, that the restaurants be closed, and we'd just sit there, all day long.[35]

—*John Lewis, on the sit-in movement*

In significant ways and at different times, young people have played a vital role in Black protest. Adults are often reticent in their recruitment, for no one wants to place their child in harm's way. But from the abolitionist movement to today, youth have refused to stay on the sidelines. Benjamin Quarles wrote of young, Black abolitionists,

Negroes of a tender age shared in the abolitionist crusade from the beginning. To enlist the sympathies and support of the children was an important phase of most of the reform movements in pre-Civil War America. "Our enterprise was a school for the young," wrote the editor of an abolitionist book for children. "The Slave's Friend," a monthly designed for juveniles and carrying pictures, hymns, and anecdotes, was distributed without charge.[36]

During the antebellum period, youth-led organizations fought for abolition. They maturely debated the hypocrisy of America as the "land of the free and home of the slave." In 1833 the Juvenile Garrison Independent Society of Boston sponsored antislavery lectures and rallies. They defined their mission as an end to racial hatred and the enslavement of Black people. Members paid four cents per meeting to raise funds for boys and girls between the ages of ten and twenty. Notable was the Pittsburgh Juvenile Anti-Slavery Society, formed on July 7, 1838, from the merger of four smaller associations in Pittsburgh, Troy, Carlisle, and Providence. They originated the "cent a week" fund-raising campaign. In 1834, a girls' abolitionist group in Providence, Rhode Island, sewed as they listened to the reading of antislavery pamphlets and newspapers. They sold their needlework to raise $90 for a local antislavery group. Students at the New York African Free School voted not to celebrate the Fourth of July until slavery ended and pledged to venture south once their classes were over to liberate their enslaved brethren.[37]

The experiences of parents who had escaped bondage informed the attitudes of their descendants. They were extremely empathetic concerning the well-being of enslaved family members. Many were aware that the freedom they enjoyed was not universal. They were mindful of an enslaver's willingness to sell relatives into the deep South before they could be rescued.

During the civil rights movement, the Children's Campaign involved the recruitment of children to participate in marches and risk arrest. It was highly effective. Parents sought to deny their children permission out of fear for their safety but were unable to prevent those who slipped away, marched, and withstood police brutality. They fearlessly faced adult dangers as police dogs attacked and fire hoses blasted skin off young backs. They were arrested and stuffed into police wagons, but each day they returned.[38]

Young adults made the Student Nonviolent Coordinating Committee (SNCC) the most impactful youth-led human rights organization. On May 2, 1963, high school and college students skipped school to meet at 16th Street Baptist Church in Birmingham, Alabama. They received civil disobedience training. As demonstrators peaceably marched downtown, hundreds were arrested. The following day "Bull" Conner ordered an attack with clubs, dogs, and fire hoses. The youth sustained severe injuries as the news media filmed the carnage. Negotiations ended the campaign when on May 10 city leaders agreed to desegregate all city facilities and businesses.

The sit-in movement was a brilliant tactic, used primarily by historically Black college and university (HBCU) students. Though they gained popularity in the 1950s, these actions began in 1939 and continued until 1964. Activists sought to desegregate public pools by refusing to vacate when ordered. A pool would have a "swim-in"; beaches, a "wade-in"; a "read-in" would flood libraries; and churches would be the site of a "pray-in."

On August 21, 1939, the first recorded sit-in occurred at a library in Alexandria, Virginia, led by attorney Samuel Wilbert Tucker. Chicago experienced a similar effort in 1943, followed by two in Baltimore, Maryland (1953 and 1955). The first by HBCU students occurred when Pauli Murray, a

Howard University law student, led undergraduates to participate in sit-ins in Washington, DC, in 1943 and 1944.[39] North Carolina Central University students sat-in at the Royal Ice Cream Parlor, led by the Rev. Douglas E. Moore on June 23, 1957. The Rev. King came to Durham the following week to participate only to find the parlor closed. He spoke at White Rock Baptist Church, where he proclaimed, "Fill up the jails." He issued a call for protesters to allow themselves to be arrested in such large numbers that it would clog up the system. In 1954, Reginald Hawkins successfully integrated the Charlotte airport restaurant when, after a sit-in, he lobbied federal oversight agencies, which resulted in the airport's desegregation. Sit-ins occurred in Wichita, Kansas; Oklahoma City, Oklahoma (1958); and Miami, Florida (1959). In 1961, nine Albany State College students held a sit-in at the bus terminal, which led to the Albany movement. In 1963, 1,600 people, including North Carolina Central University students, were arrested in Durham for participating in sit-ins at the city-owned Carolina Theater.[40]

On February 1, 1960, four North Carolina A&T University students received nationwide media coverage after their sit-in at the Greensboro Woolworth lunch counter. The "Greensboro Four" were David Richmond, Franklin McCain, Ezell Blair Jr. (later Jibreel Khazan), and Joe McNeil. Franklin McCain said, "Never request permission to start a revolution. We had talked to several students about this fractured and unequal democracy and what we wanted to do about it, and, quite honestly, most people thought we were crazy."[41]

By the month's end, thirty sit-ins occurred in seven states; by June, the number reached sixty-five. Students marched in front of Mayfair Cafeterias in Greensboro and New York. College students took actions considered radical at that moment in history. A high school in Charleston, South Carolina, Burke High School, and American Baptist Theological Seminary had student participation.[42] The "Chapel Hill 9" led sit-ins comprised of white and Black students.[43] Diane Nash reflected on her experience: "After we had started sitting in, we were surprised and delighted to hear reports of other cities joining in the sit-ins. And I think we started feeling the power of the idea whose time had come."[44]

By the end of 1960, more than 70,000 students had protested with their bodies, and 3,000 risked arrest. Many were beaten yet defiantly resisted. The High Point, North Carolina, Kress five-and-dime store removed the top of lunch-counter stools to deter their presence.[45] Three women conducted a read-in at the "white only" public library and were arrested in Jackson, Mississippi, in 1961. Students punched by locals were arrested by the police. Members of the Klan assaulted them on Ax-Handle Saturday in Jacksonville, Florida, on August 27, 1960. On that day, two hundred whites attacked protesters staging a sit-in at a local whites-only lunch counter.[46] John Lewis and James Bevel were sprayed with insecticide from a fumigating machine in Nashville after a sit-in there. Their actions moved the Tennessee city to become the first southern city to desegregate its lunch counters.[47]

Young people provided a much-needed lift to every justice movement for Black rights in the history of the nation. In each century, there was great uncertainty over their safety and whether their efforts would be successful. From the cry to end slavery to the fight for voting rights, the passion of youth has found a way to be involved. The sight of water cannons and police dogs attacking young people put a chill in the hearts of Americans not used to such sights. Their participation in past movements continues to inspire the involvement of youth in the twenty-first century as the march for justice continues.

MARTYRS OF THE CIVIL RIGHTS MOVEMENT

Lord, what have I done to deserve this?[48]
　　—*Ben Chester White, a martyr of the civil rights movement*

To be a Black activist in 1960s America was one of the most dangerous undertakings one could pursue. Between 1954 and 1968, it is impossible to estimate the number of men, women, and children brutalized in the quest for justice. The most famous killing, of course, was that of Martin Luther King Jr., assassinated on April 4, 1968, in Memphis, Tennessee, at the Lorraine Motel. Other victims' identities are known, but most simply disappeared in a day when it was life-threatening to be a Black woman or man with a voice.

Often there was no reason for these attacks other than a rabid hatred of Black people. Ben Chester White, a caretaker at a plantation with no prior involvement in civil rights, was apprehended and murdered in 1966.[49] His death served as a threat to local activists. In 1955, educators Harry and Harriette Moore were the only couple martyred during the movement, murdered on Christmas Day when a bomb exploded underneath their bedroom floor. On September 25, 1961, in Liberty, Mississippi, civil rights leader Herbert Lee was murdered in daylight in front of witnesses by a state legislator who claimed self-defense. A witness who refused to testify was shot the day he prepared to leave town to protect his life. On March 23, 1964, in Jacksonville, Florida, Johnnie Mae Chappell was murdered by white men looking to kill any Black person they encountered. Vernon Dahmer, his children, wife, and elderly aunt had their home set afire as shots peppered every room. One daughter was badly burned, and her father, Vernon, died twelve days later from injuries he sustained. In Natchez, Mississippi, in 1967, NAACP treasurer Wharlest Jackson was killed by a car bomb for accepting a promotion at his day job that was reserved for whites. Medgar Evers, director of the Mississippi NAACP, was murdered in Jackson, Mississippi, on June 12, 1963. He was shot outside of his home with his wife and children inside. They rushed out to find him dying in the driveway.[50]

Children were not exempt. On September 15, 1963, at 10:22 a.m., four girls, Addie Mae Collins, Cynthia Wesley, Carole Robertson, and Carol Denise McNair, were murdered by an explosion under the east steps of the 16th Street Baptist Church in Birmingham, Alabama. Three of the girls were fourteen; McNair was just eleven. Martin Luther King offered the sermon at three of the funerals. The blast injured fourteen adults while the younger sister of Addie Mae Collins, Sarah Collins, lost her right eye. The adult Collins lamented years later, "You go into church to praise God, and you come out without your sister."[51]

That same day two other teens were murdered in Birmingham: Virgil Ware was thirteen, and Johnny Robinson was sixteen.[52] While visiting his grandparents in Mississippi in 1955, fourteen-year-old Emmett Till was murdered by two white men who thought it honorable to kill a child for looking at a white woman. The boy was kidnapped by the woman's husband, tortured, and shot in the head. His body was chained to a cotton gin and thrown into the Tallahatchie River. When his body was discovered days later, it was mutilated beyond recognition. His mother held an open-casket funeral so that the world could see what they did to her son.[53] Professor Timothy B. Tyson investigated the murder in 2007 and revealed that Carolyn Bryant Donham, the white woman who testified in court that the young boy made lewd comments, confessed to him, "Nothing that boy did could ever justify what happened to him."[54]

Possibly the greatest injustice was the involvement of police officers in disappearances and murders. On February 26, 1965, in Marion, Alabama, Jimmie Lee Jackson and his family were attacked by state troopers who beat and shot Jackson as he tried to protect his grandfather and mother. On June 21, 1964, in Philadelphia, Mississippi, James Earl Chaney, Andrew Goodman, and Michael Henry Schwerner were arrested by a deputy sheriff and transferred to Klansmen. While searching for the young men, authorities discovered the bodies of civil rights workers Henry Hezekiah Dee and Charles Eddie Moore. Chaney, Goodman, and Schwerner were discovered buried nearby in an earthen dam. Black officers were not immune as targets for murder. The first Black police officers hired by the Bogalusa, Louisiana, Police Department, Oneal Moore and Creed Rogers, were fired upon by a car passing their cruiser. Rogers was wounded while Moore was killed.[55]

Churches and ministers were common targets. On May 7, 1955, in Belzoni, Mississippi, the Rev. George Lee dared to register himself and Black voters. He was shot in the face from a passing vehicle. College students were also victimized without leaving campus. On February 8, 1968, a South Carolina State University student demonstration to integrate the All Star Bowling Lane turned deadly. The governor ordered 150 state troopers, the National Guard, State Law Enforcement Division agents, and sheriff's deputies to the campus. Without warning, they opened fire and killed Samuel Ephesians Hammond Jr. (age nineteen), Delano Herman Middleton (seventeen), and Henry Ezekial Smith (twenty). Twenty-seven students were wounded in what came to be known as the Orangeburg Massacre.[56] In 1970, students at Jackson State College held a rally against white supremacy and the Vietnam War. The police fired thirty-five shotgun rounds and five military carbines, killing three students and wounding twelve. On January 3, 1966, in Tuskegee, Alabama, student Samuel Leamon Younge Jr. was fatally shot by a white gas-station owner following an argument over his segregated restroom.[57]

Whites engaged in the fight for civil rights were subjected to the same fate. Paul Guihard, William Moore, Juliette Hampton Morgan, Rev. Bruce Klunder, Andrew Goodman, Michael Schwerner, Rev. James Reeb, Jonathan Daniels, and the mother of five children, Viola Gregg Luizzo, were murder victims. Episcopal seminarian Jonathan Myrick Daniels stepped in front of a shotgun aimed at seventeen-year-old Ruby Sales and took the blast's full impact. Moved by his sacrifice, she spent the rest of her life as an advocate for justice. She founded Spirit House, which combines spirituality with advocacy.[58]

In each of these cases, the murders did not have the desired effect. Many of the men killed were veterans of the U.S. military, and their murders provided emotional motivation to the marches, voter registration, and acts of self-defense. Even civilians were incensed by the murder of men who had risked their lives to serve their country. Civil cases were filed on behalf of families. Ben Chester White's family was awarded one million dollars in damages from the Klan. Two thousand marched in Natchez, Mississippi, after the murder of Wharlest Jackson. The Black community, white businesses, and municipalities offered rewards. In Bogalusa, Louisiana, over one hundred marches were held after the murder of Clarence Triggs in 1966. In the late 1960s, convictions were won in the murders of Vernon Dahmer, Willie Brewster, and a few others. Tuskegee, Alabama, responded by integrating its hotels and restaurants and in 1967 elected Lucius Amerson as the first Black sheriff in the South since Reconstruction. In 1989 the Civil Rights Memorial was constructed in Montgomery, Alabama, by the Southern Poverty Law Center. It contains the names of forty martyrs imprinted on a circular, granite memorial. Words from Amos 5:24, uttered by Martin Luther King Jr., are inscribed, "We will not be satisfied until justice rolls down like waters and righteousness like a mighty stream."[59]

THE BLACK POWER MOVEMENT

We are never going to get caught up with questions about power. This country knows what power is and knows it very well. And knows what Black power is because it's deprived Black people of it for 400 years. So it knows what Black power is. But the question is, why do white people in this country associate Black power with violence? Because of their own inability to deal with blackness. If we have said Negro power, nobody would get scared. Everybody would support it. If we say power for Colored people, everybody would be for that. But it is the word Black, it is the word Black that bothers people in this country, and that's their problem, not mine.[60]
                                          —*Stokely Carmichael in 1966*

The Black Power movement signaled the closing out of the civil rights era. Black Power ideology demanded political equality partnered with economic self-sufficiency. SNCC chairman Stokely Carmichael popularized the slogan "Black Power" at a rally for the wounded James Meredith on June 16, 1966: "We been saying 'freedom' for six years. What we are going to start saying now is Black Power. We want Black Power! What do you want? Black Power!"[61] Black power promoted business ownership and political candidacy. It embodied a love of self and the right to defend families and neighbors. No longer would an inherently racist white culture be the model for Black self-improvement. Adherents wore traditional African clothing and hairstyles and stressed the beauty of dark skin, rejecting skin lighteners and hair straighteners. Youth asserted, "Black is beautiful" as they danced to James Brown's anthem "Say It Loud, I'm Black and I'm Proud!"

The demand for Black power has existed as long as there has been Black protest. The primary goal of collective empowerment can only be achieved by dismantling the white power structure. It mirrored pan-Africanism's goal of global unity for Black and African peoples. Early precursors of the pan-African movement date back to the nineteenth century in the defiant posture of Martin Delany, the fiery publisher of the Pittsburgh newspaper *The Mystery* (1843). He is affectionately referred to as "The Father of Black Nationalism" who coined the pan-African slogan "Africa for Africans."[62] William Monroe Trotter, one of the most fearless Black leaders of any century, founded the *Boston Guardian* newspaper with the following printed announcement: "We do for colored humanity what the world has conspired to deny us. We will not apologize, and we will not retreat—the *Guardian* makes itself responsible for our collective deliverance. None are free unless all are free." According to today's *Guardian*, he "invoked a black radical tradition rooted in eighteenth-century transatlantic slave rebellion and the militant abolition of African diasporic communities throughout the Americas."[63] Marcus Garvey built an empire on a call for unity and self-reliance. SNCC, CORE, Black Muslims, the Black Panther Party, Black Women's United Front, and the Nation of Islam approved a Black Power paradigm. Stokely Carmichael and Floyd McKissick mimicked the separatist teachings of Malcolm X and ousted whites from SNCC and CORE. Martin Luther King Jr. and the NAACP rejected the slogan "Black Power" as divisive and counterproductive, but by the early 1970s the NAACP and others began appropriating its energy and rhetoric.

Malcolm X solidified the Black Power movement as its most revered spokesman. He was a member of the Nation of Islam and personally mentored by Elijah Muhammad. He succinctly expressed the pent-up anger, frustration, and resentment of Afro-Americans. In contrast to King's redemptive suffering, Malcolm urged self-defense and liberation "by any means necessary." He argued that more was at stake than the right to sit in a restaurant or even vote—of utmost importance were identity, integrity, and self-respect. He called for the establishment of viable communities without the help of whites, constructed by Black people to address their problems. He stood at odds with the civil rights movement's leaders and referred to the March on Washington as "The Farce on Washington."

The most prominent nationalist movement has been that of the Nation of Islam. African slaves introduced Islam to the United States from the moment they first walked off of slave ships. In 1913 Islam gained its footing in America through the leadership of Noble Drew Ali when he founded the Moorish Science Temple in Newark, New Jersey. His ideology of Black nationalism and self-help was centered around the religious teachings of Islam. His follower, Wallace Fard, established the Nation of Islam (NOI) in Detroit on July 4, 1930. He urged Blacks to reject Christianity as the white man's religion and to convert to being a Muslim as a means of developing racial pride. Elijah Muhammad founded a mosque in Chicago and effectively proselytized Black men through a far-reaching prison ministry with an insistence on morality and self-determination. He taught empowering ethical disciplines such as abstaining from alcohol, pork, tobacco, and drugs. To reclaim their lost identity he encouraged adherents to drop their slave names and adopt the letter "X" as a last name. His son and successor, Wallace Mohammed, reverted to orthodox Islamic practices and formed the American Muslim Mission. In 1978, after Elijah Muhammad's death, Louis Farrakhan broke with Wallace and rebirthed the Nation of Islam. Farrakhan stressed the creation of Black-owned businesses, strict discipline, and self-control by the refusal to pollute one's body with alcohol, tobacco, and illegal drugs. He created the *Final Call* paper and called a million Black men to Washington, DC.[64]

On October 16, 1995, the Million Man March became the largest protest demonstration in the nation's history. Farrakhan and the NOI organized
the event, in which 1.2 million African American men gathered for a day
of speeches. Benjamin Chavis, Cornel West, Jesse Jackson, and Al Sharpton
lobbied months before the event encouraging attendance from around the
country. The rally was a call for Black men to recommit themselves to faith,
family, and service. A million men prayed, sang, and chanted for repentance
and solidarity. Louis Farrakhan gave the keynote speech:

> Abraham Lincoln saw in his day . . . what President Clinton sees in
> this day. He saw the great divide between Black and White. Abra-
> ham Lincoln and Bill Clinton see what the Kerner Commission
> saw 30 years ago when they said that this nation was moving toward
> two Americas—one Black, one White, separate and unequal. And
> the Kerner Commission revisited their findings 25 years later and
> saw that America was worse today than it was in the time of Martin
> Luther King Jr. There's still two Americas, one Black, one White,
> separate and unequal.[65]

In 1966 the Black Panther Party for Self-Defense was the brainchild of
Huey P. Newton and Bobby Seale in Oakland, California. Newton explained
the symbol: "We use the Black Panther as our symbol because the nature of
the panther, doesn't strike anyone, but when he's assailed upon he'll back
up first, but if the aggressor continues then he'll strike back."[66] The party
signaled that it was "the vanguard."[67] Its mission was protection from police
brutality as it patrolled neighborhoods and monitored activity. Armed citizen
patrols openly brandished weapons as members dressed in black berets and
black leather jackets. The party's Ten-Point Program demanded full employment, decent and affordable housing, political empowerment, the right to
protect oneself and one's community, an immediate end to police brutality, and the equal distribution of justice.[68] The Panthers demonstrated self-
reliance by assisting needy families, providing breakfast for school children
and family health clinics in thirteen locales. By 1968, they gained widespread
support in large urban areas in Los Angeles, Chicago, New York, and Philadelphia, boasting two thousand members. The FBI targeted the party and
fed the police misinformation, which led to shootouts, arrests, and murders.
Huey Newton was sentenced to prison; Eldridge Cleaver fled, and the Panther
21 arraigned for trial. Hoover admitted with satisfaction that the FBI pitted
party members against one another by an infiltration of spies. Fred Hampton
led a promising coalition between Latinos, poor whites, and Blacks until he
was murdered by the Chicago police, asleep in bed. Police infiltration and
internal conflict caused members to refocus on organizing. Seale gave a fitting
eulogy to the party: "If there's anything I can do that would truly progress the

people, let me know. I may not be a member of the Black Panther Party, but I will always be a Black Panther. All power to the people. Peace and freedom to the world."[69]

Although most of these movements no longer carry the same relevance as they did during the 1960s, most are still attracting the support of Black people, especially in urban communities. There has been a revival of the Black Panthers in the twenty-first century. The Nation of Islam is one of the largest Black Power organizations in the nation, with millions of Black men in their ranks. Their efforts to recruit Black men in prison have been highly success-ful. Despite the media perception that Muslims are of Arabic descent, many of the Muslims in America are African American.

INNER-CITY REBELLIONS

> You do not turn any society, however primitive it may be, upside-down with such a programme if you're not decided from the very beginning, that is to say from the actual formulation of the pro-gramme, to overcome all the obstacles that you will come across in so doing. The native who decides to put the programme into practice, and to become its moving force, is ready for violence at all times. From birth it is clear to him that this narrow world, strewn with prohibitions, can only be called in question by abso-lute violence.[70]
>
> —*Frantz Fanon*, The Wretched of the Earth

The Great Migrations concentrated a mass of Blacks into urban centers across the nation. Many were confined to highly segregated, densely packed, and depredated housing units, with limited economic possibilities and savaged by police brutality. With nowhere to go and little to lose, tempers erupted, and literal explosions followed.

During the 1960s, inner-city neighborhoods erupted in insurrections, or what many whites and the media referred to as urban riots. What appeared to some as lawlessness was at its core a rebellion against white supremacy. Much of it was outrage against the lack of improvement in living conditions, inadequate health care, political inequality, low wages combined with high unemployment, lack of affordable and livable housing, inequity in education, poverty, and police brutality. A specific incident would be the spark, but the root causes often resided in the horrid conditions of structural racism.

A series of racial rebellions burst forth in cities across the nation. David R. Francis wrote despairingly,

Any American of a certain age remembers the race-related riots that tore through numerous U.S. cities in the 1960s. Between 1964 and 1971, civil disturbances (as many as 700, by one count) resulted in large numbers of injuries, deaths, and arrests, as well as considerable property damage, concentrated in predominantly black areas. Although the United States has experienced race-related civil disturbances throughout its history, the 1960s events were unprecedented in their frequency and scope. The most deadly uprisings were in Detroit (1967), Los Angeles (1965), and Newark (1967). Measuring riot severity by also including arrests, injuries, and arson adds Washington (1968) to that list. Following the death of Martin Luther King in April 1968, the riots signaled the end of the carefully orchestrated, non-violent demonstrations of the early Civil Rights Movement.[71]

The Black mecca, Harlem, exploded in 1935, with another rebellion in 1964 following the murder of teenager James Powell by a white policeman. Rochester, New York, suffered under three days of unrest that same year, resulting in the deaths of three and 350 injured. In August of that same year, Black residents rebelled amid charges of constant police brutality and burned 225 stores in North Philadelphia, the Black section of the city. Similar outrage against police violence was the cause for violent protest in Jersey City and Elizabeth, New Jersey, that same summer.

Between 1965 and 1969 rebellions caused deaths and property damage in Cleveland (1966, 1968); Newark and Plainfield, New Jersey (1967); Detroit (1967); Minneapolis-Saint Paul (1967); Chicago (1968); Washington, DC (1968); Baltimore (1968); and North Omaha (1969). The most destructive was in Watts, Los Angeles, August 11–16, 1965. After the arrest of Marquette Frye and his mother, Rena, in which police struck Marquette in the face with a police baton, six days of shooting, burning, and looting led to the deaths of thirty-four persons. Only the unrest following the 1992 acquittal of the police officers videotaped beating motorist Rodney King caused greater destruction and loss of life (63 dead, 2,383 injured, and 12,000 arrested).[72]

The country's political leadership failed time and time again to address inequity adequately. Rather than reform, the system condemned communities of color as lawless and implemented punitive criminal-justice retributions. White-owned businesses fled the inner city with few investors to take their place. Conservative lawmakers preyed on inner cities as a part of political speeches and platforms while uttering fake platitudes of keeping Americans safe. The Nixon administration used the Law Enforcement Assistance Administration to militarize local police stations, providing riot gear, automatic weapons, and armored vehicles. Liberal politicians turned away from employment and education programs to implement temporary fixes, such as welfare, for long-term problems.

BLACK FREEDOM FIGHTERS

Charles Sims is the Black man who won't turn the other cheek. He
preaches, instead, the art of self-defense.[73]

—*The Harvard Crimson*

Just as the Black Power movement rejected the methods of King, they also
dismissed peaceful tactics. They saluted Malcolm X's motif of self-defense
and resolved that nonviolence was not applicable nor reasonable in the face
of racial violence. As Malcolm X said, "Be peaceful, be courteous, obey the
law, respect everyone, but if someone puts his hands on you, send him to
the cemetery."[74] Veterans of past wars received weapons training and were
familiar with paramilitary campaigns. They relied on battlefield maneuvers to
confront local situations when legal means failed. They supervised the protection of local communities when authorities failed.

From the earliest insurrections to the turmoil of the 1960s, fighting back
was favored over noble suffering. Veterans used war techniques to battle
racists aimed at destroying lives and property. Men and women stockpiled
weapons and defended themselves in Wilmington, North Carolina (1898);
Evansville, Indiana (1903); Atlanta (1906); and Springfield, Illinois (1908).
Red Summer would have been even more catastrophic if armed and trained
Black WWI veterans did not disperse mobs intent on taking life.[75]

Robert F. Williams was born on February 26, 1925, in Monroe, North Carolina. After serving a term in the Marines, he returned to Monroe and joined the
civil rights movement as the local NAACP president. The Klan had targeted
the NAACP and decimated its ranks. But under his leadership, the Monroe
branch grew from six to over two hundred members. He joined the National
Rifle Association (NRA) and formed a regiment called the Black Guard for the
protection of Black people in Monroe. Under the umbrella of the NAACP he
trained members how to use firearms and dispel attacks. He gave protection to
those whom law enforcement failed to protect. He justified his stance by saying that the only way to combat the violence of racists was to "meet violence
with violence."[76] James Forman wrote in *The Making of Black Revolutionaries* of
Williams's legendary statement: "Since the federal government will not bring
a halt to lynching in the South, and since the so-called courts lynch our people
legally, if it's necessary to stop lynching with lynching, then we must be willing
to resort to that method. We must meet violence with violence."[77]

Maxwell Curtis Stanford Jr., Wanda Marshall, and Donald Freeman created the Revolutionary Action Movement (RAM) in 1962 in Philadelphia.
RAM adapted Maoism, Black nationalism, and Third World liberation

ideologies into political strategy and urged Blacks to defend themselves. Between 1964 and 1968 Stanford was under constant FBI surveillance. In 1966 he and fifteen others were arrested in New York City under the suspicion of planning to assassinate Roy Wilkins (NAACP) and Whitney Young (Urban League). Acquitted, he returned to Philadelphia to establish the Black Guards. In 1967 he and thirty-five other RAM members were arrested on the charge of plotting to start a race riot. He dissolved RAM in 1968, converted to Islam, and changed his name to Muhammad Ahmad.[78]

Life in Jonesboro, Louisiana, in 1964 was a terrifying experience for people denied basic public services and disenfranchised by society. The postal service openly refused to deliver mail to Black residents in Bogalusa. The Klan threatened, beat, and murdered innocents as state and federal authorities did nothing. Local World War II and Korean War veterans mobilized to teach self-defense techniques. On July 10, 1964, Earnest "Chilly Willy" Thomas, Frederick Douglass Kirkpatrick, and others organized the Deacons for Defense and Justice. These army veterans listened to police scanners, intercepted Klan communications, and rushed to areas of conflict. Their presence had an immediate impact as they patrolled so efficiently that the Klan presence ceased. Deacon Charles Sims told the *Harvard Crimson*, "'We might not have organized the Deacons if [Attorney General] Katzenbach had sent troops to Bogalusa when they were needed. . . . There's gotta be law. I'd like to take a rest, but the police won't let me. . . . I'm just doing the job no one else will do.'"[79]

On May 7, 1970, Robert Teel and his two sons murdered a Black veteran named Henry Marrow in Oxford, North Carolina. The Black community exploded as citizens capitulated to internalized rage. Marchers processed from Marrow's gravesite to the county courthouse for a rally in front of the city's Confederate monument. Public protest had little impact as an all-white jury acquitted the Teels. Black veterans responded with a military operation in downtown Oxford. White-owned businesses were set afire, targeting tobacco warehouses, symbols of the Jim Crow sharecropping system. Damages exceeded one million dollars. Historian Timothy B. Tyson, a native of Oxford, reported, "The mob had destroyed seventeen storefronts, firebombed four buildings, ransacked the grocery store, smashed a police car, and scared the hell out of most of the white people in Oxford, and some of the Black ones, too."[80]

Section 5

Protest in a Rapidly Changing World

African American Protest: 1988–2020

> Black is a color. . . . We built the country through the African slave trade. African-American acknowledges that any term that emphasizes color and not the heritage separates us from our heritage.[1]
> —*John Eligon*

> The 1960's affected large numbers of Black Americans whose lives will be filled with Black concerns, which will include, to some degree, an intense interest in what happens in Africa.[2]
> —*Roger Wilkins*

African American protest during the late twentieth and early twenty-first centuries represents Black protest going mainstream. Its impact is seen in the fact that celebrities have adopted the position that speaking out is a part of the Black experience. They challenge one another to "wake up" and get in the struggle. It has influenced the perspectives of young, white Americans who unashamedly hold up Black Lives Matter banners and challenge their parents' generation by stating that "Silence Equals Complicity." Black activists have appropriated some of the best features of past efforts at protest. Like the first enslaved Africans, they are not ashamed of a connection to the motherland. Entrepreneurs and politicians search for ways to do business with African nations. Civil rights slogans such as "Black Power" and "Black is Beautiful," while not always quoted directly, are represented in the statements, poetry, and lyrics put forth. This new generation of Black leaders openly discusses what it means to be Black in America, criticizes cultural appropriation, and tweets such as "#OscarsSoWhite." A real measure of distinction for this generation is its move away from the Black church, as members and in protest. Ministers are not looked on as the natural leaders for the community any more, and many don't even collaborate with clergy in the planning of events. Many question the relevance of Black clergy, who rarely speak out on issues of racial injustice, police shootings, or LGBTQIA+ (an inclusive acronym covering people of all genders and sexualities, such as lesbian, gay, bisexual, transgender, questioning, queer, intersex, asexual, pansexual, and allies) issues.

The post–civil rights movement brought about the most rapidly implemented political and social change in the history of the United States. The last half of the twentieth century presented a remarkable transitional period in American history wherein the United States began the transformation from a nation affirming white superiority to one issuing a repudiation of white supremacy. While almost a century separated the two, the 1960s movement was a fight to recapture rights originally gained during Reconstruction yet eliminated by discriminatory laws and policies. The civil rights legislation of the 1960s restored the intent of Reconstruction legislation. The passage of the Voting Rights Act of 1965 restored rights ensured by the Fifteenth Amendment (1870) that had been nullified by literacy tests and grandfather clauses.[3]

The shifting landscape in the country provoked an identity shift. During the 1990s, people of African descent assumed the title of African American, epitomizing the final shift. *Black* epitomized race whereas *African American* exemplified cultural heritage and biology. *African American* is generally assumed to be of recent origin, but as early as 1782, it was printed on a political pamphlet, *A Sermon on the Capture of Lord Cornwallis*, written by an anonymous "African American."[4] In 1988, Rev. Jesse Jackson assumed the mantle in the first public call to use this title, lobbying during a press conference for the adoption of *African American*. Arthur Ashe titled his 1988 book *A Hard Road to Glory: A History of the African American Athlete*. When asked about the title, he responded, "It was given a great deal of thought; it was definitely not going to be 'Black.' 'African-American' is much more appropriate and correct than 'Afro-American' or 'Black' or any other alternative. And I didn't want to leave the wrong impression with something so permanent as a book."[5]

Scholars prefer the term *African American* in written presentations and oral expressions. Institutions responded by implementing name changes as the Association for the Study of Negro Life and History became the Association for the Study of African American Life and History. *The Journal of Negro History* became *The Journal of African American History*. Since the 2010 Census, persons of African descent have been given the choice of "Negro," "Black," or "African American."

However, for many persons of African descent, they are Black, period. *Afro-American* had no real staying power, and it could be argued that *Black* never went out of use. Academics and political leaders use *African American* while the masses retain loyalty to *Black*. Research has indicated that about half prefer *Black* while the other half prefer *African American*, but most take no offense at either. Those with higher levels of education had a preference for *African American*. Members of the hip-hop community were part of the self-examination,

> It was all part of us searching for our identity as people of color, as Black and Latino people. Who are we really, you know? It wasn't enough for us to have our own culture, called hip-hop. We're like, "Wait a minute? Why don't we embrace where we came from?" You know what I mean? You started hearing a lot about Africa. I wore my African medallions. Many of us took African or Islamic names. We embraced it, and it was beautiful. It was powerful man.[6]

THE AFRICAN AMERICAN POLITICAL RENAISSANCE

> In 1965, there were no Black U.S. senators or governors, and only five members of the House of Representatives were Black. As of 2021, there is greater representation in some areas—57 House members in the new Congress are Black (not including nonvoting delegates and commissioners), putting the share of Black House members (13%) about on par with the share of the overall U.S. population that is Black.[7]

The aftermath of the civil rights movement has been considered a continuation of Reconstruction, Second Reconstruction, or Reconstruction 2.0. The U.S. House of Representatives summarized the period: "During the period from the end of World War II until the late 1960s, often referred to as America's 'Second Reconstruction,' the nation began to correct civil and human rights abuses that had lingered in American society for a century."[8] "A grassroots civil rights movement coupled with gradual but progressive actions by Presidents, the federal courts, and Congress eventually provided more complete political rights for African Americans and began to redress longstanding economic and social inequities. While African-American Members of Congress from this era played prominent roles in advocating for reform, it was largely the efforts of everyday Americans who protested segregation that prodded a reluctant Congress to pass landmark civil rights legislation in the 1960s."[9]

Connecting this period historically with the first Reconstruction was the short-lived governmental policy called affirmative action. It was an attempt to even the playing field for African American entry into prohibited professions.

First uttered by President John F. Kennedy in his 1961 Executive Order 10925, it committed the federal government to the increased hiring of African Americans. Government contractors were to "take affirmative action to ensure that applicants are employed, and employees are treated during employment, without regard to their race, creed, color, or national origin."[10] Colleges and universities affirmed policies to increase diversity among students and staff. Programs increased opportunities for people of color and white women to gain access to employment, university admission, and government contracts previously denied. Priority was by race, disability, gender, ethnic origin, and age. Millions took advantage as those who possessed the required credentials were able to enter fields previously reserved exclusively for white men. Employment was based on merit as applicants had to apply based on the same criteria as others. There was wider consideration in fields where race previously prevented even an interview. Once hired, entrants kept their jobs through competence even when their colleagues did not welcome them.

Politically, African Americans worked hard to regain political rights lost when Reconstruction ended. With amazing alacrity, there was an increase in the number daring to run for elected office and in the number of positions won. No politician was as intelligent, savvy, competent, compassionate, shrewd, or as Machiavellian as the Rev. Adam Clayton Powell Jr., the pastor of Harlem's Abyssinian Baptist Church. He became the first of his race to serve as a member of the New York city council. He advanced to the House of Representatives in 1944 and described himself as "the first bad n***** in Congress." He scripted bills criminalizing lynching, poll taxes, and religious and gender bias. He lobbed so many antidiscrimination measures that his bills were known as "The Powell Amendments." As the House Education and Labor Committee's senior member and chair, he promoted an increase in the minimum wage, school construction, and senior citizen and job programs. He often stood alone, ostracized and defiant.

In 1971 there were only eight African American mayors governing U.S. cities. By 1979 the number had increased to 135, and by the 1990s there were 340. Carl Stokes was the first to be elected when he won in Cleveland, Ohio, in 1967. On May 6, 1969, Howard N. Lee became the first African American elected as mayor of a white southern town since the end of Reconstruction, in Chapel Hill, North Carolina. In 1973, Coleman Young became the mayor of Detroit, Michigan, coinciding with Thomas Bradley in Los Angeles. In 1979, Richard Arrington Jr. was elected mayor in Birmingham, Alabama. Victories continued as Harold Washington (Chicago, 1983), Wilson Goode (Philadelphia, 1984), David Dinkins (New York, 1989), and Norman Rice (Seattle, 1989) won political office. Sharon Pratt Kelly was elected the first female mayor of a major U.S. city when elected in Washington, DC, in 1991. Freeman R.

Bosley Jr. won in St. Louis in 1993. Willie Brown was elected the first African American speaker of the California State Assembly and, in 1996, became mayor of San Francisco. In 1978, Mervyn Dymally became the lieutenant governor of California, and in 1989 L. Douglas Wilder was elected governor of the Commonwealth of Virginia.

African American members of Congress accelerated from fourteen in 1972 to forty by 1997. Oscar De Priest was the first man of color elected to Congress in the twentieth century (1919–1935). In 1968, New York Democrat Shirley Chisholm became the first African American woman elected to the House of Representatives, and in 1972 she was the first to run for president representing a major political party. Kweisi Mfume won five terms in the House of Representatives between 1987 and 1996, serving Maryland, and won again in 2020, replacing the late Elijah Cummings. In 1992 Carol Mosley Braun won as the first African American woman elected to the U.S. Senate, and Eva Clayton became the first elected to Congress from North Carolina. In 1996 Alma Adams followed in the Tarheel State. Barbara Jordan and Andrew Young were the first Southerners elected since Reconstruction. Tim Scott of South Carolina was the first African American elected to both houses of Congress. Jesse Jackson put up astounding numbers in his run for president in 1984 and 1988. In 2008 Barack Obama was elected the 44th president of the United States and was reelected in 2012.

Among Blacks, holding political office is viewed as a valued position for status and an opportunity for advancement for the race; 40 percent responded affirmatively to this belief in a 2020 Pew Research poll. The election of Kamala Harris as Joe Biden's vice president was provided as evidence of racial progress. This is not soon to dissipate as record numbers of Blacks participated in 2020 voter registration efforts, with growing percentages voting in elections. Their political strength provided the electoral college victory in Georgia that lifted Joe Biden to the presidency. Their impact was reaffirmed by the election of two Democratic senators in the state of Georgia when the Rev. Raphael Warnock was elected as Georgia's first Black senator. It is ironic that this is the same district that gave the world the Drum Major for Justice, the Rev. Dr. Martin Luther King Jr., who gave his life in the battle for the right of Blacks to vote.

THE AFRICAN AMERICAN VOTE

For all the strategic calculations, sophisticated voter targeting and relentless talk about electability in Iowa and New Hampshire, the Democratic presidential nomination will be determined by a decidedly different group: Black voters. African Americans will watch as mostly white voters in the first two contests express preferences and winnow the field—then they will almost certainly anoint the winner.[11]

For African Americans, the vote is the most revered of all citizenship rights, and its sacredness has passed down from generation to generation. Youth echo their elders when they make mention of the deaths of many who died acquiring the right to vote. Julian Bond reflected on his experience during the 1964 Freedom Summer: "When we began to go to Mississippi, the Black people we met there were not interested in lunch counters. They weren't interested in sitting in the front of the bus. There were no lunch counters. There were no buses. They wanted to vote."[12] Colin Kaepernick did not vote in the 2016 election and received immediate backlash from critics, especially commentator Stephen A. Smith:

> Him of all people, because of the position he took, because of the attention he brought to the issues. The fact that you don't even have the decency to go to the polls and activate yourself in this election. . . . I don't want to hear another word from Colin Kaepernick. It's a waste of time. . . . Because for him not to vote, as far as I'm concerned, everything he said meant absolutely nothing.[13]

That's how important voting is to African Americans.

Beginning in the decade of Reconstruction and with a restart in the 1970s, African Americans' voting power has either been a sought-after prize or a target of suppression. For many, it meant death even to dare to attempt to register. African Americans have sided with the Democratic Party since the days of President Franklin D. Roosevelt, marking a departure from the Republican Party of Abraham Lincoln. While not receiving all of the benefits of the New Deal, it was deemed a better deal than any offered by the Republicans. Eleanor Roosevelt's influence on her husband's policies was tremendous and did not escape notice. Blacks tend to vote in bulk for one party, which has been beneficial as their preference can decide who wins an election. Faced with Republicans who voice opposition to their political and social positions, they rallied for Democrats. According to Professor David Lublin,

> African-Americans overwhelmingly choose to participate in Democratic primaries and can dominate them in many majority-white districts because so many whites now vote in Republican primaries. Whites still form a majority in the general election, but Black Democratic nominees can usually retain enough white Democratic support to carry these majority-white districts with sizable Black minorities.

The defection of many white Southerners to the GOP has left Blacks in the cockpit in selected majority-white districts.[14]

The Black vote in South Carolina, followed by Georgia, Alabama, and Virginia, can make a Democratic presidential candidate a frontrunner. A June 2019 article in the *New York Times* reported that "the pursuit of African-American support in 2020 will be far more competitive than in 2016 and 2008. Hillary Clinton and Barack Obama won more than 80 percent of the Black vote in the South Carolina primary, and were propelled to the nomination largely because African-Americans in subsequent states mirrored their counterparts here."[15] In 2020 presidential candidate Joe Biden assumed frontrunner status after Blacks in South Carolina gave him his first win and the primary. Biden attributed his becoming the Democratic candidate to the Black vote. African American women have become a substantial voting bloc. Their vote won a senatorial seat in red-state Alabama for Democrat Doug Jones and gave a considerable boost to the campaigns of Stacey Abrams (Georgia) and Andrew Gillum (Florida). It led to no small degree to Biden's selection of Kamala Harris as his vice president.

In the twenty-first century, Republicans during the George W. Bush administration vocalized a desire to attract more people of color, especially African Americans. That forsaken effort has been exchanged for voter suppression, especially in the South. The Supreme Court's 2013 *Shelby County v. Holder* ruling eliminated preclearance, which had meant that southern states had to receive permission from the U.S. Attorney General before passing new voting legislation. The result was a burst of voter-suppression legislation that targeted African Americans. A voter-suppression bill signed into law by the Republican governor resulted in a lawsuit filed by the North Carolina NAACP. The 4th Circuit Court overturned the ruling stating that the legislation was to "target African Americans with almost surgical precision." Strangely drawn maps from 2010 diluted voting potency. Spiraling districts packed voters into one or two regions to weaken their impact in majority-white districts. Dilution removed the effectiveness of bloc voting in closely run races where the white vote split. The aftermath of the election of Joe Biden as president and Kamala Harris as vice president saw the introduction of over twenty new laws in forty-three states placing restrictions on the ability to vote. Georgia Republicans, after losing two Senate races, passed a highly criticized bill that affected almost every aspect of voting—from absentee ballots to voter ID cards and ballot drop boxes. Many of the elements of the bill targeted means used by Black voters.

Michelle Alexander argued persuasively that the loss of the ability to vote by people convicted of felonies disproportionately strips African American men of their voting rights. "Particularly for Black folks and poor folks of color," she wrote, "once you're saddled with a criminal record, you are stripped of the very rights supposedly won in the Civil Rights Movement, like the right to vote, the right to serve on juries, the right to be free of legal discrimination, employment, housing, access to education— basic public benefits. You really are relegated to a permanent second-class status."[16]

AFRICAN AMERICAN LITERATURE AS PROTEST

It was a seed time of diverse beginnings and internal debates in the Black communities, resurgent Black nationalism, burgeoning revolutionary impulses, a critical examination of the meaning and value of old concepts of "integration" as contrasted with the rising emphasis on self-determination and Black power. It was a time of discussions on the relationship between racial oppression and class oppression, of explorations of the relationships between the Black movements and Black consciousness in the United States and the Third World anti-colonialist aspirations and the areas of common interest of oppressed peoples and groups everywhere.[17]

The 1970s saw an explosion of creative artistry by Black artists reminiscent of the Harlem Renaissance, but one that was far more expansive. This artistic outpouring could be considered Harlem Renaissance 2.0, but it extended beyond literature, dance, and music to sports, theater, and the big screen. From the 1970s into the twenty-first century, African American artists excelled in every field of entertainment and athletics.

Literature kicked off this secondary renaissance as African American writers received unprecedented opportunities for publication. Since the release of *An Evening Thought: Salvation by Christ with Penitential Cries* (1711) by Jupiter Hammon and Phillis Wheatley's *Poems on Various Subjects, Religious and Moral* (1773), African American writers had little opportunity to be published. Not even during the Harlem Renaissance were publishing companies willing to published acclaimed writers. Writers Claude McKay (*Home to Harlem*, 1928); Richard Wright (*Native Son*, 1940); Gwendolyn Brooks (*Annie Allen*, 1950); Ralph Ellison (*Invisible Man*, 1952); and James Baldwin (*Go Tell it on the Mountain*, 1953) helped inaugurate a new era as Black writers were considered marketable. Alex Haley received critical acclaim for *The Autobiography of Malcolm X* in 1965 and his 1976 epic *Roots: The Saga of an American Family*.[18] One hundred thirty million viewers watched the 1977 ABC miniseries based on the book.

Black women writers were so productive that the 1970s were labeled the "Black Women's Literary Renaissance." Gwendolyn Brooks was the first to win a Pulitzer Prize in 1950. Maya Angelou wrote descriptively on what it meant to be an African American woman in *I Know Why the Caged Bird Sings* (1969), *And Still I Rise* (1978), and *Phenomenal Woman* (1995). Before her career was over, she wrote seven autobiographies, several books of poetry and essays, plays, and movie and television scripts and was appointed poet laureate by President Bill Clinton. In 1982, Alice Walker wrote *The Color Purple*, which won a Pulitzer Prize in 1983. In 1987, Toni Morrison startled the sensibilities of American readers by retelling the story of Margaret Garner in her novel *Beloved*. She was awarded a Pulitzer Prize for Literature (1988) and a National Book Critics Circle Award for *Song of Solomon*, and she was the first Black woman to win a Nobel Prize for Literature (1993).[19]

August Wilson was the most acclaimed and prolific dramatist of the past century. His series of highly acclaimed, prize-winning plays chronicled Black life one decade at a time: *Gem of the Ocean* (1900s), *Joe Turner's Come and Gone* (1910s), *Ma Rainey's Black Bottom* (1920s), *The Piano Lesson* (1930s), *Seven Guitars* (1940s), *Fences* (1950s), *Two Trains Running* (1960s), *Jitney!* (1970s), *King Hedley II* (1980s), and *Radio Golf* (1990s). *Fences* and *The Piano Lesson* received Pulitzer Prizes.[20] Other authors explored fiction, history, criminal justice, political science, and science fiction. Pulitzer Prizes were awarded to Charles Gordone for *No Place to Be Somebody* (1969) and to Charles H. Fuller Jr. for *A Soldier's Play*. Tony Awards went to Joseph A. Walker for *The River Niger* (1972) and to director George Wolfe for *The Colored Museum*. Terry McMillan's book *Waiting to Exhale* was translated into a movie and won an NAACP Image Award. Toni Morrison urged, "If there's a book that you want to read, but it hasn't been written yet, then you must write it."[21]

A theological sea change occurred when the Rev. Dr. James Cone wrote his precedent-setting books *Black Theology and Black Power* (1969) and *A Black Theology of Liberation* (1970).[22] He inaugurated Black liberation theology and is referred to as the Father of Black Theology. He interjected the Black church's prophetic voice into mainline Christian doctrine and introduced a God who identified with the struggles of oppressed people. His biblical dogma represented a radical departure from the theology of the white church, which projected grace and faith as the essential tenets of Christianity and was either silent or openly defensive of slavery, Jim Crow, and white supremacy. Black theology propounded that a dark child was in God's image and likeness and represented purity and cleanliness. Black theology influenced the Protestant church to prioritize social justice and thrust the church's prophetic witness against racism to the forefront.

AFRICAN AMERICAN FILM AS PROTEST

The picture's final shot is of Shaft walking alone down the street, offering a bookend of sorts with the walk he took over the opening credits. On that earlier stroll, he passes movie marquees boasting names like Robert Redford and Dean Martin. Shaft saunters right on by, leaving such square stars behind. He's taking us into a whole new era.[23]

Blacks have always loved cinema but seldom felt embraced by the negative images of themselves portrayed on the screen. Their participation would not only fulfill professional dreams but also destroy caricatures and combat racist imagery. It took tremendous resources to create films, and few had the revenue to finance projects. Whites were reluctant to cast Blacks in movies, fearing they would endure backlash from white society. Blacks in the earliest movies were criticized by their own community for accepting stereotypical roles. They were limited to playing the simpleton, the tragic mulatto, mammy, the Black brute, and Uncle Tom, and it took patience and determined effort to enter a profession slow to change. It is remarkable that there was any Black presence in film, but actors were determined to enter the industry despite the difficulty and hardship experienced.

The Black presence in cinema dates back to 1877 with a short film of a Black jockey riding a racehorse. Thomas Edison was an early experimenter in films and depicted Black soldiers in battle in the Spanish-American War. The first Black director was Oscar Micheaux, a maker of silent movies and then talkies. Between 1918 and 1951, he compiled a library of films that he wrote, acted in, and directed. Secondary to making movies, he wanted to destroy racial stereotyping of Black people. One of his protégés was a young Paul Robeson, who would go on to become a famous actor, musician, and civil rights activist. The first three decades of the twentieth century provided few roles outside of vaudeville and blackface. The forties and fifties introduced Black faces on camera, but most were shown as domestics in demeaning positions. Black actors did their best to limit the number of derisive roles accepted, but opportunities were few and far between. Breakout performances occurred during the 1950s as Nat "King" Cole, Paul Robeson, Woody Strode, Lena Horne, and Dorothy Dandridge made way for Bill Cosby, Greg Morris, Diahann Carroll, and Sidney Poitier to achieve celebrity status.[24]

"Blaxploitation" movies were Black-themed movies with Black stars that captured the heart and hard-earned dollars of African American moviegoers during the seventies. They were labeled "Blaxploitation" by Junius Griffin, president of the Beverly Hills chapter of the NAACP, as a criticism of the genre. More than two hundred films blasted their way onto theater screens. While the vast majority were action films (e.g., *Shaft*, 1971), subgenres ran the gamut from drama (*Sounder*, 1972) to horror (*Blacula*, 1972), westerns (*Buck and the Preacher*, 1972), comedy (*Watermelon Man*, 1970), tragedy, historical fiction, and sports.

African Americans flocked to movie theaters and waited anxiously for the next to arrive. Dr. Henry Louis Gates reflected in his memoir, "Politics aside, though, we were starved for images of ourselves and searched TV to find them."[25] These were the first large-scale productions with depictions of African Americans in starring roles other than a maid or clown. Never before in cinematic history had the industry presented Black actors as protagonists and antagonists. These were no buffoonery, blackface, or minstrel shows. They were films with confident Black men (and occasionally women, notably Pam Grier) taking control of their destinies. MGM marketed *Shaft* as "a hard and handsome breed of Black man spawned amongst the violence and danger of the innards of Harlem in which he now moves with self-assured ease. He's also a cat who moves easily in 'Whitey's trough.'"[26] A memorable line from the movie was, "When you lead your revolution, whitey better be standing still because you don't run worth a damn no more." Most were low budget but contained messages that resonated with audiences. They personified a moral confrontation between good and evil. Screen protagonists were everyday people fighting against an unjust system. Black heroes stood up on behalf of Black people and fought back against whitey. African Americans stood, clapped, laughed, and shouted acclaim. Audiences cheered when Pam Grier shot white men in the groin in symbolic revenge for those previously violated. Richard Roundtree, who achieved stardom as the title character in *Shaft*, reflected in 2000, "Timing is everything and at the time, there was a need for a hero with my paint job. Shaft didn't take guff from anyone, and that's what made it work."[27]

But not all cheered, including Jesse Jackson, who criticized the genre as portraying Black people negatively. He and others complained that drug dealers (*Superfly*), pimps, and prostitutes did not represent the complexity of Black life and that movie studios pimped the African American community as a source of revenue. Many were highly profitable, as *Shaft*, produced for $500,000, grossed $13 million for MGM, saving the company. Huge profit margins awakened Hollywood to the ticket-buying power of Black audiences. The period ended, however, not because of Black audiences but, as usual, because Hollywood turned its back on Black cinema. Rather than invest in high-quality films, Hollywood simply stopped making them. But even though the industry moved on, African Americans continued to appear on both sides of the camera. Richard Roundtree, Pam Grier, Fred Williamson, Judy Pace, Ossie Davidson, Jim Kelly, and Ron O'Neal continued to act, produce, and direct with careers far beyond the 1970s. Many advanced to shape films from the director's chair. Fred Williamson produced over a dozen films, and Rudy Ray Moore started his own series, *Dolemite.* Acclaimed actor Sidney Poitier starred in three flicks with Bill Cosby and as a cowboy in *Buck and the Preacher.*[28]

The success of Black actors is the legacy of the Blaxploitation era. Directors Spike Lee and John Singleton made movies relevant to the Black experience. Eddie Murphy joined the staff of *Saturday Night Live* and as a movie star made billions. Denzel Washington won Oscars in 1989 and 2001. *Black Panther* (2018) had a Black director (Ryan Coogler) and Black actors Chadwick Boseman, Michael B. Jordan, Lupita Nyong'o, and old-school favorites Angela Bassett and Forest Whitaker. It was nominated for seven Academy Awards, three Golden Globes, and eight Grammy Awards. It was the first comic-book adaptation nominated for Best Picture and the first Marvel Cinematic Universe film to win an Academy Award.[29] When Boseman unexpectedly died in August of 2020, ABC took the unusual step to show *Black Panther* with no commercial interruptions followed by a salute to his life.

AFRICAN AMERICAN MUSIC AS PROTEST

> Many in the world of Hip-Hop have begun to believe that the only way to blow up and become megastars is by presenting themselves in a negative light. The two recently slain hip-hop artists, Tupac and Notorious B.I.G., as well as other Rap artists who have come under criticism like Dr. Dre, Snoop Dogg, Ice Cube, or whoever you want to name, talk positively in some of their records, but those records have to be picked by the industry executives and program directors to be magnified. . . . The media just doesn't focus on those positive songs; they'd rather dwell on the negative.[30]
>
> —*Hip-hop artist Chuck D*

African American producers, singers, and lyricists have a history of activism. William C. Anderson wrote, "Black existence is an act of rebellion in and of itself, most especially in art. Black people have sung songs amid the persistent onslaught of struggle in the United States."[31] Protest music protruded from every musical genre's lifeblood. As each evolved, artists gave voice to the cry of oppressed people through song. While some are silent in the face of problems, most of today's artists demonstrate a willingness to risk their careers and marketability. To be fair, up until the past few decades, few were financially independent, and the cost to one's career and life were more immediate. Actor, singer, and orator Paul Robeson paid a stiff price for his activism, being branded a communist, which destroyed his career. Yet his life was an inspiration for Black performers such as Lena Horne, who admired his bravery and outspoken activism.[32] Today, the percentage of celebrities who refuse to remain silent is astounding. Some make statements on police violence, injustice, and public policy as commonly as they comment on their industry. Many established charities/nonprofits, donated financially, and volunteered as the faces of various causes and were publicly outspoken.[33] That continues today. Nina Simone wanted to know, "I choose to reflect the times and the situations in which I find myself. That to me is my duty. . . . So I don't think you have a choice. How can you be an artist and not reflect the times?"[34]

Since the onset of tunes attributed to the descendants of Africa, music has never been the same. *History Detectives* reported, "The most important influence on 20th-century music? African Americans and the musical culture they brought to this country—developed within the bonds of slavery."[35] Whether the performer was enslaved, a fugitive, impoverished, prosperous, or incarcerated, music soothed a pain-filled existence. From the struggling bluesman to the King of Pop, the sounds by African-descended musicians influenced the ways that music was heard and experienced. Steven Lewis wrote,

> African American influences are so fundamental to American music that there would be no American music without them. . . . Their work songs, dance tunes, and religious music—and the syncopated, swung, remixed, rocked, and rapped music of their descendants—would become the *lingua franca* of American music, eventually influencing Americans of all racial and ethnic backgrounds.[36]

Artists reinterpreted musical styles from the past and regurgitated them as new genres. The hearts and souls of African American musicians birthed spirituals, gospel, ragtime, doo-wop, swing, blues, rock, jazz, soul, rhythm and blues, funk, reggae, disco, and rap/hip-hop. Each innovation was influenced by the artists who came before, yet each new generation spawned music the world had never heard before, and each added a new element to what came before.

Spirituals are the bedrock of Black music. While anonymous, they are potent testimonies to a people whose spirits remained unbroken and for whom the desire for justice was never conquered. When the searing sun demanded endurance from field hands, the singing of spirituals gave strength to persevere. When a heart broke due to the sale of a daughter or death of a son, singing gave hope for a reunion beyond the suffering of this world. When it took every ounce of self-restraint in the face of injustice, the spirituals assured that there would be another day, the Day of the Lord, which prophesied vengeance and retribution. Faith music survived because the enslaved survived.

These songs were devised by a largely illiterate people as a tool of communication and sung in the presence of drivers, overseers, and masters unable to discern their coded communication. William C. Anderson, in "Sounds of Black Protest Then and Now," wrote, "It's important to note that the act of this singing was more than entertainment for plantation overseers or solely expressions of sadness. In its purest form, the slave's singing was an act of protest. Its beauty and expression transcends the pervasive hell that was the environment that allowed them to be enslaved."[37] The songs released from the lips of enslaved people elicited a means to express what they dared not say outright. Outrage, pain, and despair were expressed through repetitive lyrics rich in symbolism adapted from biblical stories. Frederick Douglass, in his speech "My Bondage and My Freedom" (1855), reflected on his experience singing spirituals: "A keen observer might have detected in our repeated singing of 'O Canaan, sweet Canaan, I am bound for the land of Canaan,' something more than a hope of reaching heaven. We meant to reach the North, and the North was our Canaan."[38] Harriet Tubman lifted the spiritual "Go Down Moses" as a signal to runaways that the time to depart had arrived. Coded lyrics communicated the moment for a planned escape in "Steal Away" or "Wade in the Water." "The Gospel Train" and "Swing Low Sweet Chariot" signaled that an operator of the Underground Railroad approached. Signal songs communicated where to meet as map songs gave direction: "Follow the Drinking Gourd" (the North Star) and "I Looked over Jordan" (the Mississippi or Ohio River).[39]

Descendants of the enslaved crooned the Blues as both lament and protest. Blues musicians used harmonies inherited from spirituals, maintaining a sense of lament with an aura of hopefulness.[40] The blues, "Black Survival Music,"[41] personified what it meant to live Black in America. Song lyrics were a revelatory, personal confession of life's trials. They reflected a singer's narrative that no matter how hard he tried, fate was arrayed against him. Songs were representative of the pains and sorrows of the race, which enhanced their widespread appeal. Seldom were lyrics outwardly political, yet the listener knew that something deeper was implied than one's personal pain. Songs represented every man's pain and spoke to the Black man's dilemma. The Rev. Marvin A. McMickle wrote,

> The blues was not so much about the music as it was about the lyrics that gave expression to the life experiences of those who sang those songs. The blues was about hard times, broken hearts, unfaithful spouses, mean treatment from white people, lonely nights, too much whiskey, and too little money. The blues was B. B. King feeling so

unloved that he questioned if even his mother loved him. The blues was Louis Armstrong lamenting the state of race relations in the United States by asking, "What did I do to be so Black and Blue?" The blues was Lou Rawls complaining that trouble never seemed to end, and that each day of the week brought another bad situation.[42]

Political lyrics lamented Alabama's history of injustice highlighted in J. B. Lenoir's "Alabama," Lead Belly's "Scottsboro Boys," and John Lee Hooker's "Birmingham Blues."[43] Fats Waller's wail of "What Did I Do to Be So Black and Blue?" (1929) became a hit on the lips of Louis Armstrong (1957) and Lou Rawls (1962). The Negro national anthem, "Lift Every Voice and Sing" (1900), written and composed by the brothers James Weldon and John Rosamond Johnson, evolved into a song of protest, faith, and nationalism. First performed at an anniversary event to celebrate the birth of President Abraham Lincoln, it was sung at church services and graduations. In 1920 the NAACP embraced it as its official song and dedicated it as the Black national anthem. In 2012, mourning the death of Trayvon Martin, it was sung around a campus flagpole. In 2018 Beyoncé included it in her Coachella performance in celebration of Black culture and historically Black colleges and universities.[44] In 2020 the National Football League acknowledged regret at its mishandling of the Colin Kaepernick protest and played it before every game at the start of the season.

From the end of the nineteenth century until the 1940s, ragtime emerged as one of the most popular musical fields. Scott Joplin, the king of ragtime, and Ernest Logan were its originators. Joplin published his incredible opera *Treemonisha* in honor of his mother in 1910 and in protest that his music, and ragtime in general, was not considered a genuine American music creation worthy of inclusion in music's canon of artistic greats.

From the roaring twenties came the Jazz Age, acknowledged by many as the truest American art form. Jazz emerged as a marriage between blues and ragtime. Its improvisation gave artists a sense of autonomy as they were no longer bound to a musical script. The feeling of nonconformity and self-expression was immense as artists could take a song and refashion it.[45] The first financially successful protest song was Billie Holiday's 1939 "Strange Fruit." This antilynching anthem, with its harrowing, shadowy effect, had a haunting impact on listeners and Holiday herself. On several occasions, she wept after walking offstage, and friends pondered that the song impacted her mentally. Dorian Lynskey wrote, "During the 50s, she performed it less often and, when she did, it could be agonizing to watch. Her relationship with it became almost masochistic. The worse her mood, the more likely she was to add it to the set, yet it pained her every time and prompted walkouts by racist audience members."[46] The 1930s was the decade of boogie-woogie dance music and bebop. During the 1940s, rhythm and blues (R&B) extended a soulful rendition of love songs for the nation to enjoy. The 1950s produced soul and rock and roll. Soul music converged gospel with rhythm and blues and challenged segregation as young people danced the night away interracially.[47]

The civil rights movement was a breeding ground for freedom songs blended from gospel and soul music. They were mostly adapted from familiar hymns, such as "We Shall Overcome," "We Shall Not Be Moved," and "Ain't Gonna Let Nobody Turn Me Round." The 1962 Freedom Singers and Mavis Staples inspired audiences at rallies and concerts. [48] Nina Simone lamented "I Wish I Knew How It Would Feel to Be Free" and "Backlash Blues." "Mississippi G**d***" mourned Medgar Evers's 1963 murder and the 16th Street Baptist Church bombing.[49] In 1967, Aretha Franklin demanded "Respect" as an avid supporter of the civil rights movement. "Dancing in the Streets" by Martha and the Vandellas camouflaged rebellion and street protest as dance music. The Godfather of Soul, James Brown, declared, "Say It Loud—I'm Black and I'm Proud" (1968). That same year Curtis Mayfield and the Impressions triumphantly declared, "We're a Winner," and urged people to "Just Keep on Pushing." In 1969 Les McCann and Eddie Harris complained about the Vietnam War when they sang, "Compared to what? Folks don't know just what it's for." That year Syl Johnson bemoaned, "Is it because I'm Black?" Former Black Panther leader Elaine Brown bewailed her country in "Seize the Time" (1969).

The 1960s ushered in an era when Black music became the measurement by which others ascribed excellence. Motown hits topped the charts. For the first time Black ownership of record companies became a reality as Sussex, Stax, Tabu, Atlantic Records, and Philadelphia International Records sought to rival Motown. Black producers Quincy Jones and Clarence Avant worked deals behind the scenes, and their influence extended beyond music into politics and cinema.[50] Motown and Berry Gordy affected the nation in ways far beyond music production. Motown promoted integration and presented Blacks as fashionably stylish. Music enticed young whites to dance unashamedly to tunes sung by Black artists, and it forced record companies to admit crossover potential.[51] For the first time, Blacks influenced the production and distribution of their music due to technological advances in mass media production. Under the marketing strategy "Radio, Records, and Retail," radio stations demoed new music, creating an audience before the records were available for purchase. While the music was new, innovative, electric, and danceable, it still needed a vehicle to drive it before the public ear. That vehicle was the TV show *Soul Train*, and the engineer was Don Cornelius. Nelson George commented,

Soul Train was the weapon of the Civil Rights Movement that it didn't know it had, which was joy. Before *Soul Train* there had never been a weekly program show on national TV that featured Black people, for Black people, by Black people. Never anything close to it really. And the amount of white people who would experience Black culture for the first time in an undiluted way, that was, *Soul Train* was that for them. and they couldn't get enough of it.[52]

The 1970s saw the rise of funk as a combination of soul, jazz, and R&B. The seventies had a number of protest hits. The Supremes released "Stoned Love" in 1970. Inspired by Sam Cooke's "A Change Is Gonna Come," Marvin Gaye released *What's Going On* (1971) as a concept album on the evils of pollution, racism, and war. Motown's most political album also became its fastest seller to a public hungry for music with a message.[53] The Meters urged unity in "A Message from the Meters." Composer and producer Curtis Mayfield provoked one's conscience as a regular element in his repertoire. His songs "(Don't Worry) If There Is a Hell Below, We Are All Going to Go" (1970) and "Mighty Mighty (Spade and Whitey)" provided listening audiences with apocalyptical warnings. Sly and the Family Stone rebelled in "Don't Call Me N*****, Whitey" and pushed acceptance in "Everyday People" (1969). Gil-Scott Heron popularized the multigenerational phrase "The Revolution Will Not Be Televised" (1971). Edwin Starr's "Stop the War Now" and "War" (1970) were the most popular antiwar songs. "War! What is it good for?"—with the responding answer "Absolutely nothing!"— was covered by the Temptations and Bruce Springsteen.

"Young, Gifted, and Black" was sung by Nina Simone and Donny Hathaway in 1970 and Aretha Franklin in 1972. Hathaway promoted hope in "Someday We'll All Be Free." Etta James proclaimed, "Tell It Like It Is," and the Chi-Lites declared in their third studio album, *(For God's Sake) Give More Power To The People* (1971). The Isley Brothers chanted, "Fight The Power," and the O'Jays released "Give the People What They Want." The Temptations had a string of hits that invoked societal criticism: "Psychedelic Shack," "Ball of Confusion" (1970), and "Message from a Black Man" (1969). Johnny Taylor thundered, "I Am Somebody!" (1971), and Eddie Kendricks begged, "My People Hold On" (1972). Segments of Time poignantly sent a "Song to the System" (1972), decrying racism and exploitation. William De Vaughn told Black people to "Stand tall" and "Be Thankful for What You Got" (1974). Billy Paul's "Am I Black Enough for You?" (1973) asked a pivotal question of both white and Black America. The Honey Drippers demanded, "Impeach the President."[54] In the lead track of their album by the same name, Parliament renamed Washington, DC, "Chocolate City" (1975). "Wake Up,

Everybody" (1975), by Harold Melvin & the BlueNotes, softly pulsated for a positive awakening while the Last Poets roused Black consciousness with "Wake Up, N******."

Stevie Wonder, throughout his career, seamlessly combined music and activism without missing a harmonic beat. "Do Yourself A Favor," "Sunshine in Their Eyes," "Big Brother" (1972), and "Living for the City" (1973) evoked dissent. He called for Martin Luther King's birthday to be a national holiday in "Happy Birthday" (1980) and disparaged South Africa in "It's Wrong, Apartheid" (1985). When the song was banned in South Africa, Wonder responded by getting arrested for protesting apartheid in Washington, DC.[55] Throughout the seventies, reggae was synonymous with protest. Gregory Isaacs sang of the "Black Liberation Struggle" in a "Slave Market." Bob Marley lifted the strongest, clearest voice for human rights and an end to injustice. His followers were as attracted to his song lyrics as to his musical melodies as he urged his listeners to resist oppression.[56]

The eighties and nineties saw a succession of funk and R&B artists with more of a mind to dance their troubles away. The music industry was opening up, and lucrative contracts were signed. The two biggest stars of that era caused the most controversy as Prince and Michael Jackson sampled justice and faith themes. Prince's "Sign O' the Times" (1987) addressed drug addiction, HIV, and gang violence. Jackson recorded an ultraradical video for "They Don't Care about Us" (1996) from two different locations, in Brazil[57] and later from a prison with inmates as his choir. The prison version began with the caption "This film is not degrading to any one RACE, but pictorializes the injustices to ALL mankind. May GOD grant us PEACE THROUGHOUT the world."[58] It has proven to be his most militant and transparent statement as he addressed racism, police brutality, white supremacy, and hate groups. The folksy Tracy Chapman's "Behind the Wall" spoke of freedom from love's pain and society's abuse. "We Are the World, USA for Africa" (1985), the brainchild of Michael Jackson and Lionel Ritchie, was a philanthropic effort with little focus on the world's responsibility to eliminate the root causes of hunger. Common, Lauryn Hill, and Queen Latifah ("U.N.I.T.Y.") filtrated their productions with a cry for justice. Common successfully embraced the dual identities of activist and artist to challenge a society indifferent to poverty and race.

The eighties and nineties also gave witness to the rise of rap music to musical dominance. Rap originated in the sixties and seventies when the New York DJ Kool Herc started a revolution using two turntables and two copies of the same record. He would isolate the instrumental portion of a piece that emphasized the drum beat, or break, and by switching from one break to another or elongating the break, he created dance music from past hits. Originating in

inner-city communities, rap provided talented young people an opportunity
to enter the tightly controlled music industry. Even as its popularity grew, it
met with cynicism, scorn, and denial that it was artistry. It was not until 1983
that MTV would show any Black music videos (i.e., Michael Jackson's "Billie
Jean" and "Thriller"), and not until the following year did Run-D.M.C.'s rap
video appear.

In 1979 the first crossover rap hit, "Rapper's Delight" by the Sugarhill
Gang, alerted the industry to potential revenue. The Big Apple birthed the
earliest artists, followed by West Coast rappers who orated a harsher reality.
Female rappers mixed rhymes and beats quite successfully. "Ladies First" cel-
ebrated the accomplishments of Black women and announced to the world
that women rappers were here to stay.[59] Record companies also proliferated:,
Uptown Records (Andre Harrell); Death Row Records (Suge Knight and Dr.
Dre); No Limit Records (Percy "Master P" Miller); Bigtyme Recordz and
Bad Boy Records (Sean Combs); Roc-A-Fella Records (Jay-Z); and Undeas
Recording (Lance Rivera).[60]

In These Times published online that "not surprisingly, hip-hop has led the
way—not just through a predictable barrage of tweets by musicians and artists, but a sustained, meaningful wave of creativity and outspokenness engaging with a bold, sometimes chaotic movement."[61] Rap's most ardent agent
was Chuck D and Public Enemy ("Fear of a Black Planet," 1990), who has
rapped politically for thirty years. "The Message," by Grandmaster Flash, was
an obviously direct protest song. NWA's "F*** Tha Police" exposed police
brutality directed at young Black men on the streets of Los Angeles. KRS res-
urrected Malcolm X in "By All Means Necessary" (1988) and "Stop the Violence" (1988). Lil Wayne and Kanye West earlier in their careers broached
politics even though both were later ridiculed for nonsensical statements.
Lil Wayne mocked President George Bush in "Georgia Bush" (2006) over
his slow response to Hurricane Katrina, and Kanye West charged during a
live television fund-raiser for Katrina victims that "George Bush doesn't care
about Black people." Jasiri X filmed his video for "The Whitest House" in
front of 1600 Pennsylvania Avenue.[62] Notable are the lyrics of Lil Boosie's
"F*** the Police," Archie Eversole's "We Ready," D'Angelo's "Black Mes-
siah," Janelle Monae's "Hell You Talmbout," Bibi Bourelly's "Chains," and
Joe Budden's "Freedom Freestyle."

Kendrick Lamar is relentless as the unchallenged "Prophet of Rap" with
a career both prophetic and financially profitable. His tracks in *Alright, To
Pimp a Butterfly*, and *Freedom* address police brutality and the Black Lives
Matter movement. "Freedom's" video projected images of injustice visualized in the gripping disbelief of Philando Castile's girlfriend brought home
by Jesse Williams's BET Awards speech.[63] Black Clevelanders protested the

murder of fourteen-year-old Tamir Rice by chanting the lyrics to Kendrick Lamar's "We gon' be alright!"[64] Rapper Vince Staples is quoted in a 2017 *Rolling Stone* as saying,

> As far as musicians, unless you're talking some U2 shit, I don't know who more confidently tries to do something or say something to change the communities more than rappers. Whether it's Brand Nubian, whether it's Talib Kweli or Mos Def, whether it's Pharcyde or it's Tupac, whether it's Dr. Dre who released "Express Yourself" telling kids not to do drugs, because it will give them brain damage. We're not new to this.[65]

Rap protest music split into two branches, conscious and political rap. KRS declared that the intent of the 1988 "Stop the Violence" video was "to show the unity. We know exactly who we are. This is what it means to be conscious, to be awake, to be aware."[66]

Political rappers pushed a justice agenda as represented by the poetry and music of the Last Poets, Chuck D and Public Enemy, Brand Nubia, the Poor Righteous Teachers, King Sun, A Tribe Called Quest, De La Soul, the Jungle Brothers, X Clan, the Blackwatch Movement, Arrested Development, the Jungle Brothers, and Native Tongues.[67] Rap production companies financed the music, and Def Jam and Luke Records made millions. Hip-hop culture impacted American and international culture in fashion and language. America has become a hip-hop nation with media personalities and politicians utilizing hip-hop slang.

Today's African American artists live in a period where protest is ingrained into music. They pumped up the volume by interjecting lyrical commentary on injustice in American society. Many are as prone to interject controversial lyrics into their music as they are to rock beats. They have ventured far beyond anything witnessed before as their music parallels strongly worded public statements. Militant songs lay bare injustices and leave no doubt as to their message. Kristin Corry reflected that "Beyoncé, Solange, Kanye West, Frank Ocean, and Rihanna released provocative, forward-thinking albums during the rise of the Trump candidacy, driving home the Black music's legacy of being firmly grounded in protest music."[68] D'Angelo mused that

> Black Messiah is, I think, the most sociopolitical stuff I've done on record. . . . The Black Lives Matter movement is going on, young black men and women are getting killed for nothing. I've always been a big reader and fan of history, and I love the Black Panthers. I'm not trying to be like a poster child or anything of the movement, but definitely a voice as a black man, and as a concerned black man and as a father, as well.[69]

Black women have been almost forced into artistic activism due to sexual exploitation and misconduct directed their way. According to director Sharon Lewis, "When we see Black women in film and in television, the first thing that happens is we applaud. We made it, we're being actually seen. The second thing, is an analysis happens. How are we being portrayed? When I see Black women in any kind of TV or film, it's an act of protest because I know how long and how hard you have to fight to even get there."[70] Rhiannon Giddens has an awakening catalog including "Cry No More" and "Black Myself." Hers is a musical recounting of the Black experience with a particular focus on enslaved resilience, and her video "At the Purchaser's Option" is a subtle yet powerful experience of musical storytelling. She sits motionless in a chair as a slave ad hangs ominously above her head.[71] "Slave Driver" recounts the slave ship experience and the "crack of the whip."

Beyoncé Gisell Knowles-Carter ascended to the throne vacated by Prince and Michael Jackson as the most talked-about entertainer. Her "Formation" Super Bowl performance propelled protest music to the forefront of cultural conversation. When criticized that she had an antipolice bias, she stated plainly, "Let's be clear: I am against police brutality and injustice. Those are two separate things. If celebrating my roots and culture during Black History Month made anyone uncomfortable, those feelings were there long before a video and long before me."[72] *Lemonade* normalized the Black female experience.[73]

The rampant use of deadly force by police against Black men had artists paying homage to those slain. Eric Garner's family released "I Can't Breathe." Prince memorialized Freddie Gray in "Baltimore." Daye Jack and Killer Mike collaborated in "Hands Up," and Z-Ro featured Mike Dean on "No Justice No Peace." Christian Scott decried police brutality in "K.K.P.D. [Ku Klux Police Department]." Jay-Z's "Spiritual" focused on the disillusionment caused by calling the names of Trayvon Martin, Michael Brown, and Sandra Bland as a chorus sang, "Say his name; Say her name!" Beyoncé, in her "Forward" video, recruited the mothers of Trayvon Martin, Eric Garner, and Michael Brown to hold pictures of their murdered sons. Following the murders of Alton Sterling and Philando Castile, she admonished, "It is up to us to take a stand and demand that they stop killing us." Miquel asked, "How many people must die before law enforcement changes?. . . I'm tired of human lives turned into hashtags and prayer hands. I'm tired of watching murderers get off."[74]

Janelle Monae has been more than consistent in her statements against police shootings. "Hell You Talmbout" reset a previously released number as a seven-minute-long anthem.[75] She stated on NBC's *Today Show*, "Yes, Lord, God bless America. God bless all who've lost lives to police brutality. We want white America to know that we stand tall today. We want Black America to know that we stand tall today. We will not be silenced."[76] J Cole demonstrated in Ferguson following the murder of Michael Brown and released "Be Free," which he performed on the *Late Show with David Letterman* in 2014. He mourned the murder of young Black men "regardless of the race of the person who killed them."[77] Tom Morello proposed "Marching on Ferguson." Blood Orange memorialized Sandra Bland in "Sandra's Smile": "You watched her pass away the words she said weren't faint. Closed our eyes for a while, but I still see Sandra's smile." He wondered, "Do You See My Skin Through the Flames?" as *Freetown Sound* referenced Black Lives Matter. Usher and Nas teamed up on "Chains" with a video montage to those killed by police. Solange Knowles, *A Seat at the Table* (2016), explored the meaning of Blackness in America in "F.U.B.U. (For Us By Us)." In another song she warned, "Don't Touch My Hair."

Scholar-musician Rhiannon Giddens said the following about her song "Cry No More":

> The massacre at the AME church in Charleston is just the latest in a string of racially charged events that have broken my heart. There are a lot of things to fix in this country, but history says if we don't address this canker, centuries in the making, these things will continue to happen. No matter what level privilege you have, when the system is broken everybody loses. We all have to speak up when injustice happens. No matter what.[78]

Celebrity protest has dramatically increased in recent years with African American artists intertwining activism and artistry answering the call to be woke. Being woke is a political term of African American origin. Merriam-Webster defines it, "to be aware of and actively attentive to important facts and issues, especially issues of racial and social justice." Woke artists desire to practice their artistry while changing society. They want to use their platform as an opportunity to empower others.

THE POWER AND PROTEST
OF THE AFRICAN AMERICAN ATHLETE

Records aside, Black athletes have had a major impact on Black American history. In the early 1940s, for example, the black labor leader, A. Philip Randolph made the integration of major league baseball a test of the nation's intentions regarding discrimination in employment. The phrase "if he's (a Black man) good enough for the Navy, he's good enough for the majors" became an oft-heard slogan for many.[79]

—*Tennis star and activist Arthur R. Ashe Jr.*

Long before the twenty-first century, athletes adopted the mantle of activist athletes. The effort on the part of Blacks to integrate the world of American sports was an act of protest, even on the part of those who just wanted to play. Since the beginning of the country's history, sports have made celebrity-heroes out of athletes. Paul Robeson, Jackie Robinson, Jim Brown, Muhammad Ali, Kareem Abdul-Jabbar, and others excelled in their sport and became national celebrities. They also advocated for American racism's dismantlement. Their personhood and the game itself carried influence far beyond the playing field. Blacks knew that if they could get on the playing field, the court, or the diamond, everyday life in America would be impacted. African American athletes called for the country to live up to its creeds, similar to their enslaved ancestors. They advocated for America to fulfill the dream of itself: To make America great for the first time in its treatment of people of color.[80] The effort to play has been relentless, and when exiled from playing with white athletes, Blacks created their own arenas of athletic competition across the many spectrums of the wide world of sports.

In a remarkable way, the Black protest against athletic segregation has been a civil rights movement in and of itself, predating those of a more obvious nature against slavery and Jim Crow. Before the abolitionist movement got under way, Blacks dominated the sport of horse racing. Racing fans and riders were familiar with the saying "All are equal on the turf and under it." Blacks were eventually ostracized from the world of horse racing because they demolished this myth completely and dominated it with wins.[81] But thoroughbred horse racing lacks any significant African American presence whatsoever today. Edward Hotaling writes, "Most people are oblivious to the fact that, two centuries before Jackie Robinson, blacks competed alongside whites in America's first favorite pastime. They are unaware of it because the black jockeys were not only ridden out of their profession but written out of history. . . . This is not black history. It is not white history. It is American history, never told before."[82]

Between the 1600s and the War to End Slavery, horse racing was a southern sport, and most of the first professional jockeys and trainers were of African descent, both enslaved and free. Some managed to purchase freedom from racing proceeds or were emancipated by owners. Austin Curtis won so many races between 1770 and 1790 that he was emancipated. The first Kentucky Derby, held on May 17, 1875, in Lexington, Kentucky, was won by Oliver Lewis. Thirteen of the fourteen jockeys in that race were African American. They won eight of the first sixteen derbies and five national championships, accounting for the most wins in 1884–1885. Riders of repute were Charles Stewart, Simon, and Pike Barnes. The greatest rider of his day, Isaac "Honest Ike" Murphy, was the only rider to win the derby, the Kentucky Oaks, and the Clark Stakes, and the first to win successive derbies (1890 and 1891). When the Jockey Hall of Fame opened in Saratoga Springs, New York, he was among the first to be voted into membership. After winning consecutive derbies, jockey Jimmy Winkfield's life was threatened by the Klan, and he fled the country. In Europe, he won the Grand Prix de Baden, the Polish Derby, the Moscow Derby, and other races. After years of intolerance by white jockeys, Henry King in 1921 was the last African American rider in the Kentucky Derby until the year 2000.[83] No longer would men of color be allowed to ride at the derby, a legacy of absence which largely continues to this day as few African Americans ride in the derby.

Early African American competitors on the world stage were successful when allowed to play. They ran face-first against the force of fans who booed and hurled racist expletives. In the theater of international competition, African American achievements on the field were remarkable. In 1899 Marshall "Major" Taylor became the first African American world champion in any sport. He set seven cycling world records fifty years before Jackie Robinson integrated baseball and at a time when cycling was more popular than baseball. He wrote in his autobiography, "I am writing my memoirs . . . in the spirit calculated to solicit simple justice, equal rights and a square deal for the posterity of my downtrodden but brave people, not only in athletic games and sports, but in every honorable game of human endeavor."[84] In 1904, George Poage was the first African American to compete in the Olympics when he won two bronze medals in St. Louis, thirty-two years before Jesse Owens. In 1908, Olympian John Taylor was the first to win a gold medal in any sport when he won in track and field.

Wilma Rudolph was the first African American woman to win three gold medals in a single Olympics at the 1960 games in Rome. In 1968, James Kanati Allen became the first African American male gymnast named to the U.S. Olympic team. Simone Biles is the most decorated gymnast in world history, with twenty-five Olympic and world championship medals as of 2021. At the 1948 Olympics, Alice Coachman became the first African American woman to win Olympic gold; she was elected to eight different Halls of Fame. She wrote, "I made a difference among the Blacks, being one of the leaders. If I'd have gone to the games and failed, there wouldn't be anyone to follow in my footsteps."[85] At the 1968 Summer Olympics in Mexico City, Tommie Smith and John Carlos, winners of gold and bronze medals, raised black-gloved fists in a Black Power salute. The United States Olympic Committee immediately expelled them, and their actions inhibited them professionally for the rest of their lives. Regardless, runners Lee Evans, Larry James, and Ron Freeman wore black berets when accepting their track medals. At the 1972 Munich Olympics, runners Vince Matthews and Wayne Collett gave the Black Power salute as the crowd booed. The International Olympic Committee barred both.

Tennis and golf have been among the most difficult sports to integrate. Tennis courts were among the most difficult to step upon. Rather than being deterred, all-Black tennis associations were formed to teach young people to play. In 1917, Lucy Diggs Slowe became the first African American woman to win a major sport's title in the American Tennis Association. Ora Mae Washington, born in 1898, won the American Tennis Association (ATA) title, twelve doubles titles, and three mixed doubles championship. She played for twelve years as an undefeated champion. Althea Gibson was the first African American woman to win the French Open (1956), Wimbledon (1957–58), and the U.S. Open singles championships (1957–58). Arthur Ashe was the first African American man to win the U.S. Open (1968) and Wimbledon (1975) and the first to participate in the Davis Cup competition. In 2002, Venus Williams started the year ranked number one with sister Serena and ended the year ranked number one. In 2003 Serena won the career Grand Slam title. In 2009 they were the first African Americans and African American sisters to be named the year-end International Tennis Federation doubles world champions. Serena Williams declared, "The day I stop fighting for equality and for people that look like you and me will be the day I'm in my grave."[86]

One of the most stubborn holdouts was the sport of golf. *Golf History Today* magazine reprinted a 1971 letter from Rose Elder to Clifford Roberts, tournament chairman of the Master's Golf Tournament, in which she wrote,

> You also said "There is no doubt that when Blacks make the same efforts in golf as in other athletic fields they'll have a place here. But few are making a serious effort." I am sure you will admit it is comparatively easy for a young black boy to go to a basketball court, football, or baseball field. It is not that easy for that same lad to go to a country club and play golf every day. Right in Washington, D.C., there are places where Lee is not allowed to play because he is a black. So you see, Mr. Roberts, it is difficult except for the most dedicated blacks to make a "serious effort to play."[87]

Ann Moore Gregory was "The Queen of Negro Golf." She played for over fifty years and won over three hundred gold tournaments and four hundred trophies. From 1945 onward, she was often the only African American woman among the white players. Charlie Sifford was the first African American to join the PGA Tour in 1961 and won it in 1967. He was inducted into the World Golf Hall of Fame in 2004. Althea Gibson was the first African American woman to join the Ladies Professional Golf Association in 1964. Lee Elder was the first to play in a men's major golf championship, the Masters. In 1994 Tiger Woods won the U.S. Amateur Championship, in 1997 the

Masters, and the following year he became the first African American to play in the Presidents Cup. His eighty-two professional wins are second only to Sam Snead in golf history.

Even today the sports of hockey, NASCAR racing, and rowing have the lowest percentage of a Black presence of any sport. The Black Ice Hockey and Sports Hall of Fame displays the history of African American ice hockey. Twenty-five years before the Negro Major Leagues there was the Colored Hockey League, which predated even the National Hockey League (NHL). Writers Darril and George Fosty recalled of the Colored Hockey League of the Maritimes, formed in Nova Scotia in 1895 by Henry Sylvester, "The sons and grandsons of runaway American slaves . . . transformed . . . this winter game from the primitive gentleman's pastime of the nineteenth-century to the modern fast-moving game of today."[88] Eddie Martin, the captain of the Halifax Eurekas, perfected the slap shot. Henry "Braces" Franklyn pioneered defending the goal in a butterfly position by dropping to one's knees to prevent the puck from going into the net. On January 18, 1958, Willie O'Ree became the first Black to play in the National Hockey League for the Boston Bruins, followed in 1974 by Mike Marson. In 2003, Canadian Grant Fuhr, the first Black hockey player to win the Stanley Cup, was inducted into the Hockey Hall of Fame.[89] Only seventy Black players have played in the NHL's hundred-year history.

In 1963, Wendell Scott became the first NASCAR Grand National winner; he was inducted into the NASCAR Hall of Fame in 2015. Frank Scott, son of Wendell Scott, in an NPR "Morning Edition" interview (January 30, 2015) stated, "Daddy said, 'Look, if I leave in a pine box, that's what I gotta do. But I'm gonna race.'"[90] In 1981, Willy T. Ribbs was the first Black man to qualify for the Indianapolis 500. In 2020, after the reoccurring protests over the murder of George Floyd, NASCAR banned Confederate flags from races.[91] The first African American rowing team in the United States was the 1998 Manley High School team in West Chicago, coached by Marc Manley.[92]

During their heydays, both boxing and baseball were America's favorite pastimes. Each one first allowed Black participation but later rescinded the privilege. As each prohibition was subsequently stripped away, however, the Black athlete's status was a way to fight the stigma of inferiority. Even when society was slow to change, each victory gave hope and encouragement to the masses of Black people who applauded their heroes' every win. The Black athlete desired to change America for the better.

Before the great American War to End Slavery, Blacks fought to enter the boxing ring. In a day when no other sport carried any real significance, boxing was America's pastime. Boxing was the ultimate symbol of white manhood, and the boxing champion upheld white supremacy. Blacks were barred from fighting for championships until the twentieth century, but even then the idea that African Americans would compete, nonetheless hold the belt, caused a reaction nationwide. In 1902 Joe Gans became the first African American lightweight boxing champion; in 1908 Jack Johnson won the heavyweight championship. As angry whites rioted, paperboy Louis Armstrong remembered running for his life. Johnson confessed, "The search for the white hope not having been successful, prejudices were being piled up against me, and certain unfair persons, piqued because I was champion, decided if they could not get me one way, they would another."[93] Henry Armstrong was the only champion of three different divisions simultaneously. In 1954 he was inducted into the Boxing Hall of Fame.[94]

The list of African American boxing champions contains some of the most masterful athletes in sport's history. Muhammad Ali is the only heavyweight to win the title three times. In 1967 Ali aroused the ire of white America when he refused to register for the draft during the Vietnam War. "The Greatest" litigated the irony of enlisting Black men to fight against people of color in a racist war. "My conscience won't let me go shoot my brother, or some darker people, or some poor hungry people in the mud for big powerful America. . . . And shoot them for what? They never called me n*****, they never lynched me, they didn't put no dogs on me, they didn't rob me of my nationality, rape and kill my mother and father. . . . Shoot them for what?"[95]

Always in the background, an important goal was racial acceptance of a people denied their humanity. To change the country, one had to first win on the athletic battlefield as it presented a visual attack on the myth of white superiority and Black inferiority. Before the civil rights movement, the Black press colluded with Branch Rickey to change American society when Rickey broke Major League Baseball's color barrier by signing Black player Jackie Robinson. They wrote exhaustively of the exploits of Robinson to enhance his appeal. Baseball was celebrated as America's favorite pastime, and its most celebrated commissioner was a white supremist who died just years before Jackie Robinson was introduced. Baseball, more than any other sport, reflected the country's history. African Americans were initially allowed to play, then were banned, and later were reinstated. Baseball historian Bruce Chadwick wrote, "American baseball was never just a game, it was the passion of the nation, and as long as it was segregated the entire nation would be. Generations of black ballplayers tried to end that segregation, but after knocking at the major league doors and being ignored, they played baseball where they could."[96]

Jackie Robinson is acknowledged as the first African American Major League baseball player in 1947, but others had already run the bases. In the 1860s, the National Association of Base Ball Players (NABBP) was formed and included John W. "Bud" Fowler in 1878 and Moses Fleetwood Walker in 1884. Walker was the first to play in a game almost seven decades before Robinson. By 1889, all players of color were exiled.[97] Andrew "Rube" Foster, the "Father of Black Baseball," lived only fifty-one years but is considered the greatest professional pitcher, coach, and owner-manager of all time.[98] Charles E. Whitehead, in his book *A Man and His Diamonds*, wrote, "In the annals of baseball there are certain names such as Cy Young, Kenesaw Mountain Landis, Connie Mack, and John McGraw that are immediately recognized, even today. Yet, there was one baseball great, Andrew 'Rube' Foster, who was reported to be greater than any of the aforementioned, but who because of his race is today almost forgotten."[99] In 1920 Foster convinced eight owners to establish an eight-team Negro National League (NNL). He trained his teams to excel in pitching with an offensive style of play based on speed and intellect. His innovations used "bunt and run" and "hit and run" strategies that still exist in professional baseball. He was the first to play night games and arranged East-West all-star contests. The Chicago American Giants and Kansas City Monarchs brought in more fans with larger gate receipts than most white teams. He was inducted into the Baseball Hall of Fame in Cooperstown in 1981.[100] In 1924, a second league, the Eastern Colored League (ECL), was formed. Gus Greenlee had a lineup of the most electrifying baseball players the game had ever seen: Leroy "Satchel" Paige, Josh Gibson, Roy Campanella, James "Cool Papa" Bell, and Ted "Double-Duty" Radcliffe. Between 1946 and 1959, every major-league team signed at least one Black player, which depleted the ranks of the Negro Leagues. In 1963, in Kansas City, the last Black all-star game was held, where it had all begun.

In 1946, John Roosevelt "Jackie" Robinson was drafted by Brooklyn Dodgers president Branch Rickey to play in the major leagues. He was the first African American to win the Most Valuable Player (MVP) award and was inducted into the Baseball Hall of Fame in 1962. Satchel Paige was the first Black pitcher and joined the Hall of Fame in 1971. In 1956, Don Newcombe of the Dodgers won the Cy Young Award and was the National League's most valuable player. John Jordan "Buck" O'Neil of the Chicago Cubs was the first major-league coach. "Hammering" Hank Aaron hit his 755th home run on April 8, 1974, breaking the record of Babe Ruth. Barry Bonds became the all-time home-run hitter when he blasted his 756th home run on August 7, 2007. Comer Cottrell was the first Black major-league minority owner of a pro baseball team in 1989. When Jackie Robinson was honored during the 1972 World Series in Cincinnati, he said, "I'm going to be tremendously more pleased and more proud when I look at that third base coaching line one day and see a black face managing in baseball."[101] In 1975 Frank Robinson became the first Black general manager for the Cleveland Indians, and in

1996, Bob Watson was a general manager who won the World Series with the New York Yankees.

In the realm of college football, Fritz Pollard of Brown University became the first African American football player to play in the Rose Bowl in 1916. Duke Slater played with the University of Iowa and was named to the College Football Hall of Fame in 1951. In 1961 Ernie Davis won the Heisman Trophy at Syracuse University. Willie Jeffries was the first head coach in Division I-A football for Wichita State University in 1979. The year 2019 was the "Year of the Black Quarterback." *First Take* host Molly Qerim Rose declared that "the top five QBRs [Quarter Back Ratings] in the NFL right now all belong to African American quarterbacks: Dak [Prescott], Russell [Wilson], Patrick [Mahomes], Lamar [Jackson], and then, Deshaun Watson."[102]

The African American football player revolutionized the game, but he first had to step on the field. Blacks were determined to earn the right to play, but once in the game, they were determined to make a difference. The Syracuse 8 sat out the 1970 football season in protest. They called for the hiring of Blacks as coaches, increases in health care, academic support of student athletes regardless of color, and fair treatment for all.

At the first snap, African Americans were sidelined. For example, the position of quarterback was reserved for white men, for African Americans were considered too stupid: slow in thought, all brawn, and no brain. This last reserve of white supremacy lingered as late as 2018 when Hall of Fame general manager Bill Polian stated that Heisman Trophy–winning quarterback Lamar Jackson should be converted into a wide receiver. It had been the normal repositioning for Black quarterbacks drafted into the NFL, but the next year Jackson, as a quarterback, was the league's MVP.[103] Fritz Pollard and Bobby Marshall were the first Black NFL players in 1920 with the Rock Island Independents. In 1951 Bernie Custis was the first Black quarterback to start a professional football game, with the Hamilton Tiger-Cats. In 1975 Franco Harris earned a Super Bowl MVP with the Pittsburgh Steelers. Deacon Jones is the measure by which all defensive ends are measured. Jerry Rice was the greatest wide receiver while quarterback Doug Williams had a superb Super Bowl performance. Jim Brown and Walter "Sweetness" Payton are arguably the greatest running backs ever to play. Two-sport players Bo Jackson and Deion Sanders played football and baseball in the same seasons. Ozzie Newsome of the 2002 Baltimore Ravens became the first Black NFL general manager. Only a select few have held head coach positions. Fritz Pollard, Art Shell, Dennis Green, Marvin Lewis, Hue Jackson, Tony Dungy, Lovie Smith, Jim Caldwell, and Mike Tomlin are nine of the twenty-four total. In 1921 Fritz Pollard was the player-coach of the Akron Pros. Art Shell became the first Black NFL coach in today's era with the Los Angeles Raiders. In 2007 Lovie Smith and Tony Dungy made league history as the first two Black head coaches to lead teams at the same time in the Super Bowl; Dungy was the first to win. Johnny Grier wore pinstripes as the first Black NFL referee in 1988, and in 2008, Mike Carey became the first Black to referee a Super Bowl. In 1967 Emlen Tunnell was the first to be inducted into the Pro Football Hall of Fame.

The killing of Michael Brown in Ferguson provoked the hometown team, the St. Louis Rams, to react. On November 30, 2014, five players walked out of the tunnel using the "Hands Up, Don't Shoot" gesture during a game against the Oakland Raiders. On December 7, players wore t-shirts reading "I Can't Breathe" in response to the choking death of Eric Garner. Player Davin Joseph wore the quote on his cleats during pregame warmups. He tweeted an image of his shoes before the game with the message "R.I.P. Eric Garner." Tight end Jared Cook wrote the phrase on his wrist tape. Detroit Lions running back Reggie Bush emblazoned "I Can't Breathe" in black across his blue warm-up top. Receiver Kenny Britt wrote the names of Michael Brown and Trayvon Martin on his blue-and-gold cleats.[104] Cleveland Browns cornerback Johnson Bademosi wore it on the back of his shirt before a game. On December 14, Browns' player Andrew Hawkins walked onto the field wearing a t-shirt printed with "Justice for Tamir Rice and John Crawford" and on the back "The Real Battle of Ohio."[105]

Coach Clarence "Big House" Gaines said, "It's impossible to overemphasize the impact that black athletes have had on basketball. We have been a part of the game since 1904. . . . Black athletes have moved on to dominate the sport at the prep, college, and professional levels."[106] In the college ranks, in 1966 Texas Western became the first university to field five Black players on a Division I team in the championship game, against Kentucky. Will Robinson of Illinois State University became the first Black NCAA Division I basketball coach in 1970. Clarence Gaines, the head coach at Winston-Salem State University, became the first Hall of Fame head-coach inductee. Coach John Thompson won a Division I NCAA basketball tournament with Georgetown University in 1984. Ora Mae Washington played basketball for the Germantown Hornets, winning the national championship with a record of 22–1. She moved to the Philadelphia Tribunes in 1932 and won ten straight "Women's Colored Basketball World Championships." She led the team in scoring and briefly served as head coach. She was known as "the best Colored player in the world." In 1986, she became a member of the Temple University's Sports Hall of Fame and the Women's Basketball Hall of Fame in 2009.

The National Basketball League (NBL) was formed as a segregated league in 1946, the same year Jackie Robinson integrated baseball, and three years later, basketball remained largely segregated. Sportswriter Heather Gilligan described the sentiment of the day: "Black athletes did not have the intellect needed to win in a fast-paced sport like basketball; they had small lungs and heavy bones and an inability to jump; they weren't coachable."[107] As in baseball, integration was attempted but failed. African Americans were added to a few teams, but four players recruited were cut by year's end. Harry Haskell Lew became the first Black professional basketball player with the New England Professional Basketball League in 1902. He remembered his first game: "All those things you read about Jackie Robinson, the abuse, the name-calling, extra effort to put him down . . . they're all true. I got the same treatment and even worse."[108]

For fifty years, however, being eliminated from professional basketball did not prevent Blacks from playing the game. The years from 1904 to 1950 are known as the "Black Fives Era," "Early Black Basketball," or "Black Basketball." In 1904 Dr. Erwin B. Henderson introduced basketball to Black neighborhoods in Washington, DC, where he established the first Black High School Athletic Association. His efforts resulted in the creation of the "Black Fives" in Washington, New York City, Chicago, Pittsburgh, Philadelphia, and Cleveland. Teams included the Washington Bears, the 12 Streeters, the Philadelphia Panthers, the Los Angeles Red Devils, and the New York Renaissance (Rens). The latter won 2,588 of 3,117 games from 1923 to 1948, winning 88 games in 86 days with a record of 112 out of 120 games. The season culminated with the Rens winning the "Colored Basketball World Championship" in 1939 and 1940. UCLA coach John Wooden played against the Rens and extolled, "To this day, I have never seen a team play better team basketball. They had great athletes, but they weren't as impressive as their team play. The way they handled and passed the ball was just amazing to me then, and I believe it would be today."[109] In 1948, the Harlem Globetrotters and the Minneapolis Lakers, the all-white, champions of the NBA, played an exhibition game. Widely ridiculed due to the antics of the Globetrotters, the game was viewed by the sports world as a publicity stunt. The Globetrotters won by two points, 61–59, as well as winning the second game in 1949. These games ended any contention that Blacks could not play and helped to dismantle segregated basketball.[110]

In 1950, NBA teams selected Nat "Sweetwater" Clifton (New York Knicks), Chuck Cooper (Boston Celtics), and Earl Lloyd (Washington Capitols). Cooper was the first to be drafted while Lloyd was the first to play in a game on October 31, 1950. Their presence was soon felt. New York Knicks player Willis Reed received the NBA's All-Star MVP honor, Finals MVP (1969–70), and the overall MVP. The Boston Celtics were the first team to draft a Black player, start five Blacks, and hire a Black head coach. Bill Russell won eleven championships with the Celtics and became the league's first Black coach. In 1972 Bob Douglas became the first Black to enter the Basketball Hall of Fame as a sport's contributor, followed by Bill Russell as the first Black player to be inducted. Robert Johnson bought the Charlotte Hornets/Bobcats/Hornets in 2002 and became the first Black majority owner of any professional team outside of baseball's Negro Leagues. In 2004 Joe Dumars of the Detroit Pistons was the first Black NBA general manager to win an NBA championship. Players of the caliber of Bill Russell, Wilt Chamberlain, Oscar Robertson, George Gervin, Walt Frazier, Willis Reed, Elvin Hayes, Elgin Baylor, and Julius Erving introduced a new style of play. They took the game from the floor into the air, made it faster and visually electrifying. George Gervin's "finger-roll," Kareem Abdul-Jabbar's "sky-hook," Earvin "Magic" Johnson's passes, Dominique Wilkins's and Shawn Kemp's amazing dunks, and Reggie Miller's three-pointers made every play a must-see. Michael Jordan made everyone want to "be like Mike" by winning six championships and selling basketball shoes.

While Muhammad Ali's actions are the most renowned, Jackie Robinson, Bill Russell, and Kareem Abdul-Jabbar were advocates far beyond their years as athletes. In 1961 Bill Russell and two other Black pro players refused to play for the Boston Celtics after experiencing discrimination in a Kentucky restaurant.[111] Kareem reacted to the 1967 ruling of the NCAA basketball rules committee to outlaw the dunk during a basketball game by saying, "To me, the new no-dunk rule smacks a little of discrimination. Most of the people who dunk are Black athletes."[112]

When a Black athlete uses his or her celebrity to address issues beyond the playing field, the result can be a hailstorm of criticism. A genuine risk threatens the careers of those who dare to engage in public protest. As of 2021, Colin Kaepernick had yet to play football after his protest. Malcolm Jenkins opined to ESPN,

> While our main focus is always on the community and those systemic oppressions, how we can leverage our relationships, our access and resources to help people in everyday communities, there is still a responsibility to speak out on Colin Kaepernick, who started this movement and still doesn't have a job. . . . I wholeheartedly believe he is being blackballed, to speak out in support of Eric Reid, who put his job on the line to fight for those who didn't have a voice. I have always maintained every chance I get to say, Colin Kaepernick started this, Eric Reid deserves a job, Colin Kaepernick deserves a job. I can turn on the tape this week and our opponent and see Colin Kaepernick deserves a job.[113]

Today's athletes have seemingly considered the cost and deemed it worth the risk. In March 1996, the National Basketball Association suspended Denver

Nuggets' Mahmoud Abdul-Rauf for a game for refusing to stand during the national anthem. He revealed to the *New York Times* that he opposed standing for a symbol of racist oppression. He was twenty-nine years of age and averaged 19.2 points per game with 6.8 assists. After the 2000–2001 season, he never played in the NBA again. He lost millions, received death threats, had the letters *KKK* spray-painted on his property, and had his home ignited by arson. In an *Undefeated* interview, he expressed no regrets and applauded Kaepernick's efforts and others: "It's good to continue to draw people's attention to what's going on whether you're an athlete, a politician, or a garbage man. These discussions are necessary. Sometimes it takes people of that stature, athletes, and entertainers because the youth are drawn to them, [more than] teachers and professors, unfortunately."[114]

When the Chicago Bulls won their second title, Craig Hodges, a Muslim, was outspoken against racial and religious hatred. While attending a 1991 White House reception, he wore a dashiki and handed President Bush a letter charging the nation with racism. The Bulls cut him, and no team would return his calls. He never played another NBA game. He stated in a later interview,

> We can't be sitting around, watching. We have to put our lives into the movement if we want it to sustain itself and to get to the point where we get solutions as opposed to continuing to have conflicts about the same issue. . . . The choice that I made was: I wanted to be on the right side of history. When people are oppressed, somebody has to stand up. . . . One of the things that gasses me, man, is: How could Donald Sterling be a racist and get two billion dollars? But Mahmoud Abdul-Rauf, Craig Hodges and other unnamed players I'm sure who have been discriminated against—our careers ended and [we weren't] compensated at all for it. We sacrificed.[115]

NBA player Carmelo Anthony marched in Baltimore to protest the death of Freddie Gray. While no one has directly linked it to his activism, he was out of the NBA for a full year before the Portland Trailblazers signed him. He told *Yahoo Sports*, "I think it was more so of everything else outside of basketball."[116]

The WNBA and female college basketball players were engaged in protest before Kaepernick took a knee. Four Minnesota Lynx players—Lindsay Whalen, Maya Moore, Rebekkah Brunson, and Seimone Augustus—wore shirts reading, "Change Starts with Us: Justice & Accountability" during a pregame press conference. New York Liberty players wore black t-shirts printed with *#BlackLivesMatter* and *Dallas5* (five murdered police officers) on July 10, 2016. Other teams wore plain black shirts to promote peace. Tina Charles wore one when accepting her Player of the Month trophy. When her entire team wore Black Lives Matter shirts, they received a fine, which was

later rescinded.[117] Tamika Catchings responded, "We thought it was important to have a voice about something greater than basketball. . . . I am very
proud of our team—as people—to be able to stand together for something we
believed in." WNBA player Marissa Coleman from the Indiana Fever said,
"I've been told to stay in my lane and 'just play basketball.' Basketball is what
I do, not who I am. I will not be confined to the lines of my sport. Those who
expect my teammates and to me to simply play basketball are missing out on
some phenomenal and educated women. Women who impact their communities in many ways. I have a platform, and it would be a disservice not using
it."[118] On November 29, 2014, Ariyana Smith of Knox College walked onto
the basketball court with her hands raised into the air and lay down for four
and a half minutes.[119]

Kelsey Bone was the first WNBA player to join Kaepernick's kneeling as
she took a knee in every game during the 2016 season. In the WNBA playoff opener against the Phoenix Mercury, her entire team knelt during the
national anthem. During a Phoenix Mercury playoff game, the Indiana Fever
team knelt during the playing of the anthem, joined by two opposing players,
Mistie Bass and Kelsey Bone. New York Liberty players locked arms during
the second round as Brittany Boyd bowed her head while the anthem played.
Mistie Bass kneeled alongside Kelsey Bone. Said Bone, "I have cousins, I
have brothers, I have uncles, I have a father. So for me, it hits close to home.
It's happening everywhere and I think it's something we need to talk about
and something that needs to be addressed."[120] Later she said, "I'm kneeling
because people who look like me, when they encounter the cops, there is usually some form of brutality, whether it's warranted or not. When that brutality happens, those cops are not then held accountable for their actions. . . .
This is a movement of alarm. 'Hello, wake up. Do you see us? Do you hear
us? We are not trying to go back to where we've come from.'"[121] WNBA
players wore t-shirts endorsing Rev. Raphael Warnock in his 2020 Senate run
against the Atlanta Dream owner, including Dream players.[122]

No superstar athlete in recent years has been as vocal as the NBA's LeBron
James, who addresses justice as often as he plays the game. James contemplated, "What are we doing to create change? Let's use this moment for all
professional athletes to educate ourselves, explore these issues, speak up, use
our influence, and renounce all violence. And most importantly, go back to
our communities and invest our time, our resources, help rebuild them, help
strengthen them, help change them. We all have to do better."[123] Back in
2012, James, Dwyane Wade, and eleven other members of the Miami Heat
wore hoodies in response to the death of Trayvon Martin. James shared a
photo with the hashtag *#WeAreTrayvonMartin* and wore "RIP Trayvon Martin" on his sneakers and posted on Instagram a drawing of Mike Brown and

Trayvon Martin walking arm in arm.[124] While with the Cleveland Cavaliers, he and Kyrie Irving and four Brooklyn Nets players, including Kevin Garnett, Deron Williams, Jarrett Jack, and Alan Anderson, wore "I Can't Breathe" t-shirts. Derrick Rose along with Kobe Bryant and the entire team wore black t-shirts embroidered with that logo.[125] James frequently criticized President Donald Trump on Twitter and became one of Trump's targets for personal attacks. When James opened his "I Promise" school, Trump tweeted that he was the only man dumber than Don Lemon, a CNN reporter who had interviewed him. Coming to LeBron's rescue was Melania Trump, whose spokesperson said she would visit the school if invited, and Michael Jordan, who praised LeBron's activism.[126] He worked to garner voter participation in the 2020 election with his "More Than A Vote" campaign.

Beginning in the 1990s, some professional teams declined invitations to the White House after winning their respective championships. Athletes voiced strong opposition to President Trump's stance on race and his offensive messaging following the murder of Heather Heyer in Charlottesville. The Golden State Warriors declined after winning both of its two NBA titles. After the 2017–18 title, they traveled to Washington, DC, and visited with former president Barack Obama.[127] After the Philadelphia Eagles announced they would not attend, Trump rescinded the invitation and announced a "Day of Patriotism." One attendee to the event was spotted taking a knee during the playing of the anthem.[128] *SBNation* wrote of the trending movement, "The presidency will continue its attack on the soul of the black athlete. Trump will always attack black athletes because they pose a threat to his form of white power. To strike back, to scold men he believes to be uppity and selfish, is to reassure his base."[129]

When asked if professional athletes should speak out, NBA player Derrick Rose responded, "I could care less about who else weighs in on this. Usually, athletes tend to stay away from this, but I just felt as if I had to do something." Said Los Angeles Rams player Davin Joseph, "I feel like we should support what we feel is right. We should always have an opinion of sticking up for people who don't have a voice." During the 2020 NBA playoffs, the Milwaukee Bucks players led a boycott after the shooting of Jacob Blake, refusing to play their scheduled game. The NBA postponed two days of games in response. The Detroit Lions cancelled practice and held a press conference. George Floyd's death caused a twitterstorm by players and coaches. The NFL, NHL, WNBA, NBA, L.A. Clippers, Golden State Warriors, Los Angeles Lakers, Brooklyn Nets, Washington Wizards, Los Angeles Dodgers, University of Kansas, and Big 12 Conference tweeted support.[130] Coco Gauff, Kavon Frazier, Caron Butler, Gabe Osabuohlen, Kendall Lamm, Ibtihaj Muhammad, LaVall Jordan, and Malcolm Brogdon participated in marches.[131] Michael

Jordan protested, "I stand with those who are calling out the ingrained racism and violence toward people of color in our country. We have had enough."[132] White players and coaches released statements. The most passionate came from Duke's Coach Mike Krzyzewski: "Black Lives Matter. Say it! Can't you say it? Black Lives Matter! We should be saying it every day. It's not political! This is not a political statement. It's a human rights statement."[133]

AFRICAN AMERICAN PHILANTHROPY AS PROTEST

> One reason little has been written about black philanthropy is that the word philanthropy evokes images of large foundations and wealthy philanthropists, which are scarce in the black community. When one expands the concept to include giving money, goods, and time, blacks emerge as having a strong, substantial philanthropic tradition.[134]
>
> —*Dr. Emmett Carson*

An ongoing debate within the Black community questions the responsibility of successful Blacks to those in the midst of poverty. An unwritten covenant demands the donation of time, money, and talent. African Americans live with a collective sense of responsibility. Accountability dates back to enslavement, where survival was achieved by banding together rather than individual isolation. Even those who argue against this sense of collective responsibility have benefited from others who assisted them.

Yvonne M. Brake interpreted the concept of "giving back" as a generational legacy. It is philanthropy through sharing one's resources for the betterment of the whole. She wrote,

> In other words, this philanthropy is seen as "giving back" because one is a part of the community and "it is the right thing to do"; it is not seen as generosity but as an African-American's obligation. As a result, many acts of philanthropy are personal and directly made to the individual in need, outside of the structure of a nonprofit organization; this informal philanthropy is a strong tradition among African-Americans.[135]

This understanding of philanthropy can be labeled as protest. Black philanthropy involves both giving and resisting. In the Black mind to help someone overcome the consequences of racism is an act of resistance. The motivation for reaching back was to assist but also to overcome the effects of white supremacy.

African Americans are estimated to be the nation's most charitable demographic.[136] A 2012 W. K. Kellogg Foundation report cited an increase in Black giving to the degree that nearly two-thirds of Black households donated $11 billion to charity.[137] A 2016 U.S. Trust Study of High Net Worth Philanthropy concluded that as an individual's income increased, so did her percentage of charitable giving. African Americans donated 25 percent more of their discretionary income to charity compared to white households. African American families tended to be better informed and monitored more closely the charities to which they gave donations. They reported greater satisfaction from giving and donated more frequently to faith-based and educational institutions. Church attendees were 25 percent more likely to donate than those who did not worship on a regular basis. They were almost twice as likely as whites to believe that their giving resulted in positive change in the world.[138]

Black celebrities can be divided into two groups: philanthropic celebrities and activist artists. Philanthropic celebrities give back through public or private donations. Many participate in hospital visitations, donate Thanksgiving meals, pay for funerals, and distribute toys at Christmas. Pro basketball star David Robinson has personally donated and raised hundreds of millions of dollars to finance the education of disadvantaged youth. The NBA named its service award the David Robinson Plaque.[139] Football player Warrick Dunn, humbly and quietly, has donated 145 homes for single-parent families through Warrick Dunn Charities.[140] A group of professional athletes initiated in 2006 Athletes for Hope to encourage other athletes to participate in philanthropy. Its stated mission is "to educate professional athletes about the importance of philanthropy and provide them with opportunities to get involved with charitable causes." Originators included Jackie Joyner-Kersee, Warrick Dunn, Muhammad Ali, Alonzo Mourning, Mia Hamm, Lance Armstrong, Andre Agassi, Andrea Jaeger, Tony Hawk, Jeff Gordon, Mario Lemieux, and Cal Ripken Jr. The Black Women in Sport Foundation (BWSF) provides opportunities for Black women and girls to transition from playing a sport to management. Philanthropic celebrities often give back without provoking controversy. They are less likely to offer public criticism and give back through charitable donations of money and time. Rarely do they offer critique or promote radical structural change. Some do not like appearing in public to showcase their service and prefer to operate behind the scenes. Others are low risk takers and do not wish to damage their brand.

Activist artists engage openly in public protest. They focus on changing the system, insisting that it is not broken but operates in the manner for which it was created. Their attention lies in identifying systemic racism as the enemy. Music mogul Jay-Z lent his tremendous clout toward the elimination of cash bail. His nonprofit FREEAMERICA called for criminal justice reform and an end to mass incarceration. Under his birth name, Shawn Carter, he wrote in *Time*,

> If you're from neighborhoods like the Brooklyn one I grew up in, if you're unable to afford a private attorney, then you can be disappeared into our jail system simply because you can't afford bail. Millions of people are separated from their families for months at a time—not because they are convicted of committing a crime, but because they are accused of committing a crime. . . . This Father's Day, I'm supporting those same organizations to bail out fathers who can't afford the due process our democracy promises. As a father with a growing family, it's the least I can do, but philanthropy is not a long fix, we have to get rid of these inhumane practices altogether. We can't fix our broken criminal justice system until we take on the exploitative bail industry.[141]

In 2018, he invested in the start-up Promise, focusing on individuals in the criminal justice system.[142]

Alicia Keys endorsed the Black Lives Matter movement as a strong advocate for justice for battered women. Other activist artists include Oprah Winfrey, Danny Glover, Jesse Williams, Chance the Rapper, Cardi B, Steph Curry, John Legend, Zendaya, Common, and Serena and Venus Williams, to name just a few.[143] Activist artists are politically outspoken and high risk takers. They participate in public rallies and use their marketing appeal for social causes. They risk damaging their marketability in the eyes of cautious advertisers who frown on public advocacy. They are less concerned about maintaining their relationships with white power brokers who strenuously protect their companies' marketing image amid concern over whites who might protest the protesters. They do not shy away from controversy, backing Colin Kaepernick, Black Lives Matter, and victims of police shootings. They are committed to impactful systemic change. Along with public advocacy, they build schools, establish foundations and nonprofits, and donate their time and millions of dollars.

Some Black celebrities cannot be pigeon-holed into one category, activist artist or philanthropic celebrity, as they transition from one to the other or simply evolve into a hybrid. LeBron James and Beyoncé are an interesting combination of both as they make charitable donations yet are outspoken on systemic problems facing the nation. Beyoncé embraces being labeled an outspoken feminist. She shared in *Elle*, "That is why I wanted to work with [the philanthropic organizations] Chime for Change and Global Citizen. They understand how issues related to education, health, and sanitation around the world affect a woman's entire existence and that of her children. . . . Working to make those inequalities go away is being a feminist, but more importantly, it makes me a humanist."[144]

THE NEW WARS ON AFRICAN AMERICANS

What has changed since the collapse of Jim Crow has less to do with the basic structure of our society than with the language we use to justify it. In the era of color blindness, it is no longer socially permissible to use race, explicitly, as a justification for discrimination, exclusion, and social contact. So we don't. Rather than rely on race, we use our criminal justice system to label people of color "criminals" and then engage in all the practices we supposedly left behind. Today it is perfectly legal to discriminate against criminals in nearly all the ways that it was legal to discriminate against African Americans. Once you're labeled a felon, the old forms of discrimination—employment discrimination, housing discrimination, denial of the right to vote, denial of educational opportunities, denial of food stamps and other public benefits, and exclusion from jury service—are suddenly legal. As a criminal, you have scarcely more rights, and arguably less respect, than a Black man living in Alabama at the height of Jim Crow. We have not ended racial caste in America; we have merely redesigned it.[145]
—*Michelle Alexander*, The New Jim Crow

America has fought wars on three fronts: wars against international enemies, wars against domestic enemies, and wars against African Americans. America has waged war, literally and figuratively, against its African American citizens. Since 1619, people of African descent have been under constant barrage by the federal government, local municipalities, and individual citizens. African Americans experienced oppression so severe that many felt as if they were treated as enemy combatants. Retired Chicago chief medical officer Linda Rae Murray commented, "Racism is not a disaster. It's something that human beings created and keep healthy. Segregation is something human beings invented, specific human beings, for specific purposes. The health inequities that exist are not accidents. They're created by people."[146]

Destabilization strategies materialized whenever African Americans demonstrated political, social, or economic gains. African Americans had to defend themselves against centuries of inequitable schools, lower wages, loan denials, and racialized policing. The power of the state legitimized voter suppression and disenfranchisement. Economic violence, legal and extralegal, decimated African American wealth. Families and individuals were denied opportunity as confiscated wealth was redistributed to white communities. Ta-Nehisi Coates determined, "America for most of its history has actively punished black ambition. The black middle class has been the field for demonstrations upon the subject of what happens to n***** with ideas. . . . It's worth considering what message a country sends to a people when it persecutes ambition."[147]

Following Reconstruction, southern states sought to reinstate conditions as close to slavery as inhumanely possible. In the early 1900s, the Great Migration was triggered by a feudal economic system and the unjust application of criminal law. The 1920s witnessed the onslaught of race massacres, the destruction of towns, and the creation of "sundown," white-only, communities. The 1930s, in the midst of the Great Depression, excluded African Americans from New Deal programs. The denial of home loans increased segregation as urban renewal decimated districts and displaced Black-owned businesses. The 1940s and 1950s persisted the economic warfare through redlining and the foreclosure on millions of acres of African American farmland. The 1960s civil rights movement produced hysteria and white flight. The 1970s and 1980s saw the emergence of a War on Drugs, which inflicted high incarceration rates during the Nixon and Reagan administrations. The War on Crime during the Clinton administration increased disproportionate imprisonment. The incarceration of African American men, labeled as lifelong felons, disrupted African American children's lives and impeded family well-being. The first decades of the twenty-first century saw the housing market crash that disproportionately impacted African Americans as subprime mortgages, "reverse redlining," resulted in home foreclosures. According to the Center for Responsible Lending, 8 percent of African Americans were victims of foreclosure between 2007 to 2009 whereas the rate for whites was half that rate.[148] Bank of America alone was fined $335 million for charging 200,000 African American and Hispanic households higher interest rates and fees than similarly situated whites.[149]

Only in the rarest periods and for the briefest moments have politicians legislated relief to rectify the damage done by these injustices.

GI Bill

On June 22, 1944, President Franklin D. Roosevelt signed into law the Servicemen's Readjustment Act, or GI Bill. It provided veterans low-interest loans (home, farm, and business), unemployment benefits, job location assistance, and college tuition. Although the bill was written to benefit all veterans, Black veterans were excluded from a fair dispersal as grants were distributed primarily to whites. By July 1956, 8 million veterans entered college or training institutions, and 4.3 million received home loans valued at

$33 billion. The white middle class thrived on GI benefits as millions got an economic boost.[150]

The country established residential zones based on race, determining where Blacks could and could not reside. In 1926 the Supreme Court backed the ruling of a lower court stating that although the zones were illegal, since private ownership controlled restrictive covenants, they were not regulated under the Fourteenth Amendment. Redlining and mortgage covenants excluded Blacks. The Veterans Administration (VA) approved restrictive covenants and prevented Blacks from acquiring loans in white areas. By 1947, of 3,200 VA-backed home loans for veterans, only two were for Black vets. In New York and northern New Jersey, from a total of 67,000 mortgages, less than 100 went to Black families. Predominantly white colleges and universities denied entry to Black vets, relegating them to Black colleges and universities, which had neither the facilities nor teachers to educate the overwhelming numbers who applied. One hundred fifty thousand veterans were denied enrollment, based not on aptitude but the inability of HBCUs to enroll them due to lack of capacity. Fifty percent had fewer than 250 students; only 5 percent were accredited; and only seven had graduate programs, with no doctoral degrees or accredited engineering programs.[151]

White, southern, Democratic congressmen limited the GI Bill's benefits exclusively to white veterans. They insisted that states manage distribution and not the federal government. While white soldiers were able to establish credit and purchase homes, Blacks had to fend in a world which segregated them socially and economically.[152]

Redlining

America generated a white middle class while intentionally excluding African Americans through redlining. The term comes from drawing red lines around communities to deny loans based upon the residents' race. A 1940 Chicago city map outlined in red areas where Black people lived and marked them as ineligible for federal home loans. Ta-Nehisi Coates wrote in an *Atlantic* article titled "The Case for Reparations" that "from the 1930s through the 1960s, black people across the country were largely cut out of the legitimate home-mortgage market through means both legal and extralegal."[153]

The 1930s Great Depression crippled the American economy. Congress passed the National Housing Act to increase home ownership, provide low-interest, long-term loans, and reduce down payments through the Federal Housing Administration (FHA). Rather than envisioning that home ownership across all demographics would benefit the American economy, leadership implemented a racist policy to increase white ownership and stifle, even decrease, ownership among Blacks. The *Underwriting Manual*, known as "The FHA Bible," promoted the policy that stability was secure when comprised of people of the same racial and social class. The federal government operated a nationwide campaign to deny home loans to Black families seeking to move into white districts. The FHA gave explicit instructions that no loans were to go to developers who built homes in integrated zones, and at resale Blacks were prohibited from purchase. Government actions implemented segregation where it had not existed before.[154] The first civilian public housing units began with white families as the intended recipients. White speculators purchased homes and sold them to Black families for twice as much as the home was worth.[155] Policies were enforced in the suburban communities of Levittown, New York City: Lakewood, Los Angeles; San Lorenzo, San Francisco; and others across the nation. A planned community outside of Stanford University was denied a loan because three of the 150 families were African American. Richard Rothstein concluded that the FHA's "whites-only policies" flung a "white noose" around the neck of Black homeownership.[156] Richard Rothstein wrote in *Crisis* magazine that "racially explicit government policy in the mid-20th century was the most powerful force separating the races in every metropolitan area, with effects that endure today."[157]

In 2014 author Jamelle Bouie wrote, "The combination of redlining, block-busting, racial covenants, and other discriminatory measures means that, even now, a majority of blacks survived with relatively minimal access to capital and mortgage loans. What's more, this systematic discrimination has left many black households unable to afford down payments or other housing costs, even if loans are available."[158] The denial of bank loans greatly reduced African American families' ability to accumulate wealth and accounts to a large degree for the wealth disparity between white and Black families. The opportunity to bequeath the financial value of a home is a rare experience for many African American families.[159]

Redlining limited African American homeownership and continues to prevent wealth accumulation. Journalist Tracy Jan examined a 2019 study by the National Community Reinvestment Coalition (NCRC) on the issuance of home mortgage and small-business loans in Baltimore. The study stated that the dominant factor in the denial of a loan was the applicant's race, regardless of earned income or the amount of savings accumulated. It confirmed that areas targeted by redlining were among the poorest in the nation and that three out of every four redlined communities experienced historical and persistent economic stresses. Residents confined to impoverished communities lack access to capital, which is a major source of economic advancement. The inability to access investment dollars makes it extremely difficult for African Americans to purchase homes, improve property, receive capital investments, open businesses, relocate to desirable localities, or bequeath wealth. The Center for Investigative Reporting revealed that in 2019, sixty-one metropolitan regions practiced redlining. They included Atlanta, Detroit, Rockford, St. Louis, Little Rock, Tacoma, San Antonio, Mobile, Greenville, and Gainesville. NCRC director Jason Richardson remarked, "It's as if some of these places have been trapped in the past, locking neighborhoods into concentrated poverty."[160]

According to the *Washington Post*, the Great Recession that began in 2008 had a disproportionately devastating impact on Black families, "forcing many out of their homes and pushing Black homeownership rates to record lows . . . homeownership levels for that group have dropped incrementally almost every year since 2004."[161] A major failure of the Obama administration during the Great Recession was the failure to demand that banks provide remedies to foreclosed families. Enormous fines were issued, but no actions taken to restore homes. In other words, nothing was done to remedy the problem these banks caused.

Urban Renewal

James Baldwin said that "urban renewal means Negro removal."[162] As cities renovated downtown centers, restoration meant the destruction of Black communities and businesses. President Harry Truman signed the Housing Act of 1949 to provide funding for the renewal of urban centers throughout the United States. The goal was to eliminate sections of impoverished cities, revitalize localities, construct public housing communities, and improve infrastructure. This noble cause was frustrated by racial politics and policies.[163] Millions of African Americans flooded northern cities to be greeted by a severe shortage of affordable housing, racial segregation, and white hostility. Rather than help immigrants find suitable housing, government authorities were more concerned with clearing out residents. Under eminent domain, authorities displaced more than a million tenants from two thousand communities and handed the property over to private contractors and universities to build offices, malls, and hospitals. Projects included Lincoln Center in New York City, the Civic Arena in Pittsburgh, and the New Jersey College of Medicine and Dentistry in Newark.

The study "Renewing Inequality" diagnosed the impact of renewal projects on people of color and the impact of redlining. Northern and southern renewal led to entrenched segregation by stuffing those displaced into crowded places. African Americans were guided to public housing and rental units, while white families were given home-ownership incentives.[164]

A particularly harmful element was the construction of highway bypasses through Black communities. Cities such as Buffalo, Durham, Tampa, Miami,

Jackson, Atlanta, Chicago, Richmond, Detroit, Baltimore, Newark, Charlottesville, District of Columbia, and New York City followed this pattern.
Newark was second only to Norfolk with seventeen renewals that displaced
22,000 African American and Puerto Rican residents. In Durham, Bypass
147 cut through the former business district of Hayti. Other North Carolina city neighborhoods affected included Greensboro's Dudley, Charlotte's
Biddleville, and Washington's High Point.[165] Detroit's Black Bottom is now
Interstate 75.[166] Lubbock, Texas, contained only a small racial-ethnic population, 3 percent, but the entirety of the 1,300 residents negatively impacted were
of color. For African Americans, urban renewal was indeed "Negro removal."

War on African American Farmers

For Black people, there was something spiritual about farming. It symbolized being whole, not controlled by another, and a sense that you possessed
worth and added value to the world. Slave farming built the country's wealth
as billions filled the coffers of southern and northern profiteers. The revenue
from tobacco, cotton, and sugar provided generational wealth with no benefit
to those who performed every modicum of labor. For the enslaved, the most
sought-after prize following emancipation was land. The unfulfilled promise
of forty acres and a mule resonated with Black men and women who fully
understood the worth of being a landowner. Land acquisition granted financial independence and represented that you were a free man. To own land
meant that you could maintain self-sufficiency for yourself and your family.[167]

African American farmers once controlled 14 million acres of farmland
in the United States. In 1920, there were nearly 950,000 Black farmers. The
Emergency Land Fund estimated that after 1950, 500,000 Black farms disappeared in just twenty-five years. Between 1950 and 1969, eight million acres
of farmland were lost or seized. According to the U.S. Census Bureau, 2,890
Black men and 237 Black women were working Alabama farms in 1970. In
1980 there were only 1,201 men and 117 women engaged in farm work.[168]
Mississippi counties, with a majority Black population, control just 2 percent
of farms. In 2020, 45,500 African American farmers constituted just 1.3 percent of farmers nationwide. According to *Modern Farmer*, "Black agriculture
was a powerhouse; per capita there were more Black farmers than white farmers. But by the turn of the 21st century, 90 percent of that land was lost. . . .
Less known is the story of those who stayed in rural areas and their efforts to
hold on to their land within a legal system that seemed designed to shift it—
and the generational wealth it represented—to white ownership."[169]

The narrative of the life and death of the African American farmer is one
of the most devastating stories in the loss of Black wealth. Author Pete Daniel

remarked, "It was almost as if the earth was opening up and swallowing black farmers."[170] The New Deal provided assistance to a nation in need of a moral and economic boost. It proved to be an asset for white farmers but forbidden fruit for farmers of color. Systemic racism at the hands of the U.S. Department of Agriculture limited any fair distribution of loans to Black farmers, who were denied loans at an unimaginable rate. Government agents who treated them fairly were rare as race trumped need. For those who managed to acquire a loan, it was so minuscule that it rarely covered expenses.[171] White agents for the Farmers Home Administration universally discriminated through the denial of loans, falsified the availability of funds, accelerated payment schedules, delayed approvals, withheld skill training, and foreclosed on property years early. Cecil Brewington of Pender County, North Carolina, reported, "Every time I walked in that office, they said, 'You can fill out the forms, but we don't have any money.'" In 1984, the U.S. Commission on Civil Rights declared that the plight of the Black farmer was "a blight on the conscience of the nation."[172] The property of African American heirs was annexed by real-estate developers and speculators.[173]

In 1999, after efforts by Democratic Congresswoman Eva Clayton and the Congressional Black Caucus, the United States government settled the largest civil suit of its kind with Black farmers for $1 billion. The USDA publicly acknowledged past discrimination but claimed it had been unaware of discriminatory practices between 1981 and 1995. While the suit settlement seems astronomical, it only amounted to $50,000 per farmer, enough to buy a tractor and some seed but not enough to recover the millions of acres of land forever lost, much of it stolen. Congresswoman Clayton shared the sentiments of many after a meeting with President Bill Clinton: "Much of the session was sharing the pain of having been discriminated against by their government."[174]

The War on Drugs

On June 17, 1971, President Richard Nixon declared a "War on Drugs." This so-called war was not to diminish the number of Americans suffering drug addiction; it was a political directive to target activist Blacks and whites who protested the Vietnam War. John Ehrlichman, counsel for the president, revealed in a 1994 interview,

> The Nixon campaign in 1968, and the Nixon White House after that, had two enemies: the antiwar left and Black people. . . . We knew we couldn't make it illegal to be either against the war or Black, but by getting the public to associate the hippies with marijuana and Blacks with heroin, and then criminalizing both heavily, we could disrupt

those communities. . . . Did we know we were lying about the drugs? Of course we did.[175]

Ronald Reagan continued the racialized war on drugs for political purposes, as summarized in an NPR interview with Michelle Alexander:

[Reagan] declared the drug war primarily for reasons of politics—racial politics. Numerous historians and political scientists have documented that the war on drugs was part of a grand Republican Party strategy known as the "Southern strategy" of using racially coded "get-tough" appeals on crime and welfare to appeal to poor and working-class whites, particularly in the South, who were resentful of, anxious about and threatened by many of the gains of African-Americans in the civil rights movement.[176]

In 1980, 40,900 people were convicted of drug offenses; by 2017, the number had increased to 452,964. Drug arrests and convictions increased by 1,000 percent, not due to increased usage but through the diversion of federal dollars to law enforcement agencies. The arrest of low-level offenders has been incentivized by the lure of funding and equipment benefits based on the number of seizures. Michelle Alexander maintained that both the Bush and Obama administrations continued these drug enforcement policies instead of putting the focus on prevention.

The War on Drugs devastated the African American populace as incarceration numbers skyrocketed. One of four African American males is under the jurisdiction of the criminal justice system. According to the Drug Policy Alliance, African Americans are more likely to be stopped, searched, arrested, convicted, and sentenced for drug crimes. Eighty percent of those in federal prisons and 60 percent in state prisons are Black or brown.[177] Attorney General Eric Holder attempted to slow the prosecution of low-level offenders and instructed prosecutors to recommend to judges shorter sentences for elderly and nonviolent offenders. Attorney General Jeff Sessions reversed his policies.

The War on Crime

President Lyndon B. Johnson said in an address to Congress, "I hope that 1965 will be regarded as the year when this country began in earnest a thorough and effective war against crime." This so-called war on crime has in reality been a war on African Americans and a war on the poor. The impact of punitive criminal justice practices has changed little since convict leasing when the aim of policing was to keep Black people in their place.[178] In her NPR interview Michelle Alexander explained,

People are swept into the criminal justice system—particularly in poor communities of color—at very early ages . . . typically for fairly minor, nonviolent crimes. [The young black males are] shuttled into prisons, branded as criminals and felons, and then when they're released, they're relegated to a permanent second-class status, stripped of the very rights supposedly won in the civil rights movement—like the right to vote, the right to serve on juries, the right to be free of legal discrimination and employment, and access to education and public benefits. Many of the old forms of discrimination that we supposedly left behind during the Jim Crow era are suddenly legal again, once you've been branded a felon.[179]

In 1969 the U.S. prison population totaled 188,000 inmates. The goal was rehabilitation, which sought to decrease recidivism and provide a path forward. Oregon, Iowa, Michigan, California, Illinois, and Minnesota reduced inmates through parole, progressive sentencing guidelines, and merit reductions.[180] Progress halted when an increase in illegal drug use resulted in public hysteria fueled by politicians and endorsed by the media. President Johnson established the Law Enforcement Assistance Administration and the Bureau of Narcotics and Dangerous Drugs agencies. President Nixon advanced the war and called for tougher enforcement. Victims' rights organizations effectively advocated for longer prison terms. By 1977 the number of prisoners had grown to 283,000. The 1984 Truth in Sentencing Laws (TIS) required prisoners to serve out most of their sentences before parole eligibility. President Ronald Reagan signed the 1986 Anti-Drug Abuse Act with mandatory minimum sentencing for drug convictions with a notable discrepancy between crack and powder cocaine. During his eight years in office, the number of prisoners doubled. Between 1975 and 1985, every state in the union instituted mandatory sentencing guidelines and eliminated discretion by parole boards even though crime rates were decreasing.

Bill Clinton signed the 1994 Violent Crime Control and Law Enforcement Act requiring mandatory sentencing, TIS, and the three-strikes provision. The 1995 Contract with America established punitive sentencing guidelines more severe than those already legislated. Program funding for prevention and treatment shifted to arrest and incarceration. Social institutions and nonprofits experienced severe funding cuts in rehab programs. The prison population swelled from 329,000 in 1980 to 949,000 in 1993 and then to 1.5 million in 1995. A 1993 poll revealed that most Americans no longer supported the pre-1970s belief that prison should rehabilitate a person. A 2016 Brennan Center study concluded that 39 percent of sentencing could have been resolved outside of the prison industrial complex.[181]

The results of the War on Crime have been devastating for African Americans. According to the Pew Research Center and the NAACP, Black communities are targeted for over-policing although drug use and distribution rates match those of whites. The Sentencing Project declared that "Police find drugs where they look for them. Inner-city, open-air drug markets are easier to bust than those that operate out of suburban basements." Blacks made up 13 percent of the U.S. population but 30 percent of those on probation or parole. When Black men and white men commit the same crime, black men, on average, receive a sentence almost 20 percent longer. Black people are three times more likely to be killed by police than white people. More unarmed black people are killed than unarmed white people.[182]

Environmental Racism

In Warren County, North Carolina, the Rev. Ben Chavis coined the term *environmental racism* in 1982.[183] Toxic dumps are located in communities of color to a far greater degree than white communities, causing a disproportionate exposure to contaminants. Hazardous sites consist of toxic transfer stations, incinerators, garbage dumps, garages, smokestacks, landfills, industrial hog and chicken farms, oil refineries, chemical plants, and radioactive-waste-storage areas. Environmental pollutants endanger African Americans' health with higher-than-normal rates of cancer, asthma, and premature death. Impacted communities include Houston (1967) and West Harlem (1968). Florida's Wedgewood had thirteen landfills. Louisiana ranks among states with the highest risks of cancer, sickness, and premature death; eighty-five miles of the state's "Cancer Alley" contain 150 industries and refineries that poison the land, air, and water with carcinogens in areas populated by Black and brown residents.[184]

American policy makers and industry leaders viewed Black, Hispanic, and poor white neighborhoods as the first option for industrial waste deposits. The U.S. General Accounting Office presented evidence that hazardous waste sites in three southeastern states were often located in or near African American communities. In 1987, the United Church of Christ verified that three out of five Black and brown Americans lived near a toxic waste site. In partnership with the Clean Air Task Force (CATF), the NAACP released a 2017 study ascertaining that African Americans were disproportionately exposed to air toxins to a greater degree than any other group. The EPA declared in 2019 that race, not class or wealth, is a greater factor in being subjected to environmental pollution.[185] That same year the state of California released a report with similar findings. An NPR report by Jonathan Lambert cites a 2019 study published in the journal *PNAS* declaring that "air pollution is disproportionately caused by white Americans' consumption of goods and services, but disproportionately inhaled by black and Hispanic Americans."[186]

It has not only been challenging to attract attention from politicians and industry but also from the environmental movement. Its focus is on damage to the environment with scant attention to the people impacted by pollution. Black leaders challenged environmental groups to diversify staff and boards and widen their focus to those whose lives were in jeopardy. There has been movement as organizations are more aware of the importance of diversity amongst their staffs and hired people of color.

Economic Racism

America has a long history of economic racism. The examples are plentiful: A bank has one set of loan qualifications for Blacks and another for whites with similar qualifications. Bank standards alternate depending on race or zip code of the applicant. A firm does not hire or promote African Americans yet employs whites with the same prerequisites. It is difficult to detect in the corridors of the private sector. Such economic discrimination is difficult to prove and prosecute, however, for state and federal governments are reluctant to take on racial bias cases. Republican administrations have also proven hostile to enforcing consumer regulations.[187]

According to a 2014 *Slate* article, "The Crisis in Black Homeownership," the Great Recession decimated African American wealth. An African American who purchased a home at the beginning of this century was twice as likely to lose that home to debt, divorce, or unemployment. The Great Recession erased half of Black wealth when the wealth gap between white and African Americans was already insurmountable. In 2005 Blacks had an average net worth of $12,124, shocking in comparison to a white net worth of $134,149. After the recession, Black wealth measured $5,677. A Brandeis University report revealed that between 2007 and 2010, "wealth for blacks declined by an average of 31%, home equity by an average of 28%, and retirement savings by an average of 35%. Whites only lost 11% of wealth, 24% in home equity, and gained 9% in retirement savings." Economists estimated that the recession cost the Black community $20 billion.[188]

This dispossession of wealth was wholly avoidable and notable for the complicit silence of politicians. There have been no efforts for compensation for financial loss, nor has the banking industry been properly prosecuted. There is ample room for judicial intervention through the enforcement of fair-play policies and the prosecution of discriminatory practices.

Corporate banks, such as Wells Fargo, New Century Financial, and Morgan Stanley, guided customers toward high-risk, subprime loans and then foreclosed on the family homes acquired by the loans. Large banking corporations escaped, but twelve employees at the Chinese American–owned bank of Abacus Federal Savings were prosecuted and marched down the courthouse hallway handcuffed as in a slave coffle.[189] Abacus was the only bank prosecuted and the first in New York since 1991. The irony is that it was Abacus who reported the fraudulent actions to regulators. There are few consequences for institutions that commit such crimes that disproportionally happen to Black people.

Economic and Environmental Racism Marry

America is preparing for the next natural disaster with minimal response to repair communities impacted by poverty that were previously damaged or destroyed by a natural disaster. Filmmaker Judith Helfand studied the 1995 deadly heat wave in Chicago and says about the resulting documentary *Cooked: Survival by Zip Code*, "This movie which started out being about one specific heat disaster, turned into something more complicated and uncomfortable, about the impact of generations' worth of racism and denial."[190]

In 1995 over 739 Chicagoans died in five days (July 14–July 20). The initial cause of death was attributed to the heat wave, but the real reason was racialized poverty. Even as the summer heat diminished, the numbers kept rising, and many believed that it could be much higher than stated. Zip codes revealed that those who died lived in the center of the city where African Americans' concentration is densest. The city responded by a slowed reaction resembling willful negligence. A city official explained,

> This is a map that has two things going on at the same time. We put the circles in those communities that have the highest poverty rates, and then we shaded in those communities that have the highest mortality rates from the heat. As you can see they have almost perfect overlaps. So, the question is, did people die of the heat, or did they die of the social conditions in these neighborhoods, and the answer is both. I mean, had the heat not occurred, they wouldn't have died that week, that's for sure. But they would have died too soon anyway.[191]

Across the country, there is high mortality rate when a natural disaster and race collide. In 2005 Hurricane Katrina devastated the city of New Orleans; two thousand people of color perished while one million sought refuge elsewhere. Today 92,000 fewer African Americans live in the city than before the hurricane. Hurricane Sandy killed 159 residents of New York and New Jersey and caused $70 billion in damages. Attention and aid were for white home owners, while African Americans' homes and structures went without repair or financial assistance. In 2017 Hurricane Maria plowed over the Caribbean island of Puerto Rico, wreaking havoc upon American citizens and killing at least a thousand residents. The Trump administration responded with inadequate aid, symbolized by a video of the president slinging rolls of paper towels at desperate citizens. In Flint, Michigan, fresh drinking water is no longer a luxury that children experience; 100,000 are exposed to contaminated water with dangerous levels of lead pouring from drains.[192] Poverty and race often equate to preventable deaths, and investment in the homes and lives of the impoverished saves lives.

Dr. Frankenstein

The relationship between the African American community and the medical community has long been fraught and filled with abuse. It is a history of fraudulent and inadequate health care. The enslaved had to develop their own medical services because they only had the services of a doctor in life-or-death circumstances, if then. Slaves developed their own cures, many dating back to Africa, and were renowned for using plants for their healing powers. Black women served as expert midwives, often rendering services to Black and white expectant mothers. When they could garner the services of white practitioners, they were frequently used as subjects of study or received lesser attention. Rachel Hardeman released the findings of her study citing evidence that the high rate of infant mortality for Black infants in Florida is influenced by the race of the doctor: "Although Black newborns are three times as likely to die as White newborns, when the doctor of record for Black newborns—primarily pediatricians, neonatologists and family practitioners—was also Black, their mortality rate, as compared with White newborns, was cut in half."[193]

African Americans have also often been the victims of unethical medical practices. J. Marion Sims, the "father of gynecology," performed gynecological-surgical experiments on twelve enslaved women without the use of anesthesia.[194] For forty years, from 1932 to 1972, the "Tuskegee Study of Untreated Syphilis in the Negro Male" involved over six hundred men as victims of an unscrupulous experiment. They were examined as research animals without treatment even after penicillin was discovered to be a cure. Men endured blindness, mental insanity, and immense pain but never received medical assistance.[195]

In 1951, Henrietta Lacks, a mother of five, became a patient at Johns Hopkins Hospital for the continuing ailment of vaginal bleeding. The discovery of a large, malignant tumor on her cervix was treated by radium treatments. Unbeknownst to her, doctors collected her cells and used them in research without her permission before her death at the age of thirty-one in 1951. The result was a multimillion-dollar biotech industry that occurred without her family's knowledge or benefit. The durability of her cells led to breakthroughs in the development of the polio vaccine, cloning, and gene mapping. The family sued to benefit in the use of her cells, which have been reproduced billions of times and sold to research centers, but have been told that they have no standing in court because the statute of limitations for medical malpractice has long expired. Lacks's only recognition has been the naming of the cells "HeLa."[196]

In 2020, the pandemic of COVID-19 swept the globe. In the United States, it hit communities of color the hardest. Blacks constitute just 13 percent of the U.S. population but 16 percent of those who have died due to the virus.[197] Of all racial-ethnic groups, African Americans reported being less likely to take the COVID-19 vaccine, at a low rate of 42 percent. Hispanics (61%), whites (63%), and Asians (83%) report being the most willing to be vaccinated. The Black rate of skepticism is compounded by the fact that 71 percent report that they know someone who has been hospitalized or died because of infection. As recently as September 2020, research into a COVID-19 drug voiced a shortage of Black volunteers. Barack Obama urged all Americans to take the vaccine and was vaccinated on camera. "I may end up taking it on TV or having it filmed, just so that people know that I trust this science."[198]

The eugenics movement in the United States victimized African American and Latina women, and poor white women. Paternalistic doctors have made unethical decisions deeming who was worthy of being a mother throughout a long history of forced sterilization. U.S. courts failed time after time to protect poor women, white or Black.[199] According to Lisa Ko of PBS's "Independent Lens," "Federally-funded sterilization programs took place in 32 states throughout the 20th century." California led the nation with 20,000 from 1909 until 1979 targeting Asian and Mexican women. Between 1970 and 1976 "between 25–50 percent of Native American women were sterilized." More women were sterilized in Puerto Rico than anywhere else in the world, at least 35 percent of the female population. Southern states practiced medical maleficence on African American women for the primary goal of population control. North Carolina led the way, paying surgeons to sterilize girls as young as nine years of age. Medical students performed so-called Mississippi appendectomies, which were in reality hysterectomies done at teaching hospitals. Federal programs sterilized between 100,000 and 150,000 poor women a year in the United States.[200]

Even in the twenty-first century, health care remains problematic for the Black community. Study after study reveals disparities in the amount of health care and the quality of treatment received. The National Academy of Medicine released a report that poverty itself is not the sole cause of a shorter Black life span and the higher rates of sickness that Blacks experience. It confirmed that whites and Blacks received different levels of health care when the only difference between patients was their race and that race impacted the treatment received from physicians. The report further stated that

> racial and ethnic minorities receive lower-quality health care (concrete, inferior care that physicians give their Black patients) than white people—even when insurance status, income, age, and severity of conditions are comparable. . . . Minority persons are less likely than white persons to be given appropriate cardiac care, to receive kidney dialysis or transplants, and to receive the best treatments for stroke, cancer, or AIDS. . . . Some people in the United States were more likely to die from cancer, heart disease, and diabetes simply because of their race or ethnicity, not just because they lack access to health care.[201]

The tragic legacy has been a distrust of the medical profession because of the generational trauma that exists in the Black community.

Gentrification

Gentrification is a phenomenon lambasted by people of color and activists in every major city. It is marketed as downtown redevelopment, while others associate it with displacement and invasion. Its impact on poor, racial-ethnic residents can lead to economically forced relocation due to the loss of a home or apartment as well as higher taxes. An influx of whites into cities results in the exodus of city residents who have lived there for generations. Spike Lee spoke in 2014 on New York City gentrification: "Why does it take an influx of white New Yorkers in the south Bronx, in Harlem, in Bed Stuy, in Crown Heights for the facilities to get better? What about the people who are renting? They can't afford it anymore!"[202]

A study from the National Community Reinvestment Coalition (NCRC) identified areas in the country where gentrification occurred and its impact. A press release from the NCRC explained that "gentrification is a term used to describe what happens when lower-income neighborhoods receive massive levels of new investment, adding amenities, raising home values, and bringing in new upper-income residents. This can lead to cultural displacement, when members of a racial or ethnic group who were longtime residents of gentrified neighborhoods are pushed out." Between 2000 and 2013, the study surveyed 935 towns and cities and 1,000 neighborhoods. Two hundred thirty communities experienced increased rent, property values, and higher taxes, resulting in the exodus of more than 135,000 residents. Washington, DC, experienced one of the highest rates of displacement in the country with Ward 6 (Capitol Hill, the Navy Yard, the Southwest Waterfront, and parts of downtown) being the hardest hit.[203]

Austin, Texas, markets itself as one of the more progressive cities in America, but residents living on Garden Street in East Austin tell a different story, as a Black exodus has been occurring for the last decade. Edward Escamillia said, "You got a 3-story home going up that's worth $380,000, right next to a home that's worth no more than $50,000. The people that are not able to afford what taxes are now are kind of being bullied out and they're getting offers that they can't refuse."[204] A 2018 University of Texas at Austin report, titled "Uprooted," concluded,

> Absent major interventions by the City of Austin and other stakeholders, these residents—who are largely low-income persons of color—will be pushed out farther away from opportunity and dislocated from their communities. In the process, neighborhoods that have historically been home to African-American and Hispanic residents will lose their cultural character and become enclaves for largely white and wealthier residents.[205]

Racist Robots

Twenty-first-century technology touches everyone as automation handles service calls and online purchases. It should trigger a decrease in discrimination as machines are not racist whereas people are. Or aren't they?

Unfortunately, human bias affects artificial intelligence technology (AI). Studies discovered that racism crept its way into AI's programs. Software designed to improve services in health care, criminal justice, and education yield racially impaired results. Computers use information programmed into data banks by racially impaired perceptions. Programmers act as parents, and their predispositions influence the conclusions of the machine, whether it is an algorithm or facial recognition.[206] *Towards Data Science* writer John Murray affirmed, "Bias is a part of life, and something that not a single person on the planet is free from. . . . This bias can, and often does, find its way into AI platforms."[207]

A *Proceedings of the National Academy of Science* (*PNAS*) study revealed glitches in speech-recognition technology that demonstrated difficulty recognizing words spoken by African Americans. Amazon, Apple, Google, IBM, and Microsoft reported similar results. Google's facial-recognition software, BERT, used by police departments, had a difficult time correctly recognizing the features of people of color.[208] A 2016 ProPublica report stated that risk-assessment software programs flagged African American prisoners as a threat, likely to commit new crimes, and recommended longer sentences. White defendants labeled as low risk received lower sentences.[209] Hospital algorithms influenced the health care of millions of African American patients.

A widely used program had discriminatory results in selecting patients to receive more personalized care even when patients had the same illness.[210]

Simple changes can have a huge impact. Stanford University recommended that tech firms increase efforts to diversify staff. Internships and vocational training opportunities should be a priority for every tech giant. CEO Arvind Krishna canceled IBM's facial recognition technology and recommended the "expansion of educational and economic opportunities for communities of color."[211] Companies should continuously examine and question results to discover partiality in algorithms. Any algorithm whose conclusions influence people's lives should be tested regularly. Carnegie Mellon's Rayid Ghani disclosed that machines can display bias, but not as much as the humans who program them.[212]

LIVING A "WOKE" LIFE
AND SOCIAL MEDIA PROTEST

> After much thought, I've decided to opt out of the 2020 WNBA season. There's work to be done off the court in so many areas in our community. Social justice reform isn't going to happen overnight but I do feel that now is the time and Moments equal Momentum. Let's keep it going![213]
> —*WNBA player Renee Montgomery, in a 2020 tweet*

The prediction many had for the twenty-first century was for a different reality, a postracial America, with race no longer a discriminating factor in employment, education, or relationships. This century has thus far proven to be anything but that. The issues are as old as the nation: police brutality, immigrant abuse, racism, xenophobia, LGBTQAI+ discrimination, redlining, voter suppression, child neglect, academic inequity, human trafficking, sexual abuse, cultural appropriation, profiling, misogyny against Black women, and many others. There is an increased sense of outrage over social injustices, with many arguing that the new is just a continuation of the old.

Protest in the twenty-first-century human rights struggle is led by so-called "woke" young people, people who have been awakened to the injustice around them. Participants are younger, energetic, inclusive, and willing to confront intolerance. They grew up in a different world from their parents and grandparents, and they recognize that America's original sin has not been eradicated. In the past, youth were allowed to participate in campaigns led by adults. Contemporary youth plan and implement rallies and create campaigns on their own. Their advocacy is enhanced by their ability to achieve a rapid response through social media. They bring to the table a greater reliance on new modes of communication and can mobilize thousands quickly. Leonard Pitts of the *Miami Herald* (April 1, 2018) wrote,

> The new movement, unlike the old, is not dominated by clergy or appeals to faith, though both do play a part. . . . The new movement is picking up where King left off, going into battle against systemic oppression: mass incarceration, police brutality, structural poverty. The one thing both movements have in common, though, is an understanding that at its most effective, protest is theater.[214]

A social media revolution has galvanized the Black community because of the ability to record incidents as they happen. Since the mid-2000s, incidences of "citizen journalism"[215] have skyrocketed due primarily to rapidly advancing technology. The advent of social media has been a godsend as video and audio evidence are readily accessible to document injustice. The technology most beneficial has been a cell phone with a built-in camera and recording capabilities.[216] The ACLU invented an app, Mobile Justice, to record police misconduct state by state.[217] Citizen journalism is thus responsible for the increasing number of police departments using dash and chest cameras on cars and officers. Because Blacks have historically been greeted with a large degree of skepticism when reporting police violence, witnesses rush to document police encounters for additional proof beyond an eyewitness report. When a Minnesota police officer shot Philando Castile, his girlfriend, Diamond Reynolds, live-streamed the aftermath on Facebook Live. Former Los Angeles Clippers owner Donald Sterling was banned for life from the NBA after his girlfriend, V. Stiviano, recorded him uttering racist epithets. And the callous murder of George Floyd by a Minneapolis police officer was painfully and excruciatingly caught on video, second by second.[218]

A 2018 Pew Research Center study polled attitudes on social media as a tool to propel incidents of social injustice to the broader public. The study disclosed that over 50 percent of respondents participated in at least one "political or social-minded activity" using social media over the past year. Democrats and those between the ages of eighteen and forty-nine were more likely to engage through technology. Fine lines existed between demographics. A majority of Blacks place a large degree of belief that their social media use gives them a chance to express their political views and to project their concerns nationwide.[219]

Not everyone agreed, however, as 77 percent of Americans voiced skepticism about how impactful social media was in creating change. Almost 71 percent responded that "social media makes people believe they're making a difference when they really aren't." The practice of supporting causes by social media or online petitions has been characterized by some as involving little effort or commitment and has been labeled "slacktivism." Whites confessed the highest level of skepticism, believing that social media has more of a negative impact than a beneficial one. African Americans reported more optimism, with 80 percent stating that social media brings attention to issues usually ignored in mainstream society.[220]

Video Protest against Police Brutality

Throughout the history of policing, African Americans have been targeted as threats to white people's peace and tranquility and subjected to investigative surveillance. In 2018 Childish Gambino, aka Donald Glover, released the stimulating song/video "This Is America." It received immediate acclaim and accumulated 63 million hits on YouTube. His critique of American culture presented a society inundated with gun violence, greed, and the devaluation of Black lives. Hayley Miller, of *HuffPost*, reflected that while Gambino dances in the foreground, the background reflects the chaos of living in America. These are "things that are plaguing Black America today. His use of duality presents the different layers representing Black entertainment dating back to Jim Crow. He exposed the fears of America that are based in white supremacy."[221] Gambino's song represents the complexity of Black life in America. The tragedy of the Black experience is that Black people have not desired anything other than the right to live fully as Americans. Yet Blackness has been presented as other, something to be despised and contained. Simply being Black in America has been enough justification for white people to react in fear that you are out of place and your behavior irregular.

Studies explored the relationship between race and treatment received at the hands of police. The darker a person's skin, the greater the chance of being stopped and experiencing violence. Black people live in a country where they constitute 13 percent of the population but 24 percent of those killed by law officers. African American women are 1.4 times more likely to be killed than other women. In 1992 Amnesty International charged that people who pose little or no threat to officers or deputies have been shot, beaten, shocked with electric stun guns and bitten by police dogs. "At times it has even amounted to torture or cruel, inhuman or degrading treatment. . . . More often than not, officers and deputies have acted with impunity, receiving little or no disciplinary action even in serious cases." The record on police brutality is appalling.[222] After the 1969 murder of Black Panther Party Chairman Fred Hampton, co-founder Bobby Seale said in an interview,

All the moves, the initiative has been on the part of the police. They murdered Fred Hampton. They are out to murder me. They'll most likely murder anybody that's Black in the country. . . . I think that the time will come when the people themselves will take the power that belongs to them into their hands, and move to guarantee life, liberty, and the pursuit of happiness.[223]

Modern technology has become an instrument of protest in the hands of African Americans able to record and broadcast any event in real time. Now equipped with an evidentiary tool to substantiate what was previously ignored or denied, people with cameras suddenly appear whenever something of a suspicious nature occurs. Handheld phones, in combination with dash cams on cars and those attached to officers' chests, are an added measure of surveillance. As soon as something happens between a police officer and a civilian, every available phone starts recording. It is beyond incidental that the Black community universally adopted videoing encounters that might turn deadly. Eyewitnesses turn video evidence over to police departments as well as to media outlets.[224] In the words of two Los Angeles residents remembering the videotaping of the Rodney King beating, "You know, this video camera revolution. Like, they got it. . . . Finally, you know what I mean? We got some evidence. We're going to expose this. This time we're gonna have justice." Congresswoman Karen Bass remarked, "This is a terrible thing to say, we all felt bad for his beating, but we cheered the fact that it was finally documented."[225]

Reports of police brutality have occurred since the creation of police departments in the early seventeenth century in Boston. The NAACP and African American newspapers consistently reported instances providing victims' names along with descriptions and names of the officers. For centuries there has been little prosecution of police officers amid the contention that Blacks were either criminals who deserved it, exaggerated excesses, or were not worth the time it would take to investigate. It took the introduction of video evidence to induce a nationwide discussion and for the white public to publicly acknowledge that something was amiss. The visual evidence has been too significant to deny and supports previously dismissed charges.[226] White Americans appeared willing to accept the reality of racialized police violence. For the first time in American history, officers are indicted on murder charges for killing African Americans.[227]

It has proven to be a combustible mixture when a Black man or woman, a white person, a phone call, and the police coalesce. Black people are suspect, and encounters can end tragically with an arrest or shooting. Most whites have no idea just how dangerous it can be to live as a law-abiding Black person in America. There exists a prolonged history of police called on African Americans regardless of how harmless the situation might be. Incidents have evolved into hashtags: *#DrivingWhileBlack* describes the risk of being pulled over by the police merely for driving a car; *#WalkingWhileBlack* involves being stopped by the police if strolling through a predominantly white neighborhood; and *#ShoppingWhileBlack* means store security following you around a store. Dr. Henry Louis Gates was confronted by a policeman while attempting to open his front door. All of these encounters carry the risk of deadly consequences.

The police are called to a dizzying array of everyday activities of people of color; often they overreact. In 2018 CNN listed actions Black people were engaged in when police were called to investigate: operating a lemonade store, golfing too slowly, barbecuing at a park, working out at a gym, moving into an apartment, mowing the wrong lawn, asking for directions, not waving while leaving an Airbnb, redeeming a coupon, selling bottled water on a sidewalk, eating lunch on a college campus, riding in a car with a white grandmother, babysitting two white children, wearing a backpack that brushed against a woman, working as a home inspector, working as a firefighter, helping a homeless man, delivering newspapers, swimming in a pool, shopping while pregnant, driving with leaves on a car, trying to cash a paycheck, and sitting in Starbucks.[228]

Black America has responded, demanding charges against the callers for making a false police report. Several states considered bills making it a criminal misdemeanor, and persons have been fired for violating company policy. Enhanced training for businesses, PSAs on the impact calling the police has on an innocent person, and political leaders' endorsing tolerance and acceptance are needed. Also effective would be public shaming of those captured on video through hashtags like *#BBQBecky*, *#PermitPatty*, and *#PoolPatrolPaula*. Starbucks had a mandatory day of racial sensitivity training for its entire U.S. staff.[229] This is America.

But too often the consequences of this type of injustice results in more than just a hashtag and leaves a Black man or woman dead. Diamond Reynolds cried as she filmed the dying Philando Castile and the officer who shot him. "They killed my boyfriend. . . . He was trying to get out his ID and his wallet out his pocket. And he let the officer know that he was — he had a firearm, and he was reaching for his wallet. And the officer just shot him. . . . I can't believe they did this!" Her daughter sought to comfort her by saying, "It's OK, mommy. It's OK, I'm right here with you."[230]

Say Her Name / Say His Name

Protests have been consistent against police brutality, but they reached a critical mass with the 2020 recording of the gruesome murder of George

Floyd and the reports of the manner of death suffered by Breonna Taylor. Taylor's killing reminded America that it is not only Black men who
die wrongfully at the hands of police. She was a nurse and former EMT
who was killed as Louisville police shot wildly into her apartment, acting
on a no-knock search warrant obtained for a person who no longer lived
at that address. On May 25, George Floyd, a father of two children, was
arrested in Minneapolis and handcuffed. As he lay on the ground Officer
Derek Chauvin pressed his knee on Floyd's neck for nine minutes and thirty
seconds until he died. Mr. Floyd told the officer twenty-seven times that he
could not breathe. In response to the two killings, protests erupted in cities from coast to coast, including Minneapolis, New York, Dallas, Denver,
Atlanta, and Louisville. Four officers were arrested.[231] Attorney Earl Gray,
an attorney for officer Thomas Lane, said on CNN's *Smerconish*, "George
Floyd killed himself. The restraint did not kill him."[232] Despite the height-
ened awareness those killings created, on August 24, 2020, Jacob Blake was
shot in the back seven times in Wisconsin as he attempted to get in his car
containing his three sons.

Policing in America is a 182-year-old-tradition established under the
mantra "To protect and serve." Relations with communities of color have
been problematic during that time, with repeated charges of police misconduct. The murder of Breonna Taylor highlighted complaints long ignored
as Blacks have documented abuse by the criminalizing of being Black in
America. During slavery vigilantes were deputized to patrol for runaways
with life-and-death authority. The earliest police departments in many
areas of the country were for the purpose of controlling the Black population. Blacks have resisted and denounced police atrocities to the point
that the outcry was focused on the charge of "police brutality" that was
used throughout the civil rights movement. During marches, protesters carried signs reading, "End police brutality," and speeches called for its end.
NBA player George Hill commented, "Police are to protect and serve, not
harass and shoot." Minneapolis mayor Jacob Frey said on the death of Mr.
George Floyd, "For the better part of the night I've been trying to find the
words to describe what happened. And all I keep coming back to is that he
should not have died. What we saw was horrible, completely and utterly
messed up. This man's life matters. He matters. He was someone's son. I
believe what I saw and what I saw was wrong at every level. This does not
reflect the values that Chief Arradondo has worked tirelessly to instill. It
does not represent the training we've invested in or the measures we've
taken to ensure accountability. Being black in America should not be a death
sentence."[233]

Black Twitter

For young African Americans, social media has become today's equivalent to the Black press. They are more likely than any other group to use social media as a source for news and to report newsworthy events. The queen of Black social online activism is Black Twitter. African Americans have the highest percentage of Twitter usage and use it to address social problems. Black Twitter is not an isolated platform that belongs to any one institution or program. It's an open network in which anyone can participate and have input. Topics include family, economics, education, politics, relationships, and especially culture. According to a 2013 Pew study, more than a quarter of all Black Internet users are on Twitter, with 30 percent being between the ages of eighteen and twenty-nine.[234] Black Twitter users not only dissect news but make it.[235] It is open to a divergence of voices, as long as they are informed. It is not kind to pretenders.

The term "Black Twitter" emerged from a 2010 article written by Farhad Manjoo, "How Black People Use Twitter," where he used the term "black-tag," which evolved to "Black Twitter."[236] He wrote,

> Black people—specifically, young black people—do seem to use Twitter differently from everyone else on the service. They form tighter clusters on the network—they follow one another more readily, they retweet each other more often, and more of their posts are @-replies—posts directed at other users. It's this behavior, intentional or not, that gives black people—and in particular, black teenagers—the means to dominate the conversation on Twitter.[237]

A study on Twitter by Brendon Meeder commented that Black people use Twitter as a social tool, such as texting to talk to one another rather than the general public. It has become a way for Black people to contest the narrative in real time.[238] Jamilah Lemieux described Black Twitter as akin to barbershop and beauty salon conversations. "There's some minor injustice that takes place: a journalist or a major outlet says something terribly offensive, we're on the attack. Or there's a grave injustice like Trayvon Martin's murder or the death of Renisha McBride, we're all there."[239]

Black Twitter, even as it has usurped the role of the Black press, has continued many of its best practices with a focus on fair representation. When members feel disrespected, they respond quickly and repeatedly. The Media Insight Project reported that only a minimum of Hispanics (33 percent) and African Americans (25 percent) trust that their communities are accurately portrayed in the media; most distrust the media to present an accurate portrayal.

TWENTY-FIRST-CENTURY MOVEMENTS

We are ready to go to Washington. . . . Now if we are going to carry on this campaign, this Poor People's Campaign, this campaign to guarantee jobs and income, we're going to need people, large numbers of people. . . . We're going to build us a town within a town. We're going to build a shanty-town in Washington. That's what we're going to do. We're going to build our own town, and let the world see how we so often have to live back home. . . . So once again we are asking you to put on your walking shoes, and walk together, pray together, struggle together, believe together, have faith together, and come on to Washington. And there will be a great camp meeting in the promised land.[240]

—Martin Luther King Jr., 1968,
"There Will Be A Mighty Wrath"

Today we face a national crisis that is in many ways an intensifying of the storm that rocked America in 1968. But too often, our attempts to diagnose what ails us cannot get past the tired debates of left-versus-right politics. King's analysis was that interlocking systems of violence, literal and metaphorical—which he called racism, poverty, and militarism—blinded most Americans to the lives of people. . . . Just as the Poor People's Campaign proposed, the Reconstruction we need now must arise from the efforts of people harmed directly by racism, poverty, environmental degradation, and the war economy. That is the inspiration for the new Poor People's Campaign: A National Call for Moral Revival, which is coordinating direct actions across the country.[241]

—Bishop William J. Barber II

Moral Monday and the Poor People's Campaign

On April 28, 2013, in Durham, North Carolina, the Rev. Dr. William Barber II preached a stirring sermon at Pilgrim United Church of Christ. Afterward, he invited participants to gather the following day at the North Carolina General Assembly's legislative building in Raleigh to participate in civil disobedience. The state had witnessed a political takeover as extremists won elections in both state houses and the governor's office, possessing a supermajority. This Republican-led political takeover passed the most draconian, despotic laws anywhere in the country, from the refusal to sign onto the Affordable Care Act to forfeiting federal unemployment benefits. On

April 29, seventeen women and men entered the building to pray, sing, and risk arrest. Moral Monday was born. Of those first seventeen, the majority were African American clergy from the ranks of the Disciples of Christ, Presbyterian, Baptist, and Pentecostal denominations. The following Monday, a press conference held at Davie Street Presbyterian Church trained those who would duplicate civil disobedience. For the next nine weeks, rallies were held at Bicentennial Park, followed by thousands who marched into the Jones Street legislative building to voice their opposition to the direction in which the state was headed. As the prison bus exited the building transporting the arrestees, the crowd shouted, "Thank you! We love you!" Over the summer, almost one thousand young, elderly, Black, Hispanic, white, Jewish, Muslim, Catholic, and Protestant arrestees participated in the movement with news coverage by MSNBC, the *New York Times*, the *Washington Post*, CNN, the *Guardian*, and others.[242] In 2017, Rev. Barber became the coconvener of the Poor People's Campaign, partnering with the Rev. Dr. Liz Theoharis. Its four-point program attacked systemic racism, ecological devastation, militarism, and false morality. On May 14, six weeks of direct action began in the District of Columbia in conjunction with protests in thirty-four state capitals. Civil-disobedience training, rallies, marches, and arrests coincided around the country.

In 2014 the Supreme Court overturned article 2 of the Voting Rights Act, which required preclearance from the Justice Department before southern states could introduce new laws governing an election. North Carolina responded immediately with vigorous restrictions to curtail the African American vote by mandating voter ID requirements and shortening the days of early voting. The NAACP joined by the U.S. Justice Department filed suit in federal court in Winston-Salem. After losing in the lower court, the appeals court ruled in favor of the plaintiffs that the law intentionally discriminated against African American voters and used race with "surgical precision" to disenfranchise African Americans.

Black youth played a vital role in the teen-led movement against gun violence in the March for Our Lives movement that began in 2018 in response to the mass killing at Marjory Stoneman Douglas High School in Parkland, Florida. They sensitized Parkland students that their experience, while painful, was not unique but shared by Black youth. Speeches mouthed by Black teens and preteens were impactful as they shared their hope for a better tomorrow. Yolanda Renee King, the granddaughter of Martin Luther King Jr., electrified the 200,000 in attendance at the March 2018 rally. "My grandfather had a dream that his four little children will not be judged by the color of the skin but the content of their character," she told them. "I have a dream

that enough is enough. And that this should be a gun-free world, period."
Naomi Walder, age eleven, from Alexandria, Virginia, spoke eloquently after
having organized a walkout of her elementary school to honor the seventeen
victims. While other walkouts lasted seventeen minutes to honor the victims,
Walder added an additional minute to hers in honor of Courtlin Arrington,
a Black student murdered while at school in Alabama. Walder said in Washington, "I am here to acknowledge and represent the African-American girls
whose stories don't make the front page of every national newspaper, whose
stories don't lead on the evening news."[243]

African American Protest for the Removal
of Confederate Flags, Statues, and Monuments

In the 1900s, groups such as the Daughters of the Confederacy and Sons
of Confederate Veterans erected memorials on state and private property
in response to the growing civil rights movement. Schools, parks, and roads
were renamed in honor of Robert E. Lee, Stonewall Jackson, and Jefferson
Davis. In a similar move, southern legislatures incorporated the flag of the
Confederacy onto state flags. It's important for white Americans to realize
that little of this was done in the immediate aftermath of the Civil War; it
began when whites saw Blacks achieving the same rights they had.

Brittany "Bree" Newsome remarked before removing a Confederate flag
in 2015, "You come against me with hatred, oppression, and violence. I come
against you in the name of God. This flag comes down today."[244] Nationwide
remonstrations endanger the symbols of the Southern mutiny against the
United States of America. Racist memorials erected throughout the country
have been targeted. Long after the war ended, Southerners proudly hoisted
the flag and constructed monuments to represent Southern dominance over
African Americans. Monuments and statues stood as visible proof of white
supremacy and a threat to any who opposed it; they were erected to intimidate
Black people and let them know that white people controlled America. At the
1913 unveiling of the so-called Silent Sam statue of a Confederate soldier
at the University of North Carolina, sponsored by the United Daughters of
the Confederacy, a featured speaker bragged that he "horsewhipped a Negro
wench (on the campus) until her skirts hung in shreds."[245]

According to the Southern Poverty Law Center's 2019 annual report,
Whose Heritage? Public Symbols of the Confederacy, there remain 1,747 Confederate symbols and memorials around the country. Seven hundred and eighty
monuments have three hundred locations in Georgia, Virginia, and North
Carolina. There are 103 public schools and three colleges with Confederate

designations. Eighty counties and cities carry such names. Nine states celebrate Confederate holidays; ten military bases carry Confederate names, as well as an unknown number of battlefields, cemeteries, and museums.[246] Eleven Confederate statues are in the U.S. Capitol Building, and Speaker of the House Nancy Pelosi has called for their removal. In December 2020, she announced the removal of the statue of Robert E. Lee, with its replacement being that of civil rights leader Barbara Johns of Virginia. She issued a statement saying,

> We relocated the Robert E. Lee statue out of a place of honor in National Statuary Hall, where a statue of Rosa Parks now proudly stands. . . . The Congress will continue our work to rid the Capitol of homages to hate, as we fight to end the scourge of racism in our country. There is no room for celebrating the bigotry of the Confederacy in the Capitol or any other place of honor in our country.[247]

Her statement referred to the National Defense Authorization Act. The U.S. military put in the 2020 budget the removal of the names of Confederate soldiers from ten military bases. Donald Trump vetoed the defense bill, but lawmakers overrode his veto. The act "mandates the removal of Confederate names, symbols, monuments and other honors from Defense Department property—including bases, buildings, streets, ships, aircraft, weapons and equipment—within three years and tasks the eight-member panel with carrying it out. The bill exempts Confederate grave markers from the review."[248]

Not even churches are exempt. During the Jim Crow era, white mainline denominations followed suit and endorsed the false supposition that the Civil War was not fought to maintain the institution of slavery but was over states' rights and southern independence. *Christianity Today* noted, "The separation from the Presbyterian Church in the U.S.A. and the formation of the Presbyterian Church in the Confederate States occurred in 1861."[249] Throughout the 1950s and 1960s Confederate memorials were placed inside of churches and on property. Within the last decade congregations have acted to remove Confederate symbols. Episcopalian churches placed plaques and stained-glass windows in reference to Robert E. Lee and other Confederate leaders, but decisions for removal have recently been implemented. St. Paul's Episcopal, "The Cathedral of the Confederacy," replaced kneelers, bookplates, and plaques containing the Confederate flag. Robert E. Lee Memorial Church in Lexington, Virginia, became Grace Episcopal Church. The Washington National Cathedral removed the windows of Lee and Jackson in 2017. Christ Church in Alexandria, Virginia, relocated a sanctuary plaque with the likeness of Lee. All Saints' Chapel at the University of the

South, Sewanee, Tennessee, removed Confederate banners but retained a stained-glass window with the Confederate seal. St. John Episcopal Church in Montgomery, Alabama, removed both a Jefferson Davis plaque and a pew dedicated by a prolynching segregationist. The Southern Baptist Convention passed a resolution to its members asking "brothers and sisters in Christ discontinue the display of the Confederate battle flag."[250] First Presbyterian Church of America, in Augusta, Georgia, moved a plaque and kneelers embroidered with the Confederate flag and its coat of arms.[251]

African Americans have taken a leading role in the removal movement. As noted earlier, Bree Newsome scaled a flagpole at the South Carolina state capitol and took down the Confederate flag. Takiyah Thompson toppled a Confederate statue outside of the Durham, North Carolina, County Courthouse. Gerald Griggs and the Georgia NAACP announced a "War on the Confederacy" on the eve of the 2019 Super Bowl. On April 30, 2018, Maya Little poured a mixture of her blood and red paint on the Silent Sam statue at the University of North Carolina, Chapel Hill. Student activists leveled the statue that August and removed its pedestal. Alumna Michelle McQueen took a selfie on the spot and remarked, "This is a day that I celebrate unity."[252]

The 2015 murder of nine African Americans at Mother Emanuel A.M.E. Church in Charleston, South Carolina, prompted the removal of 114 Confederate symbols within a year. The states of South Carolina and Alabama removed all Confederate flags from state properties. New Orleans removed four monuments. States removed Confederate monuments and flags from license plates. In 2020 Mississippi removed the battle flag from its state flag; the University of Mississippi and the University of Southern Mississippi had removed all state flags from their campuses earlier. The Southern Poverty Law Center noted in early 2021 that 168 Confederate symbols were taken down across the country in 2020, all but one being removed after the killing of George Floyd.

It was a movement propelled by young people across the nation. In many ways, it gave rise to a multiracial protest movement wherein youth from a generation not burdened by the experience and lessons of racial segregation were able to distinguish more honestly between history and distortion. The excuses of political correctness, southern historical distortions of the "Lost Cause," and veiled support for white supremacy simply do not sway generations born or raised with Barack Obama as president. Black young people have been determined not only to participate but to offer critical leadership in different regions, counties, and cities. They are a new generation of protest leaders who demand an end to racial injustice and are already tired of issues they inherited, issues that should have been resolved long ago.

#BLM

We are clear that all lives matter, but we live in a world where that's not actually happening in practice. So if we want to get to the place where all lives matter, then we have to make sure that Black lives matter, too.[253]

—Alicia Garza

In 2013, Alicia Garza, Patrisse Cullors, and Opal Tometi, Black queer women, ushered in #BlackLivesMatter. They acted out of anger in response to the acquittal of Trayvon Martin's murderer, George Zimmerman.[254] According to BuzzFeed, Garza wrote a "love letter" to Black people in 2013, first using the phrase Black Lives Matter.[255] Patrisse Cullors put #BlackLivesMatter into a hashtag. Opal Tometi organized people online under BLM. According to the Black Lives Matter Web page, "Black Lives Matter is an ideological and political intervention in a world where Black lives are systematically and intentionally targeted for demise. It is an affirmation of Black folks' humanity, our contributions to this society, and our resilience in the face of deadly oppression."[256]

The *New Yorker* claimed that BLM has become the "largest Black-led protest campaign since the 1960s."[257] BLM championed that Black lives do matter, and because they matter, solutions that work for Black folks must come from Black folks. The Movement for Black Lives platform, titled "A Vision for Black Lives: Policy Demands for Black Power, Freedom, and Justice," listed six core demands, with forty associated policy recommendations. It called for an end to the militarization of police departments, cash bail, and private schools, and key issues centered around police brutality, criminal justice reform, environmental racism, economic injustice, commonsense gun laws, LGBTQAI+ rights, and the 2020 election.[258]

The ACLU differentiates between Black Lives Matter movement as opposed to the organization: "The organization is a global decentralized network with over 30 chapters across the world. Black Lives Matter, the movement, is a broad conceptual umbrella that refers to the important work of a wide range of Black liberation organizations."[259] The BLM movement mobilized the Black Lives Matter Network and the Movement for Black Lives, as well as influenced fifty other networks or organizations. It impacted the religious community as churches hung banners which read, "Black Lives Matter" on grounds visible to the public. Almost everyone has an opinion on the movement, either positive or negative, with few feeling neutral. It has generated conversations on police reform and the devaluation of Black lives.[260] Patrisse Cullors said, "[BLM] has popularized civil disobedience and the need to put our bodies on the line. With things like the Women's March, and Me Too, and March for our Lives, all of these movements, their foundations are in Black Lives Matter."[261]

The Black Lives Matter movement and community activists called for police reform through the defunding of departments. Defunding does not mean the abolishment of law enforcement but involves financial divestment from police departments and redirecting investment to social services departments. A 2017 study by the Center for Popular Democracy identified that police budgets consume 20 to 45 percent of a city's budget. Reallocated funds transferred to other programs increase social services, education, mental health, and affordable housing opportunities. Additional funding can potentially reduce crime and decrease instances of police misconduct. A 2015 study by the Urban Health Lab showed that rehabbing abandoned housing units led to a significant drop in crime rates, gun assaults, and nuisance misdemeanors in Philadelphia. Instead of sending in armed and militarized police to handle domestic conflicts, trained mental health professionals should respond to such emergency calls. According to the Treatment Advocacy Center, people with mental illness are sixteen times more likely to be killed by law enforcement in response to a 911 call. Professional estimates suggest that as high as 50 percent of those killed by police suffered from some form of mental illness. Experts suggest that a more appropriate response to calls that someone is suffering from mental anguish should be answered by a health professional rather than law enforcement officers.[262]

AFRICAN AMERICAN LGBTQIA PROTEST

Biggest obstacle I ever faced was my own limited perception of myself.[263]

—RuPaul

By 2020 the Black LGBTQ protest movement had a strong head of stream. The LGBTQ movement has its origins in the June 2, 1969, Stonewall Inn uprising in New York City. But when Black activists first started becoming engaged in protests, the white LGBTQ community wouldn't give them a seat at the table. In the 1980s the Black queer woman Audre Lorde, an activist and writer, gave the movement momentum. More recently, a unique coalition of Black gays, lesbians, and transgender people formed a natural alignment with the Black Lives Matter movement as two of that movement's founders identify as queer, Alicia Garza and Patrisse Cullors. Together they addressed racism, secure housing and employment for Black trans individuals, defunding the police, and the decriminalization of sex work. They demanded attention to the deaths of transgender men and women, including Tony McDade, Nina Pop, Riah Milton, Dominique "Rem'mie" Fells, and Muhlaysia Booker.[264]

The Black LGBTQ youth community reflects all of the diversity of wider American society. Self-reporting reveals that 31 percent identify as gay or lesbian; 35 percent, as bisexual; 20 percent, as pansexual; 9 percent, as queer; 33 percent, as transgender and nonbinary; and 25 percent use nonbinary pronouns. A sizable percentage report struggling with their mental health with thoughts of self-harm, suicide, anxiety disorder, and severe episodes of depression.[265]

Their protest is paying off. June has been established as Pride Month for the Lesbian, Gay, Bisexual, Transgender, and Queer community. A video titled "Putting Protest Back in Pride" promoted the right of the community to protest against injustice.[266] The June 2020 Black Trans Lives Matter "Brooklyn Liberation" rally in New York City had 15,000 marchers.[267] The slogan "For All Black Lives" has become common to include the lives of trans men and women. Another slogan reads, "To be a Black queer woman in Amerikkka is a triple threat . . . and NOT in a good way."[268]

It is troubling that the most prophetic branch of Christianity, the Black church, is the most socially conservative when it comes to gay rights. Gay activists have long complained about the lack of support from the Black church. There is irony in a church birthed in the call of liberty being accused of siding with the oppressive theological lens projected by white evangelicals who have never been allies to Black liberation—trans, gay, or straight. Both Adam Clayton Powell Sr. and his congressman son Powell Jr. preached that homosexuality was a perversion. The LGBTQ Human Rights Campaign (HRC) released the video *Stone of Hope* to enlist the support of Black churches for LGBTQ issues. Featured in the film is Rev. Howard-John Wesley, the pastor of Alfred Street Baptist Church, who shares how his opinions have evolved over the years from intolerance to acceptance. HRC President Alphonso David released a statement saying, "Black LGBTQ people of faith have always been an integral part of the Black Church's movement work, charting a course from oppression to liberation . . . [but] have often been written out of the story."[269]

THE TALK

Black parents have the talk w/ their kids on how to conduct themselves around cops, so they don't get shot. If we can have THE TALK, #America can have A TALK, as responsible parents on keeping their kids safe from society & keeping society safe from their kids. #DLHughleyShow.[270]

—*Comedian D. L. Hughley*

"The Talk" between African American parents and their children is not new, as Black parents have always sought to teach their children how to navigate life in America. They desired to diminish generational trauma inherited by past experiences of racism. Slaves taught their children how to manipulate plantation owners and the system. Jim Crow parents taught children to be mindful when frequenting segregated venues and the proper etiquette when shopping in stores. Duke University's project *Behind The Veil* reported, "One thing we found is that parents were extremely resourceful about telling their children, 'Look when we go downtown, we can't drink out of this water fountain, we can't go to the restaurant, but that doesn't mean that you're a second-class human being.'"[271] The current rendition of the Talk is the conversation in which parents warn their children how to respond to encounters with the police before they turn deadly.

Black parents have always had to talk to their children about racism. The talk is part of a survival mentality, developing the ability to outwit one's oppressor into thinking that compliance means subservience. It teaches skills necessary to succeed in a hostile world, using one's wits and historical memory. Nat Turner's mother, born in Africa, taught him what it meant to be free. Martin Luther King Jr. spoke with his daughter about why she could not go to the amusement park Funtown in Atlanta, Georgia.

One area of misunderstanding is that each family's talk contains the same details. Black parents teach their children what they think will bring them home safely. Some children are instructed to look straight ahead, not get angry, comply, and keep their hands on the steering wheel. Parents inform children to call immediately if stopped. Some instruct them to drive to a well-lit area. Some say not to stop the car but call 911. Some parents instill the ability to question authority. Hari Ziyad, in "Black Youth Project," wrote, "My mother told me that I should always fight for what I believe in, whether it brings me personal hardship or not."[272]

OBAMA AS "DREAM" AND TRUMP AS "NIGHTMARE"

The law is also memory; the law also records a long-running conversation, a nation arguing with its conscience. *We hold these truths to be self-evident.* In those words, I hear the spirit of Douglass and Delany, as well as Jefferson and Lincoln; the struggles of Martin and Malcolm and unheralded marchers to bring these words to life.[273]

—*President Barack Obama, in his memoir* Dreams from My Father

"African American men and women have persevered to enrich our national life and bend the arc of history toward justice. From resolute Revolutionary War soldiers fighting for liberty to the hardworking students of today reaching for horizons their ancestors could only have imagined, African Americans have strengthened our nation."[274] Barack Obama was the first person of African American descent elected to the presidency of the United States of America. In 2008 he received 95 percent of the Black vote, followed by 93 percent in 2012. His election was the most emotional, electrifying, and inspirational moment since the announcement of the Emancipation Proclamation. The long-awaited, unbelieved moment had arrived. The impact that his election will have on future generations cannot be measured. His two terms were empty of controversy, and his family life was a model for all. He did not embarrass those who placed their hope and confidence in him. Past stereotypes could not be applied as he was nonthreatening, intelligent, and punctual.

African Americans, for the first time, felt included in the American family. In some way, it was proof that their lives mattered even amid ongoing racism. An overriding reason for this positive impression has to be examined generationally. Anyone over sixty is a living witness to the changes in American society. For those who did not grow up in legally enforced segregation, Obama's election generated hope as many saw themselves reflected in the First Family. His girls were young enough to remind them of their children. He was the father figure so many young Black men never had. His wife Michelle could be anyone's auntie.

Obama was not a perfect president, and some African Americans are more enamored with him as a former president than they felt under his presidency. He reprimanded Blacks with a Booker T. Washingtonian challenge to pick oneself up by one's bootstraps. Andrew Jackson II of Louisiana was twenty-seven when Obama was elected, and four years later, he reflected, "We thought our dreams would be more visible under Obama. They're not." His sixty-five-year-old mother, Brenda Jackson, disagreed, "He was able to accomplish all that he could accomplish. He was a man of grace."[275]

President Obama is a member of the family and shall be revered for making the American dream appear truer than at any time in the Black experience. He offered a sense that this land is indeed home. All the centuries of protest, struggle, and prayers of the slaves culminated in his election. The fight is not over, but there is progress. Run, Michelle, run!

Donald Trump's presidency, by contrast, was a nightmare for African Americans. He challenged African Americans to vote for him: "You're living in poverty; your schools are no good; you have no jobs, 58 percent of your youth is unemployed—what the hell do you have to lose?"[276] The 45th president, for African Americans, was the worst possible candidate and has proven to be the worst president in the history of the United States. Donald J. Trump turned out to be the most blatantly racist, misogynistic, xenophobic, nihilistic, and dangerous man to win the nation's highest office. While it is hard to fathom, he materialized every fear voiced during his candidacy, but the reality is far worse. In 2018 he demeaned three African American reporters, all women, in three days. He called Abby Phillip's question "stupid," referred to April Ryan as a "loser," and said Yamiche Alcindor was a "racist." He has shown disdain for congresswomen Maxine Waters and Frederica S. Wilson.[277] Defying reality he stated, "The African American people have been calling the White House. They have never been so happy with what a president has done."[278]

African Americans responded to the president by punishing him in polls and the voting booth. The 2016 presidential election awarded Trump 8 percent of the Black vote while Hillary Clinton received 89 percent. A 2019 Quinnipiac University poll registered an 84 percent disapproval rating among Blacks contrasted by 6 percent approval. When asked if he was a racist, 80 percent responded in the affirmative while 11 percent responded no. Other media outlets reflected similar polling. Fox News registered 75 percent disapproval, with 22 percent approval, and the *Washington Post* registered 81 percent disapproval countered by 18 percent approval.[279] A 2020 *Washington Post* Ipsos poll revealed that 92 percent of African Americans registered to vote supported Joe Biden over Trump, and half did not care who his running mate would be. Final turnout revealed that 90 percent voted for the Biden-Harris ticket with 8 percent voting for Trump.[280] Ninety percent thought Trump has a bias against Blacks, with 86 percent saying he has done nothing to reduce discrimination. Black voters turned out in record numbers to vote for the Biden-Harris ticket.[281]

The 2020 election became a referendum on the presidency of Donald Trump for Black America. Many stated they wanted to provide an answer to his 2016 question to Black Americans, "What do you have to lose?" The defeat of Trump was caused to a large degree by the large percentage of voters of color who turned out in huge numbers to vote for the Biden-Harris ticket in key states. Their voting strength enabled the Democrats to gather more votes than ever cast in a presidential election. Nine out of ten Black voters voted for the Democrats. They were instrumental in Biden's win in critical areas with large Black populations. Pivotal were the Black votes cast in Wayne County, Michigan (Detroit); Milwaukee County, Wisconsin; Philadelphia; and Georgia. Kamala Harris rallied women of color as an inspiration and motivation to vote. Black women, led by Stacey Abrams in Georgia, registered voters and led a resurgence of the Black vote that had been lost in the 2016 election.[282] The increase in voting worked for both parties, as Trump's percentages among African Americans grew by three percentage points between 2016 and 2020, by three percentage points among Hispanics, and by five points in the Asian American community.[283] For Black people, however, the January 6 insurrection proved that their perceptions about the 45th President were correct. After the president initiated the tear-gassing of peaceful protesters over racialized police violence on Black Lives Matter Plaza and then supported the violent rioters of the Capitol, it was clear that their issues were not his. No matter his rhetoric, he always spoke and acted against their interests. And only a relative few breached the Capitol on January 6.

2020: "WHAT A YEAR!"

Black women, Asian, white, Latina and Native American women throughout our nation's history who have paved the way for this moment tonight. . . . Tonight, I reflect on their struggle, their determination and the strength of their vision—to see what can be unburdened by what has been. And I stand on their shoulders. . . . But while I may be the first woman in this office, I will not be the last. Because every little girl watching tonight sees that this is a country of possibilities.[284]

—*Kamala Harris, on the night of her election as vice president*

The year 2020 was one of the most momentous years in the history of the United States and for the African American community. COVID-19 shut the nation down, disrupted the economy, overburdened hospitals and staff, and imposed a disparate death rate among Blacks and Hispanics. The issue of racial justice rose to the forefront of the nation's awareness as the murders of George Floyd and Breonna Taylor resulted in protest marches that numbered in the hundreds of thousands. The 2020 presidential election propelled Joe Biden to the presidency and elected Kamala Harris as the first multiracial vice president. These interlocking events held African Americans in the center as they were impacted directly by overpolicing, negligence, incompetency, unequal access to medical care, and a higher rate of job loss, and the Black voice was a part of the protest and advance.

COVID-19

When COVID-19 infected the United States, tragedy was compounded when those hit hardest by the virus were Black and brown. Race and poverty reflect long-standing systemic inequalities and are preexisting conditions for COVID-19. Prior health conditions compromise the bodies' efforts to fight off the virus. When much work transitioned to virtual work from home settings, Blacks held jobs for which they could not work from home in service industries, hospitals, grocery stores, and food service. The infection and death rates reflected the nation's disparities. In many states, Black and brown people had a higher rate of infection and death compared to whites. Milwaukee tracks the racial breakdown of those infected by COVID-19. The city reports that 81 percent of those who have died are Black though Blacks constitute only 26 percent of its population. In Michigan, Blacks comprise 14 percent of residents and 40 percent of those who have died.[285] One-third of Chicago's residents are African American, yet they constituted 72 percent of those who died. In Illinois, 15 percent of the population represented 43 percent of deaths and 28 percent of infections. Similar stats were seen in North and South Carolina, Wisconsin, Louisiana, Alabama, and Mississippi.[286] In New York City, Blacks and Latinos died at twice the rate of whites. *Mother Jones* reported,

> This disease is not an equal-opportunity disease. Black people are contracting the coronavirus and dying from the disease at higher rates than other people. This disproportionate effect is a social issue in the guise of an epidemiological one. Black Americans . . . are more likely to be uninsured. They're more likely to work a low-paying job. They're more likely to suffer from heart disease, asthma, cancer, and other conditions. . . . It's because of straightforward social choices such as where toxic dumps get sited, where new highways get built, and where Black people have historically been permitted to live. [287]

In Michigan, five-year-old Skylar Herbert was the first child to die in the state.[288] Michigan Congresswoman Rep. Rashida Tlaib became emotional as she spoke of her death on the House floor.[289] The youngest to die in Georgia was a seven-year-old unnamed boy.[290] Kimora "Kimmie" Lynum was the youngest to die in Florida.[291] Eight-year-old Aurea Soto Morales was the youngest victim to die in North Carolina.[292] All were African American or Hispanic.

The Black community exploded in outrage as the government responded with an anemic plan that failed to address the impact race and age played in the spread and severity of the disease. Activists called as early as March for the Centers for Disease Control (CDC) to release the racial statistics on the rates of infection. Calls for racial breakdowns were backed up by similar calls from the Lawyers' Committee for Civil Rights Under Law and four hundred medical professions.[293] Elizabeth Warren joined Senators Kamala Harris and Cory Booker to request that the Trump administration collect and release statistics on the treatment and deaths of those infected.[294] New York Governor Andrew Cuomo stated, "You know, it always seems that the poorest people pay the highest price. Why is that?"[295] By April 8, 2020, the CDC released a limited data drop revealing that 33 percent of those hospitalized for coronavirus infection were Black, 8 percent Hispanic, and 45 percent white.[296] Almost a year later, the death rate for Blacks due to COVID-19 is 166 per 100,000 cases and deaths; for whites it is 116; for Hispanics it is 141.[297]

CONCLUSION: WHAT COMES NEXT?

Am I my brother's keeper? I have to be. The poor people, who live just above the welfare and relief, have to live by that old saying, "I can see farther over the mountain than the man who is standing atop of it." We know and see the problems, because we have to live so close to them. We know that we have a sense of responsibility, and we (some of us) have tried to instill some of the ambitions we could not realize into our children.[298]

—*Helen Howard*

America is a nation born and nurtured in the spirit of protest. People of African descent have not been immune to that spirit and, at important junctures, have led the way. The demand for equal treatment and equity in the distribution of justice has been a mainstay of the Black experience. There runs a continuous thread of Black protest throughout American history. African Americans, especially the younger generation, organized protests in small towns, college campuses, and the nation's largest cities. From rebellions on slave plantations, anti-discrimination lawsuits, the civil rights movement, Confederate statues protests, and Black Lives Matter marches, Black voices have cried out for an end to white supremacy. Journalist Thomas Sugrue wrote, "2020's uprising resembles those of 1919, 1943, and 1968 in certain respects; they grow out of simmering hatreds seeded by the long, festering history of white violence and police brutality against African-Americans that has taken hundreds of lives per year, including Floyd, Breonna Taylor, and Ahmaud Arbery, three of the most recent victims."[299]

To understand Black protest is to see it from the eyes of those most impacted by racism. Blacks have never wanted anything more than that which was due them as members of American society. Protest has centered around the demand for equal justice, humane treatment, and the ability to live a life of dignity. White supremacy was created to provide cover for the economic greed that slavery produced. Arrogant pride whitewashed American history to produce a narrative that highlighted the accomplishments of whites, while other contributions were appropriated or erased.

So what is Black protest? It is truth telling. It understands that America has always been a nation of contradictions, hypocrisy, and illusion. America has never lived up to its proclamations of liberty and justice for all, but African Americans have found American democratic ideas to be worth fighting for. The focus of protest has never been to change the nation's creed but to compel the country to live up to its own values and professed beliefs. Black protest is inclusion. The goal has never been, for the majority of Black people, to separate from other races but to ensure that a diversity of people are afforded opportunity and access to life's benefits and blessings. Black protest is confrontation. It is standing in the face of racism, misogyny, homophobia, and xenophobia and saying, "No!" Black protest is a promotion of equity in education. The Black experience has valued the acquisition of equal and quality education for all children. It understands that children must be taught to think and acquire the skills necessary for a productive life. It has learned this lesson by being denied literacy and equitable facilities and knows firsthand the harm prohibitions can do. Black protest means reciprocity. It understands that our futures are intertwined and that what impacts one people will impact the other; that when resources and opportunities are equally shared, there is mutual benefit for all of society. It declares that no nation can long survive with barriers barring the achievement of segments of its citizenry and that a dog-eat-dog mentality is self-destructive. It is the rejection of leaders who seek popularity by pointing to others as the enemy and source of economic and social problems. Black protest seeks unity.

The protest movements of the twenty-first century are the children of the multitude of Black protests dating back to the fifteenth century. Every racial, ethnic, gender, and sexual identity fight for human rights has been affected. A link can be drawn from the abolitionist movement to the suffrage protests. The 1950s emergence of the civil rights movement influenced the 1960s protest against the Vietnam War and the gay rights movement. There appears to be an acknowledgment of new and demonstrative ways, as young whites pour onto the streets in support of Black Lives Matter marches.

Black protest must continue to evolve and adapt to a rapidly changing and expanding global community. It must form new organizations and establish coalitions with other partners who share issue interconnectivity. Today's protest will continue to evolve due to the impact of social media. Those most affected by racism, economic disparity, and educational inequity must join forces and continue the work of justice for those left out and left behind. An important linkage is joining forces with working-class whites, a partnership desired by Martin Luther King Jr. and Fred Hampton, which has yet to be established. This merger would determine elections, be an effective community-organizing agency, and transform this nation. Thus far no leader nor institution has found that magic potion, but it does exist. If the country is to have a future consistent with its heralded democratic legacy, protest must expand its connections and create a prophetic voice for the powerless.

Notes

Introduction

1. Joanne Grant, ed., *Black Protest* (New York: Ballantine Books, 1968), 7, 14.
2. President Donald Trump made this comment on August 19, 2017, during a political rally for Alabama Republican Senate candidate Luther Strange. See www.theguardian.com/sport/2017/sep/22/donald-trump-nfl-national-anthem -protests.
3. Jackie Robinson, *I Never Had It Made: An Autobiography of Jackie Robinson* (New York: Harper Perennial, 2003).
4. Steve Wulf, "Athletes and Activism: The Long, Defiant History of Sports Protests," January 30, 2019, https://theundefeated.com/features/athletes-and -activism-the-long-defiant-history-of-sports-protests/.
5. Zach Johnk, "National Anthem Protests by Black Athletes Have a Long History," *New York Times*, September 25, 2017. Johnk documented protests by African American athletes between 1968 and 1996 and observed that such protests "have a long history in the United States and an equally lengthy tradition of angering mostly white fans, sports officials and politicians." See www.nytimes .com/2017/09/25/sports/national-anthem-protests-black-athletes.html.
6. Ralph Wiley, "An Athlete with the Freedom to Speak," ESPN.com, 2003, http://www.espn.com/page2/s/wiley/030228.html. Wiley wrote on the protest by white student-athlete Toni Smith, who would turn away from the American flag during the playing of the national anthem before her college games. He wrote, "Things you'd want your own 21-year-old daughter to do." He died in 2004 of a heart attack at age 52.
7. "Carlos Delgado: Colin Kaepernick's Actions Rooted in American Ideals," ESPN online, September 26, 2016, https://www.espn.com/mlb/story /_/id/17648761/carlos-delgado-12-years-later-colin-kaepernick-protest-ideals. Delgado confided that he thought that it was important that athletes use their platform to speak on issues of justice. "But I think it is important that athletes, who have this platform, where they can reach millions of people, they should use it. If your principles indicate that you want to do something or must do it, you should act, whether you act alone or with others."
8. Mark Fainaru-Wada, "The Revival of Mahmoud Abdul-Rauf," ABC News, February 17, 2017, abcnews.go.com/Sports/revival-mahmoud-abdul-rauf /story?id=45562375; and Jesse Washington, "Still No Anthem, Still No Regrets For Mahmoud Abdul-Rauf," The Undefeated, September 1, 2016, https://theundefeated.com/features/abdul-rauf-doesnt-regret-sitting-out -national-anthem/.

9. The *Milwaukee Journal Sentinel*, September 25, 2017, ran an article by Kevin Spain (*USA TODAY* Sports) on Ed Reid explaining his frustration to the negative reaction to his protest.

10. Steven R. Cureton, *Black Vanguards and Black Gangsters: From Seeds of Discontent to a Declaration of War* (Lanham, MD: University Press of America, 2011), 2.

11. Johnk, "National Anthem Protests."

12. Ryan Phillips, "Brent Musburger Takes Shot at 49ers for Anthem Protests," *The Big Lead*, October 8, 2017, https://www.thebiglead.com/posts/brent -musburger-takes-shot-at-49ers-for-anthem-protests-01dmfv3pa2mb. Phillips criticized Musburger for throwing shade on the NFL 49ers through Twitter. *Deadspin, The Nation, New York Daily News*, and *Yahoo Sports* all have called for Musburger to apologize to Smith and Carlos.

13. A. J. Perez, "Muhammad Ali Award Caps Big Year for Colin Kaepernick," *USA Today*, December 6, 2017, https://www.usatoday.com/story/sports/nfl/2017 /12/06/muhammad-ali-award-caps-big-year-colin-kaepernick/925995001/.

14. Sean Gregory, "Colin Kaepernick Wins Amnesty International's Highest Honor," *Time*, April 21, 2018, https://time.com/5248606/colin-kaepernick -wins-amnesty-internationals-ambassador-of-conscience-award/.

15. Morgan Jerkins, "What Colin Kaepernick's National Anthem Protest Tells Us about America," *Rolling Stone*, August 29, 2016, https://www.rollingstone .com/culture/culture-sports/what-colin-kaepernicks-national-anthem-protest -tells-us-about-america-247887/.

16. Robyn C. Spencer, "From Jimi Hendrix to Colin Kaepernick: Why Black Americans' Patriotism Often Looks like Protest," September 29, 2017, https://www.washingtonpost.com/news/post-nation/wp/2017/09/29/why-black -americans-patriotism-has-often-looked-like-protest/.

17. Michael Tesler, "To Many Americans, Being Patriotic Means Being White," *Washington Post*, Oct 13, 2017, https://www.washingtonpost.com/news /monkey-cage/wp/2017/10/13/is-white-resentment-about-the-nfl-protests -about-race-or-patriotism-or-both/?utm_term=.663605e9786a.

18. Netflix documentary by Liz Garbus, *What Happened, Miss Simone?* (2015).

19. Michael Harriot, "The FBI Admits Black Lives Matter Was Never a Threat. It's White People You Should Be Worried About," The Root, June 11, 2019, https://www.theroot.com/the-fbi-admits-black-lives-matter -was-never-a-threat-i-1835417043.

20. Anti-Defamation League, "The Purpose and Power of Protest," https://adl .org/education/resources/tools-and-strategies/the-purpose-and-power-of -protest.

21. Lerone Bennett Jr., *Confrontation: Black and White* (London: Penguin Books, 1965), 2.

22. Darren Sands, "What Happened to Black Lives Matter?" BuzzFeed News, June 21, 2017, https://www.buzzfeednews.com/article/darrensands/what -happened-to-black-lives-matter.

23. Black abolitionists charged colonists of racist intent as their goal was to eradicate slavery and remove Blacks from the country. See C. Eric Lincoln and Lawrence H. Mamiya, *The Black Church in the African American Experience* (Durham, NC: Duke University Press, 1990), 45.

24. Rebecca Roberts, "'I Have a Dream' Speech, in Its Entirety," *Talk of the Nation*, NPR, January 18, 2010, https://www.npr.org/2010/01/18/122701268 /i-have-a-dream-speech-in-its-entirety.

25. Henry Highland Garnet, "An Address to the Slaves of the United States," *Electronic Texts in American Studies* 8 (August 16,1848), digitalcommons.unl .edu/cgi/viewcontent.cgi?article=1007&context=etas. The speech, given during the 1843 National Negro Convention in Buffalo, New York, called for open slave rebellion and failed endorsement by one vote. Frederick Douglass spoke against it.

26. Vincent Harding, *There Is a River: The Black Struggle for Freedom in America* (New York: Vintage Books, 1981), 14–15.

27. Frederick Douglass, "What to the Slave Is the Fourth of July?" (speech, Corinthian Hall, Rochester, New York, July 5, 1852), teachingamericanhistory.org /library/document/what-to-the-slave-is-the-fourth-of-july/.

28. President Abraham Lincoln wrote a letter to his friend Joshua Speed on August 24, 1855, from Springfield, Illinois, challenging him on his proslavery stance. Retrieved from http://www.abrahamlincolnonline.org/lincoln /speeches/speed.htm.

29. *The Herald-Sun*, sect. E2, November 8, 1998. Graduate students from Duke, North Carolina Central University, and the University of North Carolina recorded the oral histories of 1,200 African Americans who lived in the Jim Crow South from the 1880s to the 1950s. The interviews covered twelve Southeastern states and were done between 1994 to 1997. The project, *Behind the Veil: Documenting African-American Life in the Jim Crow South*, is the largest collection of photographs, recordings, and documents of life under southern segregation and is stored in the John Hope Franklin Research Center for African and African-American Studies. In 2001 a book and CD compilation was published, *Remembering Jim Crow*. See http://scriptorium.lib.duke.edu /franklin/.

30. Edward E. Baptist, *The Half Has Never Been Told: Slavery and the Making of American Capitalism* (New York: Basic Books, 2016).

31. Henry Louis Gates Jr. *Colored People: A Memoir* (New York: Vintage Books, 1995), 201.

32. Eugene D. Genovese, *Roll, Jordan, Roll: The World the Slaves Made* (New York: Vintage Books, 1972), xv.

33. Gates, *Colored People*, xvi.

34. Adaobi C. Iheduru, "Examining the Social Distance between Africans and African Americans: The Role of Internalized Racism" (PhD diss., Wright State University, 2013), https://corescholar.libraries.wright.edu/cgi/viewcontent .cgi?article=1802&context=etd_all.

35. Ben L. Martin, "From Negro to Black to African American: The Power of Names and Naming," *Political Science Quarterly* 106, no. 1 (Spring 1991): 83, https://www.jstor.org/stable/2152175.

36. Garbus, *What Happened, Miss Simone?*

37. Lucy M. Salmon, *Why Is History Rewritten? North American Review* 195, no. 675 (1912): 228–31, https://www.jstor.org/stable/25119698?seq=4#meta data_info_tab_contents.

38. Lerone Bennett Jr., "What's in a Name? Negro vs. Afro-American vs. Black," *Review of General Semantics* 26, no. 4 (December, 1969): 403, https://www.jstor .org/stable/42574587?seq=1#metadata_info_tab_contents.

39. Bennett, "What's in a Name?"

40. Tom W. Smith wrote that Blacks were insistent on providing their own labeling and identifies the transition from "African" to "Colored" to "Negro."

"Changing Racial Labels: From 'Colored' to 'Negro' to 'Black' to 'African American,'" *Public Opinion Quarterly* 56, no. 4 (Winter 1992), https://www .jstor.org/stable/2749204?seq=1#page_scan_tab_contents.

41. Bennett, *Confrontation*, 55.
42. Martin, "From Negro to Black," 85, 92.
43. University of Missouri political science professor Ben L. Martin referred to a 1974 Roper Center for Public Opinion Research poll that by 1974 a majority of Black Americans said they preferred the term "Black" to "Negro." See Martin, "From Negro to Black."
44. Bennett, "What's in a Name?"
45. D'Vera Cohn, "Race and the Census: The 'Negro' Controversy," Pew Research Center, January 21, 2020, https://www.pewsocialtrends.org/2010 /01/21/race-and-the-census-the-negro-controversy/.
46. Barbara Kiviat, "Should the Census Be Asking People if They Are Negro?" *Time*, January 23, 2010, http://content.time.com/time/nation/article/0,8599 ,1955923,00.html.
47. "Census to Replace 'Negro' with 'Black' or 'African-American,'" *New York Post*, February 25, 2013, https://nypost.com/2013/02/25/census-to-replace -negro-with-black-or-african-american/.
48. Bennett, "What's in a Name?"
49. Bennett, "What's in a Name?"
50. "Don't Call Me African-American," *New African*, https://newafricanmagazine .com/3168/, reported on resistance to the title and described a meeting in South Africa between African American and African mayors.
51. "Negro, Black and African American," *New York Times*, December 22, 1988, http://www.nytimes.com/1988/12/22/opinion/negro-black-and-african -american.html.
52. Smith, "Changing Racial Labels."
53. Martha S. Jones, "What's in a Name? 'Mixed,' 'Biracial,' 'Black,'" CNN, February 19, 2014, https://www.cnn.com/2014/02/19/living/biracial -black-identity-answers/index.html.
54. John H. McWhorter, "Why I'm Black, Not African American," *Los Angeles Times*, September 8, 2004, https://www.manhattan-institute.org/html/why-im -black-not-african-american-0153.html.
55. Cydney Adams, "Not All Black People Are African American. Here's the Difference," CBS News, June 18, 2020, https://www.cbsnews.com/news/not-all -black-people-are-african-american-what-is-the-difference/.
56. Bettye Collier-Thomas and James Turner, "Race, Class and Color: The African American Discourse on Identity," *Journal of American Ethnic History* 14, no. 1 (Fall, 1994): 13, https://www.jstor.org/stable/pdf/27501932.
57. Jones, "What's in a Name?"

Section 1: The Age of Exploitation in the New World

1. Lerone Bennett Jr., *Confrontation: Black and White* (London: Penguin Books, 1965), 25.
2. Bennett, *Confrontation*, 4.
3. Bennett, *Confrontation*, 20.
4. S. G. F. Brandon and Friedrich Heer, eds., *Forty Centuries: From the Pharaohs to Alfred the Great* (London: Weidenfeld, 1970), 18.
5. Genesis 43:32.

6. Gilder Lehrman Institute of American History, *Iberian Roots of the Transatlantic Slave Trade, 1440–1640*, http://ap.gilderlehrman.org/history-by-era/origins-slavery/essays/iberian-roots-transatlantic-slave-trade-1440-1640.

7. New York Public Library Online, Schomburg Center for Research in Black Culture, *African Origins in the U.S.*, http://abolition.nypl.org/print/us_slave_trade/.

8. August Meier and Elliott Rudwick, *From Plantation to Ghetto*, rev. ed. (New York: Hill and Wang, 1970), 25, 26.

9. Edward E. Baptist, *The Half Has Never Been Told: Slavery and the Making of American Capitalism* (New York: Basic Books, 2016), xxi.

10. Reverend Peter Fontaine, *Defense of Slavery in Virginia (1757)*, http://pshs.psd202.org/documents/bmiller/1502456905.pdf.

11. A. Troy Thomas, director and producer, *Liberty & Slavery: The Paradox of America's Founding Fathers*, a 2016 documentary.

12. Meier and Rudwick, *From Plantation to Ghetto*, 27.

13. Meier and Rudwick, *From Plantation to Ghetto*, 28, 32.

14. Meier and Rudwick, *From Plantation to Ghetto*, 5, 29.

15. Meier and Rudwick, *From Plantation to Ghetto*, 33.

16. Meier and Rudwick, *From Plantation to Ghetto*, 32.

17. Vincent Harding, *There Is a River: The Black Struggle for Freedom in America* (New York: Vintage Books, 1981), 8.

18. Meier and Rudwick, *From Plantation to Ghetto*, 36.

19. Harding, *There Is a River*, 36.

20. Bennett, *Confrontation*, 19.

21. William Loren Katz, *The Black West: A Documentary and Pictorial History of the African American Role in the Westward Expansion of the United States* (New York: Touchstone, 1987), 10.

22. Jeffrey J. Crow, Paul D. Escott, and Flora J. Hatley, *A History of African Americans in North Carolina* (Raleigh: North Carolina Office of Archives and History, 1992), 1.

23. Benjamin Quarles, *The Negro in the Making of America* (New York: Maxmillan, 1969), 29.

24. Bennett, *Confrontation*, 19.

25. Harding, *There Is a River*, 26.

26. Harding, *There Is a River*, 29.

27. Harding, *There Is a River*, 44.

28. Meier and Rudwick, *Plantation to Ghetto*, 61.

29. Bennett, *Confrontation*, 14.

30. Bennett, *Confrontation*, 4.

31. Catherine Clinton, *The African American Experience: 1565–1877* (Fort Washington, PA: Eastern National, 2004), 3.

32. *The New York Times 1619 Project*, August 18, 2019, cover page.

33. Bennett, *Confrontation*, 14.

34. Bennett, *Confrontation*, 40.

35. Bennett, *Confrontation*, 16.

36. Bennett, *Confrontation*, 41.

37. *Slavery in the Colonies*, Lumen, https://courses.lumenlearning.com/boundless-ushistory/chapter/slavery-in-the-colonies/.

38. Clinton, *African American Experience*, 2.

39. Meier and Rudwick, *Plantation to Ghetto*, 41–42, 51–54.

40. Baptist, *The Half.*
41. The Revolutionary War is referred to as the War of Liberation, upholding the perspective of colonial free and enslaved Africans. Historians Lerone Bennett Jr. and Henry Louis Gates both refer to the Civil War in similar terms, as the War to End Slavery.
42. John Hope Franklin, *From Slavery to Freedom: A History of Negro Americans* (New York: Vintage Books, 1969), 72.
43. Quarles, *Negro in the Making*, 33–37.
44. Bennett, *Confrontation*, 16–18.
45. Quarles, *Negro in the Making*, 38.
46. Bennett, *Confrontation*, 22–23.
47. Crow, Escott, and Hatley, *A History*, 8.
48. The Old Testament book of Genesis in chapters 9–10 presents a genealogy listing the tribes/nations that were descended from the sons of Noah. The children of Ham, who settled Africa and parts of Arabia, were cursed to be the servants of his brothers for observing his father's drunken nakedness and not covering him up.
49. Cain Hope Felder, *Troubling Biblical Waters: Race, Class, and Family* (Maryknoll, NY: Orbis Books, 1989), 40.
50. Quarles, *Negro in the Making*, 35.
51. Quarles, *Negro in the Making*, 34–36.
52. Becky Little, "Who Was Jim Crow?" *National Geographic*, August 6, 2015, https://www.nationalgeographic.com/news/2015/08/150806-voting-rights-act-anniversary-jim-crow-segregation-discrimination-racism-history/.
53. William Ferris and Charles Reagan Wilson, eds., *Encyclopedia of Southern Culture* (New York: Anchor Books, 1989), 365.

Section 2: The Protest of the Enslaved

1. Lerone Bennett Jr., "What's in a Name? Negro vs. Afro-American vs. Black," *Review of General Semantics* 26, no. 4 (December 1969): 403, https://www.jstor.org/stable/42574587?seq=1#metadata_info_tab_contents.
2. "Freedom and Bondage in the Colonial Era," PBS, Africans in America Narratives, http://www.pbs.org/wgbh/aia/part2/2narr1.html.
3. "Freedom and Bondage."
4. Bennett, "What's in a Name? Negro vs. Afro-American vs. Black."
5. Listed as a Tubman quote in the Harriet Tubman Underground Railroad Museum located at Church Creek, Maryland.
6. Martin Magnusson, "'No Rights Which the White Man Was Bound to Respect': The Dred Scott Decision," American Constitution Society, March 19, 2007, https://www.acslaw.org/expertforum/no-rights-which-the-white-man-was-bound-to-respect/.
7. Benjamin Quarles, *The Negro in the Making of America* (New York: Macmillan, 1969), 30.
8. Jeffrey J. Crow, Paul D. Escott, and Flora J. Hatley, *A History of African Americans in North Carolina* (Raleigh: North Carolina Office of Archives and History, 1992), 56–57.
9. Eugene D. Genovese, *Roll, Jordan, Roll: The World the Slaves Made* (New York: Vintage Books, 1972), 423, xvi.
10. August Meier and Elliott Rudwick, *From Plantation to Ghetto*, rev. ed. (New York: Hill and Wang, 1970), 56.

11. Federal Writers' Project, *Slave Narratives: A Folk History of Slavery in the United States from Interviews with Former Slaves*, vol. 4, *Georgia Narratives*, pt. 2 (Washington, DC: Library of Congress, 1941), 119, https://memory.loc.gov/mss/mesn/042/042.pdf; Federal Writers' Project, *Slave Narratives* 11:2, 156, https://www.loc.gov/resource/mesn.112/?sp=160; Federal Writers' Project, *Slave Narratives* 11:1, 190, https://www.loc.gov/resource/mesn.111/?sp=194.

12. Joseph A. Bailey, "'Seasoning' the Slaves," February 19, 2009, https://blackvoicenews.com/2009/02/19/qseasoningq-the-slaves/.

13. Thomas Clarkson, *An Essay on the Slavery and Commerce of the Human Species, Particularly the African*, pt. 3, chap. 4 (orig. pub. London: J. Phillips, 1786), Online Library of Liberty, oll.libertyfund.org/titles/clarkson-an-essay-on-the-slavery-and-commerce-of-the-human-species.

14. Lerone Bennett Jr., *Confrontation: Black and White* (London: Penguin Books, 1965), 26.

15. Frederick Douglass's speech "Life with a Slave-Breaker" (1833), https://www.originalsources.com/Document.aspx?DocID=4V1GSGVSDGJRBTT.

16. Douglass, "Life."

17. Daily Kos, "Black History: Slave Factories, the Middle Passage and Seasoning Camps," March 25, 2008, https://www.dailykos.com/stories/2008/3/25/483725/-.

18. Kunta K. Kinte, "Roots: Your Name Is Toby!" YouTube video, https://www.youtube.com/watch?v=1CpJpGF8lS8.

19. Ben L. Martin, "From Negro to Black to African American," *Political Science Quarterly* 106, no. 1 (Spring, 1991): 83, https://www.jstor.org/stable/2152175?seq=1#page_scan_tab_contents.

20. Belinda Hurmence, *My Folks Don't Want Me to Talk about Slavery* (Winston-Salem, NC: John F. Blair Publisher, 1984), 7.

21. Belinda Hurmence, *We Lived in a Little Cabin in the Yard* (Winston-Salem, NC: John F. Blair Publisher, 1994), 29.

22. Catherine Clinton, *The African American Experience: 1565–1877* (Fort Washington, PA: Eastern National, 2004), 23–24.

23. Hurmence, *We Lived*, 30. Hurmence recorded the words of Elizabeth Sparks, as told to Claude J. Anderson as a part of the Federal Works Project.

24. Crow, Escott, and Hatley, *A History*, 54.

25. Belinda Hermence, *Before Freedom* (Winston-Salem, NC: John F. Blair Publisher, 1989), 22.

26. Hurmence, *Before Freedom*, 188–89.

27. Meier and Rudwick, *Plantation to Ghetto*, 66.

28. Genovese, *Roll, Jordan, Roll*, 303.

29. Joanne Grant, *Black Protest* (New York: Ballantine Books, 1968), 45–49.

30. Bettye Collier-Thomas and James Turner, "Race, Class and Color: The African American Discourse on Identity," *Journal of American Ethnic History* 14, no. 1 (Fall 1994): 13, https://www.jstor.org/stable/pdf/27501932.

31. Collier-Thomas and Turner, "Race, Class and Color."

32. Collier-Thomas and Turner, "Race, Class and Color."

33. Collier-Thomas and Turner, "Race, Class and Color."

34. From the Monticello Web site. "The Life of Sally Hemings: Drawn from the Words of Her Son Madison Hemings," www.monticello.org/sallyhemings/.

35. Jean P. Fisher, "History in Black & White," *The Herald-Sun*, November 8, 1998, sect. E1. Graduate students from Duke, North Carolina Central University, and the University of North Carolina recorded the oral histories of 1,200 African Americans who lived in the Jim Crow South from the 1880s to the 1950s. The interviews covered twelve Southeastern states and were done between 1994 to 1997. The project, *Behind the Veil: Documenting African-American Life in the Jim Crow South*, is the largest collection of photographs, recordings, and documents of life under southern segregation and is stored in the John Hope Franklin Research Center for African and African-American Studies. In 2001 a book and CD compilation was published, *Remembering Jim Crow*, http://scriptorium.lib.duke.edu/franklin/.

36. "Rodney Harrison Sorry for Saying Colin Kaepernick is 'Not Black,'" ESPN, August 30, 2016, https://www.espn.com/nfl/story/_/id/17423939/rodney-harrison-apologizes-saying-colin-kaepernick-san-francisco-49ers-not-black.

37. Clay Skipper, "How Patrick Mahomes Became the Superstar the NFL Needs Right Now," *GQ*, July 14, 2020, https://www.gq.com/story/patrick-mahomes-cover-profile-august-2020.

38. Genovese, *Roll, Jordan, Roll*, 427.

39. Darryl Lyman, *Great African American Women* (New York: Random House, 1999), 33.

40. "Narrative of W. L. Bost, Enslaved in North Carolina, ca. 1849–1865," interview by Federal Writers' Project, September 1937, Asheville, North Carolina, National Humanities Center Resource Toolbox: The Making of African American Identity, vol. 1, 1500–1865, http://nationalhumanitiescenter.org/pds/maai/enslavement/text1/wlbost.pdf.

41. James A. Haught, "Institute: It Springs from Epic Love Story" (*West Virginia History Journal* 32, no. 2 [January 1971]:101–7) tells the fascinating story of the relationship of an enslaved woman, Mary Barnes, who married her owner, Samuel I. Cabell. He left her and their eleven surviving children his estate. While living, he educated all of their children in Ohio. He was murdered by local whites in 1865. The family's property became the site of West Virginia State College. Retrieved from http://www.wvculture.org/history/journal_wvh/wvh32-2a.html.

42. Hurmence, *We Lived*, 55–56.

43. "Isiah Jefferies, Gaffney, South Carolina, August 23, 1937," Library of Congress, https://www.loc.gov/resource/mesn.143/?sp=20&st=text.

44. Federal Writers' Project, *Slave Narratives* 14:1, 156, https://www.loc.gov/resource/mesn.141/?sp=153.

45. Edward Ball, "Retracing Slavery's Trail of Tears", *Smithsonian*, November 2015, https://www.smithsonianmag.com/history/slavery-trail-of-tears-180956968/.

46. Genovese, *Roll, Jordan, Roll*, 416.

47. Edward E. Baptist, "'Cuffy,' 'Fancy Maids,' and 'One-Eyed Men': Rape, Commodification, and the Domestic Slave Trade in the United States," *The American Historical Review* 106, no. 5, (December 2001): 1619, 1633, and 1645, https://www.jstor.org/stable/2692741?read-now=1&refreqid=excelsior%3A71d0e01fcdb67d5cb6d3f71705d837be&seq=15#page_scan_tab_contents.

48. Jacob Manson interview, Genealogy Trails History Group, "Slave Narratives: 'M,'" http://genealogytrails.com/ncar/wake/slavery_narratives_m.html.

49. Tiye A. Gordon, *The Fancy Trade and the Commodification of Rape in the Sexual Economy of 19th Century U.S. Slavery* (Canton, NY: St. Lawrence University, 2009), 2–3, scholarcommons.sc.edu/cgi/viewcontent.cgi?article=4647 &context=etd.

50. Edward E. Baptist, *The Half Has Never Been Told: Slavery and the Making of American Capitalism* (New York: Basic Books, 2016).

51. Lerone Bennett Jr., *Before the Mayflower: A History of Black America* (New York: Penguin Books, 1995), 116.

52. Collier-Thomas and Turner, "Race, Class and Color," 11.

53. Federal Writers' Project, *Slave Narratives: A Folk History of Slavery in the United States from Interviews with Former Slaves*, vol. 11, *North Carolina Narratives*, pt. 1 (Washington, DC: Library of Congress, 1941), 219–20, https://memory.loc.gov/mss/mesn/111/111.pdf.

54. Gordon Lloyd and Jenny S. Martinez, "The Slave Trade Clause," Interactive Constitution, https://constitutioncenter.org/interactive-constitution /interpretation/article-i/clauses/761.

55. Marie Jenkins Schwartz, "'Good Breeders,'" Slate, August 24, 2015, slate .com/human-interest/2015/08/how-enslaved-womens-sexual-health-was -contested-in-the-antebellum-south.html.

56. Documentary *Liberty & Slavery: The Paradox of America's Founding Fathers*, 2016.

57. Meier and Rudwick, *Plantation to Ghetto*, 55.

58. Henry Wiencek, *The Hairstons: An American Family in Black and White* (New York: St. Martins Press, 1999).

59. Curtis Bunn, "6 Startling Things about Sex Farms during Slavery That You May Not Know," *Atlanta Black Star*, November 26, 2014, atlantablackstar.com /2014/11/26/6-startling-things-about-sex-farms-during-slavery-that-you-may -not-know/.

60. Hurmence, *We Lived*, 34.

61. Federal Writers' Project, *Slave Narratives* 11:1, 360.

62. Federal Writers' Project, *Slave Narratives* 11:1, 184–85.

63. Meier and Rudwick, *Plantation to Ghetto*, 66.

64. Crow, Escott, and Hatley, *A History*, 58–59.

65. Crow, Escott, and Hatley, *A History*, 35–36.

66. Crow, Escott, and Hatley, *A History*, 59.

67. Federal Writers' Project, *Slave Narratives* 11:2, 364–65, https://www.loc.gov /resource/mesn.112/?sp=368.

68. "Narrative of W. L. Bost."

69. Michael Trinkley, "South Carolina Slavery: Buying and Selling Human Beings," SCIWAY (South Carolina Information Highway), https://www .sciway.net/afam/slavery/flesh.html.

70. Hurmence, *We Lived*, 34–35.

71. Ball, "Retracing Slavery's Trail of Tears."

72. Meier and Rudwick, *Plantation to Ghetto*, 56.

73. Hurmence, *We Lived*, 46.

74. Sydney Trent, "Slavery Cost Him His Family. That's When Henry 'Box' Brown Mailed Himself to Freedom," *Washington Post*, December 28, 2019, https://www.washingtonpost.com/history/2019/12/28/slavery-cost-him-his -family-thats-when-henry-box-brown-mailed-himself-freedom/.

75. Federal Writers' Project, *Slave Narratives* 11:2, 25–26, http://lcweb2.loc.gov /mss/mesn/112/112.pdf.

76. Hurmence, *Before Freedom*, 146.
77. James Mellon, *Bullwhip Days: The Slaves Remember; An Oral History* (New York: Avon Books, 1988), 18.
78. Mellon, *Bullwhip Days*, 9.
79. Daina Ramey Berry, *The Price for Their Pound of Flesh: The Value of the Enslaved, from Womb to Grave, in the Building of a Nation* (Boston: Beacon Press, 2017). Audiobook.
80. Posted in the *New York Review of Books*: "The Slave Revolts," March 3, 1988, https://www.nybooks.com/articles/1988/03/03/the-slave-revolts/.
81. Bennett, *Confrontation*, 35.
82. David Robertson, *Denmark Vesey: The Buried Story of America's Largest Slave Rebellion and the Man Who Led It* (New York: Vintage Books, 1999), 60.
83. Crow, Escott, and Hatley, *A History*, 21.
84. The American Battlefield Trust Web site, "Purged Away with Blood," www.battlefields.org/learn/articles/purged-away-blood.
85. Bennett, *Before the Mayflower*, 110.
86. Bennett, *Before the Mayflower*, 115; and Robertson, *Denmark Vesey*, 76.
87. Crow, Escott, and Hatley, *A History*, 21.
88. Bennett, *Before the Mayflower*, 110.
89. Alice H. Bauer and Raymond Bauer, "Day to Day Resistance to Slavery" (*Journal of Negro History* 27, no. 4 (October 1942): 388, https://www.jstor.org/stable/2715184.
90. Robertson, *Denmark Vesey*, 35.
91. Joanne Grant, *Black Protest* (New York: Ballantine Books, 1968), 19–22.
92. Bennett, *Before the Mayflower*, 116.
93. Grant, *Black Protest*, 48–49.
94. Bennett, *Before the Mayflower*, 108.
95. Hurmence, *Before Freedom*, 145.
96. Robertson, *Denmark Vesey*, 59.
97. Jill Lepore, *New York Burning: Liberty, Slavery, and Conspiracy in Eighteenth-Century Manhattan* (New York: Vintage Books, 2006).
98. William Loren Katz, *The Black West: A Documentary and Pictorial History of the African American Role in the Westward Expansion of the United States* (New York: Touchstone, 1987), 4.
99. Katz, *Black West*, 3.
100. Quarles, *Negro in the Making*, 28.
101. Claudia Sutherland, "Haitian Revolution (1791–1804)," Blackpast, July 16, 2007, https://www.blackpast.org/global-african-history/haitian-revolution-1791-1804/.
102. AllGreatQuotes as well as BrainyQuotes listed this as a Toussaint Louverture quote. See www.brainyquote.com/authors/toussaint-louverture-quotes.
103. Bennett, *Before the Mayflower*, 124–25.
104. Meier and Rudwick, *Plantation to Ghetto*, 53.
105. Peniel E. Joseph, "Haiti's Revolt Inspired U.S. Black Activists," CNN, January 27, 2010, https://www.cnn.com/2010/OPINION/01/26/joseph.african.americans.haiti/index.html.
106. Henry Louis Gates Jr., "What Was America's First Black Town?", PBS, https://www.pbs.org/wnet/african-americans-many-rivers-to-cross/history/what-was-americas-1st-black-town/.
107. Katz, *Black West*, 16–17.

108. Quarles, *Negro in the Making*, 23.
109. Harding (*There Is a River*, 11–15) and Eric Robert Taylor (*If We Must Die: Shipboard Insurrections in the Era of the Atlantic Slave Trade* [Baton Rouge: Louisiana State University Press, 2006]) both provide ship names, with Taylor providing a more extensive list throughout his work.
110. Stanley Elkins, *Slavery: A Problem in American Institutional and Intellectual Life* (Chicago: University of Chicago Press, 1976), 102.
111. Taylor, *If We Must Die*, 175, 209.
112. Taylor, *If We Must Die*, 167.
113. Harding, *There Is a River*, 10.
114. Harding, *There Is a River*, 10.
115. Meier and Rudwick, *Plantation to Ghetto*, 34.
116. Harding, *There Is a River*, 34–35.
117. Meier and Rudwick, *Plantation to Ghetto*, 35.
118. Harding, *There Is a River*, 10.
119. Harding, *There Is a River*, 34.
120. Harding, *There Is a River*, 21.
121. John Anderson, "The Tryal Slave Ship Rebellion, 1805," BlackPast, September 30, 2014, https://www.blackpast.org/global-african-history/tryal-slave-ship-rebellion-1805/.
122. Harding, *There Is a River*, 14.
123. Harding, *There Is a River*, 12.
124. Harding, *There Is a River*, 12.
125. Harding, *There Is a River*, 13.
126. Bennett, *Before the Mayflower*, 116.
127. Marc Newman, "Slavery and Insurrections in the Colonial Province of New York," National Council for the Social Studies, 1995, http://www.socialstudies.org/sites/default/files/publications/5903/590301.html.
128. Harding, *There Is a River*, 30.
129. Bennett, *Before the Mayflower*, 125–26, 131–39.
130. Herbert Aptheker and C. Vann Woodward engaged in a public dispute over the number and nature of slave revolts in the United States (see "The Slave Revolts," *New York Review*, March 3, 1988, https://www.nybooks.com/articles/1988/03/03/the-slave-revolts/).
131. The Civil War is referred to as the War to End Slavery.
132. Crow, Escott, and Hatley, *A History*, 24–25, 42–47.
133. Stephen Kinzer, "Charleston's Slavery Past," *The News & Observer*, Sunday, August 19, 2001.
134. Grant, *Black Protest*, 37.
135. Grant, *Black Protest*, 37.
136. Robertson, *Denmark Vesey*. Also notable is the retelling by Bennett in *Before the Mayflower*, 127–31.
137. Leon A. Waters, "Louisiana's Heroic Slave Revolt," Zinn Education Project, January 8, 1811, https://www.zinnedproject.org/news/tdih/louisianas-slave-revolt/.
138. Daniel Rasmussen, *American Uprising: The Untold Story of America's Largest Slave Revolt* (New York: Harper Perennial, 2012).
139. Grant, *Black Protest*, 51.
140. Harding, *There Is a River*, 18.
141. Taylor, *If We Must Die*, 344.

142. Grant, *Black Protest*, 51–52.
143. Grant, *Black Protest*, 52
144. Grant, *Black Protest*, 53.
145. Grant, *Black Protest*, 52.
146. Grant, *Black Protest*, 82.
147. Crow, Escott, and Hatley, *A History*, 20–21.
148. Albert J. Raboteau, *Slave Religion: The "Invisible Institution" in the Antebellum South* (Oxford: Oxford University Press, 1978), 92.
149. W. E. B Du Bois, *The Souls of Black Folk*, https://www.gutenberg.org/files/408 /408-h/408-h.htm.
150. Matthew 23:3.
151. Federal Writers' Project, *Slave Narratives*, 11:1, 217.
152. Federal Writers' Project, *Slave Narratives*, 11:2, 345.
153. James H. Cone, *Black Theology & Black Power* (New York: Seabury Press, 1969).
154. Leviticus 25.
155. Ephesians 6:5 and Colossians 3:22.
156. Jean P. Fisher, "History in Black & White," *The Herald-Sun*, November 8, 1998, sect. E1.
157. Gayraud S. Wilmore, *Black Religion and Black Radicalism: An Interpretation of the Religious History of African Americans* (Maryknoll, NY: Orbis Books, 1998), 30.
158. Charles Johnson, Patricia Smith, and the WGBH Series Research Team, *Africans in America: America's Journey through Slavery* (San Diego: Harcourt Brace, 1998), 161, 164.
159. Henry Wiencek, "The Dark Side of Thomas Jefferson," October 2021, https://www.smithsonianmag.com/history/the-dark-side-of-thomas-jefferson -35976004/.
160. Edward Ayres, "African Americans and the American Revolution." American Revolution Museum at Yorktown, https://www.historyisfun.org/learn /learning-center/colonial-america-american-revolution-learning-resources /american-revolution-essays-timelines-images/african-americans-and-the -american-revolution/. Ayres is the historian for the American Revolution Museum at Yorktown and is ardent in pointing out America's failure to recognize the role African Americans played in the nation's fight for independence.
161. Elizabeth M. Collins, "Black Soldiers in the Revolutionary War," February 27, 2013, https://www.army.mil/article/97705/Black_Soldiers_in_the _Revolutionary_War.
162. Quarles, *Negro in the Making*, 46–47.
163. Henry Wiencek, *An Imperfect God: George Washington, His Slaves, and the Creation of America* (New York: Farrar, Straus & Giroux, 2003), 215–17.
164. Clinton, *African American Experience*, 12.
165. Clinton, *African American Experience*, 13.
166. Clinton, *African American Experience*, 13.
167. Elizabeth M. Collins, "Black Soldiers in the Revolutionary War," U.S. Army, March 4, 2013, https://www.army.mil/article/97705/black_soldiers_in_the _revolutionary_war.
168. Wiencek, *Imperfect God*, 243.
169. Wiencek, *Imperfect God*, 244.
170. Colette Coleman, "Seven Black Heroes of the American Revolution," History, February 17, 2021, https://www.history.com/news/black-heroes-american -revolution.

171. Quarles, *Negro in the Making*, 50–51.
172. Clinton, *African American Experience*, 15.
173. Richard Newman, "Not the Only Story in 'Amistad': The Fictional Joadson and the Real James Forten," *Pennsylvania History: A Journal of Mid-Atlantic Studies*, Spring 2000, https://www.jstor.org/stable/27774258.
174. Wiencek, *Imperfect God*, 215–20.
175. Jeffrey J. Crow, "African Americans and the Revolution," NCPedia, Fall 1992, https://www.ncpedia.org/history/usrevolution/african-americans.
176. Quarles, *Negro in the Making*, 56.
177. Frank Martin, director, documentary *For Love of Liberty: The Story of America's Black Patriots* (February 2010).
178. Wiencek, *Imperfect God*, 190, 191.
179. Wiencek, *Imperfect God*, 192.
180. Wiencek, *Imperfect God*, 260–61.
181. Wiencek, *Imperfect God*, 44
182. Bennett, *Confrontation*, 41.
183. Benjamin Quarles, *Black Abolitionists* (Boston: Da Capo Press, 1969), 15, 18, 31.
184. Meier and Rudwick, *Plantation to Ghetto*, 74–75.
185. The Zinn Education Project provides a comprehensive list of Black abolitionists. See www.zinnedproject.org/materials/black-abolitionists/.
186. Bennett, *Confrontation*, 49–51.
187. Henry Weeden wrote this letter to a U.S. Marshal. "An African American Protests the Fugitive Slave Law, 1850," https://www.gilderlehrman.org/content/african-american-protests-fugitive-slave-law-1850.
188. Meier and Rudwick, *Plantation to Ghetto*, 125, 129.
189. Mary Prince, *The History of Mary Prince: A West Indian Slave Narrative* (New York: Penguin Classics, 1831).
190. James Oliver and Lois E. Horton, "A Federal Assault: African Americans and the Impact of the Fugitive Slave Law of 1850," *Chicago-Kent Law Review* 68, no. 3 (1993): 1181, scholarship.kentlaw.iit.edu/cgi/viewcontent.cgi?article=2905&context=cklawreview.
191. National Park Service, *Underground Railroad* (Washington DC: U.S. Government Printing Office, 1998), 45.
192. National Park Service, *Underground Railroad*, 47.
193. "The Long Road to Freedom," *The Herald-Sun*, January 18, 1998, sect. H1.
194. "The Long Road."
195. "The Underground Railroad in Niagara, Canada," *The Carolina Times*, March 14, 1998, 2.
196. Meier and Rudwick, *Plantation to Ghetto*, 126–28.
197. PBS documentary *Redeeming Uncle Tom: The Josiah Henson Story* (2019).
198. Eric Foner, *Gateway to Freedom: The Hidden History of the Underground Railroad* (New York: W.W. Norton & Co., 2016).
199. "The Long Road."
200. Marcia Y. Riggs, ed., *Can I Get A Witness? Prophetic Religious Voices of African American Women: An Anthology* (Maryknoll, NY: Orbis Books, 1997), 21.
201. Nell Irvin Painter, *Sojourner Truth: A Life, A Symbol* (New York: W.W. Norton & Co., 1997), 160–61.
202. Painter, *Sojourner Truth*, 220–33, 272.
203. David W. Blight, *Frederick Douglass: Prophet of Freedom* (New York: Simon & Schuster, 2018), 752–62.

204. Catherine Clinton, *Harriet Tubman: The Road to Freedom* (New York: Back Bay Books: 2005).
205. Frederick Douglass, "(1868) Letter from Frederick Douglass to Harriet Tubman," BlackPast, August 26, 1868, https://www.blackpast.org/african -american-history/1868-letter-from-frederick-douglass-to-harriet-tubman/.
206. Joseph Glatthaar, *The Civil War's Black Soldiers*, National Park Service Civil War Series (Conshocken, PA: Eastern National, 2016), 5.
207. Bennett, *Confrontation*, 62.
208. David W. Blight, *Frederick Douglass' Civil War: Keeping the Faith in Jubilee* (Baton Rouge: Louisiana State University Press, 1991), 148.
209. Abraham Lincoln, "Letter to Horace Greeley," August 22, 1862, Abraham Lincoln Online, http://www.abrahamlincolnonline.org/lincoln/speeches /greeley.htm.
210. Katherine Calos, "Black Soldiers in the Civil War: Who Did They Fight for and Why?" *Richmond Times–Dispatch*, March 14, 2015, https://www.richmond .com/black-soldiers-in-the-civil-war-who-did-they-fight-for-and-why/article _317568c2-1ba4-5f88-a18a-45d24a900a22.html.
211. Harding, *There Is a River*, 228–31.
212. James M. McPherson, "Who Freed the Slaves?," *Proceedings of the American Philosophical Society* 139, no. 1 (March 1995), https://www.jstor.org/stable /986716.
213. Bennett, *Before the Mayflower*, 193.
214. United States Senate, "The Confiscation Acts of 1861 and 1862," https://www .senate.gov/artandhistory/history/common/generic/ConfiscationActs.htm.
215. Harding, *There Is a River*, 232.
216. Harding, *There Is a River*, 231.
217. Harding, *There Is a River*, 231.
218. Clinton, *African American Experience*, 39–42.
219. History.com editors, "Fort Pillow Massacre," History.com, June 21, 2019, https://www.history.com/topics/american-civil-war/fort-pillow-massacre.
220. "General Lee's Views on Enlisting the Negroes," *Century Magazine* 36, no. 4 (August 1888), https://encyclopediavirginia.org/entries/general-lees-views-on -enlisting-the-negroes-century-magazine-august-1888/.
221. Calos, "Black Soldiers."
222. Calos, "Black Soldiers."
223. Calos, "Black Soldiers."
224. Bill Mears and Barbara Starr, "Slave in Jefferson Davis' Home Gave Union Key Secrets," CNN, February 20, 2009, https://www.cnn.com/2009/US/02 /20/spy.slaves/.
225. Jeffrey J. Crow, "African Americans and the Revolution."
226. Thad Morgan, "How a Black Spy Infiltrated the Confederate White House," History.com, April 31, 2018, https://www.history.com/news/female-spies -civil-war-mary-bowser-elizabeth-van-lew.
227. Mears and Starr, "Slave in Jefferson Davis' Home."
228. Clinton, *African American Experience*, 39–42.
229. McPherson, "Who Freed the Slaves?"
230. "Civil War," The Lehrman Institute, http://www.mrlincolnandfreedom.org /civil-war/.
231. John A Latschar and Robert K. Sutton, *The Reconstruction Era* (Fort Washing- ton, PA: Eastern National Publishers, 2016), 173.

232. Bennett, *Confrontation*, 71.

233. Bennett, *Confrontation*, 70.

234. Bennett, *Confrontation*, 73.

235. Rayford W. Logan, *The Betrayal of the Negro: From Rutherford B. Hayes to Woodrow Wilson* (New York: Collier Books, 1969), 37.

236. Federal Writers' Project, *Slave Narratives*, 11:2, 123.

237. Rick Beard, John Latschar, and Robert Sutton, *Slavery in the United States: A Brief Narrative History* (Fort Washington, PA: Eastern National Publishers, 2013), 56.

238. Euell A. Nielsen, "The New York City Draft Riots (1863)," Blackpast, November 10, 2017, https://www.blackpast.org/african-american-history /new-york-city-draft-riots-1863/.

239. Meier and Rudwick, *Plantation to Ghetto*, 174.

240. T. W. Gilbreath, *The Freedmen's Bureau Report on the Memphis Race Riots of 1866* (May 22, 1866). See teachingamericanhistory.org/library/document/the -freedmens-bureau-report-on-the-memphis-race-riots-of-1866/.

241. Michael Stolp-Smith, "New Orleans Massacre (1866)," Blackpast, April 7, 2-11, https://www.blackpast.org/african-american-history/new-orleans-massacre -1866/.

242. Meier and Rudwick, *Plantation to Ghetto*, 172–75.

243. Meier and Rudwick, *Plantation to Ghetto*, 174.

244. Sheren Sanders, "The Meridian Race Riot (1871)," Blackpast, January 11, 2018, https://www.blackpast.org/african-american-history/meridian-race-riot -1871/.

245. Meier and Rudwick, *Plantation to Ghetto*, 172–73.

Section 3: Protesting Reconstruction's Failures

1. John Hope Franklin, *Reconstruction after the Civil War* (Chicago: University of Chicago Press, 1961), 133.

2. Bettye Collier-Thomas and James Turner, "Race, Class and Color: The African American Discourse on Identity," *Journal of American Ethnic History* 14, no. 1 (Fall 1994): 14, 19,www.jstor.org/stable/pdf/27501932.

3. Kee Malesky, "The Journey from 'Colored' to 'Minorities' to 'People of Color,'" NPR, March 30, 2014, https://www.npr.org/sections/codeswitch /2014/03/30/295931070/the-journey-from-colored-to-minorities-to-people -of-color.

4. Lerone Bennett Jr., "What's in a Name? Negro vs. Afro-American vs. Black," *Review of General Semantics* 26, no. 4 (December 1969): 404, https://www.jstor .org/stable/42574587?seq=1#metadata_info_tab_contents.

5. Bennett, "What's in a Name?"; "'Negro' with a Capital 'N.,'" *New York Times*, March 7, 1930, https://www.nytimes.com/1930/03/07/archives/negro-with-a -capital-n.html.

6. Nancy Coleman, "Why We're Capitalizing Black," *New York Times*, July 5, 2020, https://www.nytimes.com/2020/07/05/insider/capitalized-black.html.

7. Federal Writers' Project, *Slave Narratives: A Folk History of Slavery in the United States from Interviews with Former Slaves*, vol. 11, *North Carolina Narratives*, pt. 1 (Washington, DC: Library of Congress, 1941), 361, https://memory.loc .gov/mss/mesn/111/111.pdf.

8. Lerone Bennett Jr., *Confrontation: Black and White* (London: Penguin Books, 1965), 71.

 9. Rayford W. Logan, *The Betrayal of the Negro: From Rutherford B. Hayes to Woodrow Wilson* (New York: Collier Books, 1969), 25.

10. David Brussat, "Hardscrabble and Snowtown," *Architecture Here and There* (blog), November 23, 2019, architecturehereandthere.com/2019/11/23/hard scrabble-and-snowtown/. Brussat links to an essay by a lawyer, John Crouch, about articles in the Providence *Beacon* from the period of the riots that are incendiary and exhibit a remarkable bias toward both the white crowd and Black residents. The *Beacon*'s publisher, William Spear, describes Blacks as "naturally vicious and wicked," "profligate," and "worthless," yet "innocent as lambs." He decries the "indiscriminate 'atrocities' of an 'abandoned and profligate mob.'" John Crouch, "Providence Newspapers and the Racist Riots of 1824 and 1831," https://archive.md/TR0S.

11. August Meier and Elliott Rudwick, *From Plantation to Ghetto*, rev. ed. (New York: Hill and Wang, 1970), 79.

12. *Born in Slavery: Slave Narratives from the Federal Writers' Project, 1936–1938*, Library of Congress, 114, http://fairfieldgenealogysociety.org/Members _Only/PDF/Books/Slave-Narratives.pdf.

13. Logan, *Betrayal of the Negro*, 21.

14. Samuel Thomas, "Testimony of the Assistant Commissioner of the Bureau of Refugees, Freedmen and Abandoned Lands," Digital History, 1895, https://www.digitalhistory.uh.edu/disp_textbook.cfm?smtID=3&psid=4560.

15. Equal Justice Initiative, *Lynching in America: Confronting The Legacy of Racial Terror* (2017), eji.org/reports/lynching-in-america/.

16. Netflix documentary *Quincy* by Rashida Jones (2018).

17. Equal Justice Initiative, *Lynching in America*.

18. Ida B. Wells, 1900 speech "Lynch Law in America," BlackPast, July 13, 2010, https://www.blackpast.org/african-american-history/1900-ida-b-wells-lynch -law-america/.

19. Black Excellence team, "The Silent Parade of 1917: Why the Forgotten March Matters," Black Excellence, August 2019, https://blackexcellence.com /the-silent-parade-of-1917/.

20. Black Excellence team, "Silent Parade."

21. Alexis Newman, "New York City NAACP Silent Protest Parade (1917)," BlackPast, March 26, 2017, https://www.blackpast.org/african-american -history/naacp-silent-protest-parade-new-york-city-1917/.

22. Bennett, *Confrontation*, 76.

23. Adrienne LaFrance and Vann R. Newkirk II, "The Lost History of an American Coup D'État," *The Atlantic*, August 12, 2017, https://www.theatlantic.com /politics/archive/2017/08/wilmington-massacre/536457/.

24. LaFrance and Newkirk, "The Lost History."

25. Bennett, *Confrontation*, 79.

26. Meier and Rudwick, *Plantation to Ghetto*, 179.

27. Carter G. Woodson, "The Negro Church: An All-Comprehending Institution," *The Negro History Bulletin*, October 1939, 7, as cited by Michele M. SimmsParris in her manuscript "Comment: What Does It Mean To See A Black Church Burning?" *Journal of Constitutional Law* (1998): 1:1, 142, https://scholarship.law.upenn.edu/cgi/viewcontent.cgi?article=1471&context=jcl.

28. E. Franklin Frazier, *The Negro Church in America* (New York: Schocken Books, 1963), 29–46.

29. C. Eric Lincoln and Lawrence H. Mamiya, *The Black Church in the African American Experience* (Durham, NC: Duke University Press, 1990), xii.

30. "Burning of Black Churches Is Old Tactic: Arson Attacks in South Show a Racist Past Still Smolders," *Baltimore Sun*, June 13, 1996, https://www.baltimoresun.com/news/bs-xpm-1996-06-13-1996165001-story.html.

31. SimmsParris, "What Does It Mean?"

32. Chris Kromm, "Charleston and the South's Sordid History of Attacks on Black Churches," *Facing South*, June 18, 2015, https://www.facingsouth.org/2015/06/charleston-and-the-souths-sordid-history-of-attack.

33. Moira Lavelle, "The Fire Last Time: The 1990s Wave of 145 Church Burnings—Map," The World, July 3, 2015, https://www.pri.org/stories/2015-07-02/fire-last-time-1990s-wave-145-church-burnings-map.

34. Emma Green, "Black Churches Are Burning Again in America," *The Atlantic*, June 25, 2015, https://www.theatlantic.com/national/archive/2015/06/arson-churches-north-carolina-georgia/396881/.

35. Stephen C. Fehr, "U.S. Historic Trust Puts Black Churches on Endangered List," *Washington Post*, June 18, 1996, https://www.washingtonpost.com/wp-srv/national/longterm/churches/reaction.htm.

36. Gerda Lerner, ed., *Black Women in White America: A Documentary History* (New York: Penguin Random House, 1972), 152, 155.

37. William Ferris and Charles Reagan Wilson, eds., *Encyclopedia of Southern Culture* (New York: Anchor Books, 1989), 223–25, 318.

38. Michelle Alexander, *The New Jim Crow: Mass Incarceration in the Age of Colorblindness* (New York: New Press, 2012), 156–57.

39. "Convict Leasing and Chain Gangs," *Mississippi Encyclopedia*, mississippiencyclopedia.org/entries/convict-leasing-and-chain-gangs/.

40. Herbert Aptheker, ed., *A Documentary History of the Negro People in the United States: 1910–1932* (Charleston, SC: Citadel Press, 1973), 119–20.

41. Thomas N. Maloney, "African Americans in the Twentieth Century," eh.net/encyclopedia/african-americans-in-the-twentieth-century/.

42. Maloney, "African Americans."

43. Richard Wormser, *The Rise and Fall of Jim Crow: The African-American Struggle against Discrimination, 1865–1954* (New York: Franklin Watts, 1999), ebook.

44. Meier and Rudwick, *Plantation to Ghetto*, 80–81.

45. Tsahai Tafari, "The Rise and Fall of Jim Crow," Thirteen, WNET New York. See www.thirteen.org/wnet/jimcrow/print/p_struggle_president.html.

46. Wormser, *Rise and Fall of Jim Crow*.

47. David Levering Lewis, ed., *W. E. B. Du Bois: A Reader* (New York: Henry Holt and Co., 1995), 319.

48. Bennett, *Confrontation*, 88–102, 110.

49. W. E. B. Du Bois, *The Souls of Black Folk* (Chicago: A. C. McClurg & Co., 1903).

50. Meier and Rudwick, *Plantation to Ghetto*, 3.

51. Du Bois, *Souls of Black Folk*.

52. Du Bois, *Souls of Black Folk*, 110.

53. Bennett, *Confrontation*, 91.

54. Quarles quoted in Bennett, *Confrontation*, 91.

55. *Birth of a Movement*, documentary directed by Bestor Cram and Susan Gray (Northern Lights Productions, 2017).

56. North Carolina Congressman George White's farewell congressional speech in 1901 after being voted out of Congress by his political colleagues. See "(1901) Congressman George H. White's Farewell Address to Congress," BlackPast, January 28, 2007, https://www.blackpast.org/african-american -history/1901-george-h-whites-farewell-address-congress/.

57. Statement inserted on the unnumbered page before the table of contents of W. E. Burghardt Du Bois's *The Negro Church* (Atlanta: Atlanta University Press, 1903).

58. Meier and Rudwick, *Plantation to Ghetto*, 84.

59. Meier and Rudwick, *Plantation to Ghetto*, 83.

60. Meier and Rudwick, *Plantation to Ghetto*, 83–85.

61. Bennett, *Confrontation*, 44.

62. Meier and Rudwick, *Plantation to Ghetto*, 88.

63. Gayraud S. Wilmore, *Black & Presbyterian: The Heritage and the Hope* (Louisville, KY: Geneva Press, 1983), 64.

64. Pagan Kennedy, *Black Livingstone: A True Tale of Adventure in the Nineteenth-Century Congo* (London: Penguin Books, 2002).

65. Lerner, *Black Women*, 102–3.

66. Meier and Rudwick, *Plantation to Ghetto*, 94.

67. Marshall Brown, "Preservation Matters: The First African American High School in Frederick," *The Frederick News Post*, September 23, 2019, sect. A7.

68. Meier and Rudwick, *Plantation to Ghetto*, 96.

69. *You Belong to Me: Sex, Race and Murder in the South; The Ruby McCollum Story*, documentary written and directed by John Cork (Marina Del Rey, CA: Vision Films, 2015).

70. Susie King Taylor, *Reminiscences of My Life: A Black Woman's Civil War Memoirs.* (Athens: University of Georgia Press, 1902), 37.

71. Darryl Lyman, *Great African American Women* (New York: Random House, 1999), 153.

72. Shomari Wills, *Black Fortunes: The Story of the First Six African Americans Who Survived Slavery and Became Millionaires* (New York: Amistad Press, 2019).

73. Beverly Bunch-Lyons studied the evolution of Black-owned funeral homes in the state of North Carolina. See "'Ours Is a Business of Loyalty': African American Funeral Home Owners in Southern Cities," *Southern Quarterly* 53, no. 1 (Fall 2015): 58, ncr.vt.edu/docs/53.1.bunch-lyons.pdf.

74. Meier and Rudwick, *Plantation to Ghetto*, 99.

75. Muriel Miller Branch, "Maggie Lena Walker (1864–1934)," April 12, 2010, https://www.encyclopediavirginia.org/Maggie_Lena_Walker_1864-1934#start _entry.

76. Henry Louis Gates Jr., ed., *African Americans: Voices of Triumph; Leadership* (New York: Time-Life Books, 1994), 75–76.

77. Alexa Benson Henderson, "Atlanta Life Insurance Company," *New Georgia Encyclopedia*, April 1, 2003, https://www.georgiaencyclopedia.org/articles /business-economy/atlanta-life-insurance-company.

78. Gates, *African Americans: Voices*, 96–111.

79. E. Franklin Frazier, *Black Bourgeoisie* (New York: Free Press: 1957).

80. William B. Gatewood, *Aristocrats of Color: The Black Elite, 1880–1920* (Fayetteville: University of Arkansas Press, 1990).

81. Edward Ball, *The Sweet Hell Inside: A Family's History* (New York: William Morrow, 2001).

82. Wills, *Black Fortunes.*

83. Independent documentary, *The Black Miami*, produced by Michael Williams and Carlton Smith (2014).

84. Judith Lynn Howard, "A Rich Black History: Former Slave's Atlanta Mansion Preserves a Slice of Upper-Class Life," *The News and Observer*, Sunday, November 16, 1997, sect. 6H.

85. Mark Whitaker, *The Untold Story of Smoketown: The Other Great Black Renaissance* (New York: Simon & Schuster, 2018).

86. Meier and Rudwick, *Plantation to Ghetto*, 90.

87. Meier and Rudwick, *Plantation to Ghetto*, 91.

88. Meier and Rudwick, *Plantation to Ghetto*, 92.

89. John Lewis, "Speech at the March on Washington (28 August 1963)," Voices of Democracy, https://voicesofdemocracy.umd.edu/lewis-speech-at-the -march-on-washington-speech-text/.

90. Meier and Rudwick, *Plantation to Ghetto*, 109–10.

91. Miranda Booker Perry, "No Pensions for Ex-Slaves: How Federal Agencies Suppressed Movement to Aid Freedpeople," *Prologue Magazine* 42, no. 2 (Summer 2010), https://www.archives.gov/publications/prologue/2010 /summer/slave-pension.html.

92. Stephanie Christensen, "Niagara Movement (1905–1909)," Blackpast, December 16, 2007, https://www.blackpast.org/african-american-history /niagara-movement-1905-1909/.

93. Quarles, *Negro in the Making*, 173–74.

94. PBS, "Marcus Garvey: Look for Me in the Whirlwind," *American Experience*, https://www.pbs.org/wgbh/americanexperience/features/garvey-his-own -words/.

95. Quarles, *Negro in the Making*, 195–97.

96. Brian Scott MacKenzie, "Freedom Is Never Granted; It Is Won," *Medium*, April 15, 2017, https://brianscottmackenzie.medium.com/freedom-is-never -given-it-is-won-51e697b0b9ff.

97. American Public Media, "Dorothy Height: Speech Delivered at the First Scholarly Conference on Black Women," American RadioWorks, November 13, 1979, http://americanradioworks.publicradio.org/features/blackspeech /dheight.html.

98. *National Council of Negro Women Handbook*, 6. See https://ncnw.org/files /NCNW_Handbook_2017_withAppendices.pdf.

99. Wiley A. Hall, "Urban League, NAACP Should Work Together," *Baltimore Sun*, June 15, 1995, https://www.baltimoresun.com/news/bs-xpm-1995-06-15 -1995166171-story.html.

100. Bennett, *Confrontation*, 47.

101. Clint C. Wilson II, "Overview of the Past 182 Years of the Black Press," National Newspaper Publishers Association. See nnpa.org/black-press -history/.

102. Smithsonian: National Museum of African American History & Culture, "Special Collection: 75 Years of *Ebony* Magazine," December, 2020. See https://nmaahc.si.edu/explore/collection/75-years-ebony-magazine.

103. Carl Senna, *The Black Press and the Struggle for Civil Rights* (New York: Franklin Watts, 1944), 125.

104. Alison Flood, "Travel Guides to Segregated US for Black Americans Reissued," *The Guardian*, December 19, 2017, https://www.theguardian.com

/books/2017/dec/19/travel-guides-to-segregated-us-for-black-americans
-reissued.

105. Juan Williams, *Eyes on the Prize: America's Civil Rights Years 1954–1965* (New York: Penguin Random House, 1987), 130.

106. David Fishman, "Distinguished Civil Rights Activist Diane Nash to Address Northwestern," *The Daily Northwestern*, December 4, 2015, https://dailynorthwestern.com/2015/12/04/campus/distinguished-civil-rights-activist-diane-nash-to-address-northwestern/.

107. Stuart A. Rose Manuscript Archives & Rare Book Library under City Directories: Directories of Localities for African American Communities, Emory Libraries, Atlanta, Georgia.

108. A fuller listing is contained in the Stuart A. Rose Manuscript Archives & Rare Book Library under "City Directories: Directories of Localities for African American Communities."

109. Lerner, *Black Women*, 383–84.

110. Afi-Odelia Scruggs, "Exodus: Blacks Fled the South in Droves More Than a Century Ago, Seeking True Freedom," *USA Today*, March 6, 2019, https://www.usatoday.com/story/news/investigations/2019/03/06/black-migrations-black-history-slavery-freedom/2807813002/.

111. Meier and Rudwick, *Plantation to Ghetto*, 55.

112. Ball, "Retracing Slavery's Trail of Tears."

113. Meier and Rudwick, *Plantation to Ghetto*, 57.

114. Ball, "Retracing Slavery's Trail of Tears."

115. Quarles, *Negro in the Making*, 95–96.

116. Quarles, *Negro in the Making*, 95-96.

117. Library of Congress, "The African-American Mosaic: Anti-Colonization Song," https://www.loc.gov/exhibits/african/afam005.html.

118. Quarles, *Negro in the Making*, 96.

119. Joseph Glatthaar, *The Civil War's Black Soldiers*, Civil War series (Fort Washington, PA: Eastern National Park and Monument Association, 1996), 9.

120. Clinton, *African American Experience*, 53.

121. Jeffrey J. Crow, Paul D. Escott, and Flora J. Hatley, *A History of African Americans in North Carolina* (Raleigh: North Carolina Office of Archives and History, 1992), 120.

122. Anna Khomina, "The Homestead Act of 1862: Dreams and Realities," 2021, https://ushistoryscene.com/article/1862-homestead-act/.

123. Topher Wilson, "Hiram Young: Kansas City's First 'Colored Man of Means,'" *Martin City Telegraph*, February 28, 2016, https://martincitytelegraph.com/2016/02/28/hiram-young-kansas-citys-first-colored-man-of-means/.

124. Clinton, *African American Experience*, 52.

125. "Black Towns," Encyclopedia.com, https://www.encyclopedia.com/history/encyclopedias-almanacs-transcripts-and-maps/black-towns.

126. Isabel Wilkerson, *The Warmth of Other Suns: The Epic Story of America's Great Migration* (New York: Random House, 2010), 538.

127. Wilkerson, *Warmth of Other Suns*, 539.

128. Marcus Gee, "Another Great Migration Is under Way: Black Americans Are Leaving Big Cities for the Suburbs," *The Globe and Mail*, April 29, 2018, https://www.theglobeandmail.com/world/article-another-great-migration-is-under-way-black-americans-are-leaving-big/.

129. Paul Overberg and Greg Toppo, "After Nearly 100 Years, Great Migration Begins Reversal," *USA Today*, February 2, 2015, https://www.usatoday.com/story/news/nation/2015/02/02/census-great-migration-reversal/21818127/.
130. Overberg and Toppo, "After Nearly 100 Years."
131. Wilkerson quoted in Overberg and Toppo, "After Nearly 100 Years."
132. "Words of the Week," *Jet Magazine*, April 7, 1966, 30.
133. William Loren Katz, *The Black West: A Documentary and Pictorial History of the African American Role in the Westward Expansion of the United States* (New York: Touchstone, 1987), xiii.
134. Katie Nodjimbadem, "The Lesser-Known History of African-American Cowboys," *Smithsonian*, February 13, 2017, https://www.smithsonianmag.com/history/lesser-known-history-african-american-cowboys-180962144/.
135. Jen Fifield, "Black Cowboys Were Common in the Old West. Here's a Piece of Their Forgotten History," *AZCentral*, March 17, 2019, https://www.azcentral.com/story/news/local/arizona-history/2019/03/17/black-cowboys-were-common-old-west/3180296002/.
136. Katz, *Black West*, 54–56.
137. Nodjimbadem, "The Lesser-Known History of African-American Cowboys."
138. Thad Morgan, "Was the Real Lone Ranger a Black Man?" History, August 31, 2018, https://www.history.com/news/bass-reeves-real-lone-ranger-a-black-man.
139. Lillian Schlissel, *Black Frontiers* (New York: Aladdin Paperbacks/Simon & Schuster, 2002), 9, 54.
140. William Loren Katz, *Black Indians: A Hidden Heritage* (New York: Aladdin Paperbacks, 1997), 108–11, 137.
141. W. E. B. Du Bois, "The Upbuilding of Black Durham: The Success of the Negroes and Their Value to a Tolerant and Helpful Southern City," electronic edition, docsouth.unc.edu/nc/dubois/dubois.html. The University of North Carolina's Web page, Documenting the American South, contains the whole of Du Bois's assessment of the prosperity achieved by African Americans in Durham, North Carolina.
142. Norman L. Crockett, *The Black Towns* (Lawrence: KS: Regents Press of Kansas, 1979), xii.
143. "Historic Black Towns and Settlements—Oklahoma 2021!" HBTSA: Historic Black Towns and Settlements Alliance, hbtsa.org.
144. Crockett, *The Black Towns*.
145. Larry O'Dell, "All-Black Towns," *The Encyclopedia of Oklahoma History and Culture*, https://www.okhistory.org/publications/enc/entry.php?entry=AL009.
146. Brandee Sanders, "History's Lost Black Towns: Fort Mose, Fla.: The First 'Emancipation Proclamation,'" The Root, January 27, 2011, https://www.theroot.com/historys-lost-black-towns-1790868004.
147. DeNeen L. Brown, "All-Black Towns Across America: Life Was Hard but Full of Promise," *Washington Post*, March 27, 2015, https://www.washingtonpost.com/lifestyle/style/a-list-of-well-known-black-towns/2015/03/27/9f21ca42-cdc4-11e4-a2a7-9517a3a70506_story.html.
148. National Museum of American History, "The Migration of Free Frank McWorter," https://americanhistory.si.edu/many-voices-exhibition/peopling-expanding-nation-1776-1900/western-migration/free-frank-mcworter; and the New Philadelphia Web page, http://newphiladelphiail.org.
149. Martha Waggoner, "Historic Princeville Plans Heritage Tourism Site," *The Herald-Sun*, August 8, 1999, sect. B8.

150. Rob Christensen, "A Forgotten North Carolina Leader," *The News & Observer*, February 25, 2001, sect. 5G.

151. DeNeen L. Brown, "Black Towns, Established by Freed Slaves after the Civil War, Are Dying Out," *Washington Post*, March 27, 2015, https://www.washingtonpost.com/local/black-towns-established-by-freed-slaves-after-civil-war-are-dying-out/2015/03/26/25872e5c-c608-11e4-a199-6cb5e63819d2_story.html.

152. Melanie S. Hatter, "Some Say He Was Touched by God," *Roanoke Times & World News*, December 23, 1993. sect.1.

153. *The News & Observer*, "West Side Story," Tuesday, March 2, 1999, sect.1E.

154. E. R. Shipp, "A Journey into Georgia's Black History," *The Atlanta Journal and Constitution*, September 18, 1988, sect. 3.

155. *The Black Miami*.

156. *The Black Miami*. These words are from a historical placard labeled "Charles Avenue."

157. *The Black Miami*.

158. Deneen L. Brown, "Remembering 'Red Summer,' When White Mobs Massacred Blacks from Tulsa to D.C.," *National Geographic*, June 19, 2020, https://www.nationalgeographic.com/history/2020/06/remembering-red-summer-white-mobs-massacred-blacks-tulsa-dc/.

159. Gregory Mixon and Clifford Kuhn, "Atlanta Race Riot of 1906," *New Georgia Encyclopedia*, September 23, 2005, https://www.georgiaencyclopedia.org/articles/history-archaeology/atlanta-race-riot-1906.

160. William H. Black quoted in Coshandra Dillard, "An Armed White Mob in Texas Massacred Their Black Neighbors in 1910, and None of Them Were Prosecuted," Timeline.com, October 6, 2017, timeline.com/slocum-massacre-texas-mob-4a212c1e63e7. The sheriff was quoted in the August 1, 1910, edition of the *New York Times*. He lost his bid to be reelected and never served as sheriff again in Anderson County, Texas, E. R. Bills wrote in his 2014 book, *The 1910 Slocum Massacre: An Act of Genocide in East Texas*.

161. Brown, "Remembering 'Red Summer.'"

162. Robert Stephens, "The Truth Laid Bare," *Pegasus: The Magazine of the University of Central Florida*, Fall 2020, https://www.ucf.edu/pegasus/the-truth-laid-bare/; and Gillian Brockell, "A White Mob Unleashed the Worst Election Day Violence in U.S. History in Florida a Century Ago," *The Washington Post*, November 2, 2020, https://www.washingtonpost.com/history/2020/11/02/ocoee-florida-election-day-massacre/.

163. Maggie Astor, "What to Know About the Tulsa Greenwood Massacre," *New York Times*, June 20, 2002, https://www.nytimes.com/2020/06/20/us/tulsa-greenwood-massacre.html.

164. James W. Loewen, "Sundown Towns and Counties: Racial Exclusion in the South," *Southern Cultures* 15, no. 1 (Spring 2009), https://www.jstor.org/stable/pdf/26214270.pdf.

165. James W. Loewen, *Sundown Towns: A Hidden Dimension of American Racism* (New York: New Press, 2018).

166. Elliot Jaspin, *Buried in the Bitter Waters: The Hidden History of Racial Cleansing in America* (New York: Basic Books, 2008).

167. David Bianculli, The 'Racial Cleansing' That Drove 1,100 Black Residents Out of Forsyth County, GA," NPR, December 8, 2017, https://www.npr

.org/2017/12/08/569156832/the-racial-cleansing-that-drove-1-100-black
-residents-out-of-forsyth-county-ga.

168. Loewen, *Sundown Towns.*

169. Abigail Higgins, "Red Summer of 1919: How Black WWI Vets Fought Back against Racist Mobs," *History*, July 26, 2019, https://www.history.com/news/red-summer-1919-riots-chicago-dc-great-migration.

170. David F. Krugler, *1919, The Year of Racial Violence: How African Americans Fought Back* (Cambridge: Cambridge University Press, 2015), 13.

171. Brown, "Remembering 'Red Summer.'"

172. Krugler, *1919*, 3.

173. Brown, "Remembering 'Red Summer.'"

174. Brown, "Remembering 'Red Summer.'"

175. Brown, "Remembering 'Red Summer.'"

176. Higgins, "Red Summer of 1919."

177. Krugler, *1919*, 4.

178. Quarles, *Negro in the Making*, 193.

179. Alain Locke, *Voices of the Harlem Renaissance: The New Negro: An Interpretation* (Old Saybrook, CT: Konecky & Konecky, 2019), xii, 4, 8, 10.

180. David Driskell, David Levering Lewis, and Deborah Willis Ryan, *Harlem Renaissance: Art of Black America* (New York: Studio Museum in Harlem, 1987), 106.

181. Gregory Holmes Singleton, "Birth, Rebirth, and the 'New Negro' of the 1920s," *Phylon* 43, no. 1 (1982): 29–30, https://www.jstor.org/stable/274597.

182. Driskell, Lewis, and Ryan, *Harlem Renaissance*, 63.

183. Eva Goldberg, "What Ever Happened to Hazel Scott?" YouTube, https://www.youtube.com/watch?v=o_WJ4PpxWaE.

184. Driskell, Lewis and Ryan, *Harlem Renaissance*, 106.

185. Documentary, *For Love of Liberty: The Story of America's Black Patriots* (2010), directed by Frank Martin.

186. *For Love of Liberty.*

187. "African Americans in the White House," DocSouth, *Documenting the American South*, docsouth.unc.edu/highlights/whitehouse.html.

188. Robert B. Edgerton, *Hidden Heroism: Black Soldiers in America's Wars* (New York: Basic Books, 2002), 9.

189. Newsroom, "A Soldier's Story: Cathay Williams Defied Her Time to Become the Only Known Female Buffalo Soldier," *Wounded Warrior Project*, https://newsroom.woundedwarriorproject.org/Cathay-Williams-The-Only-Known-Female-Buffalo-Soldier.

190. Henry Louis Gates, ed., *African Americans: Voices of Triumph: Perseverance.* (New York: Time-Life Books: 1994). 165.

191. Gustav Person, "Aileen Cole Stewart: Black Pioneer of the Army Nursing Corps," U.S. Army, February 18, 2010, https://www.army.mil/article/34605/aileen_cole_stewart_black_pioneer_of_the_army_nursing_corps.

192. Gates, *African Americans: Voices*, 165–67.

193. Vietnam War Commemoration, "Interview with Doris Allen," May 1, 2014, https://www.vietnamwar50th.com/assets/1/28/Allen_Doris_Captions_Transcript.pdf.

194. David Wright and David Zoby, *Fire on the Beach: Recovering the Lost Story of Richard Etheridge and the Pea Island Lifesavers* (New York: Scribner, 2000), 176–77.

195. Edgerton, *Hidden Heroism*, 72.
196. Edgerton, *Hidden Heroism*, 86–87.
197. Edgerton, *Hidden Heroism*, 98.
198. Tom Clavin and Phil Keith, *All Blood Runs Red: The Legendary Life of Eugene Bullard—Boxer, Pilot, Soldier, Spy* (New York: Hanover Square Press, 2019).
199. Edgerton, *Hidden Heroism*, 95.
200. History Channel Vault documentary, *African American Soldiers of D-Day*. Mr. Price was in the 327th Quartermaster Service Company, Illinois.
201. Edgerton, *Hidden Heroism*, 154–55.
202. Edgerton, *Hidden Heroism*, 142–45.
203. Maria Höhn, "African-American GIs of WWII: Fighting for Democracy Abroad and at Home," *MilitaryTimes*, January 30, 2018, https://www.militarytimes.com /military-honor/black-military-history/2018/01/30/african-american-gis-of-wwii -fighting-for-democracy-abroad-and-at-home/.
204. *For Love of Liberty.*
205. *For Love of Liberty.*
206. History.com Editors, "Works Progress Administration (WPA)," History, June 10, 2019, https://www.history.com/topics/great-depression/works -progress-administration.
207. Ira Katznelson, *When Affirmative Action Was White* (New York: W.W. Norton & Co., 2006).
208. See fdr4freedoms, "13: African Americans and the New Deal: A Historic Realignment in Americans Politics," https://fdr4freedoms.org/wp-content /themes/fdf4fdr/DownloadablePDFs/II_HopeRecoveryReform/13_African AmericansandtheNewDeal.pdf.
209. Richard Rothstein, "We Can End Racial Segregation in America," *Jacobin Magazine*, July 22, 2019, https://www.jacobinmag.com/2019/07/desegregation -color-of-law-public-housing.
210. Richard Rothstein, *The Color of Law: A Forgotten History of How Our Government Segregated America* (New York: Liveright, 2017).
211. Katznelson, *When Affirmative Action Was White*, offers great information on federal government's role in racial segregation throughout the country.
212. Charles Lane, "The New Deal as Raw Deal for Backs in Segregated Communities," *Washington Post*, May 25, 2017, https://www.washingtonpost.com /opinions/the-new-deal-as-raw-deal-for-blacks-in-segregated-communities /2017/05/25/07416bba-080a-11e7-a15f-a58d4a988474_story.html.
213. Lane, "The New Deal."
214. Tom Sugrue, *Sweet Land of Liberty: The Forgotten Struggle for Civil Rights in the North* (New York: Random House, 2009).
215. David Liebers, "The Forgotten Struggle for Civil Rights in the North: An Interview with Thomas Sugrue," History News Network, n.d., http://hnn.us /articles/57703.html.

Section 4: The Civil Rights and Black Power Movements

1. James Cone, *Martin & Malcolm & America: A Dream or a Nightmare* (Maryknoll, NY: Orbis Books, 1991), 2–3.
2. Students for a Democratic Society, "Huey Newton Talks to the Movement about the Black Panther Party, Cultural Nationalism, SNCC, Liberals, and White Revolutionaries," Michigan State University Archive Library, August 1968, https://archive.lib.msu.edu/DMC/AmRad/hueynewtontalks.pdf.

3. Lerone Bennett Jr., "What's in a Name? Negro vs. Afro-American vs. Black," *Review of General Semantics* 26, no. 4 (December 1969): 400, https://www.jstor.org/stable/42574587?seq=1#metadata_info_tab_contents.

4. Bennett, "What's in a Name?," 403.

5. Juan Williams, *Eyes on the Prize* (New York: Penguin Random House, 1987), xi.

6. Jarvis DeBerry, "David Duke Denies Being Racist; George Wallace Son Says His Daddy Wasn't That Bad," Nola.com, January 16, 2015, https://www.nola.com/opinions/article_1efb4c40-f4d2-54e9-b952-9859f788306c.html.

7. Blair Kelley, *Right to Ride: Streetcar Boycotts and African American Citizenship in the Era of Plessy v. Ferguson* (Raleigh: University of North Carolina Press, 2010).

8. August Meier and Elliott Rudwick, *From Plantation to Ghetto*, rev. ed. (New York: Hill and Wang, 1970), 81–82.

9. *Freedom Riders*, documentary directed by Stanley Nelson Jr. and produced by Firelight Media for PBS American Experience (2010).

10. Williams, *Eyes on the Prize*, 60–89.

11. Williams, *Eyes on the Prize*, 122–61.

12. Martin Luther King Jr., "Letter from a Birmingham Jail [King, Jr.]," April 16, 1963, African Studies Center, University of Pennsylvania, https://www.africa.upenn.edu/Articles_Gen/Letter_Birmingham.html.

13. Williams, *Eyes on the Prize*, 197–205.

14. North Carolina State University professor Jason Miller researched King's speeches for a connection with the poems of Langston Hughes. See Michael Hill, "Martin Luther King, Jr.: Speech in Rocky Mount, N.C., November 1962," NCpedia, April 8, 2016, https://www.ncpedia.org/martin-luther-king-jr-speech-rocky-mount-1962.

15. "Savannah's Proud Past," *The News & Observer*, August 12, 2001, sect. 4H.

16. Steve Carmody and Emma Winowiecki, "Before 'I Have a Dream,' There Was the 'Great Walk to Freedom' in Detroit," Michigan Radio, January 16, 2017. You can listen to the entire 35-minute speech at www.michiganradio.org/post/i-have-dream-there-was-great-walk-freedom-detroit.

17. Henry Hampton, Sarah Flynn, and Steve Fayer, *Voices of Freedom: An Oral History of the Civil Rights Movement from the 1950s through the 1980s* (New York: Bantam Books, 1990), 228.

18. Williams, *Eyes on the Prize*, 252–87.

19. Stanford University, "Southern Christian Leadership Conference (SCLC)," The Martin Luther King, Jr. Research and Education Institute, https://kinginstitute.stanford.edu/encyclopedia/southern-christian-leadership-conference-sclc.

20. Ralph Abernathy's recorded speech at a mass meeting in Birmingham, Alabama in 1963, *Lest We Forget, Volume 2*, Smithsonian Folkways Recordings/Folkways Records, https://www.youtube.com/watch?v=TIXwxBxs8Bg.

21. Stanford University, "A Creative Protest," The Martin Luther King, Jr. Research and Education Institute, https://kinginstitute.stanford.edu/king-papers/documents/creative-protest

22. Williams, *Eyes on the Prize*, 145.

23. PBS Documentary *Freedom Summer* (2014).

24. *Freedom Summer*.

25. Williams, *Eyes on the Prize*, 288.

26. Michelle Obama, *Becoming* (New York: Crown Publishers, 2018).

27. Gerda Lerner, ed., *Black Women in White America: A Documentary History* (New York: Penguin Random House, 1972), xxv.
28. Lerner, *Black Women*, 157.
29. *Freedom Summer.*
30. Lerner, *Black Women*, 156.
31. Danielle L. McGuire, *At the Dark End of the Street: Black Women, Rape, and Resistance—A New History of the Civil Rights Movement from Rosa Parks to the Rise of Black Power* (New York: Vintage Books, 2020), 15.
32. McGuire, *At the Dark End of the Street*, xvii–xviii.
33. Lerner, *Black Women*, 210.
34. *Freedom Summer.*
35. Hampton, Flynn, and Fayer, *Voices of Freedom*, 57.
36. Benjamin Quarles, *Black Abolitionists* (Boston: Da Capo Press, 1969), 29.
37. Quarles, *Black Abolitionists*, 29–30.
38. Frankye Adams-Johnson, "Daughter of a Sharecropper," 2012, https://www.crmvet.org/nars/faj12.htm. This interview was originally published in *The Nation's Longest Struggle: Looking Back on the Modern Civil Rights Movement*, by the D. C. Everest school system of Wisconsin. It was conducted and edited by junior and senior high school students of the Everest system.
39. Flora Bryant Brown, "NAACP Sponsored Sit-Ins by Howard University Students in Washington, D.C., 1943–1944," *Journal of Negro History* 85 (Autumn 2000), https://www.jstor.org/stable/2668546.
40. Paul Bonner, "Elementary Students Walk through City's Segregated Past," *The Herald-Sun*, February 21, 1998, sect. A1.
41. Matt Cherry and Emanuella Grinberg, "Sit-In Vet: 'Never Request Permission to Start a Revolution,'" CNN, February 1, 2010, https://www.cnn.com/2010/US/02/01/greensboro.four.sitins/index.html.
42. "Sit-ins Sweep across the South (1960–1964)," Civil Rights Movement History Web site, https://www.crmvet.org/tim/timhis60.htm#1960sitins.
43. Chapel Hill Community History, "The Chapel Hill Nine Story," *Town of Chapel Hill*, https://chapelhillhistory.org/civil-rights/the-chapel-hill-nine/.
44. Diane Nash shared her experiences in Hampton, Flynn, and Fayer, *Voices of Freedom*, 58.
45. Williams, *Eyes on the Prize*, 129.
46. Destiny Johnson, "'Ax Handle Saturday': A Dark Day in Jacksonville History Occurred 56 Years Ago," First Coast News, February 17, 2017, https://www.firstcoastnews.com/article/news/ax-handle-saturday-a-dark-day-in-jacksonville-history-occurred-56-years-ago/77-309628839.
47. Danny Lyon, *Memories of the Southern Civil Rights Movement* (Raleigh: University of North Carolina Press, 1992), 11.
48. Sara Bullard, ed., *Free at Last: A History of the Civil Rights Movement and Those Who Died in the Struggle* (Oxford: Oxford University Press, 1989), 88.
49. Bullard, *Free at Last*, 88.
50. Bullard, *Free at Last*, 86–90.
51. Karyn Miller-Medzon, Ciku Theuri, and Robin Young, "4 Little Girls Died in ihe 16th Street Baptist Church Bombing in 1963. A 5th Survived," wbur.com, April 30, 2019, https://www.wbur.org/hereandnow/2019/04/30/16th-street-baptist-church-bombing-survivor.
52. Zinn Education Project, "Sept. 15, 1963: 16th Street Baptist Church Bombing," https://www.zinnedproject.org/news/tdih/16th-street-baptist-church-bombing/.

53. This became one of the most famous issues of *Jet Magazine* when on September 15, 1955, it printed the pictures of the distorted head and face of the fourteen-year-old-murder victim. His mother, Mamie Till-Bradley, refused to close the casket, declaring that she wanted the world to see what they did to her son. It shocked the nation, both white and Black. See the article "Nation Horrified by Murder of Kidnapped Chicago Youth," on pages 6–9, https://books.google.com/books?id=57EDAAAAMBAJ&printsec=frontcover &source=gbs_ge_summary_r&cad=0#v=onepage&q&f=false.

54. Timothy B. Tyson, *The Blood of Emmett Till* (New York: Simon & Schuster, 2017), 7.

55. Bullard, *Free at Last*, 64–68, 78–79.

56. "Some Shooting Victims Return to Site of Orangeburg Massacre," *The News & Observer*, February 9, 2001, sect. 7B.

57. Bullard, *Free at Last*, 84–85, 94–95.

58. Bullard, *Free at Last*, 52–55, 62–63, 66, 74–77.

59. Bullard, *Free at Last*, 81, 86, 88, 91, 104.

60. Joanne Grant, ed., *Black Protest* (New York: Ballantine Books, 1968), 465.

61. Milton Viorst, *Fire in the Streets: America in the 1960s* (New York: Simon and Schuster, 1979), 374.

62. Gerry Butler, "Martin Robison Delany (1812–1885)," Blackpast, March 3, 2007, https://www.blackpast.org/african-american-history/delany-major-martin -robison-1812-1885/.

63. Kerri Greenidge, "The Radical Black Newspaper That Declared 'None Are Free unless All Are Free,'" *The Guardian*, January 3, 2020, https://www .theguardian.com/us-news/2020/jan/03/boston-guardian-william-monroe-trotter -newspaper.

64. See Southern Poverty Law Center, "Nation of Islam," https://www .splcenter.org/fighting-hate/extremist-files/group/nation-islam.

65. Michael H. Cottman, *Million Man March* (New York: Crown Trade Paperbacks, 1995), 75.

66. PBS documentary, *Black Panthers: Vanguard of the Revolution*, directed by Stanley Nelson and produced by Firelight Films (2015).

67. *Black Panthers*.

68. "'To Determine the Destiny of Our Black Community': The Black Panther Party's 10-Point Platform and Program," History Matters, http:// historymatters.gmu.edu/d/6445/ .

69. *Black Panthers*.

70. Frantz Fanon, *The Wretched of the Earth* (New York: Grove Press, 1963), 30–31.

71. David R. Francis, "How the 1960s' Riots Hurt African-Americans," National Bureau of Economic Research, *The Digest*, no. 9 (September 2004), https:// www.nber.org/digest/sep04/w10243.html.

72. Wikipedia, "Urban Riots," https://en.wikipedia.org/wiki/Urban_riots.

73. Philip Ardery, "Charles Sims," *Harvard Crimson*, December 10, 1965, https:// www.thecrimson.com/article/1965/12/10/charles-sims-pif-youre-white-and/.

74. BBC News listed this Malcolm X quote from November 10, 1963. Retrieved from http://news.bbc.co.uk/2/hi/americas/4277981.stm.

75. David F. Krugler, *1919, The Year of Racial Violence: How African Americans Fought Back* (Cambridge: Cambridge University Press, 2015), 13.

76. Robert F. Williams, *"Negroes with Guns*: 1962, Ch. 3–5," National Humanities Center Resource Toolbox, http://nationalhumanitiescenter.org/pds/maai3 /protest/text6/williamsnegroeswithguns.pdf.

77. Cited in "Williams, Robert F. 1925—," encyclopedia.com, https://www.encyclopedia.com/history/historians-and-chronicles/historians-miscellaneous-biographies/robert-franklin-williams.

78. Jonathan Bradley, "Maxwell Curtis Stanford Jr. (A.K.A. Muhammad Ahmad) (1941–)," BlackPast, January 12, 2011, https://www.blackpast.org/african-american-history/stanford-max-1941-and-revolutionary-action-movement-ram-1962-1968/.

79. Ardery, "Charles Sims."

80. Timothy B. Tyson, *Blood Done Sign My Name* (New York: Crown Publishers, 2004), 6.

Section 5: Protest in a Rapidly Changing World

1. John Eligon, "A Debate over Identity and Race Asks, Are African-Americans 'Black' or 'black'? *New York Times*, June 26, 2020, https://www.nytimes.com/2020/06/26/us/black-african-american-style-debate.html.

2. Roger Wilkins, "What Africa Means to Blacks," *Foreign Policy*, Summer, 1974, 139, https://www.jstor.org/stable/1147934.

3. "The Civil Rights Movement and the Second Reconstruction, 1945–1968," United States House of Representatives History, Art & Archives, history.house.gov/Exhibitions-and-Publications/BAIC/Historical-Essays/Keeping-the-Faith/Civil-Rights-Movement/.

4. John Overholt, in "Exploring the Origins of "African American" (Holton Library Blog, April 23, 2015), cites this sermon, which is now digitized. See blogs.harvard.edu/houghton/exploring-the-origins-of-african-american/.

5. Isabel Wilkerson, "'African-American' Favored by Many of America's Blacks," *New York Times*, January 31, 1989, https://www.nytimes.com/1989/01/31/us/african-american-favored-by-many-of-america-s-blacks.html.

6. Netflix documentary *Hip Hop Evolution* (2014).

7. Anna Brown and Sara Atske, "Black Americans Have Made Gains in U.S. Political Leadership, but Gaps Remain," Pew Research Center, January 22, 2021, https://www.pewresearch.org/fact-tank/2021/01/22/black-americans-have-made-gains-in-u-s-political-leadership-but-gaps-remain/.

8. "The Civil Rights Movement."

9. "The Civil Rights Movement."

10. The Web page BlackPast posted the entirety of Executive Order 10925. See www.blackpast.org/african-american-history/john-kennedy-s-executive-order-10925-1961/.

11. Errin Haines, "Analysis: Black Votes Will Define Electability for Democrats," ABC News, September 5, 2019, abcnews.go.com/Politics/wireStory/analysis-black-votes-define-electability-democrats-65400505.

12. *Freedom Summer* (2014), PBS documentary directed by Stanley Nelson Jr.

13. Melanie Arter, "ESPN's Stephen A. Smith Blasts Kaepernick for Not Voting: 'A Flaming Hypocrite' Who 'Betrayed His Cause,'" CNS News, November 10, 2016, https://www.cnsnews.com/news/article/melanie-hunter/espns-stephen-smith-blasts-kaepernick-not-voting.

14. David Lublin, "Savvy Black Strategy in Georgia," *The News & Observer*, Friday, October 30, 2002.

15. Jonathan Martin and Astead W. Herndon, "'The Black Vote Is Not Monolithic': 2020 Democrats Find Split," *New York Times*, June 22, 2019, https://www.nytimes.com/2019/06/22/us/politics/black-voters-south-carolina-democrats-primary.html.

16. "Michelle Alexander: Who We Want to Become: Beyond the New Jim Crow," *On Being* with Krista Tippett, April 21, 2016, onbeing.org/programs/michelle -alexander-who-we-want-to-become-beyond-the-new-jim-crow/.

17. Abraham Chapman, ed., *New Black Voices: An Anthology of Contemporary Afro-American Literature* (New York: New American Library, 1972), 28.

18. "Black Authors That Impacted the Culture of the USA," EssayService.com, https://essayservice.com/black-authors; and "The Black Arts Movement," *Britannica*, https://www.britannica.com/art/African-American-literature/The -Black-Arts-movement.

19. History.com Editors, "Black Women in Art and Literature," *History*, August 21, 2018, https://www.history.com/topics/black-history/black-women-in-art -and-literature.

20. "August Wilson," *August Wilson Theater*, https://www.august-wilson-theatre .com/awards.php.

21. "Toni Morrison Legacy," Spelman College, https://www.spelman.edu /academics/majors-and-programs/english/toni-morrison-tribute.

22. Black Theology & Black Power, "Biography of James Cone," Northwestern University, https://jameshcone.northwestern.edu/biography-of-james -cone/.

23. This quote is from an online review of the movie *Shaft* on the Web site Larsen on Film, http://www.larsenonfilm.com/shaft.

24. Kevin L. Carter, "African American Culture," *The News & Observer* special, 1998, 9.

25. Henry Louis Gates Jr., *Colored People: A Memoir* (New York: Vintage Books, 1995), 19.

26. Yvonne Sims, "Blaxploitation Movies" *Encyclopedia Britannica*, https://www .britannica.com/art/blaxploitation-movie.

27. Bill Higgins, "Hollywood Flashback: 'Shaft' Ignited a Blaxploitation Movie Craze in 1971," *Hollywood Reporter*, June 8, 2019, https://www.hollywood reporter.com/news/shaft-ignited-a-blaxploitation-movie-craze-1971-1214925.

28. Rosanne Salvatore, "'Blaxploitation' Stars: Where Are They Now?" *New York Daily News*, https://www.nydailynews.com/entertainment/watn-photos /blaxploitation-stars-gallery-1.51536.

29. For a list of accolades received by *Black Panther* see https://en.wikipedia.org /wiki/List_of_accolades_received_by_Black_Panther_(film).

30. Chuck D, with Yusuf Jah, *Fight the Power: Rap, Race and Reality* (New York: Delacorte Press, 1997), 3.

31. William C. Anderson, "Sounds of Black Protest Then and Now," Pitchfork, September 16, 2015, pitchfork.com/thepitch/898-sounds-of-black-protest -then-and-now/.

32. Documentary *How It Feels to Be Free* (PBS American Masters, 2021).

33. Leonard Pitts Jr., "Black Activists of the 21st Century Are Taking It beyond 'Takin' It to the Streets,'" *Miami Herald*, April 1, 2018,www.miamiherald.com /opinion/opn-columns-blogs/leonard-pitts-jr/article207648769.html.

34. Netflix documentary by Liz Garbus, *What Happened, Miss Simone?* (2015).

35. "20th Century Music," *History Detectives*, PBS, https://www.pbs.org/opb /historydetectives/feature/20th-century-music/.

36. Steven Lewis, "Musical Crossroads: African American Influence on American Music," *Smithsonian Music*, September 2016, music.si.edu/story/musical -crossroads.

37. Anderson, "Sounds of Black Protest."

38. Frederick Douglass, "My Bondage and My Freedom" (1855). Retrieved from http://nationalhumanitiescenter.org/pds/maai/enslavement/text5/douglassship yardlabor.pdf.

39. Lerone Bennett Jr., *Confrontation: Black and White* (London: Penguin Books, 1965), 34.

40. "20th Century Music."

41. Anderson, "Sounds of Black Protest."

42. Rev. Dr. Marvin A. McMickle, "Why I Don't Sing The Blues," *Christian Citizen*, December 13, 2018, christiancitizen.us/why-i-dont-sing-the-blues/. McMickle wrote this article during the season of Advent, advising Christians to be undefeated by sorrow. I use this quote as it was wittingly written but question McMickle's stance on the rejection of the blues as a sign of defeatism. Joy and sorrow often exist hand in hand. I can sing the blues to express my despair at my situation but still maintain a determination to fight the good fight of faith. Biblical blues are called lamentations and are a legitimate response to the human experience.

43. McMickle, "Why I Don't Sing The Blues."

44. Samantha Schmidt, "'Lift Every Voice and Sing': The Story behind the 'Black National Anthem' That Beyoncé Sang," *Washington Post*, April 16, 2018, https://www.washingtonpost.com/news/morning-mix/wp/2018/04/16 /lift-every-voice-and-sing-the-story-behind-the-black-national-anthem-that -beyonce-sang/.

45. Carter, "African American Culture," 6–7.

46. Dorian Lynskey, "Strange Fruit: The First Great Protest Song," *The Guardian*, February 16, 2011, https://www.theguardian.com/music/2011/feb/16 /protest-songs-billie-holiday-strange-fruit.

47. Documentary *Mr. Dynamite: The Rise of James Brown* (2015).

48. Bridgett Henwood, "The History of American Protest Music, from 'Yankee Doodle'to Kendrick Lamar," Vox.com, May 22, 2017, https://www.vox.com /culture/2017/4/12/14462948/protest-music-history-america-trump-beyonce -dylan-misty.

49. Garbus, *What Happened, Miss Simone?*

50. Documentary *The Black Godfather: Clarence Avant* (2019).

51. Carter, "African American Culture," 12.

52. *The Black Godfather;* Nelson George is a music and culture historian.

53. Charles Leonard, "Political Songs/What's Going On—Marvin Gaye," New Frame, June 14, 2019, https://www.newframe.com/political-songs-whats -going-on-marvin-gaye/.

54. The Honey Drifters' song called for the impeachment of President Richard Nixon. Listen to the song on Youtube at "The Honey Drippers—Impeach the President 1973,"https://www.youtube.com/watch?v=F6vIGGK-rao.

55. Aaron Leaf, "Thirty-One Years Ago Today Stevie Wonder's Music Was Banned in South Africa," OkayAfrica.com, March 26, 2016, https://www .okayafrica.com/twenty-two-years-ago-today-stevie-wonders-music-banned -south-africa/.

56. Chanté Griffin, "The Music of Black Liberation." *New Internationalist*, October 31, 2018, newint.org/features/2018/10/31/four-songs-black-liberation.

57. See Michael Jackson's video "They Don't Care about Us" (Brazil Version, Official Video) on YouTube at https://www.youtube.com/watch?v= QNJL6nfu__Q.

58. See Michael Jackson's "They Don't Care about Us" (Prison Version) at https://www.youtube.com/watch?v=t1pqi8vjTLY.

59. Netflix documentary *Hip Hop Evolution* and "The 20 Best Female Rappers of All Time," XXL, April 30, 2014, https://www.xxlmag.com/20-best-female -rappers/.

60. *Hip Hop Evolution* and "The 20 Best Female Rappers."

61. Alexander Billet, "The New Anthems of Resistance: Hip-Hop and Black Lives Matter," *In These Times*, August 21, 2015, inthesetimes.com/article/18333/hip -hop-black-lives-matter-kendrick-lamar-janelle-monae.

62. John W. Miller, "We're in the New Age of Protest Music," *American Magazine*, January 25, 2020, https://www.americamagazine.org/arts-culture/2020 /01/25/were-new-age-protest-music.

63. Nicole Falcone, "Kendrick Lamar as a Modern Day Prophet," Medium.com, November 28, 2016, medium.com/@nicolefalconee/kendrick-lamar-as-a -modern-day-prophet-bbefb0955602.

64. Jeremy Gordon, "Kendrick Lamar's 'Alright' Chanted by Protesters During Cleveland Police Altercation," Pitchfork, July 29, 2015, https://pitchfork .com/news/60568-kendrick-lamars-alright-chanted-by-protesters-during-cleve land-police-altercation/.

65. Corbin Reiff, "Vince Staples on Rap Activism: 'It's Bigger Than Whoever the President Is,'" *Rolling Stone*, February 15, 2017, https://www.rollingstone .com/music/music-features/vince-staples-on-rap-activism-its-bigger-than-who ever-the-president-is-110302/.

66. *Hip-Hop Evolution*.

67. Carter, "African American Culture," 3.

68. Kristin Corry, "The 2010s Were the Decade When Black Protest Music Went Mainstream," Vice.com, November 11, 2019, https://www.vice.com/en_us /article/bjw4j4/the-2010s-were-the-decade-when-black-protest-music-went -mainstream.

69. James Hendicott, "D'Angelo on the Black Lives Matter Movement: 'Music Absolutely Has the Power to Change Things,'" NME, September 4, 2015, https://www.nme.com/news/music/dangelo-2-1226687.

70. Documentary *How It Feels to Be Free*.

71. Rhiannon Giddens, "At The Purchaser's Option," from her album *Freedom Highway* (Nonesuch Records). Watch the video on Youtube at www.youtube .com/watch?v=6vy9xTS0QxM.

72. Tamar Gottesman, "Exclusive: Beyoncé Wants to Change the Conversation," *Elle*, April 4, 2016, https://www.elle.com/fashion/a35286/beyonce-elle-cover -photos/.

73. Gottesman, "Exclusive: Beyoncé."

74. Brittany Spanos and Sarah Grant, "Songs of Black Lives Matter: 22 New Protest Anthems," *Rolling Stone*, July 13, 2016, https://www.rollingstone .com/music/music-lists/songs-of-black-lives-matter-22-new-protest-anthems -15256/beyonce-feat-kendrick-lamar-freedom-33813/.

75. Katie Presley, "Janelle Monae Releases Visceral Protest Song, 'Hell You Talmbout,'" NPR, August 18, 2015, https://www.npr.org/sections /allsongs/2015/08/18/385202798/janelle-mon-e-releases-visceral-protest -song-hell-you-talmbout.

76. Martin Pengelly, "NBC Appears to Silence Janelle Monae during Black Lives Matter Speech," *Guardian*, August 16, 2015, https://www.theguardian

.com/music/2015/aug/16/nbc-today-show-janelle-monae-cut-off-black-lives
-matter.

77. Kory Grow, "J. Cole Mourns Michael Brown in Somber New Song 'Be Free,'" *Rolling Stone*, August 15, 2014, https://www.rollingstone.com/music/music -news/j-cole-mourns-michael-brown-in-somber-new-song-be-free-169276/.

78. Katie Presley, "First Watch: Rhiannon Gidden's Stunning Charleston Response," NPR, July 15, 2015, https://www.npr.org/2015/07/15/422949419 /first-watch-rhiannon-giddens-stunning-charleston-response.

79. Arthur Ashe, *A Hard Road to Glory* (New York: Amistad Press, 1988), xv.

80. Sunni M. Khalid, "Black Athletes Have Always Been at Forefront of the Struggle," The Undefeated, July 14, 2016, theundefeated.com/features/black -athletes-have-always-been-at-forefront-of-the-struggle/.

81. Edward Hotaling, *The Great Black Jockeys: The Lives and Times of the Men Who Dominated America's First National Sport* (Rockland, CA: Prima Publishing, 1999), 73.

82. Hotaling, *Great Black Jockeys*, 1.

83. Hotaling, *Great Black Jockeys*, 1–7.

84. "Major Taylor, World-Famous Black Athlete in 1899, Dies in Obscurity in 1932," New England Historical Society, https://www.newenglandhistoricalsociety .com/major-taylor-the-cyclists-jackie-robinson-in-1892/.

85. "Alice Coachmen—Gold Medal Moments," YouTube, https:www.youtube .com/watch?v=n8GdDQocz2c.

86. Mark McCormick, "Black History Month: The Best African American Tennis Players," Bleacher Report, February 26, 2010, bleacherreport.com/articles /352672-black-history-month-the-best-african-american-tennis-players.

87. The letter was written by Rose Elder, the widow of golf great Lee Elder, and was dated April 8, 1971. An excerpt appeared in the article "1971: Wife of African-American Pro Writes to the Chairman of the Masters," *Golf History Today*, golfhistorytoday.com/1971-mrs-lee-elder-roberts-masters/.

88. Darril Fosty and George Fosty, *Black Ice: The Lost History of the Colored Hockey League of the Maritimes, 1895–1925* (Halifax, NS: Nimbus Publishing, 2008).

89. Gilman W. Whiting, "Only the Puck Was Black: A Story of Race and the NHL," The Conversation, February 19, 2015, theconversation.com/only-the -puck-was-black-a-story-of-race-and-the-nhl-37450.

90. "African-American NASCAR Driver Raced Like 'A Great Artist,'" January 30, 2015, https://www.npr.org/2015/01/30/382444955/african-american-nascar -driver-raced-like-a-great-artist.

91. Harry Edwards in an interview conducted by Sunni M. Khalid, "Black Athletes Have Always Been at Forefront of the Struggle," The Undefeated, July 14, 2016, theundefeated.com/features/black-athletes-have-always-been -at-forefront-of-the-struggle/.

92. Documentary by Mary Mazzio, *A Most Beautiful Thing* (2020). Executive producers were Grant Hill, Dwyane Wade, 9th Wonder, and Common, who also narrated.

93. WETA, "Knockout: Failing to Defeat Him in the Ring, His Enemies Take to the Courts," PBS, https://www.pbs.org/weta/unforgivableblackness/knockout/.

94. Art Rust and Edna Rust, *Art Rust's Illustrated History of the Black Athlete* (New York: Doubletree & Co., 1985), 139–53, 180–83.

95. DeNeen L. Brown, "'Shoot Them for What?' How Muhammad Ali Won His Greatest Fight," *Washington Post*, June 16, 2018, https://www

.washingtonpost.com/news/retropolis/wp/2018/06/15/shoot-them-for-what
-how-muhammad-ali-won-his-greatest-fight/.

96. Bruce Chadwick, *When the Game Was Black and White* (New York: Abbeville Press, 1992), 13–14.

97. John Harris, "Moses Fleetwood Walker Was the First African American to Play Pro Baseball, Six Decades before Jackie Robinson," The Undefeated, February 22, 2017, theundefeated.com/features/moses-fleetwood-walker-was-the-first -african-american-to-play-pro-baseball-six-decades-before-jackie-robinson/.

98. Negro Leagues Baseball Museum eMuseum, "Andrew 'Rube' Foster," www .nlbemuseum.com/nlbemuseum/history/players/fostera.html.

99. Alyson Footer, "Negro Leagues' Legacy Begins with Foster," sfgiants.com, May 20, 2014, https://www.mlb.com/giants/news/negro-leagues-founder -rube-foster-left-lasting-legacy/c-76057332.

100. Tim Odzer, "Rube Foster," Society for American Baseball Research, sabr.org /bioproj/person/fcf322f7.

101. Peter Dreier, "Jackie Robinson: A Legacy of Activism," Prospect.org, January 31, 2019, https://prospect.org/civil-rights/jackie-robinson-legacy -activism/.

102. Molly Qerim Rose made this statement on *First Take* on Nov. 11, 2019.

103. Jarett Bell, "Bill Polian: 'I Was Wrong' for Saying Lamar Jackson Should Be a Wide Receiver in NFL," *USA Today*, November 6, 2019, https://www .usatoday.com/story/sports/nfl/ravens/2019/11/06/lamar-jackson-bill-polian -wide-receiver-nfl-draft-ravens/4169975002/.

104. "NFL Players Sporting 'I Can't Breathe' Message," ESPN.com, December 7, 2014,http://www.espn.com/espn/wire/_/section/nfl/id/11993819

105. Pat McManamon, "Police Decry Andrew Hawkins Protest," ESPN.com, December 14, 2014, https://www.espn.com/nfl/story/_/id/12030748/andrew -hawkins-cleveland-browns-wears-protest-shirt-police-seek-apology.

106. Coach Gaines won 828 games over forty-seven years as the coach of Winston Salem (NC) State University. He wrote the foreword to Arthur Ashe's *A Hard Road to Glory*, xviii.

107. Heather Gilligan, in "The Black-Versus-White Basketball Game That Integrated the Sport" (LEVEL, medium.com, February 27, 2018), timeline.com /globetrotters-mn-lakers-game-segregation-basketball-874bf15f832.

108. Meserette Kentake, "Harry Lew: The First African-American Professional Basketball Player," Kentake Page, January 4, 2016, https://kentakepage.com /harry-lew-the-first-african-american-professional-basketball-player/.

109. Rhiannon Walker, "When the First All-Black Professional Basketball Team Dominated . . . Back in the '20s," The Undefeated, February 15, 2017, theundefeated.com/features/when-the-first-all-black-professional-basketball -team-dominated-back-in-the-20s/.

110. Sharon Brown, "The Harlem Globetrotters Were Often Victims of Racism off the Court and behind the Scenes," The Undefeated, February 13, 2017, https://theundefeated.com/features/the-harlem-globetrotters-behind -the-scenes/.

111. Martenzie Johnson, "Bill Russell, Activist for the Ages," The Undefeated, July 12, 2019, theundefeated.com/features/bill-russell-activist-for-the-ages/.

112. Johnny Smith, "The Reign of Lew Alcindor in the Age of Revolt," The Undefeated, March 30, 2018, theundefeated.com/features/lew-alcindor-kareem -abdul-jabbar-ucla-boycot-1968-olympics/.

113. Tim McManus, "Eagles' Malcolm Jenkins Says Colin Kaepernick Deserves NFL Job, Points to Jaguars," ESPN, October 24, 2018, https://www.espn.com/nfl/story/_/id/25074947/malcolm-jenkins-philadelphia-eagles-says-jacksonville-jaguars-proof-colin-kaepernick-deserves-job.

114. Jesse Washington, "Still No Anthem, Still No Regrets For Mahmoud Abdul-Rauf," The Undefeated, September 1, 2016, theundefeated.com/features/abdul-rauf-doesnt-regret-sitting-out-national-anthem/.

115. Alex Squadron, "Former Chicago Bull Craig Hodges Tells His Story, Opens Up about NBA Activism," SLAM, April 11, 2019, https://www.slamonline.com/nba/craig-hodges-story/.

116. James Herbert, "Blazers' Carmelo Anthony Says the Reasons He Went Unsigned for So Long Were 'Outside of Basketball,'" CBS Sports, November 22, 2019, https://www.cbssports.com/nba/news/blazers-carmelo-anthony-says-the-reasons-he-went-unsigned-for-so-long-were-outside-of-basketball/.

117. Mike Prada and Tom Ziller, "The WNBA Has Been at the Forefront of Protesting Racial Injustice," SBNation, September 24, 2017, https://www.sbnation.com/2017/9/24/16357206/national-anthem-protest-wnba-history-donald-trump.

118. Marissa Coleman, "Indiana Fever Player: Why I Took A Knee during National Anthem," Indy Star, Sept. 22, 2016, https://www.indystar.com/story/opinion/2016/09/22/indiana-fever-player-took-knee/90852194/.

119. Dave Zirin, "Interview with Ariyana Smith: The First Athlete Activist of #BlackLivesMatter," The Nation, December 19, 2014, https://www.thenation.com/article/archive/interview-ariyana-smith-first-athlete-activist-blacklivesmatter/.

120. Giselle Cancio and Lindsey Wisniewski, "Mercury's Kelsey Bone to Take Anthem Protests into WNBA Playoffs," September 16, 2016, AZCentral, https://www.azcentral.com/story/sports/wnba/mercury/2016/09/16/mercurys-kelsey-bone-take-anthem-protests-into-wnba-playoffs/90522428/.

121. Lindsay Gibbs, "The First WNBA Player to Join Kaepernick's Protest Refuses to Stop Kneeling," ThinkProgress, June 22, 2018, https://archive.thinkprogress.org/the-first-wnba-player-to-join-kaepernicks-protest-refuses-to-stop-kneeling-6b6e01d3ab2c/.

122. Cindy Boren, "A WNBA Owner Dismissed Player Protest. Now They're Campaigning for Her Senate Opponent," Washington Post, August 5, 2020, https://www.washingtonpost.com/sports/2020/08/05/wnba-players-are-so-livid-sen-kelly-loeffler-team-owner-theyre-backing-her-opponent/.

123. Lesley Messer and David Caplan, "ESPYS 2016: LeBron James, Dwyane Wade, Chris Paul and Carmelo Anthony Call for an End to Violence," ABC-News, July 13, 2016, https://abcnews.go.com/Entertainment/espys-2016-lebron-james-dwyane-wade-chris-paul/story?id=40563702.

124. Jason Reid, "With Trayvon Martin Tribute, Dwyane Wade, LeBron James Take Strong Position," Washington Post, March 27, 2012, https://www.washingtonpost.com/sports/wizards/with-trayvon-martin-tribute-dwyane-wade-lebron-james-take-strong-position/2012/03/27/gIQAyNU4eS_story.html.

125. "LeBron James, Kyrie Irvie Irving, More Wear 'I Can't Breathe' Shirts," Sports Illustrated, December 8, 2014, https://www.si.com/nba/2014/12/09/lebron-james-kyrie-irving-i-cant-breathe-eric-garner.

126. Brian Stelter and Nicole Chavez, "Michael Jordan Pushes Back after Trump Attacks LeBron James, Don Lemon," CNN, August 4, 2018, https://www.cnn .com/2018/08/04/politics/trump-lebron-james-tweet/index.html.

127. Cork Gaines, "Championship Teams Visiting the White House Has Turned into a Mess—Here Is How Trump and the Teams Have Wrecked the Tradition," Insider, June 26, 2019, https://www.businessinsider.com/championship -teams-trump-white-house-2019-4.

128. Rafi Schwartz, "Hero Ruins Donald Trump's Patriotism Fest by Taking a Knee during the National Anthem," Splinter, June 5, 2018, https:// splinternews.com/hero-ruins-donald-trumps-patriotism-fest-by-taking-a-kn -1826580838.

129. Tyler Tynes, "President Donald Trump Replaced Eagles' Celebration With Parody of Patriotism," SBNation, June 6, 2018, https://www.sbnation.com /2018/6/6/17431132/donald-trump-philadephia-eagles-celebration-white-house -parody-of-patriotism.

130. Tim Daniels, "LeBron, Colin Kaepernick, Michael Jordan, More Speak on George Floyd's Death," Bleacher Report, https://bleacherreport.com/articles /2894017-lebron-james-joe-burrow-more-athletes-speak-out-on-george-floyds -death. *USA Today*, June 9, 2020, listed twenty-one photos in "Athletes, Coaches Speak on George Floyd, Racial Injustice," https://www.usatoday .com/picture-gallery/sports/2020/06/03/george-floyd-death-athletes-coaches -speak-out/3132940001/.

131. Jori Epstein, Jeff Zillgitt, and Aria Gerson, "Fear, Despair, Outrage, Hope: Athletes Open Up on Why They Joined Protests," *USA Today*, June 6, 2020, https://www.usatoday.com/story/sports/nfl/2020/06/06/athletes-protests -george-floyd-death/3147154001/.

132. Mark Medina, "Michael Jordan Speaks Out on George Floyd Death and Protests: 'We Have Had Enough,'" *USA Today*, May 31, 2020, https:// www.usatoday.com/story/sports/nba/2020/05/31/michael-jordan-statement -george-floyd-protests-we-have-had-enough/5302335002/.

133. Adam Zagoria, "Duke's Coach K Says 'Black Lives Matter' Is 'Not A Political Statement; It's A Human Rights Statement,'" *Forbes*, June 27, 2020, https:// www.forbes.com/sites/adamzagoria/2020/06/27/dukes-coach-k-says-black-lives -matter-is-not-a-political-statement-its-a-human-rights-statement/#1b454 7102188.

134. Allegra Mangione, "The History of Black Philanthropy," *Zim Consulting*, February 22, 2021, https://www.zimconsulting.com/single-post/the-history -of-black-philanthropy.

135. Mangione, "The History of Black Philanthropy."

136. Shena Ashley and Joi James, "Despite the Racial Wealth Gap, Black Philanthropy Is Strong," *Urban Wire* (blog), Urban Institute, February 28, 2018, https://www.urban.org/urban-wire/despite-racial-wealth-gap-black -philanthropy-strong.

137. Lou Carlozo, "Black Americans Donate to Make a Difference," *Reuters*, February 23, 2012, https://www.reuters.com/article/us-usa-blacks-donors/black -americans-donate-to-make-a-difference-idUSTRE81M1WI20120223.

138. W. K. Kellogg Foundation, *Cultures of Giving: Energizing and Expanding Philanthropy by and for Communities of Color* (January, 2012), 5, http://www .d5coalition.org/wp-content/uploads/2013/07/CultureofGiving.pdf.

139. Chris Wyatt ("Charity Admiral David Robinson," *Upscale*, February 2, 2014) highlighted Robinson's cofounding the Admiral Center in 2008 as a fundraising endeavor that solicited financial donations from celebrities to "create sustainable social change." Retrieved from http://upscalemagazine.com /charity-admiral-david-robinson/.

140. Dan Carson, "Warrick Dunn's Charity Has Gifted 145 Homes to Single-Parent Families," Bleacher Report, October 13, 2015, bleacherreport.com /articles/2578793-warrick-dunns-charity-has-gifted-145-homes-to-single -parent-families.

141. Shawn Carter, "Jay Z: For Father's Day, I'm Taking On the Exploitative Bail Industry," *Time*, June 16, 2017, time.com/4821547/jay-z-racism-bail -bonds/.

142. Phineas Rueckert, "Jay-Z Is Investing in a Company That Helps People Pay for Bail and Stay Out of Prison," Global Citizen, March 20, 2018, https:// www.globalcitizen.org/en/content/jay-z-investment-promise-incarceration/.

143. "Fight the Power: Celebrity Activists Who Say it Loud," BET online, November 4, 2018, https://www.bet.com/celebrities/photos/2013/02/from -paul-robeson-to-kerry-washington-celebrity-activists.html#!051518-celebs -from-paul-robeson-to-kerry-washington-celebrity-activists-8.

144. Gottesman,"Exclusive: Beyoncé."

145. Michelle Alexander, *The New Jim Crow: Mass Incarceration in the Age of Color-blindness* (New York: New Press, 2012), 2.

146. *Cooked: Survival by Zip Code* (2020), documentary by filmmaker Judith Helfand.

147. Ta-Nehisi Coates, "How the Housing Market Has Hindered the Wealth of Black Americans," *The Atlantic*, February 5, 2013, https://www.theatlantic .com/politics/archive/2013/02/how-the-housing-market-has-hindered-the -wealth-of-black-americans/429999.

148. Tony McCullen, "The 'Heartbreaking' Decrease in Black Homeownership," *Washington Post*, February 28, 2019, https://www.washingtonpost.com /news/business/wp/2019/02/28/feature/the-heartbreaking-decrease-in-black -homeownership/.

149. Richard Rothstein, "A Comment on Bank of America/Countrywide's Discriminatory Mortgage Lending and Its Implications for Racial Segregation," Economic Policy Institute, January 23, 2012, https://www.epi.org/publication /bp335-boa-countrywide-discriminatory-lending/.

150. YouTube documentary by Malik Hubbard and Ke'Von Singleton, "Uneducated and Unwelcome: The GI Bill in the Segregated South," https://www .youtube.com/watch?v=_qpSlDo4Vd0.

151. Hubbard and Singleton, "Uneducated and Unwelcome."

152. Erin Blakemore, "How the GI Bill's Promise Was Denied to a Million Black WWII Veterans," History.com, September 30, 2019, https://history.com /news/gi-bill-black-wwii-veterans-benefits.

153. Ta-Nehisi Coates, "The Case for Reparations," *The Atlantic*, June 2014, https://www.theatlantic.com/magazine/archive/2014/06/the-case-for-reparations/361631/.

154. Tracy Jan, "Redlining Was Banned 50 Years Ago. It's Still Hurting Minorities Today," *Washington Post*, March 28, 2018, https://www.washingtonpost .com/news/wonk/wp/2018/03/28/redlining-was-banned-50-years-ago-its-still -hurting-minorities-today/.

155. Helfand, *Cooked*.

156. Richard Rothstein, "We Can End Racial Segregation in America," *Jacobin*, July 22, 2019, https://www.jacobinmag.com/2019/07/desegregation-color-of -law-public-housing.

157. Richard Rothstein, "No Blacks Allowed,"*The Crisis Magazine*, October 2017.

158. Jamelle Bouie, "The Crisis in Black Homeownership: How the Recession Turned Owners into Renters and Obliterated Black American Wealth," Slate, July 24, 2014, slate.com/news-and-politics/2014/07/black-homeownership-how -the-recession-turned-owners-into-renters-and-obliterated-black-american -wealth.html.

159. Aaron Glantz and Emmanuel Martinez, "Modern-Day Redlining: How Banks Block People of Color from Homeownership," *Chicago Tribune*, February 17, 2018, www.chicagotribune.com/business/ct-biz-modern-day-redlining -20180215-story.html.

160. Jan, "Redlining was Banned."

161. McMullen, "The 'Heartbreaking' Decrease in Black Homeownership."

162 James Baldwin was interviewed by Kenneth Clark in 1963. See Vince Graham, "Urban Renewal . . . Means Negro Removal," YouTube, June 3, 2015, https:// www.youtube.com/watch?v=T8Abhj17kYU.

163. Greg Miller, "Maps Show How Tearing Down City Slums Displaced Thousands," *National Geographic*, December 15, 2017, https://www.national geographic.com/news/2017/12/urban-renewal-projects-maps-united-states/.

164. Katharine Schwab, "The Racist Roots of 'Urban Renewal' and How It Made Cities Less Equal," Fast Company, January 4, 2018, https://www.fastcompany .com/90155955/the-racist-roots-of-urban-renewal-and-how-it-made-cities -less-equal.

165. Jim Schlosser, "Dudley Residents Applying for Historic District Status," *Greensboro News & Record*, February 15, 1987, sect. D1.

166. "How the Razing of Detroit's Black Bottom Neighborhood Shaped Michigan's History," Michigan Radio, February 11, 2019, https://www.michiganradio .org/post/how-razing-detroit-s-black-bottom-neighborhood-shaped -michigan-s-history.

167. Brian Barth, "How Did African-American Farmers Lose 90 Percent of Their Land?" *Modern Farmer*, August 19, 2019, https://modernfarmer.com/2019/08 /how-did-african-american-farmers-lose-90-percent-of-their-land/.

168. "Blacks Leave Farms for Greener, Urban Pastures," *Atlanta Journal and Constitution* , Sunday, December 3, 1989, sect. M-3.

169. Barth, "How Did African-American Farmers Lose?"

170. Pete Daniel, *Dispossession: Discrimination Against African American Farmers in the Age of Civil Rights* (Raleigh: University of North Carolina Press, 2013).

171. Vann R. Newkirk II, "The Great Land Robbery: The Shameful Story of How 1 Million Black Farmers Have Been Ripped from Their Farms," *Atlantic*, September 2019, www.theatlantic.com/magazine/archive/2019/09/this-land -was-our-land/594742/.

172. James Rosen, "Seeds of Change," *The News & Observer*, December 14, 1999, sect. 20A. In response to this article, former agent Robert P. Bryan Sr. wrote in a Sunday, December 20, letter to the editor, "Your Dec. 14 article 'Seeds of Change' contained more than an element of truth regarding Black farmers and their financial resources over the years. . . . I worked with that agency from 1941 to 1955 in Halifax, Jones, and Bertie counties. In those days the majority of our clientele consisted of Blacks (referred to

as 'colored' in those days). We were restricted to making farming and real estate loans only to those individuals who could not secure adequate credit from other sources. . . . I cannot approve or disapprove of those tactics because I have already left when I saw too many departures from the laws and regulations."

173. Leah Douglas, "African Americans Have Lost Untold Acres of Land over the Last Century: An Obscure Legal Loophole Is Often to Blame," The Nation, June 26, 2017, https://www.thenation.com/article/african-americans-have -lost-acres/.

174. James Rosen, "Farmers Give Clinton an Earful: Blacks Seek Help Resolving Claims," The News & Observer, Sunday, December 18, 1999, sect. 1A.

175. Mark J. Perry, "The Shocking Story behind Richard Nixon's 'War on Drugs' That Targeted Blacks and Anti-War Activists," American Enterprise Institute, June 14, 2018, https://www.aei.org/carpe-diem/the-shocking-and -sickening-story-behind-nixons-war-on-drugs-that-targeted-blacks-and-anti -war-activists/.

176. David Davies, "Legal Scholar: Jim Crow Still Exists in America," NPR Fresh Air Interview with Michelle Alexander, January 16, 2012, https://www.npr.org /2012/01/16/145175694/legal-scholar-jim-crow-still-exists-in-america.

177. "Race and the Drug War," Drug Policy Alliance (blog), https://www .drugpolicy.org/issues/race-and-drug-war.

178. Elizabeth Hinton, "From 'War on Crime' to War on the Black Community," Boston Review, June 21, 2016, http://bostonreview.net/us/elizabeth-hinton -kerner-commission-crime-commission.

179. Davies, "Legal Scholar."

180. Caitlin Curley, "Tough on Crime: How the United States Packed Its Own Prisons," Genbiz.com, October 3, 2015, http://www.genfkd.org/tough-on -crime-united-states-packed-prisons.

181. Curley, "Tough on Crime."

182. Radley Balko wrote an extensive article, over twenty pages, documenting racial disparities in the criminal justice system ("There's Overwhelming Evidence That the Criminal Justice System Is Racist. Here's the Proof," Washington Post, June 10, 2020). See www.washingtonpost.com/graphics/2020/opinions /systemic-racism-police-evidence-criminal-justice-system/.

183. Brian Palmer, "The History of Environmental Justice in Five Minutes," NRDC .org, May 18, 2016, https://www.nrdc.org/stories/history-environmental-justice -five-minutes.

184. Connor Maxwell, "America's Sordid Legacy on Race and Disaster Recovery," Center for American Progress, April 5, 2018, https://www.americanprogress .org/issues/race/news/2018/04/05/448999/americas-sordid-legacy-race -disaster-recovery/.

185. Phil McKenna, "EPA Finds Black Americans Face More Health-Threatening Air Pollution," Inside Climate News, March 2, 2018, insideclimatenews.org /news/01032018/air-pollution-data-african-american-race-health-epa-research.

186. Jonathan Lambert, "Study Finds Racial Gap between Who Causes Air Pollution and Who Breathes It," NPR, March 11, 2019, https://www.npr.org /sections/health-shots/2019/03/11/702348935/study-finds-racial-gap-between -who-causes-air-pollution-and-who-breathes-it.

187. Bouie, "The Crisis in Black Homeownership."

188. Bouie, "The Crisis in Black Homeownership."

189. Patrice Taddonio, "After the Crash, Big Banks Got Bailouts. Abacus Faced Charges," PBS.org, September 12, 2017, https://www.pbs.org/wgbh/frontline /article/after-the-crash-big-banks-got-bailouts-abacus-faced-charges/.

190. Helfand, *Cooked*.

191. Helfand, *Cooked*.

192. Maxwell, "America's Sordid Legacy."

193. Tonya Russell, "Mortality Rate for Black Babies Is Cut Dramatically When Black Doctors Care for Them after Birth, Researchers Say," January 13, 2001, https://www.washingtonpost.com/health/black-baby-death-rate-cut-by-black -doctors/2021/01/08/e9f0f850-238a-11eb-952e-0c475972cfc0_story.html.

194. DeNeen L. Brown, "A Surgeon Experimented on Slave Women without Anesthesia. Now His Statues Are under Attack," *Washington Post*, August 29, 2017, https://www.washingtonpost.com/news/retropolis/wp/2017/08/29/a -surgeon-experimented-on-slave-women-without-anesthesia-now-his-statues -are-under-attack/.

195. Centers for Disease Control and Prevention, "U.S. Public Health Service Syphilis Study at Tuskegee: The Tuskegee Timeline," https://www.cdc.gov /tuskegee/timeline.htm.

196. DeNeen L. Brown, "Can the 'Immortal Cells' of Henrietta Lacks Sue for Their Own Rights?" *Washington Post*, June 5, 2018, https://www.washingtonpost .com/news/retropolis/wp/2018/06/25/can-the-immortal-cells-of-henrietta -lacks-sue-for-their-own-rights/.

197. John Elflein, "Distribution of COVID-19 (Coronavirus Disease) Deaths in the United States as of January 13, 2021, by Race," Statista.com, January 18, 2021, https://www.statista.com/statistics/1122369/covid-deaths-distribution -by-race-us/.

198. Brakkton Booker, "Survey Finds Asian Americans Are Racial or Ethnic Group Most Willing to Get Vaccine," NPR, December 4, 2020, https://www.npr .org/sections/coronavirus-live-updates/2020/12/04/943213216/survey-finds -asian-americans-are-racial-or-ethnic-group-most-willing-to-get-vacc.

199. Sandrine Piorkowski Bocquillon, "Sterilization in the United States: The Dark Side of Contraception," Open Edition Journals, August, 2018, https:// journals.openedition.org/rrca/1169?lang=en.

200. Lisa Ko, "Unwanted Sterilization and Eugenics Programs in the United States," PBS.org, January 29, 2016, https://www.pbs.org/independentlens /blog/unwanted-sterilization-and-eugenics-programs-in-the-united-states/.

201. Khiara M. Bridges, "Implicit Bias and Racial Disparities in Health Care," American Bar Association, *Human Rights Magazine*, vol. 43, no. 3, https://www .americanbar.org/groups/crsj/publications/human_rights_magazine_home /the-state-of-healthcare-in-the-united-states/racial-disparities-in-health -care/.

202. Chris Michael and Ellie Violent Bramley, "Spike Lee's Gentrification Rant-Transcript: 'Fort Green Park Is Like the Westminster Dog Show,'" *The Guardian*, February 26, 2014, https://www.theguardian.com/cities/2014/feb /26/spike-lee-gentrification-rant-transcript.

203. Alyssa Wiltse-Ahmad, "Study: Gentrification and Cultural Displacement Most Intense in America's Largest Cities, and Absent from Many Others," National Community Reinvestment Coalition, March 18, 2019, ncrc.org /study-gentrification-and-cultural-displacement-most-intense-in-americas -largest-cities-and-absent-from-many-others/.

204. "Austin Neighborhood Named Top 10 Fastest-Gentrifying Neighborhood in America," KVUE News, April 26, 2019, https://www.kvue.com/article/money/economy/boomtown-2040/austin-neighborhood-named-top-10-fastest-gentrifying-neighborhood-in-america/269-78a5ac78-a8ef-4503-9200-d869ecffdc98.

205. Brandon Formby, "Report Says Gentrification Threatens to Displace Austin's Low-Income Residents, Communities of Color," *Texas Tribune*, September 18, 2018, https://www.texastribune.org/2018/09/18/gentrification-threatens-austins-low-income-residents-and-communities-/.

206. Brian Resnick, "Yes, Artificial Intelligence Can Be Racist," Vox.com, January 24, 2019, https://www.vox.com/science-and-health/2019/1/23/18194717/alexandria-ocasio-cortez-ai-bias.

207. John Murray, "Racist Data? Human Bias Is Infecting AI Development," Towards Data Science, April 24, 2019, https://towardsdatascience.com/racist-data-human-bias-is-infecting-ai-development-8110c1ec50c.

208. Jay Greene, "Microsoft Won't Sell Police Its Facial-Recognition Technology, Following Similar Moves by Amazon and IBM," *The Washington Post*, June 11, 2020, https://www.washingtonpost.com/technology/2020/06/11/microsoft-facial-recognition/.

209. Julia Angwin, Jeff Larson, Surya Mattu, and Lauren Kirchner, "Machine Bias," ProPublica, May 23, 2016. The report provided ample evidence of the harm done to defendants based on their race even when algorithms were utilized by police departments and judges hoping to remove race from the justice system. See www.propublica.org/article/machine-bias-risk-assessments-in-criminal-sentencing.

210. Heidi Ledford, "Millions of Black People Affected by Racial Bias in Health-Care Algorithms," *Nature*, October 24, 2019, https://www.nature.com/articles/d41586-019-03228-6.

211. Hanna Ziady, "IBM Is Canceling Its Facial Recognition Programs," CNN, June 9, 2020, https://www.cnn.com/2020/06/09/tech/ibm-facial-recognition-blm/index.html.

212. Ledford, "Millions of Black People."

213. Chris Bumbaca, "Renee Montgomery Opts Out of 2020 WNBA to Focus on Social Justice: 'It's That Real,'" *USA Today*, June 22, 2020, https://www.usatoday.com/story/sports/wnba/2020/06/22/renee-montgomery-atlanta-dream-sits-out-racial-reform-social-justice/3233266001/.

214. Leonard Pitts Jr., "Black Activists of the 21st Century Are Taking It beyond 'Takin' It to the Streets,'" *Miami Herald*, April 1, 2018, https://www.miamiherald.com/opinion/opn-columns-blogs/leonard-pitts-jr/article207648769.html.

215. Leopoldine Iribarren, "The Impact of 'Citizen Journalism' on the Public Sphere," Medium.com, February 3, 2019, https://medium.com/@LeopoldineIL/the-impact-of-citizen-journalism-on-the-public-sphere-c1a5586cdac9.

216. Brian Shelter, "Philando Castile and the Power of Facebook Live," CNN Business, July 7, 2016, money.cnn.com/2016/07/07/media/facebook-live-streaming-police-shooting/index.html.

217. The ACLU Web site allows users to download the Mobile Justice app to report incidents in their state. See https://www.aclu.org/issues/criminal-law-reform/reforming-police/aclu-apps-record-police-conduct.

218. Joseph Zucker, "Clippers Owner Donald Sterling Banned for Life from NBA for Racist Remarks," Bleacher Report, April 29, 2014, bleacherreport.com

/articles/2042902-clippers-owner-donald-sterling-banned-for-life-from-nba-for-racist-remarks.

219. Onica Anderson, Skye Toor, Lee Rainie, and Aaron Smith, "Public Attitudes toward Political Engagement on Social Media," Pew Research Center, July 11, 2018, https://www.pewresearch.org/internet/2018/07/11/public-attitudes-toward-political-engagement-on-social-media/.
220. Anderson et al., "Public Attitudes."
221. Hayley Miller, "Childish Gambino's 'This Is America' Video, Explained," Huffpost.com, May 15, 2018, https://www.huffpost.com/entry/childish-gambino-this-is-america_n_5af05c12e4b041fd2d28d8e9.
222. "United States of America: Torture, Ill-Treatment and Excessive Force by Police in Los Angeles, California," Amnesty International, May 31, 1992, https://www.amnesty.org/en/documents/amr51/076/1992/en/.
223. PBS documentary *Black Panthers: Vanguard of the Revolution*, directed by Stanley Nelson and produced by Firelight Films (2015).
224. Cecilia Lei, "Majority of Black Americans Value Social Media for Amplifying Lesser-Known Issues," NPR, August 5, 2018, https://www.npr.org/2018/08/05/635127389/majority-of-black-americans-value-social-media-for-amplifying-lesser-known-issue.
225. Documentary *Burn MotherFucker Burn!* directed by Sacha Jenkins.
226. Katie Nodjimbadem, "The Long, Painful History of Police Brutality in the U.S.," *Smithsonian*, July 27, 2017, https://www.smithsonianmag.com/smithsonian-institution/long-painful-history-police-brutality-in-the-us-180964098/.
227. "George Floyd: Timeline of Black Deaths Caused by Police," BBC News, June 26, 2020, https://www.bbc.com/news/world-us-canada-52905408.
228. Brandon Griggs, "Living while Black," CNN, December 28, 2018, https://www.cnn.com/2018/12/20/us/living-while-black-police-calls-trnd/index.html.
229. Lilly Price, "'Black People Aren't Believed': Videos Exposing Everyday Racism Hailed as New Activism," KCENTV, July 16, 2018, https://www.kcentv.com/article/news/nation-now/black-people-arent-believed-videos-exposing-everyday-racism-hailed-as-a-new-activism/465-806ec607-108a-496f-8963-367a5b3064ec.
230. The *StarTribune* published online the entire transcript of the Philando Castile shooting "Philando Castile: Transcript of Facebook Live Shooting Aftermath," *StarTribune*, July 7, 2016,www.startribune.com/transcript-of-facebook-live-shooting-aftermath-video/385850431/.
231. Hannah Gold, "Everything We Know about the Killing of George Floyd," The Cut, August 10, 2020, https://www.thecut.com/2020/08/man-pinned-down-by-minneapolis-police-officer-dies.html.
232. *Smerconish*, "Officers' Defense: George Floyd 'Killed Himself,'" CNN Videos, https://www.cnn.com/videos/tv/2020/08/22/officers-defense-george-floyd-killed-himself.cnn.
233. CBS Minnesota, "'Being Black in America Should Not Be a Death Sentence': Officials Respond to George Floyd's Death," WCCO, May 26, 2020, https://minnesota.cbslocal.com/2020/05/26/being-black-in-america-should-not-be-a-death-sentence-officials-respond-to-george-floyds-death/.
234. Saraya Nadia McDonald, "Black Twitter: A Virtual Community Ready to Hashtag Out a Response to Cultural Issues," *Washington Post*, June 20, 2014, https://www.washingtonpost.com/lifestyle/style/black-twitter-a-virtual

-community-ready-to-hashtag-out-a-response-to-cultural-issues/2014/01/20
/41ddacf6-7ec5-11e3-9556-4a4bf7bcbd84_story.html.

235. McDonald, "Black Twitter."

236. Farhad Manjoo, "How Black People Use Twitter," Slate, August 10, 2010, slate.com/technology/2010/08/how-black-people-use-twitter.html.

237. Manjoo, "How Black People Use Twitter."

238. Manjoo, "How Black People Use Twitter."

239. McDonald, "Black Twitter."

240. The *Atlantic* did a special edition, the *King Issue*, which printed his speech given in Eutax, Alabama, on March 20, 1968. See www.theatlantic.com/magazine /archive/2018/02/martin-luther-king-jr-poor-peoples-campaign/552539/.

241. William J. Barber II, "America's Moral Malady," special issue, *The Atlantic*, 2018, https://www.theatlantic.com/magazine/archive/2018/02/a-new-poor -peoples-campaign/552503/.

242. The author was present during the founding and implementation of the Moral Monday Movement. He was one of the original seventeen arrested and the first arrested on the one-year anniversary.

243. Tonya Pendleton, "Meet Naomi Wadler, the 11-Year-Old Whose March Speech Moved Millions," blackamericaweb.com/2018/03/26/meet-naomi -wadler-the-11-year-old-whose-march-speech-moved-millions/.

244. Lottie Joiner, "Bree Newsome Reflects on Taking Down South Carolina's Confederate Flag 2 Years Ago," Vox.com, June 27, 2017, https://www.vox.com /identities/2017/6/27/15880052/bree-newsome-south-carolinas-confederate -flag.

245. Antonia Noori Farzan, "'Silent Sam': A Racist Jim Crow–era Speech Inspired UNC Students to Topple a Confederate Monument on Campus," *Washing- ton Post*, August 21, 2018, https://www.washingtonpost.com/news/morning -mix/wp/2018/08/21/silent-sam-a-racist-jim-crow-era-speech-inspired-unc -students-to-topple-a-confederate-monument-on-campus/.

246. Southern Poverty Law Center 2019 Annual Report, *Whose Heritage? Public Sym- bols of the Confederacy* (Montgomery: Southern Poverty Law Center, 2019), 9.

247. Speaker Pelosi's press release on December 21, 2020: "Pelosi Statement on Removal of Robert E. Lee Statue from the U.S. Capitol," https://www.speaker .gov/newsroom/122120.

248. Connor O'Brien, "The Pentagon Has 3 Years to Strip Confederate Names from Bases. Here's What Comes Next," Politico.com, January 5, 2021, https://www.politico.com/news/2021/01/05/pentagon-confederate-name -bases-455180.

249. Christianity Today staff, "Heritage and Mission: Southern Presbyteri- ans and Evangelism," *Christianity Today*, January 2, 1961, https://www .christianitytoday.com/ct/1961/january-2/heritage-and-mission-southern -presbyterians-and-evangelism.html.

250. Meg Kinnard, "Episcopalians Struggle with History of Confederate Sym- bols," *The Times and Democrat*, September 22, 2017, thetandd.com/lifestyles /episcopalians-struggle-with-history-of-confederate-symbols/article_928e68a2 -6e9f-5910-bda7-4c92f4542cb5.html.

251. Kate Shellnutt, "Should Churches Keep Their Civil War Landmarks? How Historic Congregations Grapple with Confederate Legacy," *First Presbyterian Augusta*, June 19, 2017, https://firstpresaugusta.org/christianity-today-quotes -dr-robertson/.

252. Alan Blinder and Jesse James Deconto, "'Silent Sam' Confederate Statue Is Toppled at University of North Carolina," *New York Times*, August 21, 2018, https://www.nytimes.com/2018/08/21/us/unc-silent-sam-monument-toppled.html.

253. Attributed to Alicia Garza, https://www.brainyquote.com/authors/alicia-garza-quotes.

254. Mehgan Gallagher, "Black Lives Matter: The 21st Century Civil Rights Movement?" O'Neill Institute, October 12, 2018, oneill.law.georgetown.edu/black-lives-matter-the-21st-century-civil-rights-movement/.

255. Jelani Cobb, "The Matter of Black Lives," *New Yorker*, March 14, 2016, https://www.newyorker.com/magazine/2016/03/14/where-is-black-lives-matter-headed.

256. "HerStory," Black Lives Matter, blacklivesmatter.com/herstory/.

257. Cobb, "Matter of Black Lives."

258. Jamilah King, "How Black Lives Matter Has Changed US Politics," *New Internationalist*, March 5, 2018, https://newint.org/features/2018/03/01/black-lives-matter-changed-politics.

259. Frank Leon Roberts, "How Black Lives Matter Changed the Way Americans Fight for Freedom," ACLU, July 13, 2018, https://www.aclu.org/blog/racial-justice/race-and-criminal-justice/how-black-lives-matter-changed-way-americans-fight.

260. Adia Robinson, "After 5 Years, Black Lives Matter Inspires New Protest Movements," ABC News, July 21, 2018, abcnews.go.com/Politics/years-black-lives-matter-inspires-protest-movements/story?id=56702439.

261. Adia Robinson, "After 5 Years, Black Lives Matter Inspires New Protest Movements," ABC News, July 21, 2018, https://abcnews.go.com/Politics/years-black-lives-matter-inspires-protest-movements/story?id=56702439.

262. Bourbiza, "Did George Floyd, Daniel Prude Change 911 Mental Health Call Response?" Salten News, April 2021, https://salten.cz/2021/04/05/did-george-floyd-daniel-prude-change-911-mental-health-call-response/.

263. RuPaul (@RuPaul), "Biggest Obstacle I Ever Faced Was My Own Limited Perception of Myself," Twitter, April 30, 2014, 9:04 a.m., https://twitter.com/RuPaul/status/461491403718402048.

264. Sony Salzman, "From the Start, Black Lives Matter Has Been about LGBTQ Lives," ABC News, June 21, 2020, https://www.abcnews.go.com/US/start-black-lives-matter-lgbtq-lives/story?id=71320450.

265. "All Black Lives Matter: Mental Health of Black LGBTQ Youth," The Trevor Project, October 6, 2020, https://www.thetrevorproject.org/2020/10/06/all-black-lives-matter-mental-health-of-black-lgbtq-youth/.

266. Antonia Hylton, "Black Lives Matter Forces LGBTQ Organization to Face Its History of Racial Exclusion," NBC News, June 22, 2020, https://www.nbcnews.com/feature/nbc-out/black-lives-matter-forces-lgbtq-organization-face-its-history-racial-n1231816.

267. Salzman, "From the Start."

268. Hailey Branson-Potts and Matt Stiles, "All Black Lives Matter March Calls for LGBTQ Rights and Racial Justice," *Los Angeles Times*, June 15, 2020, https://www.latimes.com/california/story/2020-06-15/lgbtq-pride-black-lives-controversy.

269. Adelle M. Banks, "Human Rights Campaign Urges Black Church LGBTQ Acceptance Via Video," Religion News Service, February 24, 2021, https://

religionnews.com/2021/02/24/human-rights-campaign-urges-black-church-lgbtq-acceptance-via-video/.

270. DL Hughley (@RealDLHughley), "Black Parents Have the Talk w/Their Kids on How to Conduct Themselves around Cops So They Don't Get Shot," Twitter, August 26, 2019, 11:44 p.m., https://twitter.com/RealDLHughley/status/1166194827165405184.

271. Jean P. Fisher, "Oral History Exhibit Records Life under Segregation, during the Years between Slavery and Civil Rights," *The Herald-Sun*, November 8, 1998, sect. E1. Graduate students from Duke, North Carolina Central University, and the University of North Carolina recorded the oral histories of 1,200 African Americans who lived in the Jim Crow South from the 1880s to the 1950s. The interviews covered twelve Southeastern states and were done between 1994 to 1997. The project, *Behind the Veil: Documenting African-American Life in the Jim Crow South*, is the largest collection of photographs, recordings, and documents of life under southern segregation and is stored in the John Hope Franklin Research Center for African and African-American Studies. In 2001 a book and CD compilation was published, *Remembering Jim Crow* (New York: The New Press, 2014), http://scriptorium.lib.duke.edu/franklin/.

272. Hari Ziyad, "How the Myth That All Black Parents Give Kids 'the Talk' About Police Is Used to Silence Resistance," Black Youth Project, October 29, 2019, http://blackyouthproject.com/how-the-myth-that-all-black-parents-give-kids-the-talk-about-police-is-used-to-silence-resistance/.

273. Barack Obama, *Dreams From My Father* (New York: Crown Publishers, 1995), 437.

274. Transcript of the "Obama Administration Record for the African American Community" from his online archives, https://obamawhitehouse.archives.gov/sites/default/files/docs/african_american_community_record.pdf.

275. Jaweed Kaleem, Kurtis Lee, and Jenny Jarvie, "Obama's Legacy: America Just Spent 8 Years with a Black President. For Many African Americans, It Meant One Big Thing: Freedom to 'Dream,'" *Los Angeles Times*, January 16, 2017, https://www.latimes.com/projects/la-na-obama-african-americans/.

276. Trump said this at a campaign rally in a predominantly white suburb of Lansing, Michigan. See Ashley Killough and Tom LoBianco, "Trump Pitches Black Voters: 'What the Hell Do You Have to Lose?'" CNN, August 19, 2016, https://www.cnn.com/2016/08/19/politics/donald-trump-african-american-voters/index.html.

277. Paul Farhi, "'What a Stupid Question': Trump Demeans Three Black Female Reporters in Three Days," *Washington Post*, November 9, 2018, https://www.washingtonpost.com/lifestyle/style/what-a-stupid-question-trump-demeans-three-black-female-reporters-in-two-days/2018/11/09/272113d0-e441-11e8-b759-3d88a5ce9e19_story.html.

278. Daniel Dale, "Fact Check: No, African Americans Are Not Happy with Trump," CNN, July 30, 2019, https://www.cnn.com/2019/07/30/politics/fact-check-african-americans-trump-approval/index.html.

279. William Cummings, "A Majority of Voters Say President Trump is a Racist, Quinnipiac University Poll Finds," *USA Today*, July 31, 2019, https://www.usatoday.com/story/news/politics/2019/07/31/donald-trump-racist-majority-say-quinnipiac-university-poll/1877168001/.

280. Joshua Jamerson and Douglas Belkin, "Black Americans Largely Rebuked Trumps's Overtures, Helped Lift Biden," *Wall Street Journal*, November 10,

2020,https://www.wsj.com/articles/black-americans-largely-rebuked-trumps
-overtures-helped-lift-biden-11605021114.

281. Kat Stafford, Aaron Morrison, and Angeliki Kastanis, "'This is Proof': Biden's
     Win Reveals Power of Black Voters," AP News, November 9, 2020, https://
     apnews.com/article/election-2020-joe-biden-race-and-ethnicity-virus-outbreak
     -georgia-7a843bbce00713cfde6c3fdbc2e31eb7

282. Stafford, Morrison, and Kastanis, "'This is Proof.'"

283. Musa al-Gharbi, "White Men Swung to Biden. Trump Made Gains with
     Black and Latino Voters. Why?" *The Guardian*, November 14, 2020, https://
     www.theguardian.com/commentisfree/2020/nov/14/joe-biden-trump-black
     -latino-republicans.

284. "Read the Transcript of Kamala Harris's Victory Speech in Wilmington,
     Del.," *Washington Post*, November 7, 2020,https://www.washingtonpost.com
     /politics/2020/11/07/kamala-harris-victory-speech-transcript/.

285. UNC African, African American and Diaspora Studies, "COVID-19
     Resources," https://aaad.unc.edu/covid-19-resources/.

286. Edwin Rios, "Black People Are Dying from COVID-19 at Higher Rates Because
     Racism Is a Preexisting Condition," *Mother Jones*, April 9, 2020, https://www
     .motherjones.com/coronavirus-updates/2020/04/black-people-are-dying-from
     -covid-19-at-higher-rates-because-racism-is-a-pre-existing-condition/.

287. Rios, "Black People Are Dying."

288. Jasmin Barmore, "5-Year-Old with Rare Complication Becomes First Michi-
     gan Child to Die of COVID-19," *Detroit News*, April 19, 2020,https://www
     .detroitnews.com/story/news/local/detroit-city/2020/04/19/5-year-old-first
     -michigan-child-dies-coronavirus/5163094002/.

289. Thomas McKiniess, "Tlaib Chokes up in Tribute to Detroit Girl Who
     Died from Coronavirus," Roll Call, April 23, 20202, https://www.rollcall
     .com/2020/04/23/tlaib-chokes-up-in-tribute-to-detroit-girl-who-died-from
     -coronavirus/.

290. Jamiel Lynch, "A 7-Year-Old Boy in Georgia Died of COVID-19, the Young-
     est Victim in the State," CNN, August 6, 2020, https://www.cnn.com/2020
     /08/06/us/georgia-boy-covid-19-death/index.html.

291. Denise Royal and Rosa Flores, "A 9-Year-Old Who Died of Coronavirus
     Had No Known Underlying Health Issues, Family Says," CNN, July 26,
     2020, https://www.cnn.com/2020/07/25/us/kimora-lynum-dies-of-coronavirus
     /index.html.

292. Gloria Rodiguez, "'It's a Nightmare I Never Imagined Living': Durham Fam-
     ily Mourns Death of 8-year-old, First Child to Die from COVID-19 in North
     Carolina," ABC 11 Eyewitness News, June 9, 2020, https://abc11.com/aurea
     -soto-morales-child-coronavirus-covid-19/6239463/.

293. Elizabeth Cooney, "'We're Flying Blind': African Americans May Be Bear-
     ing the Brunt of COVID-19, but Access to Data Is Limited," STAT, April 6,
     2020, https://www.statnews.com/2020/04/06/flying-blind-african-americans
     -disparities-covid-19-data-limited/.

294. Zack Budryk, "Cuomo Vows to Investigate Racial Disparities in COVID-19
     Deaths: 'Why Do the Poorest People Always Pay the Highest Price?'" The
     Hill, April 8, 2020, thehill.com/homenews/state-watch/491797-cuomo-on
     -disproportionate-minority-covid-deaths-why-do-the-poorest. Also see Jason
     Silverstein, "Democrats Demand Data on Racial Disparities in America's
     Coronavirus Response," CBS News, March 31, 2020, https://www.cbsnews

.com/news/democrats-demand-data-on-racial-disparities-in-americas-corona virus-response/.

295. Budryk, "Cuomo Vows to Investigate."
296. Cheyenne Haslett, "CDC Releases New Data as Debate Grows over Racial Disparities in Coronavirus Death," ABC News, April 8, 2020, https:// abcnews.go.com/Politics/cdc-releases-data-debate-grows-racial-disparities -coronavirus/story?id=70041803.
297. Keon L. Gilbert, Ruqaiijah Yearby, Amber Johnson, and Kira Banks, "For Black Americans, COVID-19 Is a Reminder of the Racism of US Healthcare," *The Guardian*, February 22, 2021, https://www.theguardian.com/commentisfree / 2021/feb/22/black-americans-covid-19-racism-us-healthcare.
298. Gerda Lerner, ed., *Black Women in White America: A Documentary History* (New York: Penguin Random House, 1972), 311.
299. Thomas J. Sugrue, "2020 Is Not 1968: To Understand Today's Protests, You Must Look Further Back," *National Geographic*, June 11, 2020, https://www .nationalgeographic.com/history/2020/06/2020-not-1968/.

Bibliography

Alexander, Michelle. *The New Jim Crow: Mass Incarceration in the Age of Colorblindness.* New York: New Press, 2012.

Ashe, Arthur. *A Hard Road to Glory.* New York: Amistad Press, 1988.

Ball, Edward. *The Sweet Hell Inside: A Family History.* New York: William Morrow, 2001.

Baptist, Edward E. *The Half Has Never Been Told: Slavery and the Making of American Capitalism.* New York: Basic Books, 2016.

Beard, Rick, John Latschar, and Robert Sutton. *Slavery in the United States: A Brief Narrative History.* Fort Washington, PA: Eastern National, 2013.

Bennett, Lerone, Jr. *Before the Mayflower: A History of Black America.* New York: Penguin Books, 1995.

———. *Confrontation: Black and White.* London: Penguin Books, 1965.

———. *Ebony Pictorial History of Black America.* Nashville: Southwestern Co., 1971.

Berry, Daina Ramey. *The Price for Their Pound of Flesh: The Value of the Enslaved, from Womb to Grave, in the Building of a Nation.* Boston: Beacon Press, 2017.

Blight, David W. *Frederick Douglass' Civil War: Keeping the Faith in Jubilee.* Baton Rouge: Louisiana State University Press, 1991.

———. *Frederick Douglass: Prophet of Freedom.* New York: Simon & Schuster, 2018.

Bullard, Sara, ed. *Free At Last: A History of the Civil Rights Movement and Those Who Died in the Struggle.* Oxford: Oxford University Press, 1989.

Bunch-Lyons, Beverly. "'Ours is a Business of Loyalty': African American Funeral Home Owners in Southern Cities." *The Southern Quarterly* 53, no. 1 (2015): 57–71.

Chadwick, Bruce. *When the Game Was Black and White.* New York: Abbeville Press, 1992.

Chapman, Abraham, ed. *New Black Voices: An Anthology of Contemporary Afro-American Literature.* New York: New American Library, 1972.

Chernow, Ron. *Grant.* London: Penguin Books, 2017.

Clavin, Tom, and Phil Keith. *All Blood Runs Red: The Legendary Life of Eugene Bullard—Boxer, Pilot, Soldier, Spy.* New York: Hanover Square Press, 2019.

Clinton, Catherine. *The African American Experience: 1565–1877.* Fort Washington, PA: Eastern National, 2004.

———. *Harriet Tubman: The Road to Freedom.* New York: Back Bay Books, 2005.

Cone, James. *Martin & Malcolm & America: A Dream or a Nightmare.* Maryknoll, NY: Orbis Books, 1991.

Cottman, Michael H. *Million Man March.* New York: Crown Trade Paperbacks, 1995.

Crockett, Norman L. *The Black Towns.* Lawrence, KS: Regents Press, 1979.

Crow, Jeffrey J., Paul D. Escott and Flora J. Hatley. *A History of African Americans in North Carolina*. Raleigh: North Carolina Office of Archives and History, 1992.

D, Chuck, with Yusuf Jah. *Fight the Power: Rap, Race and Reality*. New York: Delacorte Press, 1997.

Daniel, Pete. *Dispossession: Discrimination against African American Farmers in the Age of Civil Rights*. Raleigh: University of North Carolina Press, 2013.

Driskell, David, David Levering Lewis, and Deborah Willis Ryan. *Harlem Renaissance: Art of Black America*. New York: Studio Museum in Harlem, 1987.

Du Bois, W. E. Burghardt. *The Negro Church*. Atlanta: Atlanta University Press, 1903.

———. *The Souls of Black Folk*. Chicago: A. C. McClurg & Co., 1903.

Edgerton, Robert B. *Hidden Heroism: Black Soldiers in America's Wars*. New York: Basic Books, 2002.

Fanon, Frantz. *The Wretched of the Earth*. New York: Grove Press, 1963.

Felder, Cain Hope. *Troubling Biblical Waters: Race, Class, and Family*. Maryknoll, NY: Orbis Books, 1989.

Ferris, William, and Charles Reagan Wilson, eds. *Encyclopedia of Southern Culture*. New York: Anchor Books, 1989.

Foner, Eric. *Gateway to Freedom: The Hidden History of the Underground Railroad*. New York: W.W. Norton & Co., 2016.

Fosty, Darril, and George Fosty. *Black Ice: The Lost History of the Colored Hockey League of the Maritimes, 1895–1925*. Halifax, NS: Nimbus Publishing, 2008.

Franklin, John Hope. *From Slavery to Freedom: A History of Negro Americans*. New York: Vintage Books, 1969.

Frazier, E. Franklin. *Black Bourgeoisie*. New York: Free Press, 1957.

———. *The Negro Church in America*. New York: Schocken Books, 1964.

Gates, Henry Louis, Jr. *Colored People: A Memoir*. New York: Vintage Books, 1995.

———, ed. *African Americans: Voices of Triumph; Creative Fire*. New York: Time-Life Books, 1994.

———, ed. *African Americans: Voices of Triumph; Leadership*. New York: Time-Life Books, 1994.

———, ed. *African Americans: Voices of Triumph; Perseverance*. New York: Time-Life Books, 1994.

Gates, Henry Louis, and Cornel West. *The African American Century: How Black Americans Have Shaped Our Country*. New York: Free Press, 2000.

Gates, Henry Louis, and Donald Yacovone. *The African Americans: Many Rivers to Cross*. Carlsbad, CA: SmileyBooks, 2013.

Gatewood, William B. *Aristocrats of Color: The Black Elite, 1880–1920*. Fayetteville: University of Arkansas Press, 1990.

Genovese, Eugene D. *Roll, Jordan, Roll: The World the Slaves Made*. New York: Vintage Books, 1972.

Glatthaar, Joseph. *The Civil War's Black Soldiers*. Civil War series. Fort Washington, PA: Eastern National Park and Monument Association, 1996.

Grant, Joanne, ed. *Black Protest*. New York: Ballantine Books, 1968.

Hampton, Henry, Sarah Flynn, and Steve Fayer. *Voices of Freedom: An Oral History of the Civil Rights Movement from the 1950s through the 1980s*. New York: Bantam Books, 1990.

Harding, Vincent. *There Is a River: The Black Struggle for Freedom in America*. New York: Vintage Books, 1981.

Hurmence, Belinda, ed. *Before Freedom*. Winston-Salem, NC: John F. Blair Publisher, 1989.

————. *My Folks Don't Want Me to Talk about Slavery.* Winston-Salem, NC: John F. Blair Publisher, 1984.

————. *We Lived in a Little Cabin in the Yard.* Winston-Salem, NC: John F. Blair Publisher, 1994.

Jaspin, Elliot. *Buried in the Bitter Waters: The Hidden History of Racial Cleansing in America.* New York: Basic Books, 2008.

Johnson, Charles, Patricia Smith, and the WGBH Series Research Team. *Africans in America: America's Journey through Slavery.* San Diego: Harcourt Brace, 1998.

Jones, Constance. *1001 Things Everyone Should Know about Women's History.* New York: Doubleday, 1998.

Katz, William Loren. *The Black West: A Documentary and Pictorial History of the African American Role in the Westward Expansion of the United States.* New York: Touchstone, 1987.

Katznelson, Ira. *When Affirmative Action Was White.* New York: W.W. Norton & Co., 2006.

Kelley, Blair. *Right to Ride: Streetcar Boycotts and African American Citizenship in the Era of Plessy v. Ferguson.* Raleigh: University of North Carolina Press, 2010.

Kennedy, Pagan. *Black Livingstone: A True Tale of Adventure in the Nineteenth-Century Congo.* London: Penguin Books, 2002.

Latschar, John A., and Robert K. Sutton. *The Reconstruction Era.* Fort Washington, PA: Eastern National, 2016.

Lepore, Jill. *New York Burning: Liberty, Slavery, and Conspiracy in Eighteenth-Century Manhattan.* New York: Vintage Books, 2006.

Lerner, Gerda, ed. *Black Women in White America: A Documentary History.* New York: Penguin Random House, 1972.

Lewis, David Levering, ed. *W. E. B. Du Bois: A Reader.* New York: Henry Holt & Co., 1995.

Lincoln, C. Eric, and Lawrence H. Mamiya. *The Black Church in the African American Experience.* Durham, NC: Duke University Press, 1990.

Loewen, James W. *Sundown Towns: A Hidden Dimension of American Racism.* New York: New Press, 2018.

Logan, Rayford W. *The Betrayal of the Negro.* Springfield, OH: Collier Books, 1954.

Lomax, Louis E. *The Negro Revolt.* New York: Signet, 1963.

Lyman, Darryl. *Great African American Women.* New York: Random House, 1999.

Lyon, Danny. *Memories of the Southern Civil Rights Movement.* Raleigh: University of North Carolina Press, 1992.

McGuire, Danielle L. *At the Dark End of the Street: Black Women, Rape, and Resistance—A New History of the Civil Rights Movement from Rosa Parks to the Rise of Black Power.* New York: Vintage Books, 2020.

Meier, August, and Elliott Rudwick. *From Plantation to Ghetto.* New York: Hill and Wang, 1970.

Mellon, James. *Bullwhip Days: The Slaves Remember; An Oral History.* New York: Avon Books, 1988.

Meltzer, Milton, ed. *In Their Own Words: A History of the American Negro 1865–1916.* New York: Thomas Y. Crowell Company, 1965.

Murray, Pauli. *States' Laws on Race and Color.* Athens: University of Georgia Press, 1951.

Newman, Richard, and Marcia Sawyer. *Everybody Say Freedom: Everything You Need to Know about African-American History.* New York: Plum/Penguin Group, 1996.

Painter, Nell Irvin. *Sojourner Truth: A Life, A Symbol.* New York: W.W. Norton & Co., 1997.

Penrice, Ronda Racha. *African American History for Dummies*. New York: Wiley Publishing, 2007.

Phillips, Patrick. *Blood at the Root: A Racial Cleansing in America*. New York: W.W. Norton & Co., 2016.

Pinn, Anne H., and Anthony B. Pinn. *Fortress Introduction to Black Church History*. Minneapolis: Fortress Press, 2002.

Quarles, Benjamin. *Black Abolitionists*. Boston: Da Capo Press, 1969.

———. *The Negro in the Making of America*. New York: Macmillan, 1969.

Raboteau, Albert J. *Slave Religion: The "Invisible Institution" in the Antebellum South*. Oxford: Oxford University Press, 1978.

Rasmussen, Daniel. *American Uprising: The Untold Story of America's Largest Slave Revolt*. New York: Harper Perennial, 2012.

Robertson, David. *Denmark Vesey: The Buried Story of America's Largest Slave Rebellion and the Man Who Led It*. New York: Vintage Books, 1999.

Robinson, Jackie. *I Never Had It Made: An Autobiography of Jackie Robinson*. New York: Harper Perennial, 2003.

Rothstein, Richard. *The Color of Law: A Forgotten History of How Our Government Segregated America*. New York: Liveright, 2017.

Rust, Art, and Edna Rust. *Art Rust's Illustrated History of the Black Athlete*. Garden City, NY: Doubletree & Co., 1985.

Senna, Carl. *The Black Press and the Struggle for Civil Rights*. New York: Franklin Watts, 1944.

Sklott, Rebecca. *The Immortal Life of Henrietta Lacks*. New York: Broadway Paperbacks, 2010.

Smith, Marcia A. *Black America: A Photographic Journey*. New York: Fall River Press, 2009.

Southern Poverty Law Center. 2019 Report: *Whose Heritage? Public Symbols of the Confederacy*.

Stanford, Maxwell C. *Revolutionary Action Movement (RAM): A Case Study of an Urban Revolutionary Movement in Western Capitalist Society*. Amherst: University of Massachusetts Press, 1986.

Taylor, Elizabeth Dowling. *The Original Black Elite: Daniel Murray and the Story of a Forgotten Era*. New York: HarperCollins Publishers, 2018.

Taylor, Quintard. *In Search of the Racial Frontier: African Americans in the American West 1528–1990*. New York: W.W. Norton & Co., 1998.

Taylor, Eric Robert. *If We Must Die: Shipboard Insurrections in the Era of the Atlantic Slave Trade*. Baton Rouge: Louisiana State University Press, 2006.

Taylor, Susie King. *Reminiscences of My Life: A Black Woman's Civil War Memoirs*. Athens: University of Georgia Press, 1902.

Tyson, Timothy B. *Blood Done Sign My Name*. New York: Crown Publishers, 2004.

Viorst, Milton. *Fire in the Streets: America in the 1960s*. New York: Simon & Schuster, 1979.

Watkins, Mel. *On the Real Side: Laughing, Lying, and Signifying—The Underground Tradition of African-American Humor That Transformed American Culture, from Slavery to Richard Pryor*. New York: Touchstone, 1994.

Whitaker, Mark. *The Untold Story of Smoketown: The Other Great Black Renaissance*. New York: Simon & Schuster, 2018.

Wiencek, Henry. *An Imperfect God: George Washington, His Slaves, and the Creation of America*. New York: Farrar, Straus & Giroux, 2003.

Wilkerson, Isabel. *The Warmth of Other Suns: The Epic Story of America's Great Migration*. New York: Random House, 2010.

Williams, Juan. *Eyes on the Prize: America's Civil Rights Years 1954–1965*. New York: Penguin Random House, 1987.

Wills, Shomari. *Black Fortunes: The Story of the First Six African Americans Who Survived Slavery and Became Millionaires*. New York: Amistad Press, 2019.

Wilmore, Gayraud S. *Black & Presbyterian: The Heritage and the Hope*. Louisville, KY: Geneva Press, 1983.

———. *Black Religion and Black Radicalism: An Interpretation of the Religious History of African Americans*. Maryknoll, NY: Orbis Books, 1998.

Wormser, Richard. *The Rise and Fall of Jim Crow: The African-American Struggle against Discrimination, 1865–1954*. New York: Franklin Watts, 1999.

Wright, David, and David Zoby. *Fire on the Beach: Recovering the Lost Story of Richard Etheridge and the Pea Island Lifesavers*. New York: Scribner, 2000.

Index

Printed in the USA
CPSIA information can be obtained
at www.ICGtesting.com
CBHW060314271223
2983CB00004B/23